CRICK...

un

SHARING THE ... OF CRICKET

....co.uk

Cricket United *is delighted to be associated with the publication of this highly entertaining cricket book.*

Registered charity number 306054.

Together, we are *Cricket United.* As the official charity for recreational cricket, *The Lord's Taverners* want to share the best of cricket for everyone who plays the game. Using *The Taverners'* experience in staging events for cricketers, expertise in fundraising, access to unique opportunities & discounts; *Cricket United* will help social cricketers get more from the game. So once you've enjoyed reading the book, why not check out our website and sign up for the next *Cricket United* activity planned for your area.

All proceeds from the sale of this book are being generously donated to *The Lord's Taverners* – the official charity of recreational cricket. Our mission is to improve the prospects of disadvantaged and disabled young people, engaging with them through sport. We achieve this through the provision of specially adapted minibuses, sports wheelchairs, junior cricket equipment, national junior sports competitions and development programmes.

THE LORD'S TAVERNERS

A catalogue record for this book is available from the British Library
ISBN: 978-0-9571035-2-8

Cover illustration by Philip Green
www.Cartoonwarp.com

Typeset in Times New Roman
24pt, 14pt, 12pt, 11pt, 10pt 8pt

Printed and bound in Great Britain
by Berforts Ltd, Hastings, TN35 4NR

Published by
Jibba Jabba Publishing
Container City Building
48 Trinity Buoy Wharf
London E14 0JW

AUSTRALIA BLUES
A Scot at the Ashes

David Alexander Keay

davidkeay@tiscali.co.uk

KEAY

Stuart would like to thank David.

David wouldn't like to thank anyone.

CONTENTS

PART FOUR ~ MELBOURNE

PART FIVE ~ SYDNEY

EPILOGUE ~ ALL ENGLAND

SCORECARDS

Explanatory Note

Stuart Croll went to Australia for the 2010/2011 Ashes, intent on publishing a blog and podcasting of his travels, and this is principally his story. When the workload got too much he enlisted the help of fellow Scot, David Alexander, who was also out there skulking around and complaining a lot. Much of what is in this book was compiled from Stuart's live reports, many of which David edited or added to, or features events they were either both present at, and/or later discussed between themselves. Both being grumpy North-Eastern Scots of a similar generation and pasty complexion, their general perceptions were not dissimilar. Back home, when writing commenced through the haze of heat and alcohol-impaired memory, David's accounts were needed to flesh out incidents and inevitably his opinions have coloured matters, and at times barged in wearing heavy boots. Rather than create a haphazard duologue of slightly-mismatched recollections and impressions, they have pooled their resources and created one narrator for ease of consumption. It's only fair; Stuart bought the drinks.

PROLOGUE
THE AULD ENEMY

To some Scots, the idea of supporting England in any sporting contest is as alien as the alien from the movie *Alien,* visiting Earth on a bogus passport. Nevertheless, many Scots watch England play cricket (and not just in secret with the curtains drawn and when their parents have gone out). Some have even been known to have a go at the game themselves. Scottish cricket may have passed its heyday, but it still thrives and has a great history: Freuchie, in Fife, won the National Village Championships in 1985, and the first ever celebrity team was the Allahakbarries: founded in 1880 by J.M. Barrie (Kirriemuir) and starring Sir Arthur Conan Doyle (Edinburgh). If only Sir Arthur had lived longer, he could have set Sherlock Holmes onto the Mystery of the Duckworth-Lewis System and cleared that up for us. Elementary it is not.

Since those far off days, a significant number of Scots have been capped and have even captained the England cricket team: Mike Denness most famously, but Scotland can lay claim to such stars as Tony Greig and, the architect of bodyline himself, Douglas Jardine. In fact Jardine's ashes were scattered over a hill in his beloved Perthshire, though the Australians have been strangely reticent about seeking to reclaim those.

All of which poses a conundrum for the dedicated Scottish cricket fan: which team should he support when it comes to the international arena? Ian Hamilton, the man who repatriated the Stone of Destiny from Westminster Abbey in the 1950s, once said, 'I have sometimes made snide remarks about the English that were as unworthy of me as they are of them.' There are few Scots that, hand on heart, can truly say they've not done the same; and half of them have got their fingers crossed. With regards to football and rugby, we are brought up to believe the holy commandment: whomsoever England are playing, it's your patriotic duty to support the opposition. This holds true regardless of whether they are unwashed, unsavoury or blatant cheats (frankly, that's neither here nor there): when the English don their national colours, you cheer for their opponents.

But there remains a dilemma with cricket. As a pure devotee of the game I don't have a problem supporting England at the traditional summer sport, while not giving a damn whether English teams win anything during autumn, winter, spring, blue moons, bank holiday weekends, international folk festivals or new-age celebrations of the solstice. To me this is not an anomaly, England are the nearest we have to a cricket team of our own; but to many friends – be they English, Scottish or Australian – it is as curious as a five legged purple cat.

~

It was a love affair born in Arbroath in the summer of 1974, when I was still a young lad in short trousers and struggling to come to terms with arithmetic. Scotland had just been eliminated from the football World Cup without losing a game (the sort of harrowing number puzzle that I was to endure throughout my adult life, and it never got any easier to take), so what now to do with my time? Not then continuous daytime coverage of the affluent middle classes, as they choose which unspoiled paradise to defile with a modern development they can call second home. Not then the couples from West London relocating to a Highland castle with the proceeds of the sale of their shed, or desperate people on anti-depressants selling an Edwardian neck-brace at auction in a crazed attempt to make a fiver. If you wanted to completely waste your day in the 1970s you had to work hard at it: you had to go outside and either refight old wars against Germany or find something to vandalise. Unless of course, like me, you chose to watch the cricket, the rolling news of its day.

1974 was an optimistic time for the Scots. We'd found oil, we had a couple of the best footballers on the planet, Jackie Stewart was the best driver in the world and Sean Connery was still the *real* James Bond because he was the one on TV. (Who cared about that effete pretender that was on at the cinema?) Alright, even I could see that the Bay City Rollers were for girls, but that bloke in the Sensational Alex Harvey Band (I forget his name), he was the real deal. And the clincher that this was to be my era, M. H. Denness, from Bellshill via Ayrshire, was the captain of the England cricket team.

I like to imagine Denness recited Burns in the dressing room to fire the boys up before leading them out. Possibly he did, and that's what inspired the series wins over India and Pakistan. Alas, Boycott then went off in a sabbatical huff, and sans star-player the bandwagon ground to a halt against the Aussies that winter. Denness's England were exposed as cou'rin, tim'rous beasties before the might of the Lillee and Thomson plough. Mike was sacked and forgotten after the first home Test of 1975. And soon also, Scotland had squandered their golden generation of footballers in Argentina slinking home in shame. When the referendum on devolution was finally delivered in 1979 many didn't even bother to vote: the dream was over. And, thank God, the Bay City Rollers split up.

As the years rolled by, I still sang 'Shang-a-Lang' whenever the England gang came out to bat, but it wasn't always easy. There was no tougher time to support England than during the reign of Margaret Thatcher. Not since Oliver Cromwell had Scotland so hated Westminster, and been so fearful of what might befall it next. But I stuck it out: ignoring the taunts and the playground beatings whenever a coal mine was closed or a shipyard shut down, and almost taking up baseball and applying for Canadian citizenship when the Poll Tax was announced. When Labour stalwart Dennis Skinner said he supported 'anyone but England' because cricket was just 'the Tory Party at play,' I certainly knew that he wasn't alone in that belief.

Memories linger long up North, and since the opening of the Scottish Parliament, not once, but twice, motions have been tabled by Nationalists demanding the English game of cricket be removed from Scottish television screens. Presumably they will soon be insisting that the Sassenachs shouldn't be allowed to watch anything at all on 'oor invention.' They don't want to make Scottish TV less anglicised, they want to make it more insular, more parochial. Oh lord, have these loons never seen the horrors of Irish tele? That's the land that time forgot, right there on the box, and there but for the dubious grace of presbyterian unionism goes Scotland. Take cricket off our television and I'll be voting for the Scottish Parliament to be replaced by a bouncy castle. (Actually I'd vote for that anyway, it would be more appropriate and look better too.) Fortunately, it's not a party policy, and there are plenty of SNP members who enjoy cricket and support England, and plenty that will continue to do so after independence. In truth it might be easier after division; as with Ireland, freed from centuries old antagonisms, we might all get along a lot better. But that's another story.

~

Fast forward to the sun-baked stands of the Oval in 2009, where, as a newly signed up member of Surrey CCC, I witness England regaining the Ashes. I vigorously applaud Andrew Strauss and his victorious men to the horror of my watching companion Damian, an Australian. I say horror, although it was hard to tell, what with all the horror already etched on his face from unexpectedly losing. He can't believe I am cheering for a team whose fans sing from a songbook that stretches from the droned chant of 'Mighty, Mighty, England' to 'Jerusalem' and back to 'Mighty, Mighty England' because it ain't broke.

'And did those feet in ancient times walk down Princes Street?' he asks. 'Did they—!' he answers himself, but the words are drowned by the cheers for Broad as man of the match.

Granted, there is the likelihood that any given Australian team will contain more players with Scottish heritage than England. But then again, any given Australian team could contain more players of English heritage than some recent

England sides, so that shouldn't be an issue. It's neither about heritage nor birth, nor is it about Norman Tebbit's infamous test of Englishness; it's about loving a sport over jaundiced notions of ethnic purity and bogus jingoism.

Cricket spread throughout the world via the Empire On Which The Sun Never Set; an empire that would never have stretched further than the pier at Southend but for belligerent, ingenious and officious Scots desperate to see this place that was keeping all the sunshine to itself. Scotland's regiments formed the pace attack of the British Army, its engineers were the opening partnership that laid solid foundations from Assam to the Yukon, and Scottish law-makers umpired events on some of the stickiest wickets. Scots unfurled the flag in the morning and bugled it down at night. The flag of the Union has no place at Wembley, but should still be flying at Lords and not the cross of St. George.

That's what I say, but Damian is unconvinced, and points out that the Union Flag is still right there, on the flag of Australia, see? I point out he can talk, he's a republican at heart, he just doesn't want another bloody politician as his head of state. Suffice to say there was a lot of pointing, and not all of it cementing our friendship. One thing led to another beer, and so was issued the challenge that became the quest: did I have sufficient courage in my convictions to put my neck on the block and take my loyalty abroad, behind enemy lines and with only Sassenachs as allies? As a child I'd believed that a Scottish cricket fan could support the England cricket team, sometimes taking my life in my hands to do so. If some of my own side question my loyalty, if neutral observers express distaste, how would 'the Auld Enemy' themselves greet me? Friend or Foe? There was only one way to find out. And so I shook hands at the Oval in 2009 and promised to enlist. The following year I became a signed-up member of the Barmy Army and joined the departing ranks when they headed to Australia for the 2010/11 Ashes Down Under. This is what happened next.

PART ONE ~ BRISBANE

Chapter 1
AIRBORNE TROOPS
(Tuesday 23rd Nov)

Early morning, Heathrow Airport, preparing to embark on the trip of a lifetime: ten thousand miles to watch the Ashes in the golden sun of Australia. I'm dressed in my regular travel clothes of light beige flannels and white shirt, with a cream sweater over my shoulders: I'm like a fat football fan in an Arsenal shirt, hoping I'll get a game if someone comes off injured. Amazingly I'm the best dressed person here. For some reason I was expecting finely attired colonial administrators in linen and smart panamas, but instead the departure lounge resembles a low-budget costume drama. In their hot-pants and black tights, and all already wearing neck pillows, the female proto-passengers that surround me resemble transvestite Elizabethan courtiers. I'm aware it's a long flight, but this mob appear to be expecting a two month voyage round the Cape taking out a few Spaniards on the way. The men are worse: in crumpled leisurewear they look like recent and unwilling arrivals to a health farm.

Not for the first time I lament this fallen nation of scruff-bags. I haven't been so disappointed in my compatriots since I went to a mid-week Prom in black tie and found myself adrift in a sea of acrylic and anorak. I don't know any of these people but – with that positive, cheery attitude that Scottish football managers have popularised around the world – I already hate them. An intense emotional reaction I accept. With a cholesterol count that reads like a decent batting average, I'm going to have to learn some tolerance over the next seven weeks if I'm to survive.

For the sake of my blood pressure I follow my doctor's orders and contemplate more calming thoughts, of cricket and its love of numbers. In fairness my doctor didn't say think of stats, he just urged me to focus on things that relax me rather than my next indignant, unpublished letter to *The Times*, in much the same way that men occasionally visualise bad refereeing decisions to delay the inevitable conclusion. But it distracts admirably, for as the great Australian journalist Peter Lalor observed, averages and personal figures are as central to the game as leather, willow and rain; although Lalor didn't mention the rain, on account of writing from an Australian perspective. Records are admired, memorised and endlessly recounted by all cricket fans even without request (especially without request); and one figure above all others is bandied about between fans of both sides whenever an Ashes series looms: David Boon's 52.

Fifty-two. It doesn't sound a lot, and there are those who have claimed 58 but, according to Lalor's definitive investigative report, 52 is the alleged number of beers the Australian cricket legend consumed on a flight between Sydney and London in 1989. Admittedly Boon wasn't yet a legend when he got on the flight, and to the cabin crew he was probably more of a saga or a brutal Viking epic, but by the time he stepped off that plane – stepped off, not even carried off – his immortality was assured. I don't know about you, but I think it's good to see journalists still willing to turn the stones for the facts that really matter. With time to kill I flick open the calculator on my Blackberry and tot up the match figures.

Even if we assume they were only 330ml cans, that's 29.33 pints; if they were Australian 375ml cans, I wouldn't give him the car keys. If he'd flushed the toilet as they passed over the Gobi desert, the flowers would have come out. In fairness, the tough Tasmanian, half batsman, half batswalrus, denies the record when the cameras are rolling, but there are plenty of witnesses and he continues to make a decent living on the after-dinner circuit, so the reputation hasn't done 'the keg on legs' any professional harm. Boonie was the last of the old generation, inheritor of the grand tradition when an Australian's moustache was for life, not just for November. Will we see his like again?

We're boarding and I quickly retire to the multi-faith prayer room at Terminal 3 to recite my habitual nervous prayer to the deity of flying: 'Please God, put the babies six or seven rows away, on the other side of the plane and with a curtain between us. And if there's a child behind me, let it be a polite Asian kid, well behaved and studying for their medical exams, and not head-butting the seat in an ADHD sugar-rush.'

Fortunately my devotion is rewarded as none are sitting near me; but my prayer to witness a booze record-attempt appears to have gone unanswered, or at least there are no obvious runners yet. However, this is a two innings flight with a change of ends in Singapore, and there's 27 long hours to go; even Kiefer Sutherland wouldn't last the journey on full tilt. Three hours in, as I head to the toilet, I spot a contender. A heavily perspiring man in an England cricket shirt, pleading to break the last cardinal rule of British society, the last remaining thing that separates us from the savages of Europe: he wants to jump the queue. He apologises, but six cans of lager are rushing through him as quickly as Ewan McGregor's dinner when the heroin wore off. A kindly Elizabethan lets him through and he vanishes inside. Six isn't such an impressive figure for a man with a figure that would impress a Samoan, but it is early days and I can tell by his ample gut our man has been training very hard for the tour; conceivably he's just warming up.

At Singapore I find him in the departure lounge and introduce myself. He's Martin, a Brummie charmer who proudly tells me he drank twelve cans of lager on the first stage of the flight: 'I would have drunk more, but I grew up on Vietnam War films, and when the stewardess asked me what I wanted another drink, all I heard was 'love you long time.''

I simper and edge slightly further away, giving myself plausible deniability should anyone from the 21st century be nearby. Investigative journalism is all very well, but if they still cane people for chewing gum, I feared the punishment for stereotyping and vicarious racism. (They don't really cane you, they only fine you; I was just stereotyping.) Martin sips another beer and I ask him for a forecast on his final score. The jockeys always know if they're riding a winner, although the horse hasn't been born that could carry this rider over a fence. Thoughtfully mulling over his mouthful, he nods sagely and replies, 'I don't make predictions but I predict it will be a lot.'

Clearly the alcohol isn't affecting the clarity of his thought or preventing him from offering Zen-like prophecies. I like Martin like a scientist likes his favourite chimp, but watching him down his beers with slow relish I know there is no way even this experienced bon viveur would catch up with Boon by the time we reach Australia. Regardless, I wish him well and the hope his future wait for the toilet isn't long time.

On the Brisbane leg of the journey I wish desperately I was sitting next to a child. Even a loud, pedantic fat kid with an assortment of unhealthy snacks to feast upon would be light relief compared to the silent pantomime unfolding beside me. We're still on the runway and my new seat-mate is finding the simple task of storing his drop-down table more puzzling than a Rubik's Cube. Having knocked it down when getting his swollen belly into his seat, he now pushes it up, and it falls back down. He pushes it up, it falls back, he pushes it up... Now, replacing a tray into the back of the seat in front of you is not a complex task, it's a simple turn and lock device, no more taxing than hitting yourself on the forehead with your palm, as I'm now doing. But somewhere between my neighbour's brain and paws, some crucial piece of information has taken a permanent detour.

Most of us have evolved to the point where such tricky tasks of manipulation are best tackled by the hands. I'd say hands are your go-to boys for this sort of task 100 times out of 100. But having failed with fingers and too constrained by economy class to bring toes into action, he decides instead to use his knee to retain the tray in position, crossing his ample legs, right over left, with the upper knee holding it in place. This is to be his tactic for the next eight hours. Initially it works. For ten minutes of those eight hours it proves to be a gold-dust plan. But, tragically uncrossing his legs to take his jumper off, Newton is vindicated and the tray clatters back down with a mocking thud. Astonishment. The only thing to equal his astonishment is my astonishment at his astonishment. We are astonished, both of us. But only one of us is now holding his pen with the malign intent of a school bully with a pair of compasses.

The plane is taxiing to the runway, and we get our final warning to mobile off, belt up and tray up before take-off. By now our 'Dame' is panicking and hurriedly tries again to store his table, only this time he leaves the recently removed jumper on the tray before attempting to raise it. Unbelievable. I've seen everything. Unless I've underestimated him, and the static charge from the acrylic will hold it up. No, the tray rebounds.

The jersey is removed and the battle goes on. I could assist, but I'm working on my silent Oliver Hardy impression at the moment, and besides I'm sentenced to eight hours of this, I want no contact with him at all. How those poor exiles transported to Australia must have suffered: they had two months at sea with no escape from those they were sat with, that's almost as bad as taking a coach from Edinburgh to Cardiff. Thankfully a stewardess passes our seats, and with a sunny smile and cheery reminder, locks the tray in place. I'm relieved, but Gravity Boy has the audacity to give one of those condescending grunts that loosely translate as 'Yeaah, I know, I knooooow, I was just doing it'. Fortunately she also spots that his seat-belt is undone, thus saving him an hour attempting to put it in a reef knot, and an unspecified amount of time removing my pen from his arm.

An eight hour flight from Singapore to Brisbane next to a numpty leaves me only one option: fill the glass, put the headphones on, listen to some music and read. For the flight I had imaginatively chosen Bill Bryson's book *Down Under*, accompanied by Men at Work's 'Down Under', certain that no-one besides me had thought of such an original mood-setter before. I glance smugly round the cabin to see an Airbusful of noses buried in a sea of books bearing the word BRYSON in large letters. And are those lips murmuring 'vegemite sandwich,' or is that my imagination? Hmmm. I may not be at the cutting edge of research but at least I'm on the right track, whereas one bloke in the next aisle is reading *Notes from a Small Island.* Either he's on the wrong flight or he's in for a confusing time when we land. I want to suggest he reads it upside down; it'll make better sense that way.

Currently, sport aside, my principal knowledge of Australia is an old folk myth carelessly dropped into my youthful brain by my siblings: if you meet a talking dog on the night of a full moon you will be turned to stone. That may sound an unlikely sequence of events, but it scared the willies out of me when I was a small child. It was my sister who first broke this crucial piece of news, and as a five-year-old I went in absolute dread of meeting dogs in case any saw fit to talk to me. After what felt like weeks of fear, my brothers attempted to coax me out of my funk by asserting the juju was only effective when the moon was at its grandest, and I could walk the streets in safety between times – because of course in those days loquacious puppies were the biggest threat on the roads. But when you're little, just as the summers seem to last forever, the moon is always full, so still I avoided anything that looked like it was about to swap, 'Woof-woof', for 'How do you do? Damn, I've done it again!'

In order to allay my fears, it was spelled out to me that as an Australian belief, such magic could only be effective in Australia. This did the trick and reassured me sufficiently to stop hiding from dogs, but I vowed there and then not to take any chances and avoid this mystical island forever. It was a mistake, the very next dog I met, a neighbour's Dalmatian, bit me on the ear, and it didn't even have the decency to say 'Sorry.' And now here I am breaking my oath and heading for the land where the finest statues are crafted by dingoes, I must be nuts. I clearly recall once asking my brother what it was the dogs said to you, and he (ignorant as ever) said it didn't matter, just the talking alone was sufficient to petrify. I realise now, they'll all be inviting you to their next exhibition of sculptural works. There's no bore like an art-bore, whatever the species or phase of the moon.

Four double whiskies and seven hours of amiable buffoonery later, and I've still found no mention whatsoever of talking dogs in this book. Either he was lucky or someone's been fibbing to me. I toss Bill aside and study the maps of Australia in my mini-atlas, loaned to me by my old flatmate Jon, who travelled this fabled land for a year after Uni. At first glance much of Australia appears covered in a fine dusting of pedantic literalism. The mountains with snow on them are The Snowy Mountains, and the great big desert is named The Great Sandy Desert; or as I call it, The Great Big Sandy Desert, because I feel they missed a trick there. (I have every intent of visiting Topless Beach if only I can find it on the map.)

Happily all is not lost. As the inestimable Mr B observed there are some wonderfully rude-sounding Aboriginal names, many of which I suspect were originally a joke on the dumb white fellas, and as genuine as a $10 boomerang. Better yet, Jon either had a very strange itinerary, or like a teenager when first handed a dictionary, he's been looking up all the dirty words and circling them. Some of these names must surely have sprung from the minds of capricious settlers going on a mapping spree when the Governor was on the loo. In Victoria you can ascend Mount Buggery and find a Chinaman's Knob, and New South Wales lowers the tone further with Delicate Nobby and a Come by Chance – and you would, if it was delicate. Meanwhile, South Australia has a Cock Wash, although whether it's drive through or done by hand I can't testify. Childish? Yes. Quite funny? Yes. The flight is flying by and my investigations haven't even taken me to Tasmania yet. When they do, it takes all the prizes without resorting to smut. Who can fail to love such gems as the optimistic Eggs and Bacon Bay, the pessimistic duo of Dismal Swamp and The End of The World, and my all-time favourite, Nowhere Else? There's nowhere else like

Nowhere Else I'm sure. And I'm equally positive I'm the one millionth customer to make that joke, do I win a prize?

My eyes move back across the map to Western Australia when I come across a town called Innaloo – and suddenly I remember Martin and David Boon's record. Martin, where's Martin? I want to get up and search him out, but this would require getting the missing link between apes and tofu to undo his seatbelt and stand up, and I only have one life so I don't want to spend it in solitary doing 'twenty-five to life'. The reason I'm drinking straight whisky is both to numb the pain and cause sufficient dehydration that I can make it to Australia without a toilet break. I do my best meerkat impression, but there's no sign of Martin. Even if I can't see his seat, I should be able to see the convoy of beer being ferried from the galley, but no show, Martin has vanished into thin air.

Strangely, I didn't see him again at any point on the tour, never found how close the big Brummie got to Boonie's record, or if he ever escaped Singapore. It's a mystery worthy of flying via Colombo. Possibly he'd been prevented from boarding for being inebriated, or perhaps he'd made one inappropriate Vietnamese joke too many and is even now languishing in a bamboo cage. I guess we'll have to wait till Sly Stallone makes a film and rescues him.

No matter, it's tray up and fasten seat belts time – and thank God my co-pilot has passed out belted in – because we are preparing for descent. Like Orpheus we are now preparing for our final descent, I'm heading Down Under, and I just hope Cerberus can keep his traps shut.

Chapter 2
SCHOOLIES, TOOLIES, PIGS N WHISTLES
(Wednesday 24th Nov - Afternoon)

'You've chosen the *worst* week to come to Brisbane.' The young, prim hotel receptionist accompanies her whisper of the words 'worst week' with a solemn shake of the head, in case I don't fully understand her meaning and might confuse it with an ethnic German sausage festival. Considering the devastating floods that will befall Queensland just a couple of months later, I'd say her chances of a future career in fortune-telling are limited, but now she is in deadly earnest. I don't know why she thinks it's so bad and I didn't choose the week, it was chosen for me by Cricket Australia, but I am too tired to point this out.

Then, like Russell Crowe confronting a member of the press, it strikes me. Obviously, by my Scottish accent she has detected a clear line of descent from William Wallace, and is warning me of the impending arrival of England's Barmy Army. She must be predicting the chaos that will ensue as a tumultuous sea of pink, singing beer-guzzlers, breaks over the shores of the Gold Coast in wave after choral wave.

'Oh it's alright, that's what I'm here for. Can't wait for it all to start,' I say brightly and with an air of eager anticipation.

'Eeeew! Gross!!' It's an unexpected response. My electronic pass-card is thrust rudely upon me, then with a dutiful after-thought, she pushes the TV channel guide in my direction and backs away. I glance down and see it is open at the erotic channels available in the hotel. Curiouser and curiouser. And not just channel 909.

'What was all that about?' I ask the smooth lad who has lithely taken her place. It would seem we crossed our wires, and

I had arrived in Brisbane during the dreaded week that the 'Schoolies' take over. This is an ancient Australian tradition going all the way back almost as far as talking dogs, back into the mists of the 1970s, when Lilleean Thomsons ruled the world. 'Schoolies Week', if you haven't guessed, is a seven day party where high school graduates celebrate the end of their exams in grand and uninhibited style. The idea was dreamt up in Queensland, and they evidently take it pretty seriously around here: state pride or state shame depending on which side of the fence you're sitting, and whether it's your garden fence they've just vomited over.

As you'd expect in the current climate of media hysteria, while the school leavers see it as their unalienable right to let loose a little, the self-styled 'moral' minority in the press have been screaming about the decline of civilisation and the loss of innocence, whilst simultaneously taking every opportunity to publish photos of teenagers in bikinis. The papers insist it's a tawdry display of alcohol and drug-abuse mingled with promiscuity; a headline guaranteed to make the squarest school-leaver head for the beach double-quick pronto, I'd have thought.

Although Schoolies Week is now a nationwide phenomenon, I'm warned by the receptionist that the Gold Coast is still the number one place to avoid: a temporary Gomorrah of drinking, sex, uninhibited nudity and general Roman debauchery. Aside from that being a great headline for any travel brochure, I'm totally untroubled by such antics. I know the 1970s of my youth were far wilder; they just weren't reported on Twitter.

'Well, there were a few rowdy teenagers on the coach into town, right enough. I just put that down to them being, you know... teenagers – on a coach. That's a pretty potent cocktail at any time of the year. I hadn't realised they were embracing a specific cause.'

'I'm really sorry about them, sir,' he says gravely, but with less disgust than my old receptionist. They're an unexpectedly uptight bunch in Australia. I thought 'no worries' was their strap-line, but I'm beginning to wonder if it's a CBT mantra their therapists have suggested they drum into themselves. Is this really the land that gave us the long-haul drinking record?

'Anything else I can help you with Sir?'

'No, no, that's great thanks,' I say, picking up my bag and flicking through my mental diary for free days to visit the Gold Coast. All in the spirit of news gathering you understand.

I nearly doze off in the lift up to the fifth floor, only shaking awake when I see the sinister wreck of a man in the mirror. It's small wonder the receptionist was disturbed: I look like Freddie Kruger's younger brother, only with slightly shorter fingernails. The bed is calling, the brain cries sleep, but my best chance of avoiding jet-lag is to hang on till early evening and then sleep till late morning.

It's always been a mystery to me why airlines do everything in their power to confuse and disorientate you. Obviously the best way to get to Australia is to leave the UK in the morning and stay awake all nineteen hours to Singapore so it's just like a having a regular day sat in front of the TV watching films, and a late-night out, with free drinks. Then hit the sack and gratefully sleep the eight hour Singapore to Australia leg, arriving around lunchtime, feeling as if you've understandably risen a little late and hungover, but otherwise absolutely in the right time frame and as fresh as a daisy. You'll be all set for a gentle first day and an early night, and by day two you should be ready for even the most depraved party. Instead, it's lights off, lights on, back and forth at all the wrong times all the way there, as they try to accelerate you through what seems more like a week than a day, leaving you irritable, sleep deprived and so confused you're seeing animals that have pouches and bounce.

Even so, I've come half way round the world for this, so despite my body moaning like a recalcitrant adolescent that won't leave its bedroom, I head out into the balmy streets of Brisbane in search of my second wind. Or at least a drink, which should be easier to find. My first port of call is already marked on the map: the official headquarters of the Barmy Army in Brisbane, the Pig 'N' Whistle Traditional British Pub. Yes, I've come half way round the world to drink in a British pub. Birds of a feather migrate together.

The River Brisbane meanders through the city, and the Central Business District that is my destination sits on a peninsula much like the Isle of Dogs. The streets of this densely-concentrated area of skyscrapers are all named after the British Royal family: William, George, Edward, Albert run one way; Alice, Margaret, Mary, Charlotte, Ann run the other; questionable recessive genes run in both directions. I stroll down Elizabeth Street, searching high and low, left and right for Dalglish Street and Gemmill Avenue but without success, so I guess their idea of royalty differs from mine.

I'm here: Eagle Street Pier, a waterfront precinct boasting unrivalled views and offering the very best shopping and dining options in the city. The Pig 'N' Whistle offers steak and chips. Yes, you can see the appeal to the homesick Pom; however, they are in fact excellent, making you doubt the claim that this is an authentic British pub. More suspicious yet, there are also friendly staff, cold beer and the unbearable heat-wave outside, none of which are really in keeping with the theme.

The pub still has a good showing of locals enjoying the relative tranquillity before the full legions of the Barmy Army descend. I know they're local by their complexions, which are reminiscent of an old leather football that's been sitting in the window of a garden shed for sixty years. Campaigners fighting the abuse of sun-beds among teenage girls should display photographs of Brisbanites in schools. Maybe it's just down to the shock of my arrival, but to me they all look like an Andy Warhol painting of W.H. Auden.

To the bar, where with the gleeful anticipation of a Guinness drinker in Dublin, I order my first pint of the local beer, the legendary Castlemaine XXXX Bitter. You have to come to Brisbane for the real deal, and this is it: and, sure enough, just as I imagined it would, it tastes super-duper extra-especially watery and insipid. Savvy readers will know XXXX is actually a lager, but I'm guessing the word lager sounded too girly for an Aussie drink. The Australian trend of calling lagers, bitter (the best seller Victoria Bitter is also a lager), suggests a fondness for old British names and ideals, even if a lighter, colder beer is more appropriate to the climate. In a foreign land the settler yearns for the familiar, and plants their garden accordingly; man said 'let there be geraniums and bitter,' and lo there were geraniums and bitter. And on the sixth day he said 'let there be rabbits' and lo, by the seventh day there were millions of the buggers. These days native flora is making a comeback and replacing the gardens and lawns that travelled the world with the Empire, but the lagers remain bitters and the leporine, feline and murine fauna appear equally ineradicable.

An example of the great dangers of introducing non-native wildlife presents itself immediately: a drunken England fan starts chatting to me. I can tell he is an England fan because he's in uniform: a Barmy Army baseball cap, a Barmy Army T-shirt, St. George's Cross shorts, trainers with white socks at half mast, and skin the colour of a freshly cooked prawn. And I can tell he's drunk because he evidently believes he's the best dressed man in Australia. Without any questioning on my part he introduces himself as Phil and provides me with a glorious insight into his own personal Australian pilgrimage.

Phil is unemployed, and a year out of university, but he's been unable to find a job in the UK to match his degree in Political Science. A shameful indictment of our society. Why can't a young educated lad get a job? And how the hell can the unemployed afford to come to Australia? Phil would make both ends of the political spectrum red with rage, blue with apoplexy and green with envy; clearly his degree has not been wasted. But just before I come over all 'Mr. Appalled of Cheltenham' – ranting about how he is getting too much of my hard-earned tax loot and should be down a mine, sweeping it with a toothbrush – he explains that the Bank of Mum and Dad have paid for his flight to Australia. More than that they've supplied pocket money and told him to find some work over here! Ah privilege, I recognise this. I swap ideological hats and my mind flashes back to the year after *my* graduation in the bleak 1980s of Thatcher's Britain. Of course, I was unemployed too, and my parents took me to Fife for a weekend in the caravan. But only after I'd first cleaned it with a toothbrush.

Phil has been in Brisbane for more than a week in the hope of finding some work but has had no luck so far. 'Wiv so many Aussies working behind the bar in Eng-ger-land, you'd fink there'd be some jobs goin' over 'ere.'

Typical stereotyping xenophobic nonsense: everyone knows the Aussies all work in IT; the South Africans and Poles have got all the bar jobs now. I don't pull him up on it.

'Mmmm,' I demur vaguely in the long practised style of one who has a father that considers the Six O' Clock News a foolish child to be chastised.

'Yeah, I might as well be unemployed in Australia watching the cricket in this wea'ver, as on the dole in Eng-ger-land in the snow.' Even when chatting, Phil pronounces England with three syllables, as though he is chanting it in tune from the football terraces of old. Though that may be due to the vast amount of alcohol he's been consuming all day on an empty stomach, because Phil's manifesto has an 'eating is cheating' policy. 'The less you eat, the easier – and consequen'ly cheaper – it is to get drunk. The drunker you are, the more you sleep, and ther'fore, the less you need to eat.' I nod, humouring him. He nods back with pride. 'It's simple maff'eh'ma'ics!' he concludes with a flourish and a large mouthful of XXXX.

On such logic were founded empires on which the glass never drained. I can't decide whether Phil is a visionary and the kind of young, thrusting go-getter, whose business acumen will assist the British economy in its recovery, or whether his fiscal policy is the very short-term nonsensical thinking that got our finances into such a mess in the first place. If only Phil had done Economics he could have cleared the matter up for me. If I understood economists. And if he wasn't so pissed.

'So Phil, what have you been doing with your time then?'

'Just drinking. And shagging Aussie birds. Nah-what-I-mean? See, wiv' an Aussie bird, every chat-up line's a winner.'

'Mmmm'

'I tell 'em that I was very moved yesterday because I visited a sacred site where many aborigines died…'

'Hmmm'

'… and when the girl nods in interest, I say, "Yeah, Brisbane police station!!"'

'Mppph!!'

'You alright, mate?'

'XXXX went down the wrong way.'   So goes the conversation, with Phil regaling me with his best material: a litany of the usual abuse and old jokes confirming Australians as stupid, uneducated, uncultured and criminal. They sound not so much chat-up lines, as pithy suicide notes, but perhaps sometimes the best way to a woman's heart is through her fist. 'I'm surprised you don't get a smack from these girls.'

'It works ev'ry time. You got to remember, I say it all wiv' a smile and bit o' cockney charm.'

Phil is from Swanley in Kent, a town that would only be within earshot of Bow Bells if they were posted on YouTube, his accent more new-fangled estuary than old-fashioned sparrow. And yet I'm starting to half-believe him; something he says has a note of truth and rings some bells of my own.

'Aussie birds are the best in bed—' Not that. Well, yes that, but not only that. '—but if they ask you if you've ever been wiv' an Aussie girl before, always say no. No. Got it?'

'No.' (We say in unison.)

''Cause then they figure they're represen'ing their country and go for the world record.'

Now this I know to be the case. Twenty years ago as a young buck in London I was a frequent worshipper at The Church, the Australian 'nightclub' in Kings Cross, that actually opened at 11am on Sundays and which was responsible for stripping away much of my small-town innocence. So I know what he is telling me is true. I also know what it is like to watch couples making out while standing in pools of vomit, and a woman urinating on stage in front of a cheering crowd, but there are some things best left out of polite conversation.

'This country's the best mate, and Aussie birds are the best. I'm 'eading down the Gold Coast next. You 'eard o' Schoolies Week?' I feign innocence but consult my mental diary. 'Loads of drunken birds desperate for some action!'

'Sounds good…'

'But you're a Toolie. Maybe better skip it, yeah?'

'A Toolie?' This sounded like fighting talk.

'Yeah, Toolie. That's what they'd call you – Too Old for School.'

'Oh. Is that all?' I say, while wondering if I had really needed to pack that cardigan as magical protection against chilly evenings.

'Well no, it means you're a right tool as well, and you shouldn't be chasing students at your age, you dirty old man, hnah hnah'

I've gone off Phil, and I resolve not to check out the Gold Coast after all. And to burn the cardigan.

'But you're twenty-two. Seems to me you're a bit of a tool yourself Phil…' The loaded sentence is wasted, the bullets fly wide.

'Nahhhh. Some of them like older blokes like me, we're more sophisticated innit?' I think that was *roughly* his reply, but it was a bit lost amidst the huge belch he let out half way through the sentence. Australia doesn't know what it has let itself in for.

Chapter 3
TOUR PARTY
(Wednesday 24th Nov - Evening)

As much as I'm enjoying these tales of alcoholic debauchery, I've agreed to meet one of my pre-arranged contacts at the Victory Hotel a couple of blocks away, so I head back down Charlotte Street and leave Phil in the company of men; it's safer that way. I'm not the only England fan heading in this direction and not the only one to see two attractive girls, busking on the street corner. It's a standard set-list but they sound pretty good and they're getting plenty of interest from passers-by. I stop to listen for a minute and watch as a small group of England lads go over to chat them up; but the girls stick to playing, trying to ignore this unwelcome form of attention. It's a common sight, male bravado, more for the benefit of each other than the buskers. I assume the boys will make a few jokes, give them a few dollars to show there are no hard feelings and leave them to sing for their supper. Instead, what follows stuns me, depresses me, appals me and makes me jealous in equal measures – quite a cocktail. The girls say they have to keep playing as they're raising money to stay in the hostel across the road for the next couple of days, to which one of the lads brightly asks,

'How much do you need?'

'$100,' comes the semi-sarcastic reply.

I like their style. But our five musketeers just glance at each other and shrug, pull out a $20 bill each, and Bob's your appalled uncle from Tunbridge Wells. Now it's the girls turn to shrug, they take the cash, pick up their kit, tell the boys they'll see them in ten minutes, and head over to the hostel to dump the guitar and freshen up! I don't often use exclamation marks but on this occasion I'll make the exception. If Phil was here I suspect he'd applaud. I half expect to see another couple of girls step into the ring and start the bidding for their favours at $50.

When I reach the hotel there's plenty of Brits in residence and, like Phil, they all appear to be pre-occupied with economics; especially the repeated claim that the British banking collapse was part of a worldwide crash. If it was worldwide then Australia must be out of this world, Brisbane seemed booming as I walked here. Some in the Australian media are rejoicing that due to the *UK's* recession (as they see it), the Barmy Army will be down in numbers by at least a battalion compared to four years ago. One of the most popular Army ditties from previous Ashes tours was: 'We're fat; we're round; three dollars to the pound!' That song will not be heard this time, and the exchange rate is on many minds.

If there's one issue to unite the Barmy Army with the Tartan Army it's the unofficial ERM of all travelling sports fans: the price of a pint abroad. Cricket fans here for the duration may find themselves shedding a few pounds of a different sort, as they find their primary waist-fuel beyond their slender means. Australia, land of the amber nectar, is not what our sons of the Empire have been expecting at all, and as they retreat from the bar like the retreat from Kabul, worried faces peer down at hands full of less change than expected or hoped for. I notice a party of Yorkshiremen poring over a receipt like Aberdonians working out their share of a high tea at Claridges.

'Your sums must be wrong,' says one, who couldn't look more shocked if Stephen King had written the tab. But it is true: initial calculations prove correct, they are going to have to halve their usual levels of consumption. Either that or sell a kidney, which will at least speed the effect they're aiming for.

I've managed to make one priceless pint last half an hour when my contact, Dan Bulmer, rolls in. Dan is one of those fortunate people being paid to follow England: he's a tour operator for Living with the Lions, the company I booked this part of my trip with. I'm hoping we'll get on well as I'd left everything so last minute that I'm going to be sharing an apartment with him in Adelaide, so if relations sour it will be an awkward two matches. Sharing football digs is one drunken night; sharing cricket digs lasts so long it requires a certificate of marriage in some countries. Fortunately over our first drink together I can tell we'll have a laugh; he loves his sport and once work is over he's intending to enjoy himself. Besides, if it does go sour and end in divorce I'll demand he keeps me in the manner to which I'm accustomed, and give me custody of the tickets.

Dan is already aware that I work as a journalist and imagines that I too am being paid for my tour. I quickly correct him because it's his round. The truth is I am contributing some articles for my journalism agency, reporting for an unpaid podcast, and writing for an unsponsored blog, but I am very much here as a fan and paying all my own bills. I feel this is the only way to get the real experience, to go through what the true fans go through; put my hand in my pocket and swelter on the unshaded stands alongside them.

'For the sake of the story it's better for me to be travelling with real people. I won't hear the best Barmy Army banter and find out if the English accept the Scots if I'm sitting in the press box eating cake with Derek Pringle, will I?'

'Um...'

'Well, I won't, will I?' I'd sworn to say this little mantra of purity every day that I'm in Oz and eventually I might, just might, believe it myself. I just had to remember not to say it out loud as people will consider me an idiot.

'Well, I think you're an idiot.'

See? The sad truth, is that despite my many begging letters to Cricket Australia, the miserable sods wouldn't give me a press pass. This felt harsh as the chief executive of Cricket Australia is called James Sutherland and the head of the communications department is Lachlan Patterson, you'd have thought with those names they might have welcomed me with open arms as one of their own. I should have changed my name to Glenn McGrath; that might have swung it.

I was disappointed but not surprised. I figured 'media

accreditation', as it is now pompously known, was in high demand. The Ashes are a big deal in the sporting world; they are Cricket's Blue Riband event. Also, knowing journalists the way I do, I knew any hack that could even vaguely claim a passing whiff of an interest in cricket would be scrabbling for an excuse for a paid holiday to Australia. For a journalist, the Ashes are like a non-league club drawing Manchester United in the cup: it's the away leg you dream of. I guarantee one or two of the press passes went to reporters who don't even understand the lbw law.

We chat over the demographics of our party, a source of interest to me. Just as I always wonder who can actually afford a house in Chelsea, wherever I am, I like to identify who 'all these people' are. At least three tourists have just been made redundant and are evidently out to make the most of the downturn. I admire their gambling 'blow the cheque' spirit, while wondering if it is a wise decision, or if their children are wearing hand-me-downs as a consequence. I doubt they're going hungry; these days 'hand-me-downs' mean Nikes more than six months old. But those three aside, Tour Rep Dan confirms my suspicions: there are some comfortable people left in our supposedly poverty stricken Isle.

Just as we were leaving the UK, the Conservative politician, Lord Young was dismissed from the government for telling the country to stop complaining, as 'you've never had it so good.' David Cameron sacked the veteran 'Enterprise Tsar' because his comments were perceived as the embodiment of an out-of-touch Westminster elite. Pretty obviously out-of-touch I thought, he was wearing a bow-tie when he said it. Surely a sacking offence in itself? To many people I knew, it was the same old Tory toffs, showing they were unaware of the pain caused by lost jobs, slashed wages and benefits, and squeezed household budgets. And the fact that fewer cricket fans are travelling to Australia compared to four years ago might seem to prove that times are tough.

But does it? Forty years ago, travelling to Australia at all was an extreme rarity and for most people a one-way trip. In truth, for a happy section of British society, Lord Young was bang on the money. The over-50s with grown-up children and secure jobs or early retirement packages, have paid off their mortgages and are doing nicely, thank you very much. These days a three- or four-week trip round the world is commonplace for some, and cricket has benefitted as much as the booming cruise industry. As soon as P&O build a liner wide enough to fit a decent cricket pitch there's a package we'll all be signing up for. And now that cricket grounds are becoming shamefully homogenous, without the trees, slopes and ditches of yesteryear, the gentle swell of the seas could provide just the variety they need. I should have suggested it to Dan at the time.

Finally the conversation turns to the series in hand.

'What do you reckon Tour Rep? 2-2?'

'Nah, 5-0 England.' Oh, here we go. I liked him and all of a sudden he has morphed into the arrogant England supporter I can't bear at football and rugby matches, he'll be making Spitfire noises in a moment. But wait, there's more: 'Australia are old and injured, they've got no proper opening batsmen and no decent spinners since Warne and MacGill quit. England are a settled team, in good nick, you watch, we're going walk it.'

Okay, okay, this isn't the rant of a delusional red and white tattooed Neanderthal believing in inherent English superiority, it's the view of someone who appreciates the game and takes his job seriously; let's be honest, if your job is chumming people to some of the world's best destinations, wouldn't you? As we natter on he reveals he hadn't expected England to win the football World Cup, and doesn't feel they'll win the Rugby World Cup either. So that's alright then. Now we are really bonding.

'So deep down, Dan, in your heart of hearts, you're a defeatist pessimist with no real belief that your teams have a hope in hell of winning anything?'

'Well, I wouldn't put it quite like that...'

'Have you ever thought about joining the Tartan Army? Seriously, you'd be right at home.'

Chapter 4
FIRST TEST, DAY ONE
NOT NERVOUS
(Thursday 25th Nov)

It is the first morning of the Ashes and I'm wide awake at 5am. I'm not alone. When I go for a walk, all around me are jet-lagged England supporters wandering aimlessly in the bright white Queensland light; their numbers can't be too depleted. I stop for breakfast in a bar and find myself surrounded by assorted postmen and street cleaners. It's quickly apparent, that for a city, Brisbane is astonishingly clean; it is as though an army of 1950s mums hold a spring-cleaning competition every night. I had exactly the same thoughts in Cape Town: whether it's civic pride, job creation schemes, or they're just not a bunch of bloody chavs like us, our old colonial towns put the cities of Britain to filthy shame. We've not considered how pleasantly we could live if we only tried. It's long amazed me how many streets in London are disgusting and run down and yet lined with BMWs; perhaps if we all spent a little less on our cars and a little more on our environment we wouldn't need to central lock ourselves away from it. Just an early morning thought.

I return to my hotel to find, sitting in reception, bold as you like, Ricky Ponting, Simon Katich, and (sporting a fine Movember moustache) Ben Hilfenhaus. Unless it's an entire squad of impressive lookalikes, I'm staying in the same hotel as the Australian team! What an unexpected result. Injury worry Michael Clarke is sitting quietly, and contentedly eating his muesli. Or at least he is until ex-international Darren Lehmann greets him with a huge welcoming slap on his dodgy back, causing the muesli to spill and heaven-knows-what to happen to his spine. Some sort of Aussie fitness test I presume. Unless

Darren's hoping to make a come-back and is taking out his rivals one by one.

The rest of the players are starting to congregate, waiting for the little mini-buses to vacate the parking lot and for their luxury coach to arrive. I do a double-take when the bowlers start boarding the first mini-bus. That can't be right? I've seen village sides in Scotland travel in more ostentatious transport; a premiership football team wouldn't carry its boots around in those. But good on them; why waste money on fripperies? No wonder the roads are so immaculate.

The boarding Aussies all reply to wishes of good luck graciously and Peter Siddle says he is not at all nervous.

'Are you nervous, Peter?'

'Not at all.'

Told you. I'm giddy with excitement, I have a scoop. Newspaper headlines screaming, '*Siddle – Not Nervous*' spin before me; a Press Award awaits. Possibly I need more sleep. Good for him, because most of us fans appear to be nervous.

That bus leaves and the batsmen ready themselves for the next one, queuing like returning holidaymakers in an airport taxi rank – and look, they've all bought souvenir bats. It's terribly cute, but it's time for me to pack my own bag and head towards the Gabba, and already the hospitality of Brisbane is showing itself off. No problem getting there: if you show your match ticket you are allowed a free trip on public transport to and from the ground. I can't see the tight-arses of Transport for London or Strathclyde Partnership for Transport allowing free travel for the spectator travelling to Lords or Hampden. They sooner blow the cash on their latest rebranding I dare say. (Partnership for Transport? God help us.)

The Gabba: 411 Vulture Street, Wooloongabba, Brisbane. The most poetically addressed sporting venue on the planet, and I'm here for the first day of the Ashes. It is the beginning of the renewing of one of the oldest rivalries in sport. Is there any other sport where the clash between two presently mid-table sides could mean so much? I've not explored the realms of Kabbadi or Camel Wrestling, but as far as most Western sports go, this is it. And it lasts for over seven weeks! That's the collected attention span of virtually half a million teenagers. But don't say cricket doesn't move with the times, seven weeks is taking it at a run. As recently as the early 1970s a tour of Australia lasted nearly four months: long enough for a young lad to go right through puberty and be thrown out the church choir. No wonder the summers seemed so endless when we were boys.

Regardless of their length, for the last couple of Ashes series Down Under, the very first morning of the very first Test has been pivotal, if that's technically possible. And if that sounds to you like an uneven degree of leverage, you'd be right; but twice in a row the first day of the Gabba Test set the tone for the entire series. Eight years ago, Nasser Hussain won the toss and fatally decided to bowl, allowing Australia to ease their way to 338 for 1; then four years later Steve Harmison – feared by batsmen everywhere and briefly the world's premier fast bowler – delivered his first ball to second slip, bringing hilarity to Australians and a dire sense of foreboding to England fans. Both times, notwithstanding some great individual performances, the English returned home well and truly drubbed. What humiliations will the opening session at the Gabbattoir heap upon the boys from Blighty this time?

Walking up Vulture Street alongside thousands of cricket fans, the excitement is getting to me. The cry goes up:

'Come on England! Come on England!'

Right, that's got to me. I can't seriously expect them to shout anything else, but it's awkward for me and for the Welsh too, who are rarely acknowledged in the England and Wales Cricket Board. So rarely indeed that it's abbreviated to ECB, writing the Welsh out of it altogether, just as they've been omitted from the Union Flag. It's a wonder they don't revolt. 'Come on United Kingdom of Great Britain and Northern Ireland!' doesn't trip off the tongue though. If they'd have a go at 'Come on Albion!' at least allow me to join in as far as 'Alba—' Plus I'm more accustomed to that, as Stirling Albion (sworn enemies of Arbroath) are the fitba' team of my University town. Hearing shouts of, 'Come on Albion!' to a side on the wrong end of a 5-0 drubbing is mother's milk to me.

There is a bit of a rumpus at the turnstiles. A kerfuffle in fact. As with all sporting venues these days, all bags are being checked and many items are on the banned list – usually alcohol, glass bottles, and sometimes professional cameras too – but it is uncommon to find that the bag itself is on the banned list. Not all bags are forbidden; those who own bags with one zip are welcomed here with open arms, but the Gabba steadfastly refuses entry to any bag with two or more zips. Two zippers: banned. By what fantastic fascistic logic is carrying a holdall with two zippers a danger to personal safety in a public place? And are they checking trousers as well? Because I am sporting a rather nifty pair with no less than five zips. Not as a Toolie statement of Punk rebellion, I should add. They secure otherwise pickable pockets and allow for easy conversion of trousers into shorts; a genius invention that I think comes slightly higher than the wheel in terms of human achievement, though I'm not convinced 'the kids' would agree.

By now a number of irate, would-be spectators are asking the Gabba turnstile staff searching questions on their reasoning, logic, and parenthood. 'Stadium policy,' is the blank blanket answer given. It is strictly speaking an answer, but it doesn't answer the question – surely the minimum requirement of any answer. However, there are many sections of society you can never win an argument with: creationists, climate-change deniers, mothers, fathers, girlfriends, or even people that are actually in the right. And at the very top of that list are security personnel. They may not know right from wrong, or even right from left, but there is no possible victory when they have the power to block you from the venue without any justification whatsoever, and are liable to do so out of sheer bloody-mindedness (the standard security reaction to complaint the world over). The fans ultimately and forlornly understand this. Not since they took down the signs saying 'No dogs, No Irish, No Gypsies' has there been a more draconian entrance policy.

Those carrying bags and backpacks with two zippers are instructed to take their offensive accessories to the long queues at the Gabba cloakroom and then return to the turnstiles without them. I glance nervously at my trousers. Realising that witnessing the opening deliveries of the First Test is crucial, a lot of punters give up and just dump their two-zippered bags on the pavement. A whole cottage industry could evolve around the weight of luggage being left; there's more baggage by the roadside than all my ex-girlfriends combined. But I keep my zippy trousers on and gird my loins for a fight.

It works. Waving my unoffending bag in the disgruntled security guards' faces, and declaiming, 'One zip! One zip!' as if heralding the second coming, I'm quickly waved through, trousers and all, without anyone once glancing at me directly. This is fortunate, as in the blistering heat I am running commando, and I discover once through the turnstiles that my flies are at half mast. Too many zips to keep track of obviously; the Gold Coast doesn't know what it is missing.

The fans who have headed to the cloakroom were obviously confident that the first ball will not be so significant this time round. If that was their belief then they were right: the first ball of these Ashes is uneventful. It is the third ball that dismisses England captain Andrew Strauss and sets the tone. His exit immediately silences the Barmy Army; and, into the preternatural silence, comes a small chant from a handful of Australian fans with memories of four years ago:

'You're fat, you're pink – your pound is on the shrink!'

Not exactly Lennon and McCartney but another early victory for the Aussies. A little moment of cricket history, missed by many who'd paid five grand to be in the cloakroom.

The second wicket falls and I chat to a few natives who are disappointed despite the early breakthroughs. Are they so accustomed to easy wins that they have become incapable of joy? It transpires the major source of their sense of anti-climax is that Pietersen and Trott won't be batting together, so they can't make jokes about them calling for a run in Afrikaans. It's been a source of controversy, but I quite like the fact that four of the England starting eleven, and five of the touring party, were born abroad. It helps my case when people argue against my right and desire to support them. As Western Province's Jonathan Trott walks back, he passes Pietermaritzburg's famous son, KP, on his way to the crease, and I stifle a mischievous urge to call out, 'Come on KwaZulu Natal': a great chant for the terraces, especially if delivered in full native style.

Lunchtime at the Gabba and there is a mass exodus to the neighbourhood pubs. I've not witnessed such a stampede towards the bars since I was at an Irish music festival and Van Morrison said, 'And now here's one from my new album.' But I remain in the stadium and blether with a couple of lads belonging to Dan B's touring party, and great company they are too, so the forty minutes fly by. Ade and Simon are friends from Warwick Cricket Club, who have forsaken family to come out together for the Brisbane and Adelaide Tests, leaving Ade's teenage son at home and consumed with envy. This is not the world I grew up in where teenagers are jealous of us toolies— sorry, oldies. I was never jealous of my father except when he got to stay up and watch Kenneth Williams on Parkinson and I was sent to bed at 9.30. Mind you, I don't recall my father ever buggering off for a three week jolly while the rest of us shivered at home so it's not surprising.

These days I can stay up as long as I like and there's nothing worth watching. No matter, we don't need TVs as we're here in the flesh and on a trip of a lifetime, and we intend to cut loose a little. The only the thing that might pee on our parade, is that we're spending all the money we've saved to put our parents into a nice retirement home, just to wet our whistles. But it is hard to keep count. The price for a beer at the Gabba is $6.60 for 425ml of lager that is less than 3% alcohol. As you can see there are three conversion rates required: dollars into pounds, millilitres into pints and shandy into beer. I don't have the desire or inclination to work out how much that all comes to in old money, but I am reliably informed by a fat bloke in a Newcastle United shirt that it is around '£5.70 for a pint of piss, man', and £9.50 to tally with a pint of the real stuff. I'm dumbfounded. It's 28 degrees and here's a Newcastle fan wearing a shirt. When it's minus five in February the entire Toon Army goes topless and treats Match of the Day to a display of their guts wobbling to the tune of 'Blaydon Races', but when it's toasty warm they come fully dressed. Evidently at these prices he is still a few fluid ounces short of the critical mass required for a striptease meltdown.

Play recommences and the second session poses a conundrum. 'How to explain cricket to a Martian or an American?' is one of the cricket lover's favourite games. An entire tea-towel industry has boomed with the funny lines about one man being in and then out, and then in again and then out again, until they are all out. Try then, explaining the following to said Martian or American: in the morning England scored a massive 86 runs and lost 2 paltry wickets and were generally regarded to have won the session; in the afternoon England scored a miserable 86 runs and lost a disastrous 2 wickets, and the session is adjudged by all to be won by Australia. Confused? To cope with the strain of the paradox, as the players take tea I seek wise counsel in the bar, where it is all explained to me perfectly. It has something to do with the hardness of the ball, the timing of the wickets, the phase of the moon and the sum of the squares on the other two sides. I forgot to make a note of it at the time, so you'll have to work it out for yourself.

Thankfully, for my poor brain and liver, during the final session of the day the game turns strongly in one team's favour. Peter Siddle arrives on the scene to win the day for Australia with a devastating display of fast bowling and the first hat-trick I've ever seen. Three wickets in three balls, and good wickets too: Cook, Prior and Broad – what a birthday present for the big Victorian. He soon adds Swann taking his tally to six for the day, and England are all out for a worryingly-fragile 260. Siddle Vicious they call him over here, a great nickname if ever there was one. I try to look smug and unsurprised. He's only confirmed what he told us at breakfast: that he wasn't feeling nervous. I'd heard it first, me me me. Maybe I should have warned the England camp.

Chapter 5
JIMMY AND NICKY
(Thursday 25th Nov - Evening)

The day is over, and once again Australia have kicked-off the series in control, but the sheer exhilaration of being in Oz has kept my spirits up. That and being a happy sort of drunk, a world away from the maudlin Scottish sot of legend. So, in fine fettle, I head to the Pig 'N' Whistle at a trot. Time is of the essence as I've got a very special guest lined up for the podcast tonight. The Barmy Army's most famous face, Jimmy, has promised to grant me an interview. Following that, Nicky Campbell, no less, wants to interview me for his *Radio 5 Live* breakfast show, and I reckon the pub would be a nice background buzz for that. It's all go.

I get there in good time, beat the rush for the bar, and wander out into the beer garden where, true to his word, is loitering Jimmy Saville, the designated driver of the Barmy Army. That's a bad analogy. The spiritual leader of the Army, that's more like it. Renowned for his strong singing voice and regaled in his St. George's Cross shirt, once white trousers and an out-sized St. George's Cross top hat, Jimmy more than any other puts the barmy in Barmy Army. He is doing this once-in-a-lifetime trip to the Ashes for the sixth time, and there's definitely something of the cat about him, so I reckon he should be good for three more.

One of his roles is to lead the Army in the stands *à la* Gareth Malone. His signature tune is the chant:

> Everywhere we go
> The people want to know
> Who we are?

Where we come from?
Shall we tell them?
Who we are?
Where we come from?
We are the England
The Mighty Mighty England
We are the Army
The Barmy Barmy Army
Andrew Strauss's Barmy Army

The song ends with a mass, repeated, fast chant of 'Barmy Army' with Jimmy bouncing from leg to leg and conducting the droning hordes – not bad for a man of 60. I'm amazed when he tells me his age as he is so slim and looks in decent physical condition. I reckon he should bring out a fitness DVD for the lucrative Christmas market, it's such a simple workout, the only exercise being singing lustily while hopping and skipping with a flag in one hand and a pint of lager in the other. It would be an instant bestseller. And he could double the running time with domesticity tips on how to keep your St. George's Cross white and get the whole thing sponsored by Ariel. Brilliant idea.

Jimmy Saville is obviously not his real name. He was so christened by those who feel he bears an uncanny resemblance to the old Saturday night icon, which he now plays up to, fake cigar and all. His real name is Victor. 'I can't think of a more inappropriate name. My parents were having a laugh; I've never won anything. I'm a loser. I'm a divorcee, I haven't seen my children for twenty years, I'm destitute; I suppose I'm a bit of a traveller. I classify myself as self-unemployed.' He smiles and continues: 'But with the Barmy Army I'm not castigated, I just have fun and play the role of the joker.'

And that's the truth of it; Victor is not a loser, not by any stretch. He's been dealt some poor cards in his life but he's making the best of them, and here he is in Australia, being bought drinks and feted in the sunshine. Recognised the world over, he's had more than fifteen minutes of fame and still has his own hair, which is more than Andy Warhol did. The official Barmy Army organisation pay Jimmy's expenses and he is good value for that money and the Barmy Army's reputation, a character in an age of corporate blandness, constantly featured on television and in the newspapers.

After another pause for him to be photographed alongside a number of devoted fans I ask him if it's right for a Scot to be supporting England in Australia. For a second he is speechless; something that, by all accounts, rarely happens. Confusion crosses his craggy features, he shakes his head. 'Noooo, you've got your own cricket team.'

'But only at one-day level,' I reply, 'not at Test level.'

He nods his head in agreement and then shakes it violently when I ask him if he'd prefer I supported Australia. And this is effectively the problem I am finding with supporting England, I am both an insider and an outsider. An England fan but not English. It's also a problem that he's communicating via head gestures when I'm holding an audio microphone in front of him.

Jimmy believes – and I may have encouraged him in this – that all Scots support anyone but England in sporting contests. But growing up in the 1970s and 80s, cricket was the only daytime television we had, except for repeats of *The Flashing Blade* and two weeks of Wimbledon. (And consequently to this day I support England at Cricket and the French at fencing; and I still hate tennis for interrupting a good thing.) I instantly became an aficionado of the old game and the endless array of eccentric characters. To me, watching the cricket on the TV during the summer holidays was infinitely better than going outside and, well, playing cricket.

Jimmy is won round by my argument. He's still nodding and I've just been ranting into my own microphone for five minutes, this is going to need editing later. Anyone would think we'd been drinking. I'd better straighten up if I am to feature on national radio. We finish our conversation and Jimmy says he hopes I will remain an England supporter. Whenever we bump into each other he promises to call himself 'See you, Jimmy.' Strange the stereotypes that linger longest in popular consciousness. Perhaps I should change my name to Russ Abbott to blend in with the Saturday Night theme.

My phone rings at the licence payers' expense and I retreat to a corner for my piece on the Nicky Campbell show. Listeners to such shows may be surprised by how these things play out from the participants' perspective, so for your illumination this is how it was from my position. It's my first time on the radio and I'm glad I've had a few drinks to steady the nerves and slur the speech – it's so important to sound relaxed on these occasions. Considering my condition it also feels vaguely obscene, like injudiciously drunk-dialling a girlfriend. I'm standing in the quietest spot of a crowded pub garden, while I gather my thoughts and prep some ideas in an effort to come across as vaguely professional. The producer comes on the line, tells me I'll be on in ten minutes, and patches me through so I am able to listen-in on the show while this happens: something I didn't expect but lets you focus.

It's a bizarre sensation, listening to an everyday British radio show through a mobile phone in a pub in Australia, surrounded by a sea of chunky men in white leisure wear. Weirder still, I'm about to be part of the event; it feels as I imagine it would if you were watching a TV drama and were suddenly able to reach inside the screen and move the scenery around. Not exactly a god in the machine, but as close as I'm likely to get.

Embarrassingly, my divine powers suddenly fail me, as shortly before I'm due on my Blackberry packs up. Dead. I try the usual hi-tech solutions – pressing the power button, taking the battery on and off, shaking it, complaining to it in a John-Cleese-style – but all to no avail. My moment of fame has gone before it arrived and the fast-breaking British nation are just going to have to wait till the book comes out for the latest from Queensland. Fair enough, they had to wait three years for Captain Cook to get back with news of its discovery, the anticipation will just add to the excitement when it hits the shelves. That's not quite what I think as I skulk back to the bar in ignominy. In actuality I'm balancing my disappointment with a relief that millions won't hear me talking like a drunk-driver telling a policeman he's only had a couple of halves.

Chapter 6
FIRST TEST, DAY TWO
THE POM FACTOR
(Friday 26th Nov)

November 26th is the anniversary of the outbreak of a little known Australian conflict from early in the Second World War. I'm only aware of it because there is a track on one of the Pogues' early albums called 'The Battle of Brisbane'. It can't have been much to sing about because it is an instrumental Irish jig, suggesting it was a fairly jolly battle with plenty of refreshment taken. Undeterred, I don my mackintosh and homburg, and begin my investigation.

It transpires it was a clash between military personnel from the US Army stationed in Brisbane on the one side, and Australian servicemen and civilians on the other. By the time the violence had calmed down two days later, one Australian had been shot dead and hundreds of soldiers from both sides had been seriously injured – the street battle to beat all street battles – so not so jolly then. What could have brought this incivility on? Surely not the usual debate between those who believe cricket is a superior game to baseball, and those who are wrong? A thousand-a-side brawl on the merits of Bradman versus DiMaggio? Official histories tend to pin the blame on the usual issues of American contempt for their allies, American lack of manners and public morals, conspicuous American wealth and goods, and consequent American appropriation of all the girls. I'm struggling to see the consistent feature here, but I'm sure Poirot would spot it.

Coincidentally, the worst of the fighting occurred at the corner of Adelaide and Creek Streets, just a short walk from the Pig 'N' Whistle pub, and as I'm still waking insanely early I take a roundabout route to the Gabba, and swing by there looking for breakfast. In the half hour or so of walking in a big loop I'm aware of the searing sun changing the complexion of my skin from a North-Eastern bluey-white to a darker pasty white and then to pink, and that's at nine in the morning. It is the hottest day so far and for all its humidity, Brisbane is not going to be the warmest stop on my trip, not by a long chalk – you can see how easily tempers might flare.

On the street corner there is not a memorial to be seen. I had hoped for a documentary film-crew or two, an Australian David Starkey and an American Simon Sharma perhaps, fighting with fists over the rights to this intriguing battle; but alas no, not a sausage. I suppose it might not be seen as something to commemorate, but I don't see why not, so long as you blame the Americans. And as they won't be reading this, let's do that. Oh, you did already. Well the sports pages are where true immortality lies, so I immediately resolve to put matters right by putting it on the blog and naming my racehorse, Battle of Brisbane. Should I ever own a racehorse, that is.

When play gets underway Australia continue to dominate, with Katich and Watson accumulating runs slowly. But Watson doesn't make it to lunch (or rather he makes it too early), and Ponting enters the stage to a cacophonous mix of cheers and boos. Not a common sound on a cricket ground. It's fair to say Ponting is not exactly a popular figure among the England supporters; he attracts little of the affection Marsh and Lillee did, even when they were sticking the boot in. This point is reinforced when just after lunch the complexion of the game changes quicker than my skin tone. Anderson grabs Ricky's wicket with a slower ball that is heading leg-side, but Ponting is over-ambitious and is out to a bad ball. There are few things more painful to a quality player, and there are hoots of derision and celebration from the Barmy Army. Katich falls soon after and suddenly England are in charge. But then, just as abruptly, Hussey steadies the ship and rocks the boat simultaneously, blasting Swann's bowling mercilessly as though it's a

Twenty/20 game. We certainly weren't expecting that. Hussey is a truly great player who has somehow remained relatively obscure outside his home country, but no question he's the biggest dog in the pack today.

The afternoon session is lively off the pitch as well, with the Queensland Constabulary forcibly – very forcibly – removing a couple of Stoke City fans from the ground: overly aggressive and drunken behaviour (the fans, not the police, although you have to wonder). An Aussie behind us tells anyone willing to listen, that the Stoke lads would be fined $2000 for being drunk. Well if they can afford to be drunk at Gabba prices they can afford to pay that fine. I was surprised to learn of this law, but in Brisbane you don't have to add a disorderly to proceedings, just being drunk is an offence.

There's always been a problem with prison overcrowding in the UK, but it would be the biggest crisis ever faced by the Ministry of Justice if simply being drunk was a crime back home. We'd have to bring back transportation just to cope with a typical Saturday night in Burnley. The high seas would be awash with boats echoing with the old seafarers cries of, 'Do you f*****g want some?' and 'Leave it Kyle, he's not worth it.'

Fortunately calm is restored when we are treated to a walkabout by the Queen, who surveys her subjects, English and Australian alike, with a regal hauteur that commands instant respect. The effect is magical, even though to everyone's dismay it turns out to be not Her Majesty, but a six-foot tall bald man in a mask, though for a moment he had us fooled.

The excitement of the session is further enhanced by the newly introduced Decision Review System. The questioning of umpire decisions and allowing television replays to be the final adjudicator is great for the fans; not since the pauses in a Harold Pinter play has there been so much drama in just waiting. Andrew Strauss, however, is as bewildered as an unimpressed critic at the first night of *The Birthday Party*. When Clarke is given 'not out' England call for the review but the replay confirms the decision and both referrals have already been squandered. The skipper couldn't have looked with more anguish at a TV screen if he had inadvertently Sky Plussed *Rosemary and Thyme* instead of *The Wire*. Adapting to this new fangled stuff is evidently going to take England as long as it took the M.C.C. to acknowledge the existence of women that do more than make sandwiches. However, Clark and North are both out before tea, leaving the match perfectly balanced. It stays like that as play ends early when the heavens open, and we surge to the gates in a raindrop-spattered wave.

I've arranged to go out with Tour Rep Dan, Ade and Simon from Warwick, and another member of their group, a civil servant who has picked up the moniker TMS. The nickname was not awarded because he is a statto-supreme or addicted to Radio 4 LW, but due to the fact that he is constantly nipping off for a cigarette and hence has become known affectionately as Test Match Smoker. Not one to judge a book by its cover, TMS prefers to judge a land by the quality of its club sandwiches. So far Brisbane, and consequently Australia, is a huge letdown to him in this regard. Let's hope he doesn't work for the FCO, or there may be a diplomatic incident brewing.

Thankfully, the rain abates and we set off on a cruise of the river. It's a fun little jaunt, with the only disappointment being a failure to spot any England players on a pedalo; they're just not built in the Flintoff mould these days. But we all enjoy gawping at the usual houses of the holy and ill-repute: City Hall, Parliament House, St. John's Cathedral, Treasury Casino (I'll leave you to figure out which are which). But the real attraction on the riverside was born after the World Expo that was held on the South Bank in 1988. Rather than redevelop the area for commercial gain, the Government were pressured into turning it into what's now the rather splendid South Bank Parklands. Twenty years later they put up the [Ferris] Wheel of Brisbane to mark the anniversary of this little demonstration of people power and to add to the spectacle.

Obviously they're just slavishly copying the homeland, as of course back in the 1950s London did a similar thing with its South Bank. Following the 'Festival of Britain' the area was redeveloped for the public good, but instead of Brisbane's approach of grass, trees and water, they used concrete, concrete and concrete. This was considered more functional by the team of architects of the, then-fashionable, Blind-And-Criminally-Insane school. We should be grateful we got a theatre and a concert hall, as by '88 the idea of using land in British cities for anything other than over-priced housing and empty office blocks would have been unthinkable. Typical of Australia, they're still lagging behind the mother country, providing public amenities and unable to see the social value of naked greed.

We stumble off the boat and into the Victory Hotel where the music is perfect for the forty-something followers of England: Neil Diamond, the Monkees and Tony Christie. They don't need a DJ, they could just stick on *Now That's What I Call Mid-Life-Crisis 57* and leave it playing. Wannabe bad-boys, Oasis, are also given a frequent airing, as they are now considered the band of choice for rotund, middle-aged men in ironed, short-sleeved shirts, who think they're hip. Liam would not be amused, but I am.

It's Friday night in sultry Brisbane, but the tourists evidently have thoughts of home. This becomes apparent when we witness an hilarious display of dancing, entirely out of time with the music, by an unfortunate Wagner lookalike on the periphery of the dance floor. X Factor fans gaze in amazement as he struts his stuff to the various beats. The ability for the British drunk to comedically improvise never ceases to amaze, and as our lad finishes his moon-dance to 'Hot Stuff' – yes, not even a Michael Jackson song – he is greeted by a cacophony of faux-Irish voices crying, 'He looks like a pop star, he acts like a pop star and the public love him!'

It isn't old classics all night: the DJ throws in a few Australian classics by Peter Andre and Kylie, demonstrating once again that the less said about the Australian contribution to popular music the better, especially when coached by English-man Pete Waterman. However, not all 'Music of Antipodean Origin' is so bad: I own a considerable number of Aussie albums that are mercifully free from his influence, and all of them written and performed by Scots. The reality is that Australia's musical top order is as Scottish as England's cricket team is South African. Their players with the best sales-averages are AC/DC opening bats Angus and Malcolm Young (Glasgow), the late lamented AC/DC fast bawler Bon Scott (Kirriemuir), all-rounder Colin Hay (Kilwinning) of Men at Work, and Jimmy Barnes – unfamiliar to British ears but huge in America and their most successful solo artist – who set sail from Glasgow at a tender age, intent on showing the Aussies how to pitch a song on a good length.

And yet despite everything we've done for them, the Australians don't act the least bit grateful. It's 2am and the bar is now showing the semi-final of the Masters' tennis between Andy Murray and Rafael Nadal, and all present are roaring the Spaniard on to deliver a drubbing to the hated Murray. The consensus of the dozen Aussies I speak to is that Andy is the 'worst kind of Englishman.' Twelve may not be a representative sample of a nation's opinion, but at that time of the morning I can't see Gallup doing any better. When I ask the reason for such antipathy, I am told that Murray is a moaner, he's a cry baby, he is the ultimate whinging Pom, but ultimately: 'We don't need a reason to hate the English.' When I highlight that he's Scottish they reply, 'Same bloody thing.'

So that's me told. Considering my cricket affiliation, I suppose I can see their point, and yet the English don't: all the English in the bar are cheering for Nadal too. This sounds like treachery. If England had any tennis players to rival us, fair enough, but since they haven't and they've not found any rent-a-Canadians recently, you'd think they'd back Murray. I used to back Tim Henman, even though he was as English as a Morris Dancer and tennis is for old ladies. When I quiz the English drunks on this I get the same old apocryphal story: they have never forgiven Murray for his infamous 'anyone but England' reply, when asked who he would be supporting at the World Cup of 2006. His oft-recounted comeback was a flippant like-for-like response to jovial ribbing he was getting from Henman and journalist Des Kelly following Scotland's failure to qualify; it was only a joke but the mud has stuck.

Besides, what they forget is that Scotland's 'anyone but England' attitude lingers because once Macbeth and Co. had dealt with the Norwegians, the belligerent southerners were the only national enemy Scotland ever had. In contrast the English spent centuries at everyone's throats and Spain runs France a close second for the prize of enduring Anglo-Enemy Number One. 'Anyone but England' is a belief held just as passionately in Madrid, Paris and Berlin as Glasgow. So why then are they cheering on a Spaniard? Have they forgotten the Armada?

The fact is, that the English don't like Murray because he's the antithesis of the strawberries-and-cream eating, straw-boater wearing British tennis ideal. They wish everyone would use wooden rackets and Jeremy Bates was still our number one. Andy is too scruffy, too snarly, too inarticulate; and he wins – and wants it – too much. As he freely admits, sport is the only string to his bow; he's a one-dimensional über-sportsman of the new breed.

Truth be told, he's just the sort bloke who would effortlessly blend into the Australian populace, but they clearly aren't won over either. Loud cheers from all sides of the Ashes fence greet his ultimate defeat. Why is it that unlike the singing, joking, English-baiting Irish – who are welcomed and supported everywhere – the singing, joking, Sassenach-teasing Scot is not? Right now you'd be forgiven for thinking Australia was discovered by Cortez, and Philip II of Spain was born in Cricklewood.

Chapter 7
FIRST TEST, DAY THREE
CARRY ON BRISBANE
(Saturday 27th Nov)

Since my arrival I have been majorly impressed with Brisbane's high standards of social responsibility. The exceptions to the rule are Sections 24 to 27 in the lower tier at the Stanley Street end of the Gabba, where the rowdiest fans gather and are allowed to drunkenly slouch behind the seating area. It's fairly foul: the floor so drenched in beer that fans wearing trainers stick to the ground and those wearing flip-flops slide for yards and end up doing the splits. The gymnastic displays are almost balletic at times; if you can imagine Nadia Comăneci attempting not to spill four pints of lager you'd not be far off.

It is from this cesspit of depravity that I see an Australian fan being ejected from the ground at ten o' clock in the morning for trying to enter the female toilets. That's impressive by any standards; you have to get up early to be that drunk before play has even started. Collared by the police he takes the concerned-citizen line of defence, and starts explaining that he was about to throw up and the Ladies was closer. Although notably, he's not now throwing up on the coppers who've stopped him; probably a wise move. He's read his rights Aussie style: they tell him he can only use the women's facilities if he's wearing a dress.

'Great, where do I get one of those?' replies our lad, lurching back towards the Ladies.

'Outside,' shouts the copper, 'and that's where you're going.'

A more entertaining removal from the stadium I couldn't have wished to witness, I give it a perfect 10.0 for artistic interpretation. My own refreshment in hand I arrive at my seat without any unfortunate triple salkos, and there, either side, are two of the largest, sweatiest England supporters on the tour. How on earth have I lucked into being between these two? They don't need bucket seats, they need skip hire. The old Barmy Army chant about being fat and round was clearly composed by these blokes. I grease myself liberally with sunblock so I can slide between them and not get stuck, but I can tell I'm in for an uncomfortable day.

And so it proves, but not as torturous as it must have been for the England team. Hussey shows what can be done on this pitch, and piles on the runs and the misery. Mr Cricket, the man with the worst nickname in sport, reaches his century before lunch, but not without controversy. In only the third over Aleem Dar gives him out lbw to a ball from Anderson, but Hussey is quick to call for a review, and he is reprieved when it's shown to have pitched outside leg-stump. Four overs later, and trapped plum in front by Anderson again, a still-chastened Mr. Dar gives him 'not out'. England threw away both their reviews yesterday, when they were still behaving like a confused dad puzzling over how to work a video camera, so the dodgy decision stands. And Hussey makes hay, lots and lots of hay.

The incident isn't shown on the big screen, but by the power of modern communication we soon all know that Hussey is a lucky man. Ade's son back in Warwick is watching the game on satellite and texting his father the replay decisions. The crowd around me are impressed: not by the wonders of technology, but by a teenage boy that watches cricket when home alone, and not the 900 channels. Had such programmes existed when I was whiling away the school holidays, I might now be on a tour of the fleshpots of Bangkok instead of at the cricket.

The Aussies are individually in strong voice today, especially when England drop catches and misfield – and there are too many such occasions. When your best success before tea is persuading the umpire to change the ball, you can tell you're in trouble. Fielding on the boundary Kevin Pietersen is the victim of some pretty meaty abuse. The more ironic sledges question why he can't get a game for South Africa and 'What's Afrikaans for "England"?' The snider ones suggest that he, not Andy Murray, is the worst kind of Englishman: he actually chose to be one. But this is to give the home crowd too much creative credit, as the most common interjections simply involve the word 'w****r' tagged at the end of any collection of words of the ticket-holder's choice.

I'm used to this at football matches, but it surprises me a bit at the cricket. It shouldn't; this is the notorious Gabbattoir, the ground Simon Jones lay on in serious injured agony, with the taunts and abuse of the Australians ringing in his ears. It doesn't surprise Kevin, who reacts with an amused smile and ends up conducting their better sing-a-longs. Now that's confidence. I consider the headline '*KP: Not Nervous!*' Why break a winning formula? If he saves the match for England it'll seem prescient; if he blows it I can follow the next day with '*KP: Over-confident!*' Such is the way the wheel of journalism turns.

The day rolls on and Haddin and a forlorn Graeme Swann join Hussey with three figures by their name, but the Barmy Army's singing only becomes louder. As Jimmy told me, real fans give more encouragement when their side is losing, and that is definitely the case at the moment. Today's favourite is to the tune of Yellow Submarine, and features the refrain:

> You all live in a convict colony,
> A convict colony, a convict colony.

In its entirety, it's one of the Army's better efforts and a hard one for the Aussies to come back to, although some wags reply with the pithy: 'You all live in a poor economy.' Simple but effective. I like it when chants from the terraces have a smidgen of political satire rather than overt hostility.

Generally, it does not appear to be in the Australian mentality to sing at sporting events, which is perhaps just as well, as some less satirical Aussies chip in with a chorus of: 'I'd rather be a Paki than a Pom.' The racist undercurrent in Australia sometimes floats rather too close to the surface. I suppose it's less hypocritical that way, to publically express what you're thinking in a way no-one in Britain would dare to these days, even if there's plenty still think it. But most of us hope that if something is submerged deep enough, for long enough, it eventually drowns and sinks without trace. How those fans will react if Australia freshens up the team and select the highly-rated Pakistani-born Usman Khawaja is anyone's guess. With perfect timing the big screen flashes up the message: *ICC Anti-Racism Code – racist comments will result in ejection from the ground with possible prosecution and life bans.* So there.

After tea, things calm down and spectating feels a lot relaxed, especially for me, as the two adjacent lard buckets have left early and I can finally breathe out as well as in. It must have been their oppressive presence (or possibly their gravitational pull) holding our boys back, as no sooner have they gone than the English bowlers finally break through and Australia slump from 436 for 5 to a miserable, miserable 481 all out – a meagre 221 ahead. Things are on the up!

Perked by the fightback and with no loss of England wickets before close, I'm ready for a Saturday night out in sunny Brisbane – which will be a lot more pleasant now the sun's gone down. Back at the hotel Ade and Simon introduce me to Brian and his wife Kymberley, who have been lighting up the tour party with their spectacular displays of drinking and exuberant banter. Only Brian is truly interested in the cricket, but he'd convinced Kym to come by telling her she'll get three sessions sun-bathing per day, Which sounds like it could lead to a lot of arguments starting with the words, 'Well it was your idea—'. But so far she's lapping it up.

Brian is a patriotic and partisan England fan. Unashamedly so. I'd go so far as to say, demonstrably. During the football World Cup the façade of his house becomes one huge St. George's Cross. I briefly consider putting a St. Andrew's Cross on my flat, but I fear it may not be worth the effort. Should Scotland ever make it to the finals again, they'll probably be on the plane home before the paint dries. And being such an overt fan has its drawbacks: the day Germany beat England 4-1, Brian had to avoid going to his local pub for fear of being accosted by the only Scot in the village. 'There's a Jock who lives round our way and he loves it when England lose, rubs it right in.'

'Shameful behaviour,' I concur, 'I can't think how he knew you were sensitive on the matter.'

He will not be quite so obviously flying the flag while he's here, as his trip has started in the best British farce tradition, and the red from his St. George's Cross towels has run in the wash and turned his England shirts a fragrant shade of pink. The more I talk to him, the more I feel Brian is writing the script for *Carry on Cricket Tour;* if only Terry Scott were still alive to play the part. Now all we need is Kym's bikini to ping off and the hotel to fall down. I suggest he put the shirts through a boil wash, and if it doesn't get the colour out, at least it'll shrink them small enough that he can give them to a jockey; pink always looks good on horseback.

Suddenly, our attention is drawn to the fact that the enemy, in the form of none other than Ricky Ponting, has entered the hotel bar. Simon and Ade sidle over and egg-on Brian to chat to him, not that he needs much encouragement. He calmly approaches the Australian Captain and rather than bellow 'Eng-er-land' in his face, very politely asks him, 'Mr Ponting, I'm very sorry to disturb you but I was just wondering whether you are allowed to have a drink during a Test match, and if that's a yes would you like to have one with me?'

If nothing else I'm glad we didn't ask Phil, my acquaintance from the Pig 'N' Whistle, I suspect his approach would have been somewhat different. Right now the excitement in the hotel bar is so great I wouldn't swap places with Phil, wherever he is. (Well, not unless he's out-numbered at least two to one by tonight's conquests, in which case I'd consider it.) Meanwhile Sir Ricky calmly surveys the English landmass that fills his field of vision and replies with equal politeness. 'Yes, we are allowed a drink, but no I won't have one with you.'

Well you can't say fairer than that. The captain plays a dead straight bat to a good length ball and it's honours even. Brian enters the annals of tour legends and Ponting has inadvertently opened the flood gates and emboldened the whole lot of us. In the nick of time other Australian players join their captain at the bar to strengthen the defence, before there's a civilized rush for autographs and photographs, which they charmingly play along with.

Ade comes back from having his photograph taken with Shane Watson to tell me that the Aussie entourage have suggested that should their team win the match tomorrow, there might be one hell of a party in the hotel afterwards. Such thrilling news prompts a few England fans to contemplate supporting the Aussies for a day. Would the prospect of a drink with the Aussie team see me change my allegiance, ask the gang? I know they are testing me, so I deny there is any chance of me doing so, while in my head quietly totting up the odds on England fighting back from a match down. At least if England do lose, a night on the tiles with the boys in baggy green on the banks of the Brisbane River would be no mean consolation.

Chapter 8
FIRST TEST, DAY FOUR
GABBA ROULETTE
(Sunday 28th Nov)

It's Sunday, and considering it's the weekend and may be a day of parties, the crowd at the Gabba is disappointingly small. Australia are in a dominant position, yet the ground is only half full. This is their national sport, isn't it? The old gag that 'it's fancy-dress day and all the Aussies have come as empty seats', does the rounds. Sports fans seem to bond over well-worn jokes, especially in the face of adversity; they're a little bit of certainty in an otherwise unpredictable sphere. I've always meant to do a PhD that determines whether the fans of teams that predominately win tell fewer jokes. Could it be that the stands of Camp Nou and Old Trafford don't require this familiar reassurance quite so frequently? There's little funny in sustained success, is that why the Australians don't laugh as often or as loudly as the Barmy Army?

Today I'm wishing I'd worn my Scotland shirt, as I definitely appear on television screens around the world. During the many breaks in play, Channel 9 cut to the crowd, and I'm a prime target for prime time; not because of my chiselled good looks, but because I'm sitting right next to a group of lads from Durham who are all dressed as babies. They've excelled themselves and frankly deserve medals, because it's the full kit – nappies, bonnets, baby bottles and dummies – and whenever they pop up on the big screen they put on a good performance. The Aussies love them too, with plenty of banter through the day and, a nice touch, a barman demanding proof of age when they try to buy drinks.

Don't tell the girls, but when men are alone together they swap fashion tips, and so I ask about the relative merits of nappies versus shorts. They tell me they all found it impossible to put them on themselves, so had to take it in turns dressing one another in their hotel rooms – a disturbing image that stays with me all morning. However, having spent many an hour pre-wedding struggling to pin my kilt and hang my sporran straight, I know how tricky these things are. I'm hoping they weren't interrupted midway, as the sight of a gaggle of half-naked young men pinning each other into giant absorbent underwear might have given the chambermaids a bit of a shock and grounds for legal action. What I forget to ask, is how they manage when they have to go to the toilet. In the circumstances that's possibly a stupid question.

As England confidently accumulate runs and begin to dominate the play, the local fans – already quiet – became quieter, and when the star of the first day, Peter Siddle, drops a catch the babies restart the continuous chant of, 'Siddle, Siddle, Siddle…' that had echoed round the stands on Thursday, only this time it comes with the cooking instructions: 'Just add irony'. This is soon followed by, 'They're here, they're there, they're every flipping where! Empty Seats! Empty Seats!'

A pedant would have suggested that the 21,677 punters who are in the Gabba today would fill any cricket ground in Britain except Lords. But nobody points it out, and even if they did it wouldn't have prevented them from singing it anyway, attendance stats not being as sacrosanct as batting averages. And yes, they really do sing 'flipping': no potty mouths in this crowd. It is good to be amongst people who actually attended Grange Hill as children.

By lunchtime England are back in the game, as Strauss and Cook have batted through the session, but with a keen sense of Schadenfreude, the highlight for the England fans is a sleeping Mitchell Johnson dropping the England captain on 69. The psychological effect that a pro- or anti- crowd can have on players is generally accepted, but in a sport where the same teams play over five days, five times in a row, such things can build to gargantuan proportions. Mitch has already been singled out as a fans' favourite on both sides, only with an entirely different appreciation of what honours such favouritism brings. He's something of a talisman to the Australians, perceived as their out-and-out match winner on his day, but 'Super Mitch' has yet to put in an appearance in this match. So far he's been more Johnson Rotten than Siddle Vicious.

I retire to the Chalk Hotel, a favourite lunchtime haunt for the Barmy Army just 200 yards from the Gabba, about as far as one can sensibly stagger after a hard morning's workout – those songs don't sing themselves. Most of us are just desperate to get out the ground. The P.A. system at the Gabba is a tad powerful for most tastes. Cricket Australia has established sponsorship deals with Vodafone, McDonalds, Johnnie Walker and KFC, so their adverts are boomed relentlessly across the stadium. It is torture, and not at all the sort of hallowed atmosphere one dreams of as a child. One wonders who benefits? Not the fans, for sure. Sponsorship brings money into the sport and that allows for more to be spent on development and training, and more money for the players, but crowds thronged to grounds just as much when the players were less well trained and paid peanuts – in fact more so. And no-one is counting the cost of what is being lost. It doesn't matter how high the standard of play is, all we want to do is watch the best players of our respective nations at any given time, and we'd be just as excited.

It's questionable if standards have risen very far anyway. Perhaps at a domestic level, and fielding has undeniably come on in leaps and spectacular bounds, but only in time to counter the run-surge generated by modern bat technology, and the reduction in boundary lengths with the ropes that allow many of those running, diving stops. The end result is the same, it all evens out. 'The Don' would still be the don in any cricketing fraternity, and I'd as happily have seen him play against poorer fielders with an old 2¼lb bat, if it meant seeing it without adverts shattering our quiet reflection in the intervals.

In cricket, reflection is important. What's the state of play? It's a question that used to be considered four times a day: start of play, lunch, tea and close. In an age of Twitter it's now dispensed 360 times a day with less and less significance or meaningful consideration. If the assessment is completely false it doesn't matter as there'll be a new prediction along in literally a minute. As Jonathan Agnew observed, journalism has become one long procession of anticipation and reconsideration all day long. Thank heavens that real fans at the ground can escape this endless barrage of corporate flatulence and media hot air by nipping across to the pub and discussing the matter in the time honoured tradition, over the cricketer's lunch of a pint of lager.

I don't believe momentum truly exists in sport – except for the luge and toboggan – but the majority view from the Chalk Hotel bar is that England are gaining momentum at a critical time. They are only 87 behind with no wickets down. As they were dismissed for 51 all-out just twenty-one months earlier in the Caribbean, it's uncertain that this is a guaranteed cushy position. But that's the beauty of cricket: you can be behind and still cause a day of arguments about who's really in the lead. It's what makes it such a social sport, and why we still need our long pauses and opportunities to reflect and digest, free from audio-visual assault.

Back at the ground, and in addition to commercial announce-ments, the Gabba P.A. is now publicising the stadium policies, such as the fine for running onto the field and the brutal *'If you throw – you go'* mantra, which informs anyone contemplating throwing an object of any description, that they will be ejected from the ground. We have all just about had enough of this being drilled into us by the electronic Sergeant-Major when we enjoy one the funniest moments of the day. After tea, with England now leading and still only one wicket down, it becomes apparent that Australia are running out of ideas and the few Aussie supporters are becoming frustrated. One female fan in desperation exhorts her team at the top of her voice to 'do something!'

The Durham Babies respond to this with a collective catty, 'Woooo!' and then one suggests, 'I'd rather you do something, pet!' There follows the usual banter practiced by cavemen and women through the ages, till the exasperated girl finally demands, 'What's bloody wrong with you?'

'I need feeding,' comes the infantile reply. A bottle of water hurtles its way towards a baby's head but is deftly caught and cries of, 'If you throw – you go' are fired back in a giggling volley. The incident lightens up an afternoon of England domination, with Trott adding a fifty to the centuries of Strauss and Cook. There will be no party in the hotel tonight after all; every silver lining has a cloud in sunny Australia too.

The official Barmy Army section is having a good day though, out-singing their opponents in the lower tier and winding up an Aussie to such an extent that he is thrown out of the ground by the local constabulary. The incident starts when the unlucky fan tries to take on the England troops with the lyrical masterpiece: 'Aussie, Aussie, Aussie – Oi! Oi! Oi!' It's a bold effort, but tragically none of the other Australians admit to knowing the words, so he's left singing it solo. The old favourite, 'Who are you? Who are you?' comes back from the Army ranks, but our plucky Anzac holds firm and lets rip the Aussie Ois again. That's when the Army unleash the classic wind-up chant, 'Does your boyfriend know you're here?'

Evidently they've found the Australian Achilles' Heel: you can mock and poke fun all you like, but even a hint of poofter is a jibe too far. It's too much and our hero's Gallipoli spirit tips into an ill-advised over-the-top and straight-at-the-cliffs manoeuvre. The red mist descends and he clambers over other spectators in an attempt to charge his detractors, bayonet fixed. Half a League! Like many a poor devil he never makes it as far as the guns; the police step in before he reaches his taunters and escort him to the exit, with the chorus of, 'Cheerio, Cheerio, Cheerio!' ringing in his ears. When can his glory fade? O the wild charge he made!

At the close of play I decide my liver has had enough punishment and it's time for a change of vices, so I pop into the Treasury Casino across the bridge from my hotel; it is heaving with England fans of a similar mind. The casino is housed in a grand old building that used to be treasury offices – hence the name, not because it's a likely source of a secure pension. The irony is not lost on most British visitors: Brisbane's treasury building had to officially change its use from financial centre to gambling den, whereas in the City of London it's one and the same thing. With casino-style banking practices so prevalent in the UK and US, maybe we should go the whole hog and follow the Australians? I'd be in favour of moving the Federal Reserve to Las Vegas – DC is a dull, dull place – although in the UK that would mean shifting the Bank of England to the pier at Blackpool, not quite such a glamorous idea.

But what a venue the Treasury Casino is, a veritable mini-Reno which allows the gambler of any level and any game of choice to enjoy themself while bringing ruin upon their household. Against the odds, I enter the building with $50 but this quickly becomes $200 thanks to bit of luck on the roulette wheel. Say what you like about gambling, but it's the one vice that occasionally gives something back. As the great man Kenny Rogers said, 'You got to know when to hold 'em and know when to fold 'em,' and while that song is about poker the sentiment remains the same and I return to the hotel with a small victory. With the huge numbers of England fans assisting the Australian economy that Sunday night, I felt it was important to take a little back for Britain. As I gaze out of my hotel window at the numerous cranes peppering the skyline, sipping an over-priced mini-bar tipple in triumph, it appears that Brisbane is a work in progress, a thriving city with a huge amount of investment pouring into it – I figure they can afford to lose a few bucks. And when I inspect the mini-bar price list the next morning, I am bloody sure of it.

Chapter 9
FIRST TEST, DAY FIVE
WIN, LOSE OR DRAW
(Monday 29th Nov)

Monday morning swings around, and following the crowd disturbances on the previous days there is an article in the *Courier Mail* demanding that segregation should be brought in to Australian cricket grounds when the Barmy Army are on tour. Apparently the Brisbane media's view of cricket supporters has not changed much since the 1950s, when the author John Kay, confronted with a sea of wire, described the Gabba as resembling a concentration camp, and its treatment of spectators as akin to a slave market. Well there is no need for segregation today as there are hardly any Australians here, the 21,000 of yesterday has dwindled to a meagre 7000, and pretty much all of them are decked out in Barmy Army leisure wear; it has turned into an away game for the Australians on the field.

After four days of hedonism, some seem to be struggling with the law of averages even more than the time difference. 'I reckon it's 50/50,' opines a near neighbour, 'it could be a win, a loss or a draw.'

My roulette wheel brain stops spinning long enough to plump the chips on 0 – a draw: a win for the house but not the punters. There are a few optimistic Barmies who are hoping for a quick-fire start to the day, an England lead of 250 and an early declaration; that way Swanny can spin Australia out in less than two sessions for the famous win. I reckon those blokes are probably a few chips down at the casino (and you can read that two ways). It's been done in the past, once or twice, the occasional blue moon, but the pitch is great and Strauss is not a gambler. He'd only bet on red if you coloured all the black numbers in with a scarlet crayon. I settle down for a long England innings till defeat is impossible, and the sort of meaningless final session that was once all too common in Test cricket.

In recent times a more attacking spirit has meant more matches finish with wins, but too often the fifth day is a drag to a non-result. This makes it hard to promote and Test cricket is already tough to sell. There's no shortage of people who would like to go, but the tickets are expensive and a match requires at least a couple of days to be taken off work, a double loss. If you come just for a single day it's like only watching twenty minutes of a football match: hard to appreciate the ebbs and flows, hard to understand the course of the game. You need to be dedicated and have either a very understanding partner, no partner, or an old, closet-lesbian partner who wears tweed and finds joy in keeping the scorecard for you.

My mind turns wistfully to the dog I have left at home. He doesn't have a passport and was never any good at keeping the scorecard anyway. I hope he hasn't already eaten his way through all seven weeks' worth of food that I put out for him. Shame I don't have a garden, but I figured filling the kitchen with cat litter to the depth of a foot was a price worth paying to free me up for this trip. That's not a true story, but it's what I've started telling people to amuse myself and to stake my claim as a more hard-core cricket fan than they are. Some galahs genuinely believe me.

'What is a galah?' I hear you squawk. I'm glad you asked. Literally it is a little pink and grey cockatoo, but in Aussie slang it means an idiot, generally of the loud-mouthed variety. The perimeter advertising hoardings have continually told us not to be a galah, as part of Queensland's *'gamble responsibly'* campaign – surely the most ridiculous plea in history. How on earth can anyone gamble responsibly? The very nature of gambling is that you're not certain of the outcome and you really shouldn't be doing it. The idea of only betting the money you can afford to lose makes little sense: if you thought you were going to lose you wouldn't gamble it; it's the absurd belief that you're the chosen one that will beat the odds that makes people gamble in the first place. I should know, I'm $150 up; I clearly am the chosen one!

However, I've heard a few tales of woe from England fans who have spent a lot more time and money in the Treasury Casino than they should have. And one fan that has lost the lot undergoes humiliation at the match today, as his mates take turns holding up a sign with 'GALAH' printed on it and a big arrow pointed at his head. Friendly fire, insult to self-inflicted injury. A trifle harsh I felt, unless they are now responsible for keeping him in beer and burgers, in which case there's not much he can say on the matter.

There's not much the unsupported Australian attack can say either. Any sledging is proving ineffective as Cook and Trott compile an almost unbelievable unbeaten 329-run partnership to follow the 188 opening partnership, and Tour Rep Dan's 5-0 prediction edges into the ball-park. Certainly 4½ nil might be on the cards even if not technically possible. All is looking peachy when the day throws up an incident I find troubling. As the England batsmen thud effortlessly through the morning and on towards tea, the English fans become cocky and start to run out of material, most of their repertoire having been composed on days when England were in a more perilous position than 500 for 1. So they start teasing the Aussie players with the chant:

'Are you Scotland in disguise?'

What? Where did that come from? Even in football that's scarcely a decent shout, as despite Scotland's abysmal record of recent years, England have hardly thrashed us, and indeed managed to lose a game at Wembley. But in cricket it's virtually meaningless. It's also divisive as there are a lot of Scotland shirts and even kilts on show in the ground today. I consider warning the Army that it's not too late for us to change our allegiance. We're used to backing the underdogs and we're just starting to feel at home in Australia. But with no reinforcements immediately nearby, I seethe quietly to myself.

As I predicted, Strauss only calls a halt to the carnage with less than an hour till tea. No hopes for a 299-run chase, and optimistic to believe the Australians can be dismissed in a session and a third. Consider how different from 1998, when Mark Taylor declared, leaving England to score 348, in an entire *day* and a third. That was positive attacking captaincy where a win was only missed by the arrival of a monsoon after lunch. But in 2010 the Aussies bat their way confidently to the close, securing a vital psychological point and the honours are shared.

Post-match dissections begin and wiser commentators than me are claiming that if there is no result at the Gabba then the odds are decent that there would be no results in any game. This seems unduly pessimistic. I remember with perfect clarity Vic Marks predicting a 1-0 result during his radio commentary of the first, second and third matches of the 2009 Ashes – a series that ended 2-1 with a dazzling win for each side in the last two matches – so I refuse to envisage such a damp squib. A drawn series would mean England retain the urn so the Aussies need to fight, but the turnaround in this match means England will be going into the next game in better heart. Me? I'm expecting fireworks in Adelaide, and I'm the chosen one, remember?

Outside Gate Six a huge St. George's Cross is unfurled. I'm wearing my Scotland shirt and can't resist a little revenge attack for the earlier chanting, so stand in front of it for a photo, trying to get in everyone else's holiday snaps as well. In doing so I receive a load of abuse, the most vocal being from TMS, which is a bit much as his real name is Donald James Campbell Logan and he wouldn't be out of place as a shortbread magnate. I consider grilling him on whether his ancestors were responsible for the Highland Clearances. Usually when you meet an Englishman with a name like that, they proudly tell you they're actually Scottish, and can trace their lineage all the way back to being conceived on a tartan rug in the back of a Range Rover in Gloucestershire. TMS, in contrast, has gone the other way and is denying his heritage three times before the cock crows.

Back at the hotel, there are more reasons to question my loyalty. I might be drummed out of the Barmy Army for saying it, I might have my membership card cut up, but Ricky Ponting is a top bloke. Considering all the stick he receives from the Barmies and the vociferous booing that accompanies his arrival at the wicket, he is wonderfully accommodating and pleasant to the England fans that are sharing the same hotel. Ricky – I feel I can call him that – and his fellow players shared the breakfast facilities with the other hotel guests throughout the match and had a drink after the game in the hotel's public bar. This evening, although there are no wild parties for us to share in, an English supporters touring party raises enough courage to ask him for a photo. After a bit of chat, where he is assured that they hadn't been the ones to boo him, he graciously obliges.

The booing of Ponting is an issue that has upset the cricket traditionalists. It's held as an example of how the loutish behaviour of the football terraces is transferring to the cricket stands; and this in turn is why a number of commentators have criticised the Barmy Army, whom they hold responsible. The perceived downside to all the songs and chants is that they wind-up the opposition fans, and rivalries can become aggressive, with drink-fuelled responses that get out of control or at least offend more delicate sensibilities. Of course, any large group of supporters is going to include a few louts, but I'm not convinced.

The behaviour of fans at many of the county grounds, particularly for one day games, has been pretty boorish at least since the early 1970s, long before the birth of the Barmy Army. Would that some of the well-documented racist abuse that used to greet the black players in the Middlesex team, had been replaced by the good natured, egalitarian singing of the England touring faithful. And disruptive incursions onto the field were once customary too, as Terry Alderman will attest. The current Barmy Army has none of the thug-like behaviour that characterized the 82/83 Ashes, where a mass pitch invasion by drunken English fans at Perth ended with Alderman's shoulder being horrifically dislocated and his career devastated. To me the discipline and pride that being part of the Barmy Army brings has played a large part in ensuring that singing and humour replace macho hooliganism.

However, there are those that like their cricket played in quieter surroundings and the relentless singing is not everyone's cup of tea. It is easy to see both sides of that argument. I found the steel drums of the West Indian supporters infuriating throughout the 80s and longed for tranquillity and polite ripples of applause. But through a long match, especially in the hottest or wettest weather, the Barmies' chorus of encouragement adds to the atmosphere and keeps the whole crowd going.

Many players, including former captain Michael Vaughan, have claimed that it absolutely assists the performance of the team. Even Ricky Ponting himself understands that. Ponting is the last of the legendary Aussie figures still performing, his isolation exacerbating his status as a target. But despite his treatment, he has praised the Barmy Army for its loyalty and support, saying on more than one occasion that they're the best fans in the world. Borrowing a truism from football, they only boo the good players.

Chapter 10
SCOTS WHA' HA'E
(Tuesday 30th Nov)

It's the morning after the match, November 30th, St. Andrews Day. I'm standing outside the Pig 'N' Whistle Traditional British Pub. True to its claim of embracing the Union, it's had a makeover in honour of the day. The St. George's Cross has been replaced with the Saltire. So clearly, as far as the management are concerned, we're all Pommies together.

Today is a day for reflection, on Brisbane and on notions of nation. At the Gabba, all the Scots I met were supporting England. All were agreed there's a bit of inter-nation banter, but English cricket fans are generally welcoming. The best evidence of this fraternity were the two standard bearers from Glenrothes CC, who proudly waved the Saltire for all five days. One was a Scot, the other English. However some English fans I've met in the bars have treated me with suspicion. Viz: 'You sweaties never support us; we'll never support you!' Fair point, simply made, I suppose. Fortunately, such responses have been in the minority.

By far the most common reaction I've received is surprise that a Scotsman is interested in cricket at all. To set the record straight I've been informing anyone who will listen that there are more cricket clubs per head of population in Scotland than in England. I was told that statistical gem in a pub many moons ago. I've never double-checked its accuracy, it could be total nonsense, but Down Under I've stated it with so much conviction that no-one has doubted me. Possibly I'm helped in my persuasive oratory by only stating it in pubs – sometimes it's better to keep the Monster in the lab in which it was conceived.

Among Australians, reaction to my affiliation has ranged from bemused to appalled. Last night I was taken to task by members of the Brisbane St. Andrews Society. Dressed in their kilts and enjoying a few drinks after their premature St. Andrews Night supper. Their secretary, Angus (what else?), told me Scottish-Australians are all supporting Australia and so should I. 'Our organisation celebrates our Scottish heritage, not a British heritage and definitely not an English heritage. As far as we are concerned England is the enemy and you can't get more English establishment than the England cricket team.'

Like Irish Americans, these boys are clearly aiming to out-do the home country in the patriotic fervour stakes. They're more Scottish than a bad goalkeeper drinking whisky at a Burns' Night supper. Although I don't agree with the sentiment, I do understand where they're coming from. I grew up in a land where there undeniably remains a residual antipathy from the bad old days of the centuries of bloodshed that Scotland suffered at the hands of perfidious Albion. But it's not that simple.

I usually explain the situation as akin to the Soviet Union in the 80s. Most people in the Republics, considering themselves hard done by, disliked Russia. Whereas most ordinary Russians, regardless of what the Kremlin was up to in their satellites – be it utilising their manpower, exploiting their resources, sacrificing their soldiers, benefitting from their strategic importance, or using them as a waste bin – generally didn't even notice the Republics enough to bother hating them. And at times England has done all of the above to Scotland. It's the high-handed presumption that rankles in Scotland, while the English blithely sail on unaware, or quoting this week's completely spurious claims of subsidy, as if these things existed in a time vacuum.

However, I don't wish to create the false impression of constant simmering hostility. Generally, people are a lot more relaxed about it than is often made out, and the border is entirely permeable in world athletics and other sports where we all compete as British individuals or team GB. And of course cricket, which exists in its own special bubble of bonhomie and grace. I genuinely can't fathom any Scots who have an antipathy towards the English cricket team. With four quasi-South-Africans and an Irishman in the squad can the current England team really be held up in the same light as Edward I, Hammer of the Scots? I'd say not. (Then again, Edward couldn't speak a word of English, kept a straight sword and had a range of cut shots easily good enough to get him a game for the Twenty/20 side, so on the other hand...)

When it comes to cricket, I'm a hundred percent behind England; but I do have sympathy with Angus's last point. The establishment – David Icke's giant lizards, the mysterious powers that be and who hold us all in thrall – have certainly never been of assistance to me or my ancestors. And it's hard to counter the argument that cricket tradition and culture help preserve the timeless myth of gentlemen and players, a genetic class system (indeed caste system) which suits those at the top of the heap very well. As Simon Hughes has highlighted, there are very few cricketing socialists.

But I had no idea when I was growing up that it *was* the game of the establishment. My favourite players were Randall, Boycott and Botham, who were all in some way anti-authority figures: eccentric, difficult, confrontational, non-reptilian; all traits I sought to cultivate through my teens with varying degrees of success. Although taking a Randallesque approach to clothing and being hailed as the Boycott of the school team (sadly not as a tenacious batsman, just nobody else liked me), I never could grow the Botham moustache – praise be for small blessings. Yes, Dennis Skinner might disagree, but even then, I instinctively knew whose side I was on. Better to be inside the tent pissing out, than outside the tent getting wet. Or for that matter, lost in a muddy field, unable to even *find* your tent among the thousands of middle-class festival goers, all braiding their hair and pretending they're rebels, yah?

My Uncle Bill is less convinced. Uncle Bill emigrated from Scotland in 1971 and has lived in and around Brisbane for the past twenty years. He left the fertile land of gentle rain and mist for a foreign shore of merciless sun and drought. Although, to be truthful, he left Dundee, and if you have ever been to Dundee you'll understand the wisdom of his decision to emigrate. I haven't seen him since I was five, but he's picking me up today. And I already know which team he is supporting in the Ashes and they're wearing the baggy green.

The Holden pulls up outside the Pig 'N' Whistle and I clamber in. Luckily he'd sent me a recent photo or I might just have got into a car with a complete stranger, which would have been embarrassing. We set off on a whistle-stop tour of the environs, pausing for breath at Brisbane's highest vantage point, Mount Coot-tha, with its spectacular views across the city and beyond. Great stuff to see at any time, but best enjoyed with your guide muttering, 'Bastard English', in an un-reformed Dundonian accent, as he points stuff out. Then north, out of the city and onto Bill's adopted hometown, Redcliffe. Here I catch up with my cousin, Moira whom I haven't seen since she was seven. Disappointingly she hasn't a clue what she did with my 1970 *Dandy* and *Beano* albums. All these years I've kept a sad space on my shelf for them in case they ever turned up, but I guess the trail has finally gone cold. Moira now has a grown-up daughter in the army, so I guess it has been a while. I briefly wonder if her daughter has seen them, or if they're being secretly hoarded for the grandkids. My collection is just not complete without them.

I like Redcliffe, it has a sleepy ambience to it (and red cliffs, but you're wise to the Australian nomenclature by now). Its claim to fame is that the Bee Gees were raised here. The sea here has no surf and therefore doesn't attract the surfers and tourists of the other Queensland coastal towns. I guess that's why they weren't called the Australian Beach Boys. Although if I recall correctly, only Dennis Wilson of the Beach Boys could actually surf, the rest were faking it, so they could fairly have been called the Bee Ws instead. Perhaps a love of the coast but an inability to surf is a prerequisite for fraternal harmonies.

As enjoyable as my day has been, gazing out over the ocean I do have a slight regret that I've not had time to hear more tales of why I'm a traitor to my skin and kin. Sad too that I haven't seen more of Queensland, like North Stradbroke Island and the

Gold Coast. Especially the Gold Coast. Was it really only eight days ago that I was mistaken for a dirty old man? Happy days. Which reminds me, I must get a new mental diary for next year.

I'm just accepting a refill of 'whisky and bastard English', when I receive a call from the *BBC*. They're giving me a second chance, and this time I am to speak up for the Barmy Army in a light-hearted debate on the fans influence at the Gabba. Hanging on the end of a phone 12,000 miles away, waiting for my segment and eavesdropping on the show, I overhear Nicky Campbell interrogating a female Muslim scholar on the issue of women's rights, within what is often perceived in the West as a misogynistic religion. Serious stuff.

I'll be following this by discussing an elderly man hopping around in a red and white Mad Hatter's topper, while scores of drunk men declare their mental martial devotion to a cricket team through the medium of song. I've finally made it to the 'and finally' section of the news. This time the phone holds up.

So here I am on national radio, at last, taking on a loud-mouthed Aussie apologist for his fellow fans poor vocal performance compared to the Barmy Barbershop 8000. The Aussie fans will come out of their shells in the next game, he claims. If they come out of their houses and turn up at the match it will be a start. Zing! I feel I hold my own and finish my piece saying that after the 1st Test I remain an England fan, despite the 'Are you Scotland in disguise' chant, which got to me, it is true.

'Bastard English,' contributes Uncle Bill helpfully and fortunately just out of phone range.

There's a perverse pride in me that for a couple of minutes I am the voice of the English nation on national radio. Is this how the Scottish aristocracy felt in 1707, when they sold their independence to the English? A moment of glory, a moment of fame and a legacy of infamy; what a parcel of rogues in a nation.

Just before I hang up, I hear the breakfast show move swiftly onto a piece about Patsy Kensit. So I wasn't quite the 'and finally', I was sandwiched between a female Muslim scholar and Patsy Kensit; an image that will last as long in the mind as grown men putting on each other's nappies, and then some.

PART TWO ~ ADELAIDE

Chapter 11
ON A WING AND A PAYE
(Wednesday 1ˢᵗ Dec)

All the direct flights from Brisbane to Adelaide are sold out. Why lay on extra flights when you can charge top dollar, fill every plane, and make others go the long way round? In fairness, flying is such an environmental disaster, I don't begrudge it. And it's no big deal: just fly to Melbourne then grab a connecting flight; not really a cause for complaint unless you're the sort of person who equates a broken-down train with a medieval plague. But it's a journey that will take most of the day and in the meantime I have to post an article for the blogging site I am working for. A straightforward assignment, so in cavalier fashion I didn't charge my laptop before leaving the hotel, and plan to write and send it from my Blackberry. No doubt there will be some, probably those still struggling in confined spaces with the vast broadsheet *Daily Telegraph*, who will find my approach of filing a report with one hand, on a device you can keep in a shirt pocket, to not be entirely in the spirit of the game. And they'll be delighted with what follows.

By the time I reach Melbourne I've finished scrawling the piece in shorthand (because the old ways haven't died quite yet), and pause to wolf a sesame bagel before tippy-typing it all onto the Blackberry. I've never quite understood the place of sesame seeds in world affairs; they've always seemed an unnecessary, messy addition that does little to enhance anything, let alone food. I didn't ask for them, I just wanted a bagel. The sesame seeds were an unrequested extra, like the unwanted garbage software that moronic PC manufacturers decorate their machines with, and that similarly gets caught in the teeth of Windows and makes people buy over-priced Macs instead. See, I should have bought an apple, not a bagel.

In my case the aversion to seeds goes back a long way. Poppy and sesame crackers used to scare me as a child; they were strange savoury things that adults pretended to enjoy, while the more sensible children were eating Ginger Nuts or Bourbons and other 'proper' biscuits. (Cheddars were also permissible, the outrageously high salt and fat content satisfying the Scottish sensibility.) But today I am too distracted by the continuous human jetsam of Melbourne Airport to have time for sesame-related suspicions, and bite into the bagel with gusto. Seeds fly everywhere. That's what seeds are good at; they're returning to their genetic roots and aiming for wide-spread distribution. Put seeds on something and at the first sign of a nibble, like 1970's teenagers caught vandalising a park bench, they scream, 'It's the fuzz, scatter! scatter!' and flee to the four corners of the world. (In this regard they are the bastard cousins of the hundreds-and-thousands used to decorate cakes.) Except, on this occasion, one, which falls into my Blackberry keyboard and seeks to propagate the species under the letter R, and from which it refuses to be budged.

When you are writing about cricket in Australia one consonant you need more than most is R. Now we'd left Queensland and with no need to report on the Sydney Mardi Gras, I could live without Q. X is a rarity, and even the oft neglected K could probably escape unused. I have enough synonyms to sneak by without a V if I'm honest. But R is always in your first XI. Andew Stauss might escape unnoticed, and Bad Haddin and Icky Ponting, sound rather better. But Stuat does not Boad well, and Matt Pio wicket-keeps for Taiwan, I believe. (I just wish I was working as a film critic: *Aging Bull* with Obet De Nio sounds rather apt, although the Danny Boyle thriller *28 Days Later* becomes an altogether less thrilling movie.) But the deadline is approaching and my malfunctioning phone is causing me consideable gief and stess. You'd think something called a Blackberry could handle a few seeds, no? (Smirking iPhone owners would do well to remember that typing anything even half as comprehensible on their toys is near impossible at any time, with or without savoury touches and greasy fingers.)

Finally I give up on the endless hunt for words without an R, and even though it is six in the morning back home, I phone a cricket-mad friend there and explain my predicament. He says if I send him the article he will be able to work out where the 'R's should go and pass it on; and that if I ever call him at 6am again he'll come round my house and set it on fire. I email the copy just as the gates for my flight are closing, and make a mental note to never again tell my friends where I live.

Arriving in Adelaide the first thing that hits you as you step out of the terminal is the heat. The second thing is a huge IKEA billboard: the dull face of globalisation writ large. I suppose having relationship problems in public on a Sunday is a universal trend, but it is disappointing. I'd hoped for *'Welcome to Adelaide'*, or a beer advert, or even one of Australia's startlingly frank warning posters shouting at me, *'If you drink, then drive, you're a bloody idiot'*. Instead I get the most boring advert for the most boring company from the most boring country. When Sweden forsook porn and decided on shelving as a better bet for export, it was a sad day for the world.

Thankfully the taxi whizzes me down the wonderfully named Sir Donald Bradman Drive to my hotel and I smile contentedly. We're back to 2lbs 4ozs of linseed treated willow, not a kilogram of flat-pack painted pine: I'm in South Australia cobber. Contentment is short-lived as the hotel is located in Hindley Street, an inauspicious name. According to the guidebooks this area is slowly shedding its sleazy image. You could have fooled me, as across the street are two strip clubs, an adult bookshop and a questionable nightclub. To say it is slowly shedding its sleazy image is a bit like saying Las Vegas is slowly shedding its reputation for gambling. I'm guessing the

Australian team will not staying at my hotel this time around.

In the hotel I bar reunite with Tour Rep Dan Bulmer, with whom I'll be sharing my two-bed apartment. He was the most optimistic England fan I met in Brisbane, and when I remind him of his 5-0 prediction, now on the scrapheap alongside Wagner in the X Factor, he remains bullish.

'If Hussey had been given out, and the umpire review system not so ridiculous we would have won – no question.'

'No question?'

'No question. The Aussies are down and out, I'm confident it will be 4-0. Mooooo!!!'

Okay, not that bullish. Such proclamations are common among sports fans the world over, but I always find them peculiar. The only time any Scot ever felt that way about his team was just before Argentina 1978 – once bitten, twice shy. But the opinion of the fans in the bar is that 'the momentum is with England'. I hear this a lot, even if I don't believe in it. A wise man on our table observes that, just as in Cardiff 18 months ago, England performed so appallingly in the first innings at Brisbane that they couldn't help but improve in the second, and thus ironically have gained the mental edge. But that is cricket, moral victories, and life's journey in a nutshell: start badly but show improvement and you'll feel better about yourself than the prodigy that fails to live up to expectations, and whom you pass on his disillusioned way down.

Dan and I retire to our beds, but neither of us gets much sleep. The club across the road bangs out music until 4am, and it's only Wednesday night. The next morning a bleary-eyed Dan agrees it was too much: 'It was so loud I thought the DJ was in the bathroom.'

'You're right, we should complain to our tour rep.'

'You can try.'

'I will. Excuse me, Mr Bulmer, I didn't get a wink of sleep last night and I paid good money for this trip! What are you going to do about it?'

'I'm very sorry about that sir. You can have my room.'

'You're not funny.'

Chapter 12
SEASIDE TRAM-RIDE
(Thursday 2nd Dec)

I'd arrived in Australia's fifth largest city thinking that it was also its most conservative and respectable. I'd expected to find a haven for ladies who wear hats, and chaps with short back and sides – or a city full of snobs as Ian Chappell described it. Possibly I've been misinformed. In Brisbane the local delicacy is Moreton Bay bugs, which sounds disgusting but is quite a tasty seafood dish. In Adelaide the local meal – to call it a delicacy would be a disservice to delicacies – is a 'pie floater': a pie in pea soup; which sounds disgusting, looks disgusting and no doubt tastes disgusting. I couldn't say because copious amounts of wine will have to be consumed before I give that culinary masterpiece a try. There's plenty to consume around here; Adelaide is the slap bang in the heartland of Australia's wine region. Maybe this is why I had curious notions of gentility. Or it may be why they're willing to eat pie floaters, who can tell? The one thing I know about the subject is that James Bond killed someone for ordering red wine with fish, so the opportunity to take a wine-tasting tour greatly appeals, if only to see how violent it gets when someone confuses a Chardonnay for a Pinot Grigio.

I have a day to settle in before the match and an opportunity to explore a little. I've made the acquaintance of many Australians over the decades, and yet I have never heard any of them extol the virtues of this city. There are well over a million residents but they seem completely cut off from the normal matrix of connections. Among my relatives and all their contacts it was the only stop on the itinerary in which nobody claimed to know anyone living here, and nor does anybody in our tour party. It undoubtedly gives the place an air of mystery, and it transpires my misgivings of last night were misplaced; the second impressions are very much positive.

A wander around the town doesn't take long; the centre of Adelaide is small, bordering on quaint, but well maintained and attractive. Just as Brisbane's main square is King George Square, Adelaide has Victoria Square, with a huge statue of Queen Victoria plonked in the middle of it – in case you thought that it might have been named after a barmaid called Vicky. It's easy to see why Bradman used to talk of a tour of England as 'going home' even though he'd never lived in Britain. Not so very long ago this was a sunny adjunct to the UK and the architectural and religious heritage is still recognisably British. There must be enough churches for the entire Barmy Army to visit all at once, should they get the urge tomorrow to pray for a win (or more likely forgiveness). The England fans I speak to say everything feels familiar, and not just the sadly ubiquitous fast food outlets.

With only three days between matches I've decide to make up for missing the Gold Coast and jump a tram to Glenelg beach. I'm not even there yet and I'm already impressed: the tram is clean, efficient and nearly as fast as a train once it's left the centre. Even without a cardigan I must be showing my age if the tram ride is more exciting to me than the prospect of the beach. The sadness comes when a fellow rider tells me that this is the only tram route still operating in Adelaide. How very British, I think, to have a good thing and scrap it for no good reason.

'No doubt in time you'll catch up with us and start spending billions putting them all back in!' I remark to my informant. He snorts and, pitying my ignorance in tram-affairs, tells me that the line has recently been extended not once, but twice, twice! (he's particular on this) and I wouldn't have been able to get on where I did, just last year. I want to ask him more, but I fear that trams have taken the place of a loving wife in this good fellow's life, and I may be opening a can of worms. In fact I already have, as, unbidden, he's begun relating the plans for future extensions and lines.

While genuinely interested I don't wish to be trapped, and am grateful when another passenger tackles him on which plans have thus far been approved, which have been mooted and which are just wishful thinking on the part of sandal wearers and tram-true-believers. I may accidentally have started a fight, as the new participant in the debate is now discussing suburban rail. I don't know if all rail-runners are on the same side or whether they're deadly rivals who squabble over the best use of a track, but either way, I suspect when the going gets tough they gang together and beat up the bus-fanciers; that's usually how these things go. I say that only when the bus, tram and train spotters unite with the mono-rail and hovercraft lobby, will the motorist finally be beaten. But weighing up my two, reserved, well-mannered lecturers, I figure the car companies don't need to worry just yet. And because I don't recognise the names of any of the suburbs or streets they're talking about I can't take a side in the discussion, and just smile wanly: for all I know they're considering the merits of running a tram between craters of the moon. Nevertheless I enjoy the twenty-minute ride and the tittle-tattle, and disembark in Glenelg.

Immediately I wonder why it isn't more famous. I could be my ignorance, but I've never heard of this place before. Everyone knows of the beaches of Sydney, most are aware of the beaches of Perth and even Melbourne, so why are the beaches of Adelaide almost unknown in the UK? I wasn't even certain Adelaide was on the coast when I left home. Either the South Australia Tourist Board is not doing its job or the locals want to keep it quiet, preferring tranquillity and quality of life to the tourist dollar. Good for them if that's the case; once a beauty spot becomes a tourist spot it's the beginning of the end. Such modern development as there is, is quite enough for me, but I fear that now they've begun to run 'Heritage' trams here on weekends, there may be a lot more on the way. And foolishly I've just told you about it, so I'm going to be partially responsible.

I like the vibe of Glenelg: it's a pleasing mixture of retirement destination, sea-side resort, affluent suburb and natural paradise. I'm covering my bases there, but I only have two hours. And after thirty minutes meditatively staring out to the shimmering sea, and another thirty minutes trying to pull my eyes away from the scantily clad girls shimmying in front of the sea, I don't have much time to get a solid impression. What all good travel writers need is a local character who can quickly fill them in on the folklore in a pithy and amusing manner. Damn, seems like the tram-ride used up all my luck up on that score. I could just grab an ice-cream and ask a passing pensioner for a history lesson but, Australian complexions being what they are, I might accidentally ask someone born in the 1980s who can't even remember when Kylie had curly hair.

To hell with it. This is the first moment I've had to draw breath since I arrived in Australia, so I walk the beach in blissful mental solitude and forget cricket entirely for a little while. Feet in the sand, head in the clouds and lost in my thoughts I can imagine myself as a romantic poet on an Aegean coast, but am no doubt mistaken for a lost seal pup amongst all that tanned flesh.

Leaving the beach with thoughts of seeking work reporting on seasides rather than these inconvenient sporting events, I get my journalist's hat back on to prep for the game. Seeking hot tips and cold refreshment I head for the Barmy Army's headquarters in Adelaide, PJ O'Brien's pub on the East Terrace. As the name suggests this is an Irish bar, and on Friday nights there is live 'Irish' music. I'm can't wait to see cover versions of Boyzone, Westlife and Samantha Mumba being given an airing. With a bit of luck someone will have a go at Orinoco Flow by Enya, truly something worth coming 10,000 miles for.

Most of the punters in O'Brien's expect an unchanged England team, or perhaps a tweak to the bowling. This is not the case with Australia. There's much excitement because Mitchell Johnson has lost his place: the first time Super Mitch has been dropped in his Test career. But it should come as no surprise, as his display at the Gabba was so toothless it could have won a gurning competition. His exclusion happily reminds me of our time in Brisbane when the Aussie team posed for photographs with the England fans in the bar. After a series of snaps Mitchell had turned to us and said that we'd better catch up with him at the next match so we could take photos of him without his 'Movember' charity moustache. As Ade remarked at the time (although thankfully not to Mitch's moustachioed face): 'Well, I'll be there, but I'm not convinced you will be.'

Adelaide is distinguished by its batsmen friendly pitches, so although South Australia was never in fact a convict colony, the likelihood is that this game will serve its time rather than run its course, with a better than even chance of no result at the end of five days. With regard to the series, this would be good for Strauss and his men, as a draw will take them two-fifths of the way to a glorious Ashes retaining triumph of nil-nil; a victory every bit as convincing as the First World War. But if you believe that a genuine 'test' should have the possibility of a loss attached, it's like sentencing the crowd to five days' batting, with the fans that keep scorecards marking runs off in their jotters as if counting days to release.

Fortunately, flat pitch or not, the scandalous notion of playing adventurously for the win began and still thrives in Australia. Since internationals began, about half of Test matches between other nations have ended in no result, and yet Australia's dead-lock rate is a meagre 26% - these boys like a fight. If Australia were playing itself you imagine they'd never manage to draw at all. This is the country that plays to conquer and destroy, and good on them. In Adelaide in 2006, England confidently declared at 551-6 in their first innings, and unbelievably still managed to lose the match. Of all the bad memories England are trying to banish, it's that defeat last time around that must cause the worst nightmares. And with six of the same players still in the team, it is here they'll be keenest to win. Just don't expect an early declaration this time around.

Chapter 13
MOTORCITY MADNESS
(Friday 3rd Dec - Morning)

Friday morning, 8am. There are heavy thunderstorms hanging over most Australian cities but Adelaide is clear and bright, yet even here you sense a storm is breaking. It's the first day of the 2nd Test, but today England and Australia are united. Both countries are under a sporting depression thanks to FIFA deciding the football World Cups of 2018 and 2022 should not be held in England and Australia respectively. Football is not coming home, nor is it being transported for sheep stealing. Their bids met with silent derision and fell in the first round of widely-alleged backhanders and sweeteners. It doesn't matter if your sport is cricket, athletics, football, boxing or even chess, chances are your governing body is rotten to the core and nobody can figure how these people got all the power and money. At least in boxing they scarcely pretend otherwise and pretty much let anyone run their own version of the show. The sooner football is taken over and run by Billy Smart's Circus the better in my opinion; it would end the pretence.

But, for now, Australia is smarting under the indignity of being considered less of a world-class country than that footballing giant Qatar. Serves them right for neglecting to build air-conditioned shopping malls for the wives of FIFA delegates. The scandal has relegated the Ashes into second place on the breakfast sports news.

Tellingly, Tour Rep Dan is more upset about Australia losing to Qatar for the 2022 Cup, than England losing to Russia for the right to host it in 2018. I suppose if your living is sporting tour parties, England isn't very exotic and another month in Australia is a nice way to earn a crust. Either that or he's worried he won't find any good bars in Qatar for his clients. More predictably, I concur with him; I didn't want England hosting either. But it has nothing whatsoever to do with Scottish jealousy. There's no doubt that England would have held one of the best tournaments ever, but on a wider social level I feel Russia will get more out of hosting its first World Cup. And there's another stronger reason: to me, England should never have placed a bid in the first place, because by offering to host, it was saying that FIFA is not a deeply shady organization and the FA is proud to do business with them. But they shouldn't be; someone has to make a stand. Even after they bid, as soon as it became apparent they weren't going to get a fair fight they should have pulled out of the race altogether. In contrast, Russia is setting records for corruption in supposed democracies, and is the perfect place for a sleazy operation like FIFA to lay its hat.

However, Dan and I both share the Australians' outrage. It's a disgrace: Qatar is not a run-down struggling place in need of rejuvenation, nor has it any footballing heritage. Ah, okay, that disqualifies Australia as well. I'll try again: not many people will turn up to watch, unlike the... er... thousands that flooded to the Gabba on the fifth day to watch their national sport? Um, just... let me have another go at this. Middle Eastern nations have no record to speak of at the World Cup, nothing but Iran's pathetic 1-1 draw with Scotland. Alright, forget I spoke, maybe I'm not so outraged, and maybe Qatar is a decent shout.

The TV is showing an interview with Sunderland manager, Steve Bruce, after it becomes apparent that the England World Cup bid had received just two votes. He sums things up neatly: 'I guess the English have to realise that nobody likes us.'

One imagines such comments normally being greeted with cheers and jeers across Australia, but the interview is being shown because Australia received just one vote. I consider it an inaccurate comparison. It's not that no-one likes Australians, it's that apart from England cricket fans, no-one really remembers they're here, tucked away at the bottom of the world. Nonetheless, with all the forlorn faces it was enough to make you feel a little sorry for Australia. For a moment. But then I remember Steve Waugh's heartless sledge to Herschelle Gibbs when he dropped a catch during South Africa v Australia in 1999 – 'You just dropped the World Cup, mate.' – and any sympathy evaporated like morning dew under the cloudless Adelaide sky. However he really worded it, sympathy is not an Aussie trait; they probably think that's what gets played at the Opera House. What you don't give, you don't get back, mate.

Switching off the babbling, over-enthusiastic shouting that typifies breakfast television the world over (but not any breakfast I've ever had) I jump into the thinnest clothes I can find ready for a long day in the sun. It's time to head to the Adelaide Oval for some live action babbling and shouting of my own, and I hope I make it there in one piece. There is trepidation in walking in this city, as the car is the star in this town; pedestrians are considered a nuisance. There are eight lanes of carriageway for me to cross between the hotel and the stadium, Adelaide is not quite as leafy and tranquil as it appears on the TV. The green man on the pedestrian crossing shows only for a micro-second, before he too legs it and is replaced by a red man that looks more like a casualty than an instruction. This is no place for the frail, the injured or the slow. I'm guessing this is how they train their Olympians, a sort of Foreign Legion for sprinters: run or die.

I should have expected it really. Those with long memories will remember this city used to host the Australian Grand Prix, and for the last one in 1995, 210,000 people paid to watch. That was a *fifth* of the population of Adelaide at the time; a city, let's not forget, that is absolutely bloody miles from anywhere. That's the equivalent of 1.5 million people showing up at Wembley for an England match, even if London was in the Shetland Isles. They do like their cars fast in South Australia. It has been suggested that the attendance was higher than normal because Bon Jovi were playing after the race, though I'm tempted to believe they might have got 300,000 attending if they weren't.

As it turns out, once you get past the train station you are safe from the roaring traffic, and you can walk there through the city's pedestrianised entertainment and cultural area, and then a lovely wander through Adelaide Parklands south of the Torrens River, with the Oval and the Cathedral in view – just as the Victorian planners intended it. The walk is so beautiful it's a shame that it is only a ten-minute stroll from the city centre to the ground. A lesson to planners everywhere: people don't mind walking a bit further if the journey is pleasant; this does not include urine filled underpasses that drag us miles out of our way.

Behold! There she is, the Adelaide Oval: the finest cricket ground in the world. The Gabba is a good venue but you could tell that other sports are played there. The home ground of South Australia however, is unique. It is still clinging on as a beautiful cricket-only venue, with a warm and genteel air of history, but alas, I've just missed the last of the glory days. The three old, red-tiled stands named after stars of long ago were demolished in 2009 to make way for a new and utterly generic Western Grandstand, this in spite of the Giffen stand being listed on the City of Adelaide Heritage Register. The solution? To preserve 'Heritage Elements': leave a few of the old bricks in place while building a new stand around them. It's the sort of half-baked political fix that that only placates, but pleases absolutely no-one, neither traditionalist nor moderniser. It's an appeasement to justify an annexation; the standard political fudge of our times. The new stand is passable, but aside from a few 'elements' it could be from any ground in the world, whereas the old ones belonged here. Other fairly recent developments work well: the Chappell and Clem Hill Stands sport the pleasing tented roof effect that particularly suits cricket grounds, and the Don Bradman Stand is decent, although, ironically, its red roof was built to blend in with the old stands that were torn down less than twenty years after it opened. For all that, for many it is still the most picturesque ground on the planet and who am I to disagree?

As a matter of fact, I'll soon be disagreeing pretty strongly, because its continued existence in even this modified state is not long for this world. While I was there plans were well underway, and have subsequently been approved, for a major redevelopment that will make a few people richer but trample over history and turn the whole place into what is effectively an Adelaide Oval Themepark. The blueprint includes a new disproportionate Southern Stand with a Welcome Plaza (a bare expanse of concrete where people can 'gather' as if they couldn't before), and a pedestrian bridge, both ideas seemingly unthinkingly lifted from the soulless MCG it seeks to emulate. Pitifully, the beautiful Edwardian scoreboard from 1911 will be left isolated and out of place, like one real tooth in a mouth of dentures. As old scoreboards are actually quite hard to follow in detail, they'd be better off re-erecting it elsewhere as a monument, rather than leaving it gazing mournfully across a world in which it no longer belongs, like a worn-out grandfather clock in a city executive's steel and glass office.

A unique building in a unique city is being homogenised and turned to sludge. Even in the artist's impressions of the redevelopment it's notable that not a single person in the new Members' Bar is actually watching the cricket. Instead they stand with their backs to it, ignoring even the TV screens, and just drinking and schmoozing while the game carries on unobserved behind them. Auspiciously the glass wall will block most of that beastly crowd noise, so business will not be interrupted.

Crucially the developers have promised to preserve the 'Heritage Views' by not building a north stand, so you'll still be able to see out of the ground towards the Cathedral and the old fig trees as you can today. That's the good news, but I'm starting to side with Alan Bennett's view that the word Heritage is repugnant, and trotted out only when something has lost all its original meaning. No doubt with the original Oval demolished, the Cathedral will not last long. That's how it goes these days: tear down one piece of a building's history and ten years later it's easier to scrap another piece as the integrity's gone anyway;

then ten years after that you demolish a neighbouring building and finally the rest of the area comes down as there's no other period buildings nearby to support their case. In the words of Robert Burns, 'An' forward, tho I canna see, I guess an' fear!'

Is any of this even necessary? The reasons for the redevelopment have nothing to do with cricket, as the 36,000 capacity with space for temporary seating can easily handle most crowds the old game can throw at it. However, there is a long and murky history concerning the non-use of the Oval for Australian Rules, and though it's hosted 'football' in the past, as I write, Adelaide's two AFL teams* share the city's other major stadium, Football Park. The whole story would fill chapters, but tellingly, in 2008 when the opposition Liberals were aiming to score cheap points, they claimed FIFA had adjudged Football Park (the fourth largest football stadium in Australia with a 51,500 capacity) to not be up to 'world standards'.

Sound familiar? Yes, it links back into Australia's now failed World Cup bid and politicians bending over for corrupt unelected ruling bodies. 'Major events will go to Melbourne and Sydney,' they screamed, 'so we too must have a new stadium to boost our economy' – forgetting that Sydney's Olympic venue is a costly white elephant. This was dismissed as drivel by Labour at the time, who sensibly said an upgrade to Football Park would do the job. Unfortunately, received wisdom is that there are no votes gained by promising nothing, the status quo can't be pitched and therefore doesn't sell. And so come the 2010 elections, Labour joined in: each party trying to win votes by outdoing the other for the biggest, shiniest redevelopment scenario for the Oval. Where there's a political will for a photo-opportunity, there's a way to crap on your history. Red or Blue, they're much the same Down Under too.

*Adelaide Football Club, The Crows, not to be confused with the long established Port Adelaide Football Club, formerly nicknamed The Magpies (a member of the crow family), but now The Power so as not to be confused with the legendary Collingwood who are also Magpies, or Paul Collingwood who supports Sunderland, enemy of the Magpies that are Newcastle. Newcastle England, not Newcastle New South Wales. Stone the crows, when it comes to names they all seem to be thieving magpies

The current plan is that both AFL teams will move to a redeveloped Oval in 2014 and the stands at Football Park will be demolished, so the owners – the South Australian National Football League – can profit: where there's brass there's muck. The actual playing space is supposed to be preserved, but no-one in their right mind wouldn't bet on it being covered in houses within a decade. Defenders of the scheme have said that having the two single-use stadiums is an historical aberration that needs to be corrected: Adelaide should only have one dual use stadium like the Gabba, the MCG and the SCG. This ignores that its single use as a cricket ground is what keeps the Adelaide Oval so special, so famous, and so far more beautiful than the MCG it seeks to imitate, and so worth coming here to see. Besides, how a city of 1.4 million sports-obsessives with year-round sunshine cannot support two major venues, is beyond me. Glasgow (population 600,000) has three large stadiums and doesn't even have a summer, let alone a summer sport. Perhaps Adelaide can't support the unrealistically inflated salaries and bonuses of the executives and overpaid stars.

The drawback to the scheme is that they can't afford it. So $535million will come out of the pockets of Adelaide's taxpayers, even those who don't watch Australian Rules, who never go near the new development or who much prefer the Oval the way it is. If the ticket payers and the rich members of the South Australia Cricket Association had to pay for it directly, one doubts if it would ever have been approved. These things only sneak through because the costs are hidden in your higher tax bill, rather than made explicit on your ticket stub or membership fee. Triple the cost of those and they wouldn't touch it. 'It will boost the local economy' usually translates as: the ordinary tax-payer will be squeezed to pay for environmental destruction that most benefits the wealthy, and to hell with anything that is pure and true and good.

But on this sunny, sunny day, as we happy few stream towards the grandest old ground in the world, and with the final approval of planning yet to be granted, I feel elated and fortunate to see it while it lasts. God bless the Adelaide Oval.

Chapter 14
SECOND TEST, DAY ONE
FACEWOK
(Friday 3rd Dec)

The consensus opinion on both the radio and on the seats next to me is that England are on the up and the Aussies are on the back foot. They've effectively admitted it by dropping both Johnson and Hilfenhaus. In the press conferences, Johnson gave one of those media-trained performances so beloved by team managers and selectors but loathed by everyone else. In his best Sport Psychologist Speak, he claimed he would return to the nets and 'turn Negatives into Positives'. When I was a kid, Jon Pertwee used to 'reverse the polarity' every Saturday night in Dr Who; Mitchell's storyline sounds only slightly less far-fetched.

Bets are being placed in the stands. At the start of the tour I predicted England would retain the Ashes after a tied series, and with one Test gone that estimate is holding up, but unlike some I think it will be 2-2 not 0-0. I feel England will win here in Adelaide and so to any that ask, in truth any who will listen, I am sticking with my prediction.

Sticking, that's the word. Hot and sticky. The key phrase that dominates the day. It is hot and sticky weather this morning. Hot and sticky sitting in the Chappell stand. Hot and sticky for the Barmy Army on the grass bank. And hot and sticky for the Australian top order, who wrap themselves in coats of armour, but are barely out there long enough to break sweat. This old ground can have witnessed few more astonishing opening half hours; it's as explosive as a port and cigar party at a fireworks factory. Ponting wins the toss and five balls later goes for a Golden Duck edging Anderson to Swann. It was a good innings by this morning's standards, as the previous delivery Katich had been run out without even facing a ball: a Diamond Duck! Another first for me and Australia are 0 for 2. Astoundingly, Clarke follows just eight deliveries later, Anderson suddenly getting all the success he deserved at the Gabba. 2 for 3 and the touring fans go bananas; for a moment barmy turns to delirious. I'm starting to think I should be more assertive in my predictions. I said fireworks when we left Brisbane and no-one listened, indeed they scoffed. But where are my doubters now? Red faced, I'll bet.

Red faces all round: for my doubters, for the Aussie batsmen and, worst of all, red faces for those in the crowd who have not sun-blocked early enough. Adelaide's weather is a whole different kettle of lobsters from Brisbane's and the sun police are out patrolling the ground seeking to prevent casualties. These are a team of volunteers with lotion handily ready for the forgetful, unprepared or plain stupid, especially handy for the Barmy Army who are located on the uncovered grass bank under that beautiful old-fashioned scoreboard. If you can take the heat it's a lovely place to stand, but the downside to being uncovered is that their songs are not being amplified by a ceiling. The other downside is that they're all currently in danger of dying from heatstroke, although with a morning like this, at least they'll die happy.

However, Australian sides don't tend to let their collapses run to calamities. Out on the sizzling square, Watson and Hussey save their team's blushes and guide them through to lunch. The Aussie Fanatics are out in strength here and Hussey gives them something to cheer about, batting steadfastly for most of the day. But when he's sent packing for 93, before you can say duckbilled-platypus, Australia are knocked over for 245. A good recovery, but we'd have taken that at the start of the day.

England survive the one over before close unscathed, but then, with temperatures still high, there's a spot of argy bargy between Ponting, Haddin and Strauss. We learn the next day that Ponting was complaining about Anderson's sledging. Had we been aware of this at the time, the hoots of derision that would have headed the skipper's way would have drowned the cheers that met his dismissal. I've always been appalled by players sledging each other, and wish dearly the ICC would put a stop to it once and for all, but for the originators of the art-form to sulk because there are other painters in the gallery these days, is rich beyond dreams.

I'm starting to have a few dreams myself, or possibly they're hallucinations. Maybe it's the heat, maybe it's the unexpected turn of events and the celebrations, but this momentous day seems to have passed in a blinding-light blur of cheering and beer. I wish I had a better record of the highlights in the crowd and the mood in the ground, wish I'd taken more notes, but journalism is starting to take a back foot to integration with the fans. They are not here to record, but simply to experience and enjoy and I'm starting to fall backwards into the welcoming arms of sporting tribalism and shared euphoria. I do at least remember the wickets tumbling, but back at the hotel bar I meet Bennett, a lanky lad from Birmingham who will never remember any of it, as he's managed to miss every wicket.

'I was twenty minutes late for the start of play and missed the big bang at the beginning; I was late back from lunch and missed one; I was trying to beat the queue at the bar before tea and missed another; it was like a conspiracy.'

'Where were you at the end?'

'I was too hot, I came back to the hotel an hour early, I didn't expect the last five to go at a gallop.'

It's a bit like sitting through a six-hour burlesque striptease in a sweaty club, but missing the ten brief flashes of boob you get from behind the feathers. But credit to Bennett, he isn't down-hearted; he now regards his absence as a lucky omen for England. Personally I can't wait to get back for the second day tomorrow, but he's decided to help the team out by going to Glenelg beach instead. If only all sacrifices were as easy to make and so well rewarded.

It's Friday night and, after a long cold shower to restore some balance to my over-heated brain, I plan to head to Barmy Army HQ, PJ O'Brien's. Unexpectedly though, many of the Barmy

Army have come to me. What is it about the 24 hour bars and strip clubs of Hindley Street that drew them here, I wonder? With the exchange rate being what it is, the most I could tip a stripper wouldn't get more than a glove removed, so instead I head out somewhere calmer with Tour Rep Dan, and we meet up with our friends from Brisbane, Ade, Simon and TMS.

Simon introduces us to the most important discovery of the tour thus far: Wok in a Box; the South Australian chain of fast food restaurants that does what it says on the carton. It's a little like Subway: you go in and say what ingredients you want, the staff throws them into a wok, and a couple of minutes later throw the steaming contents of the wok into a box, and – voilà in Cantonese – you have an excellent Chinese takeaway meal. I should say it only works if they have the ingredients to hand. Requesting black pudding, bacon, eggs, and sausages is unlikely to be successful, though I daresay a few England fans tried it on their way back from the match after a full day's drinking.

Dan is so impressed with his Box of Wok that he says he will start a chain when he gets back to the UK, presumably saving him the trouble of an unwanted trip to Qatar. It's a great idea, but unless he can afford to license the name he'll have to come up with something else, so I make a few suggestions.

'If you were doing it in Scotland, you'd have a better chance if you launched a chain called Spam in a Can' They all look at me blankly. I'm dying but I'm not beaten yet. 'How about doing it with a Korean twist, Dog in a Bag?' No-one laughs. Which is fair considering the age of the joke, but harsh if you bear in mind the late hour and the amount we've drunk. I thought audiences were supposed to be easier on holiday. Tough crowd.

Ade has displayed wonderful stamina and concentration on tour thus far, missing almost nothing of the action at the grounds or at the bars afterwards. He's a Ken Barrington-style performer and doesn't lag when others are heading back to their hotel for a sleep. While gaining the respect of his peers he has been receiving stick from his wife for his constant drinking and late nights, which is puzzling, as she is still home in Warwickshire and he has absolutely no idea how she could be following his movements Down Under. It is a mystery worthy of Morse. He is as astonished as a man who can't keep his tray up.

Well, call our happy crew the Famous Five, but to the rest of us it is less of a mystery. Apart from the obvious – that she's his wife and can guess – there's another likely explanation. It's spelled out to Ade, with the air of Peter Cook talking a one-legged man out of auditioning for Tarzan, that Simon's regular and indiscreet Facebook updates on their exploits might *perhaps* have given her some clue that they weren't spending their time taking brass rubbings in the cathedral.

Not a Facebooker himself, Ade hadn't foreseen this modern day trail of footprints leading from the scene of the crime. Simon has been foolhardy and left the revolver, the lead pipe, the spanner, and all the empty bottles in the library, and tagged them with his name. Did he think they'd get away with it?

In fairness, Simon probably knew his updates were safe from his own wife's inquiries; Facebook is where you go to stalk the ones you didn't marry and now wish you had. Surely Ade's wife should have been checking out her ex from school days, not over on Simon's page worrying about her husband's binge drinking? Fortunately I'm not so drunk myself that I suggest this pet-theory to Ade and Simon or it could have got messy. But Ade can relax, it's like booing Ricky Ponting, they only nag you if they love you, it's when they go quiet you have to worry.

We hit the bar and meet up with two others from Dan's tour group who are doing all five Test matches. Lionel is one of those cricket fans who keeps his own ball-by-ball scorecards and has to watch every delivery. Some may find this obsessive, but I love that cricket produces such characters. Short of having a video of the entire match it records a game more accurately than any other sport on earth. A proper cricket scorecard is treasured for a lifetime and a far better testimony to the fact that 'I was there' than a grainy, blurry photo taken with a mobile phone, that you show to your mates once and then forget about.

Plus it keeps the mind occupied. Lionel needs this as he is going through something of a crisis. His wife has left him so he's booked a sabbatical from his job as a Maths teacher, to run away from his worries and have a think about his next move, in between watching the cricket. I feel this is a good plan, as if nothing else it spends any spare cash he might otherwise lose later in the divorce settlement, but I keep schtum. Good plan or not, you don't make too light when a bloke is down.

Chas is from Bromley, and he too is on sabbatical, from his job at the Royal Bank of Scotland. The only problem is that he might have no job to go back to. As one of the Royal Bank of Scotland's many, many fans, I find this greatly amusing. Chas doesn't keep his own scorecards, which is just as well, or he'd probably calculate that England had made a poor score in the first innings, a worse score in the second innings, charge us for the extras, declare the match a loss and then have the captain knighted for everything he's done for the team.

Chas takes all this in good spirit and is great fun, but I can't help but be disappointed. I'd only met one other person from his hometown before, a man I'd chatted to in a pub, and he'd spoken exactly like Bromley's favourite son, David Bowie. What I'd always previously assumed was a Bowie mannerism, or at least a semi-caricature '60's-Swinging-London voice, had in fact proved to be a Bromley accent. The fellow in question had never ventured far from the town of his birth and had been surprised when I'd pointed out the vocal similarities: he thought everyone spoke like that. I'd love to have seen Bromley in the 60s, it must have been like a real life Stella Street. Sadly, as with the cockney accent that is practically extinct in the younger generation of Londoners, the Bromley accent must have faded out in recent years, as Chas (in his early 30s), really does sound just like everyone else. Another charming idiosyncrasy, another piece of who we are or were, lost forever.

After a couple of beers, Lionel goes back to his room to diligently type up his scores, but the rest of us keep drinking until we get hungry. It's not a diet plan I'd recommend. I suppose it's what people meant when they used to talk about 'stimulating the appetite'. It was a mystery to me when I was young why anyone would need or want to stimulate themselves to eat more, but sure enough, a small aperitif of six pints of lager has done the trick and we're all ravenous. We agree the only sensible thing to do is to pad up for the second innings, and see just how much Wok can be fitted in a Box; and this time there will be no early declaration. Tragically, and issues like this are always tragic if you've been drinking, Wok in a Box closed at ten o'clock. Tears are very nearly shed.

The only option is the 24 hour McDonalds which, as you might imagine, on a Friday night in glamorous Hindley Street is fairly horrific. Right next door is a place called the Daily Grind, which I'd at first assumed was another strip club, but is in fact a skateboarding shop – it was turning into a night of disappointments. You can understand my confusion by the fact that next door to that is a gift shop called Morning Glory: clearly we'd found the Australian level. This also explains why *Are You Being Served?* was one of the most popular shows in Australia.

When we arrive at the golden arches, the place is rammed. We're bantering with Aussie fans when the excitement suddenly reaches fever pitch, as we spot former England pace bowler Gladstone Small queuing up for food. I say queuing: McDonalds has never really grasped that concept successfully, and midnight on a Friday in Hindley Street is not the time that a system of first come, first served is likely to establish itself. But in the melee, Gladstone can hold his own (and a few other people's as well, judging by his famous barrel chest). Here is the man who took the match-winning catch when England last captured the Ashes in Australia, way back in 1987. A legend to us even without all the beer we'd drunk. When asked by fans to be in a photo, he shrugs his shoulders and says, of course. Such is the grace of the Gods. Gods that appear to have had a few themselves, it must be said.

Chapter 15
SECOND TEST, DAY TWO
MEN IN SKIRTS
(Saturday 4th Dec)

England are in hot pursuit of a lead on the second day of the match, and I am in even hotter pursuit of Wi-Fi across Adelaide. There are considerable advantages as well as a lot of fun to be had following the match in the stands, but not having the internet and phone perks of the press room is a disadvantage bordering on a royal pain in the arse. When your hotel does not provide such a service then you are in real trouble if you have five submissions to make per day. The only realistic option, regrettably, is to head for McDonalds and its free wireless. With my Scottish genes having already pushed the cholesterol running through my veins sky high, I'm genuinely risking my life every time I eat a hamburger for the sake of getting a blog out on time. But it's what you've got to take for the team. I just hope both my readers are grateful, and my dog enjoys hearing my voice.

After breakfasting on a McMuffin meal, I take my seat in the Chappell Stands for the day's play. Sitting next to me is Paul, whom I'd met a few times in Brisbane and am glad to catch up with him now because he has stories I want to hear. We're both expecting a good England score, as despite Australia's humiliation, the wicket is still a cracker for batting on. Paul likens it to a typical 1970s housewife: boring, predictable, reliable and no naughtiness whatsoever. I don't ask him if he is married or if old sit-coms have put him off the idea forever, but no sooner does he share his analogy than Andrew Strauss cheats on his missus (so to speak), and leaves a ball from Bollinger that hits his stumps. Whoops Vicar, where's my bails?

Paul 'fesses up to his commentator's curse moment, but it was more of a poor decision than a pitch issue. Strauss left a straight ball that didn't do much at all; it started straight, it bounced straight, it carried straight onto the off-stump. The offering of no shot in cricket has always baffled me. Not just missing the ball – I'm a star at that – but actually lifting the bat out the way as if one were politely opening a door, perhaps for an encumbered parent with a pram to stroll through. I understand the theory, not wanting to catch an edge from a ball that's moving away, but when it starts even close to the stumps it is surely foolhardy to leave it. I don't think Strauss can quite understand why he did it either. Conceivably he was scared by Doug Bollinger's face, which has so much white sunblock smeared across it he resembles the Joker more than Dennis Lillee (and by close of play had bowled more like him too – send gags about Batman to the usual address).

Paul makes for a fine companion during the day's play as he tells me more of his time working as a journalist in 1970's New York. In those days the first rule of covering an event was to vandalise a nearby public phone by removing parts, so when you had to call in your report, you could enjoy exclusive use of it by fixing it again. Smashing up other hacks' mobiles is not something you can get away with unfortunately, but it does give me the bright idea of hurling a handful of sesame seeds into the air next time I'm working on a football match. He also regales me with some fantastic stories of ambulance-chasing journalism and covering the iconic first Muhammad Ali v Joe Frazier, heavyweight title fight at Madison Square Gardens.

'Aw brilliant, that must have been amazing!'

'No, not really. I don't like boxing.'

Paul is clearly a downbeat sort of a character, like myself, and, like me, he is a member of Surrey County Cricket Club. For readers from outside the South-East, unfamiliar with the club, I should say it might not be all you expect. When I tell friends in Scotland that I am a member of Surrey, opinion swings between the view that I've 'sold out' and goes all the way across to 'I've forgotten my Scottish roots and embraced

Thatcherism' (which in Scotland is seen as being slightly worse than Satanism). Even in many parts of England it's a county that's normally pronounced, 'Surrey!!??' For most, the very mention of the place conjures up images of wealthy, striped-shirted stock-brokers swigging champagne and queuing up at the polling station to see if Adolf Hitler's name is on the ballot paper – but it's not quite like that. Granted, the club does have some very wealthy members, but the home ground, the Oval, is next to Vauxhall, which is one of the scummiest places in London and emphatically somewhere Margot and Jerry Leadbetter wouldn't be seen dead in. Nor would Tom and Barbara Good for that matter, although the pig might feel at home. Certainly trying to grow vegetables in SW8 would be aided by the ready supply of fertilizer from the transient 'residents' defecating in your front garden. It is also home to the MI6 building, and if you've ever been to Vauxhall you'll understand why James Bond needed his Walther PPK.

The Oval itself is just over the postcode border in Kennington, which is a bizarre mix of beautiful Georgian terraces filled with MPs waiting for the property prices to rise so they can make a killing, and more questionable abodes filled with hoodie overspill from Vauxhall and Elephant & Castle, who frequently are also planning on making a killing, no house sales involved. In fairness, I'm exaggerating. It's really not so bad these days, and certainly a lot nicer than it was when I first moved down, when it was a properly rough area. But I'm somewhat surprised that Surrey CCC haven't sold the land for millions and found new digs in leafier surroundings further out. And good for them that they haven't, Adelaide take note when you're next thinking about bulldozing history.

Meanwhile Trott and Cook set about proving that the pitch is as placid as Paul had predicted and, continuing their form from the Gabba, score steadily, but not without drama. Hussey drops Trott when he has scored just 10, much to the delirious delight of the baking Barmy Army. As we already touched on, there are few things more depleting to a side, and more amusing to the opposition, than dropping a catch. All you want to do is hide;

but under a blazing sun that illuminates your error and is already burning your cheeks, the humiliation is amplified and it's hard to get your tail up again. You can't even blame cold hands, which is the usual excuse. Hussey looks as though he wishes he was wearing a bear costume so no-one could see his face.

Strangely enough, that's exactly what one of the Barmy Army is wearing, and it isn't even a koala, but a species of bear suited to a temperate forest or frozen Tundra. In direct sun, when it's 39C in the shade, this is endurance above and beyond the call of the most twisted duty, this ranks with an out-and-out suicide mission. Not to be outdone, an Aussie fan has come in a somewhat more appropriate kangaroo suit; not only climatically more suitable, but with a handy pouch for keys, wallet and the mobile phone that no marsupial can be without these days.

Unfortunately there are times when the behaviour between the two sets of fans on 'the Hill' heads towards the rowdy. Alcohol and sun are a potent cocktail and the stewards and police pile in, dealing with matters pretty quickly and efficiently. They must hustle more than thirty people out of the ground through the day, the high numbers more about cutting off trouble before it starts than anything actually serious.

But there is one lad who doesn't take the prospect of ejection too well. Possibly he has something of an allergy to police; but as they descend on him he lets rip, taking them all on. Most bravery is really limited intelligence in disguise, an inability to see the possible consequences, but let's be charitable and suggest he is foolhardy. Faced with six burly coppers, he figures attack is the surest form of defence; these blokes are clearly cowards if they need to come at him mob-handed, and he isn't going to take this lying down! Actually he is going to be lying, as they bundle him over and then all sit on him. It was a noble effort and it isn't over yet. Face down on the floor, with two policemen holding his legs, one sat on his back and two handcuffing him, he fights back like the Black Knight in *Monty Python and the Holy Grail*, lifting his head as high as possible and motioning head-butts and biting towards the police. I hope he was crying 'Tis a mere flesh wound!' as they carried him out.

At close of play both the fancy-dressed fans appear to have survived their ordeal, perhaps giving us hope that global warming won't lead to mass extinction after all. England have a 72-run lead and there are a few England fans in the Chappell Stands starting to think the unthinkable: Australia might not be that good. On the headsets, commentators and experts are whispering that seditious sentiment too. The Barmy Army is chanting it at the top of their hoarse voices. They borrow another line from the football terraces and sing to the beleaguered Australian captain:

'You're getting sacked in the morning'

Alastair Cook, in contrast, will not be getting sacked. He's sailed serenely to 136 not out. Following his 235 not out in the first Test, this takes his series aggregate to 438, and we are only three-tenths of the way through.

'Cook getting out is about as rare as Lionel buying a drink,' says Chas when I bump into him in the bar.

Chas apparently believes it's rare for anyone to buy him a drink; it's a common theme. It could be his imagination, or it could be that he works for a bank and we're worried he'll only buy us one back after charging us £30 to take our order. Any moment now he's going to bill me for late buying of the round.

There are dozens of members of the Welsh Brigade of the Barmy Army milling around us, and all seem especially delighted for Cook. They claim him as one of their own, on account of his mother hailing from Swansea. A Welsh parent. Not, as I originally thought I was being told by my informant, a Welsh parrot. A small disappointment in an otherwise enjoyable day. The image of Alistair owning a red and green parrot that sits in the dressing room saying, 'Who's a pretty boyo?' is a pleasing one and another that will stick with me, in spite of its inaccuracy. So with Cook still out there (figuratively speaking, he is allowed to come off overnight, something I've had to explain to Americans before) and Pietersen unbeaten on 85, England and Wales's position couldn't be more commanding. Sitting pretty, I'd say.

Coming out the ground I run into a group of kilted men, with yellow and green faces. Curious. As well as the kilts they are wearing yellow T-shirts on which they've listed an all-time England XI and the country of those players births, it reads:

Lamb (RSA)
Greig (RSA)
Shah (IND)
Hick (ZIM)
Hussain (IND)
Smith (RSA)
Pietersen (RSA)
D'Oliviera (RSA)
Strauss (RSA)
Morgan (IRE)
Malcolm (W.I.)
Woolmer (IND)

I'm guessing it's not in batting order, as with the curious absence of Trott (RSA), obviously Strauss and Hussain should be opening. I'm also disappointed Mike Denness (SCO) hasn't made the team, but it was already too heavy with batsmen. I'd have fancied at least seeing DeFrietas (W.I.) and Small (W. I.) in there to join Malcolm: a three prong West Indian attack would add some old spice.

It transpires the lads wearing them are from the 'Down the Wicket' cricket blogging site where they vent their opinions on everything right and wrong with cricket in Australia. More of the latter right now, I helpfully suggest. They explain to me that the T-shirt and the kilt was purely to wind-up the Barmy Army. 'The English don't wear the kilt; it is the dress of their enemies.'

I think they are somewhat bemused to find me supporting England, their world-view for a short time challenged. There's a charming old-fashioned nature to Australian perceptions of Europe, and apparently they believe things have not moved on much since Braveheart. If all you have to go on is seeing blue-painted faces at Murrayfield when the rugby's on TV, I can see how that might happen. I suppose we should be grateful they take their lead from the Middle Ages, if they'd updated their references a little they might have come dressed as Napoleonic Grenadiers, or worse, SS Stormtroopers; both splendid uniforms but unsuitable to the climate.

The lads are good fun and lapping up the interest of female fans who have been asking what's under the kilt. It's a new treat for them, and they are pleasantly surprised by the reaction. No surprise for us old hands; I only wear mine when I don't have to be up for work the next day. I envy them the attention and their little toy kilts. The full rig is not only very heavy, but extremely warm to wear. A ten yard kilt in 16oz wool is designed for roasting chestnuts in drafty Scottish castles (so to speak). When I bought mine I deliberately picked an eight yard one of a slightly lighter weave, aware I'd most likely be wearing it to summer weddings, but even so it was too bulky to pack and is far too hot to wear in Australia. Unless I had ice-filled underpants to go with it, but that would defeat the whole purpose.

Coincidentally, later that evening, Dan and I finally work out that the huge contraption hanging from our ceiling is an air-conditioning unit. We've been sat sweltering in non-conditioned underpants for the past three days, and only now do we figure it out – just in time for the fresher weather blowing in this evening. It's bad enough being stupid, but when you've lashed out money to come a long way to be stupid, it's worse. I'd always sooner fall at the first than run all the way round just to fall at the last; it's so much less effort.

We don trousers and head out into Adelaide to catch up with Simon and Ade, the four of us then making for the casino to support TMS in a poker tournament. Not that we could do much supporting because by the time we enter the establishment TMS has already been knocked out. I suspect he stopped for a cigarette and they just assumed he'd folded. No matter, he was now making a killing on the blackjack tables: from the poker swings to the pontoon roundabout.

Adelaide's casino, like Brisbane's, is a very impressive building with a number of bars and restaurants as well as the many gambling areas. We explore the maze like excited schoolboys then retire to the roof-garden bar so the smokers in the party can puff away (like even more excited schoolboys). Up here there's a duo playing fairly folk-orientated music. I'm egged on to put in a request for something by the Proclaimers, but am politely refused. Whatever happened to 'the Gambler is always right'? Considering my recent Blackberry challenges, their classic song about the English accent, 'Throw the "R" Away,' would have been very appropriate.

The hours race past and suddenly it is 3am. Dan has promised he will call his girlfriend back in England tonight, but has a classic 'bloke dilemma'. Should he put off calling until the following morning and apologise for being so forgetful, or call now and have to answer questions on why he is still awake and what he is doing up at three in the morning? Ladies, this is why men often don't call for days, or indeed at all. Women so readily assume we're players or at least playing games, when in truth we're just absent-minded and a little bit scared. Men are hunters and will adapt their hunting strategy to suit their prey; but they are also cowards, and if the prey would just not be quite so critical, they may in turn find the hunter is a bit more predictable. Despite the advice of others Dan decides to make the call. All the way back to the hotel he is interrogated on why he is up so late, and worse, why and how he is able to enjoy himself without her. Schoolboy error.

Chapter 16
SECOND TEST, DAY THREE
POLICE INTERVENTION
(Sunday 5th Dec)

Everything is apparently set fair for an enjoyable morning's cricket, but we've barely started when the unthinkable happens, Alastair Cook gets out. Harris finally breaks through and he's on his way for 148. After 1053 undefeated minutes at the crease he must be due a lie-down, but we're now in unfamiliar territory.

Something else is out of place, for some reason my seat for today is well away from all the usual faces and I find myself in-between a Lancastrian and a Yorkshireman. Luckily the War of the Roses is on hold and a ceasefire has been declared, leaving me to occupy no-man's land like a UN peacekeeper, observing negotiations and checking hostilities don't resume. It's not difficult to remain neutral; when I take my seat they've already found common ground and are discussing the merits of the Superleague.

I'll be honest; Rugby League is like a religion for me: I'm completely indifferent to it. But I am aware it fills up a lot of Sundays. At first I don't mind, because they both have that lovely, clipped, Northern way of speaking and, presumably out of habit, each of these gentleman says about six words before the other takes over the subject. I find it quite restful, like an episode of *All Creatures Great and Small* after a large dinner of shepherd's pie. However, as time wears on the topic wears mighty thin, as there is plenty to talk about with regards to what's happening on the field right in front of us and before our very eyes. With the cricket? Cricket? Remember, that thing we've come all this way to see, mmm? I want to sneeze, 'Ah-Shutthehellup!!' but chicken out.

For some aural respite, and with the weather a little cooler, I desert the Chappell Stands and sweat it out on the Hill with the Barmy Army. The famous old Hill – I want to say I've been here in case they build on it one day. Once upon a time these bankings were a feature of many grounds. Before they were completely ringed with stands, venues accommodated their spectators on grass covered slopes that created natural-seeming amphitheatres. Even after seating was added, for decades Australia's grounds retained a general admission grass verge for the working man who couldn't afford entrance to the covered areas. Not surprisingly, they not only preserved cricket's special atmosphere, but became the haunt of the rowdiest and funniest local characters. Sydney's was probably the most famous, but there was one at the Gabba, and now here in Adelaide I'm standing on the last original hill remaining at a major ground. I'm glad to say the Barmies are doing the tradition proud, and with their constant stream of jokes, songs and sledges the atmosphere is just fantastic.

It alters my perspective on things, but England are unruffled by my switch of vantage point and the order on the field remains the same, Pietersen and Collingwood continuing to score freely, with KP launching gleefully into a harmless Aussie attack. I'm watching the carnage with Ross, a lad from Edinburgh no less, who is unimpressed with the Australian selection: he suggests Scotland had more of an attack in the infamous football match against the Czech Republic when they played no recognised strikers. In fairness, finding a decent striker in Scotland at the time would have required a police manhunt and the assistance of a psychic, but Ross has a point. He also has a complexion like mine. Clearly Scotsmen aren't designed for the Hill. Just ask Sean Connery: he was never the same after that film.

England are cruising and the only time the watching Australians raise their voices is when Shane Warne walks round the boundary in his role as a broadcaster. It is obvious by the amount of adverts adorned with his features that he is still worshipped in Australia, but these days the face is slightly peculiar. There's the same cheeky expression but it has a pinky-orange tint and the teeth are a glistening billiard-ball white. When he smiles he resembles a chicken tikka with a small slice cut off the surface. Either the great man must have had some cosmetic treatment, or he's suffering from a debilitating illness.

That lunchtime I jokingly write in my blog that the Aussies 'should try and persuade Warne back out of reirement, because without him they are not looking like ever bowling this England team out. After all, his hair has made a comeback, why not the man himself?' Little do I guess that many Australians are saying the very same thing and are about to launch a campaign for his re-instatement in the team. To me this is akin to wanting Churchill back as Prime Minister in 1951, when he was a chronic alcoholic. I'm not suggesting Warne has sunk so low, just that it's an idealistic vote for former glories over new blood, and that there's something of a resemblance in the physique. Experts promptly dismiss the calls as unrealistic, saying he wasn't nearly fit enough to last a full five days. Mind you, Churchill, lasted another three and a half years.

After lunch, England reign on the pitch, controversy reigns off the pitch, and by tea it is raining all over Adelaide. Back at the Gabba, when Kevin Pietersen was fielding on the boundary and receiving unrestrained abuse from the Australian fans, many watching him felt that KP was 'up for it'. He didn't get the chance to show whether he was or wasn't in that match, owing to Cook and Strauss being up for it earlier than him and eating all the porridge before he got there. But now he finally gets to answer the taunts, and by the way he's playing they can probably hear his response in Brisbane. Starting the day on 85, he thrashes the Australian attack right through two sessions. By tea he's struck an imperious 213 not out.

England have built a massive 306-run lead, and the spinner Xavier Doherty's figures are more like a bingo card than a scorecard. The only thing sparing his blushes is that the recalled Dougie Bollinger, a far more experienced campaigner and presently Australia's only bowler in the world top 10, is equally shabby; and in Dougie's case, flabby. Between the two of them they've gone for 241-1. Mitchell Johnson is no doubt out watching TV at this very moment, seeing all this as the Positive that will redeem his Negative by the time we reach Perth.

From where I sit you feel that when Pietersen scores big it lifts the crowd in an entirely different way to Cook or Trott: the general happiness turns to the certainty of euphoria. Some though, have been lifted too high. Jimmy, leader of the Barmy Army, is arrested as he leads them in one of his famous sing-a-longs. Hardly a crime. He's sitting up on someone's shoulders – no danger to anyone, and not frightening (except the crows off the crops) – when suddenly the police pounce and nick him for 'inciting the crowd'. As he points out to the constabulary, we've all seen him do the very same thing on no less than eight occasions during the first two days and he wasn't arrested then. Indeed yesterday the Aussie fans threw lager and plastic glasses at him and the police didn't step in and stop that. On the charge of inciting the crowd they might as well have arrested Kevin Pietersen, and no doubt they secretly wanted to. Jimmy and many of the Barmy Army think it's simply sour grapes because the cops' team is being hammered. If play goes on like this I can see Trott and KP being arrested, *Not the Nine O' Clock News* style, for possession of an offensive accent.

The peels of thunder are heard long before the rain falls. The players have gone safely inside for tea, we have not, when the rain arrives. After days of sweltering heat this comes as no surprise, but when it falls it's like the start of the apocalypse and we're swept away by the tide. I expect to see Noah sailing past taking cricketers on board: two openers, two middle-order batsmen, two all-rounders, two seamers, two spinners, two wicketkeepers. (Surely that was the historical precedent of taking two keepers on tour, one of whom invariably never gets a game; I can't think why else they do it now we have planes.) Some of the England fans march through the puddles to the nearby cathedral to pray for better weather tomorrow. More fans head to the adjacent Cathedral Bar but are no doubt praying for the very same thing. If after two Tests the score-line remained 0-0, it would be an outrage. Unless you're Australian, in which case it would, naturally, be a 'fair result'.

The critics of the Barmy Army should have been with me at PJ O'Brien's pub this evening. They have organized a fund-raiser for the *McGrath Foundation,* breast cancer charity, and it's a great night with every one having a splendid time in the name of a good cause. Following his wrongful arrest, upon arrival, Jimmy is given a hero's welcome. As a nice touch, an English-born Adelaide policeman comes to the bar and apologises to him in person, and peace breaks out. It's just as well the air is cleared before tomorrow. I find myself chatting with co-founder of the Barmy Army, General Dave Peacock, who remarks, 'There could have been a riot if he had been charged. A sixty-year old man like Jimmy is never going to cause any trouble.' An example of how the heavy-handed desire to impose 'order' can threaten to break it down altogether. But the sour moment has passed and grudges are laid to rest.

Chapter 17
SECOND TEST, DAY FOUR
12th MAN
(Monday 6th Dec)

With it being such a small city centre it shouldn't come as a surprise to bump into the odd cricketer here and there, and seeing Gladstone Small ordering a happy meal isn't even the highlight. This morning I'm queuing in the newsagents when I recognise the tattooed arm in front of me. None other than Mitchell Johnson is taking his 12th man duties seriously and picking up the day's papers for the team. Despite his poor performance, I thought we'd rather hit it off in the hotel in Brisbane and I'm tempted to say hello, but think better of it. Not only are we no longer in the safe and convivial surrounds of the bar, but I figure he may not wish to make chit-chat, as all we have to talk about is, 'You've been dropped and your team's getting stuffed, but anyway, how's it going?' It's probably not the most sensitive opening gambit. I suppose I could commiserate with him and attribute Cook's dominance to his absence from the team. See, I can turn Negatives into Positives too, Mitchell; it's a piece of piss this psychology.

Diplomatically, I hold my peace, and I notice he's not buying the papers, but clutching copies of *Zoo* and *Nuts* magazines. No wonder the team are so distracted from their task. Or maybe he's had enough of being 12th man and carrying drinks, and is planning to spend the morning session in the toilet. I'm still struggling for an opening line that won't embarrass him or get me punched in the face when he pays for his contraband without shame and heads off. Well, when you're a highly-paid superstar sportsman I suppose those magazines take on a different significance. They must be more like catalogues: you can just pick out one you like, ring up the magazines for the date of their next party, and like Argos they'll be there waiting for you to collect when you arrive. The rogues.

Play commences, and Strauss is evidently still haunted by the nightmare of Adelaide four years ago. 306 ahead overnight, he sends his men out to continue batting against the worst Australian attack since Joe Bugner retired. With torrential rain predicted it's a doubtful decision if you're aiming to win, but 23,872 all out is probably the sort of score he'd like. Or is the desire to reach the magical 600 clouding the skipper's judgement? I don't accept that these milestones have any psychological effect whatsoever – the Aussies are watching the clock, not the scoreboard – and Andrew evidently agrees; he stubbornly keeps the boys going all the way to 620.

Australia need 375 just to make England bat again, and fifty-two completely wasted minutes later, they emerge in pads to try and survive five and a half sessions. In the stands we nervously check our barometers, while those who bet on a 0-0 series quietly gloat. Katich has an Achilles injury and is hobbling like a fun-runner in the last mile of a marathon, but he's playing so well with a limp, we start to wonder if he's really Gordon Greenidge in disguise. Things are not looking good.

But after lunch, England's talisman, Swann gets the vital breakthrough and puts Katich out of his agony. This brings Ponting to the wicket on a King Pair. Thirteen balls later he's still not off the mark. One thing I admire about him is that even when under pressure, he doesn't rush himself, doesn't give a damn about superstitions or silly little stats. He's here to bat all day, so he's not going to hurry to break his duck. He finally opens his account with a cracking boundary, and adds another with a dominant shot shortly after. But when he's out to an ecstatic Swann the very next delivery he can scarcely believe it. He stands still in the crease for a moment as if willing the catch at slip to rewind out of the hands of Collingwood, or for the gods themselves to belatedly call no-ball. Swann's success is met with hearty renditions of 'Swann will tear you apart, again' from the joyful Barmy Army. A huge pink inflatable swan is raised aloft; you have to seriously love a player to carry one of those around with you.

It's a curious sight, and I don't mean the pink swan. For years Australian batsmen have considered it their destiny to put together match-winning scores and this iron willpower has carried them through the hottest fire. Ponting still appears to believe on his way to the crease, but the old sorcery is just no longer working when he's out there. It's like the bat has turned from magic wand to empty cigarette lighter, and he's left shaking it forlornly, wondering why it won't ignite anymore. The unhappy wizard trudges off as if his body is made of lead.

Watson is in form, and when Broad drops him off his own bowling you wonder if luck is with him today, but he reaches another 50 then once again fails to convert it to three figures. The old English disease of getting in then getting out has evidently infected the Australians.

I wander over to the Hill and catch up with Brian and Kym, who have been receiving emails and phone calls from their children who are trying to run the family business in their absence. 'One of them said he was working 24 hour days just to keep up to date!' says Kym, amused that her children have been finding it hard-going.

'Kids! They don't realise how hard the older generations work,' I reply empathically.

'I told them we've been drinking 24 hours a day and that's just as stressful.'

'Mmmm.'

Stressful indeed, but they're putting effort into their intake and thought into their strategies. Brian divulges his secret for stockpiling drinks on a slope: 'The problem is, that on the grass bank there's nowhere to rest your glasses. So what you do is, take off your trainers and place them facing uphill, then go to the bar barefoot and buy four pints of lager – they don't do *proper* beer here—' the word 'proper' is heavy with longing, so clearly the colonial trick of calling lagers 'bitters' is fooling no-one from Yorkshire '—and when you get back, deposit a glass in each shoe and have the other two glasses in each hand. Four pints at a time without spilling, and without queuing up four times and missing the sunshine.'

It definitely seems to be working, as he is concerned that his growing belly is starting to resemble Winnie-the-Pooh's. Certainly his complexion is remarkably similar to Piglet's.

After chatting to Brian I'm thirsty for a drink myself and queue up at the bar behind a Newcastle United fan in the obligatory black and white stripes. Here's a great opportunity for the podcast, to finally quiz a member of the Toon army on why they wear nothing when it's freezing, but when it's sweltering they wear their shirt. I ask my bonnie lad if he doesn't mind me putting this to him 'on air' and he agrees. So I whip out the audio recorder, and pop the question I've already prepped him with. He replies by shrugging his shoulders. Quality 'radio'. I'm none the wiser about the Geordie race, but I'm contemplating another PhD on non-verbal communication among the great apes.

Thankfully I have other interviews lined up through the Barmies' PR manager Becky Fairlie-Clarke, and my first is with her husband Allan, who is not only the creator of Battrick (the largest online cricket management game on the internet), but is in fact a Scot. In his travels with the Army, he has, of course, been on the receiving end of much good-natured banter and has, of course, been given the nickname 'Jock'. Of course. They may write the most entertaining songs in sport, but when it comes to dishing out nicknames they seem limited to about five.

It's good to chat to a countryman in the Barmies's inner circle, proving we can rise through the ranks, but I ask him his opinion on the singing of 'Are You Scotland in Disguise?' Allan is a more relaxed character than I, and thinks it is no big deal, observing that the musical leader of the Barmy Army, Billy the Trumpet, doesn't play along to it. Fair point, but has he gone entirely native since his marriage? Has he started to call Britain, England, for example? No. And what's more despite his connubial ties and supporting England at cricket, he would still never be able to do so at rugby – the wedding vows have not been written that would permit that. Thought not.

Shortly after tea with Australia still 201 runs from making England bat again, the predicted storm arrives and does what the Australians can't, it silences Billy and the Barmy Army choir, many of whom accept the early shower as an early bath and trudge out of the ground not to return. This is unexpectedly unwelcome for both sides, as Michael Clarke has returned to form and looks comfortable, playing some beautiful shots.

It rains, it hails, it blows but it blows itself out, and finally the Aussies have to come back out to a half-empty ground for a tricky little period before close. Agonisingly, just four balls from safety, Clarke is caught. Or is he? He starts to walk, then realises no decision has been given, so stops and waits while England call for the review. But his reaction has already given away the inevitable outcome: Clarke c Cook b Pietersen 80

Pietersen: the part time spinner. It's possibly the worst of all dismissals for a batsman: weather the storm of the pace attack, weather the attack of the world's best spinner, weather the weather, and then within sight of a good night's sleep, you clip an edge off the make-weight bowler and the enemy go in with their tails high and victory within their grasp.

I want England to win, I want my prediction and bet to come true, but I'd have liked the golden boy to get his century for use as anti-venom against the poisoned pens that are aimed against him at the moment. Yesterday, damning photographs appeared in the newspapers of Clarke laughing as the match slipped away. It was the kind of out-of-context shot that the press love. There always laughter at funerals when I was a kid, but in this age of 'reality' TV all are supposed to wear permanent marble faces to demonstrate their grief. As it is, I wouldn't want to be sharing a hotel with Ponting and Clarke tonight; it'll be as upbeat as a funeral parlour on the verge of bankruptcy. While the English pray for sun, Ricky will be gathering his brows like the gathering storm, nursing his depression in an effort to form clouds over the ground tomorrow.

Chapter 18
SECOND TEST, DAY FIVE
WINNERS AND LOSERS
(Tuesday 7th Dec)

If the streets of Adelaide last night were anything to go by, then the Barmy Army were having a quiet night in, in anticipation of a noisy celebratory day today. It is a beautiful morning, with none of the predicted rain clouds. Flood emergency warnings are the first story on the news, but at eight this morning it is blue, blue sky all the way. But not for Michael Clarke, who has admirably, if masochistically, apologised for not walking when caught last night. Never apologise, never explain, Michael.

Today, though, the weight is on the shoulders of Hussey, Haddin and North, as with Mitchell Johnson dropped the Aussie tail is long and vulnerable. If those three can add another 50 apiece then the home side should make it to safety and, on the page rather than in the mind, it doesn't appear so hard. They have new hope, as news is filtering through that Stuart Broad is out of this match and out of the series with a torn abdominal muscle. Will the Barmies' abstinence have been in vain? I take a deep breath, don my Scotland top and head for the ground.

'Swaaaannn!! Swaannn will tear you apaaaaaart, again!'
That's one prediction this morning, and indeed Swann does kick things off, but only until the new ball is taken. The clouds, though late getting up this morning, now start to gather menacingly, and England's chance looks like it might slip away. But, ironically, under the threatening skies the ball starts to swing and Australia are in trouble. When Finn bounces Hussey into fatally playing a shot he doesn't need to in only the sixth over, the writing is on the old Adelaide scoreboard and on the

wall for the Baggy Greens. Next Anderson swings two out in two balls, and gives Harris a king pair to remember the game by, what a recall for the poor lad. He was by far their best bowler in this game, coming out relatively unscathed from the run frenzy, but he doesn't bat nearly as well as Johnson – Mitch took 19 balls over *his* zero at the Gabba. For Harris, the toil in the field will fade from memory and it'll be the two noughts in two balls that stay with him. With the chips down, North looks like a little boy lost; the tail is exposed and falls off like a panicking lizard's. To the dancing delight of the Army, Swannie does indeed wrap it up, taking the last three wickets for a well deserved 'five-for', and the crowd on the Hill genuinely do go wild.

I'm right there among the happy throng, standing with one of the Barmy Army's most illustrious members, Adge Walton. He turns to me and with his voice breaking says, 'This is my SIXTH Ashes tour Down Under and we're AHEAD!? I don't know how to celebrate this!!'

Well, he could have fooled me. He is attired as usual in an M.C.C. Blazer, M.C.C. tie and Panama hat, only the tracksuit bottoms and trainers are giving the game away. That and the fact that he's bouncing around like a squirrel on ecstasy. He's been singing all day and now he's doing the sprinkler dance (a fashionable little 80's party-piece recently repopularised by Swann and Collingwood). I wonder if the TV cameras are on us. Because of his distinctive dress Adge is seldom off the box for long, and his phone gets a steady stream of texts from friends who are fed up of seeing his mug every time they switch on the cricket. Apparently a couple of Channel 9 commentators actually believe he is 'member', so I hope they're catching all this, it might improve the stuffy image of the M.C.C. Really he should be charging them for PR consultancy, but sadly he's unlikely to be invited to join anytime soon. As he'd told me yesterday, the hatred of the Barmy Army may be on the wane, but for the hardcore traditionalists it will always be there. But on a day like today, who cares? Not Adge: after six once-in-a-lifetime trips, England are in the lead. This one's for him.

The clouds finally remember what they came for but they're too late to spoil the party. When a massive hailstorm arrives at two in the afternoon it can't rain on our parade, the game is long over and affairs have transferred to PJ O'Brien's. The Barmy Army HQ is full to bursting, but the celebrations can't spill onto the streets on account of the forty days and forty nights of rain that have turned up, and are trying to get the job done in forty-eight hours. Undeterred, we squeeze ourselves in. There's an art to packing, and once inside I can relate to how my poor clothes have suffered on this trip. If we wanted to get the doors closed, someone would have to come and sit on the pub.

The bar has cleverly put together a CD of music the Barmy Army use for their songs. Joy Division's 'Love Will Tear Us Apart' booms out, a strangely incongruous tune for a party, but the joyful singing makes up for it. Adge continues to find new ways to celebrate creating on cardboard spoof advertisements to hang outside the pub. The one that receives the biggest cheer is, '*Spin bowler required, start immediately – contact Mr R Ponting on 0472652...*' I ask the secret of his stamina. 'Just sheer, adrenalin, it's not from the beer that's for sure. It's only 2.5%!'

He is talking about the baby lager they sell in the ground, but it's easy for us to get confused with numbers, our heads are all still upside down. It feels like midnight but it's only just seven o'clock, and England are 1-0 up. It's all very mysterious.

I have arranged to meet the gang I've spent most of the last two weeks with so, liberally lubricating myself in lager, I squirm through the throng and slip away from PJs just as KC and the Sunshine Band start singing 'Give it Up'. Quite a deft piece of song-writing that's lasted twenty-seven years and is still going strong. It's accompanied by the Barmies singing over it with one of their lesser lyrical moments:

Na-na na-na na-na na-na na
Ali Ali Cook, Ali Cook , Ali Ali Cook

I don't think that one will last three decades, but as I walk out into the night and up the street, the na-na na-na na-na na-na nas seem to follow me like smoke off into the far distance.

After regaining some energy with a Wok in a Box I make my way to the South Terrace. For Ade, Simon, Dan, TMS, Brian and Kym it is their last night in Australia, so Chas, Lionel and I plan to help see them off. We're in luck: the first hotel we hit turns out to be the temporary home of the England team, which evens up the score from Brisbane. How do we know it is their hotel? Kevin Pietersen is stood outside smoking a large cigar – to the victor the spoils. There will be some killjoys talking about bad role-models, but if you can't have a cigar after a match-winning double century, when can you? The birth of your children, career best scores, and ascending to the Cuban presidency: those are the three acknowledged occasions when you can be cut a little slack.

In the bar, Strauss, Pietersen, Trott and Panesar all pop in for a small victory tipple, as well as ex-captain Michael Vaughan. To a man they are charming and approachable. It probably helped they'd won the game, but they chat and pose for photos, and humour us politely. Judging by the dark shaky photos that I found on my camera later, some needed more humouring than others. Not me of course. I'm absolutely positive Michael Vaughan is not humouring me when he compliments me on my Scotland shirt and requests a photo of the two of us. I'm happy to oblige, I'll make time for an old cricketer down on his luck. That's my story and I'm sticking to it. And thanks to the drunken fool I handed my camera to, the photo is so damned blurred no-one will be able to dispute my interpretation of the body language between us.

None of the England boys are counting their chickens, but you can tell they fancy their chances for an Ashes win. *'Strauss, Pietersen, Trott, Panesar – Not Nervous!'* Am I too late for the first editions? Deciding that journalism is well beyond me by this point I give it a rest and we move to a pub across the road before I embarrass myself. Once ensconced with a drink and surrounded by fellow lesser mortals on an inebriated equilibrium, I get chatting to Big Frank. Big Frank (the prefix seems mandatory among his mates) was born and bred in Adelaide but works as a policeman in Melbourne, returning to see his parents – purely coincidentally – during the week of the Adelaide Test. Well that's one way of avoiding them I think, while pondering the likelihood of England playing a Test in Tayside. After decades of supporting a dominant team he can't get his head round how bad Australia are: 'Winning isn't everything, it's the only thing!'

He's hardly re-writing the lexicon of sporting wisdom with this, as it is one of the perennial quotations; its originator generally acknowledged as Vince Lombardi, the legendary American Football coach. I'm not well placed to argue with Big Vince (he's one of the most successful coaches in history) nor with Big Frank (he's rather too big for that), but as many before me have observed, the comment is unconstructive. Teams can learn from defeat and improve, and this Australian team will improve, I reassure BF. They don't have the superstars of yesteryear, but from the Sheffield Shield matches I've seen on TV there is talent bubbling under. Isn't it funny how alcohol either turns people violently antagonistic or makes them want to bond in brotherhood with complete strangers, till you find yourself talking your own side down just to be convivial?

'Frank, winning two of the next three Tests is going to be tricky, but it's not impossible!' See, I'm still gibbering. While I do honestly believe Australia might do it, I don't know why I'm being so nice to the opposition. Anyway, I've convinced Fat Frank (as he is also called, but I don't try this myself) that all is not lost, and to cheer him up further, Brian decides to croon him a version of the classic Australian folk song, 'Two Little Boys' by Rolf Harris. And if that's the penalty for defeat, Vince Lombardi had a point.

As the night draws to a close, there's one last ritual to perform: Dan and Brian are finally going to play each other at pool, a challenge match that has been two weeks in the making. Boxing promoters could have got the Klitschko brothers into a fight against each other quicker than this. Dan breaks, the balls are well spread, when suddenly the bar manager and security guard come racing over and stop the contest. Weird, nobody's been cut. The security guard shouts at Brian, 'I told you earlier, you are banned from playing pool here!'

All of us are perplexed by this sudden halt to the game. Brian, taken aback, gathers himself and politely points out that it must be a case of mistaken identity; he's never been here before. It's a strange error to make as he cuts a distinctive figure; although I suspect it could have been avoided if he'd worn one of his unique pink England shirts. I don't say this, as the granite-faced staff are having none of it – like door security the world over they are infallible – and appear about to demand that he takes his two zipped bag and leaves. Chas has a bright idea and approaches the conversation with his arms in a T shape, demanding a television review of the entire incident. It lightens our mob up, but the ensuing laughter just enrages the staff further and incredibly we are all shown the door for making a joke. Australians really do lack a sense of humour at times.

Brian is justly annoyed that his last night in Adelaide is brought to such an abrupt and unjust end, but like a batsman given a shocking lbw decision we leave without further argument and before the third umpire in blue is called. We say our farewells and retire to our beds in ill humour. It's a bitter shame. Adelaide had been such a welcoming place, but apparently the police that arrested Jimmy aren't the only sore losers in town.

Chapter 19
WEDNESDAY NIGHT FEVER
(Wednesday 8th – Saturday 11th Dec)

I've got a few days off; it's time to kick back. There are blogs to be written and I have to keep up with the team news, but there's plenty of time for properly exploring Adelaide and taking a trip out to a vineyard. So far Adelaide has felt like a city that's at ease with itself and what it has to offer. The local politicians planning their latest wrecking spree will tell you otherwise, but my inkling is that the residents don't see their town as being in competition with the other big cities. Melbourne and Sydney's rivalry is famous, Brisbane would love to join the big boys, Perth has a presence on the world stage, but in Adelaide there's no shouting from the roof-tops, no obvious metropolitan jealousy or paranoia; they appear to have a great standard of living and who cares if the rest of the world don't know?

I'm keen to see more but as soon as I wake up on Wednesday I realise something is wrong, and not just that it's nearly 1pm already; after fifteen days of virtually continuous hedonism that was to be expected. Entirely unexpectedly, I suddenly start sneezing and feeling very ill. Either I have caught flu – the real thing that decimates populations, not the man-variety – or I'm experiencing some new, psycho strain of hay fever. It's possible: everything else in this country is lethal and poisonous, I suppose its pollen could be a bit on the 'mental head-case' side. As I genuinely can't tell what has brought on the symptoms it will be a real dilemma as to which medication to take, but I figure some combination of morphine, alcohol and amphetamines should cover all bases. If only you could buy them over the counter.

Doctors are no use in these circumstances, they simply say, 'Mmmm... There's a lot of it about', or 'Mmmm... It'll just have to run its course', or 'Mmmm... Take your clothes off and bend over, this will teach you to waste my time.' Whatever, it always starts with 'Mmmm...' and goes downhill from there. So instead I head out to find a chemist, preferably one of the back-street variety that will dispense something meaty and distilled from cobra venom and shark penis. I've only gone a few hundred yards when I feel so bad that even my usual hysterical hypochondria is shocked into submission, and says, you're on your own boyo. I turn around and go straight back to bed. I may not be at Death's door but I'm convinced I'm walking up his garden path – better to get under the covers where he's less likely to find me. It's a strategy that never failed me as an adolescent; even the Grim Reaper was unwilling to poke around in a teenager's fetid bedroom.

The next few days go in a spluttering blur of codeine and napping. Many of the Living with the Lions crew have already departed and aren't replaced, so the hotel empties out. Besides, I'm in no mood for seeing people, nor in any state for forging new friendships with strangers and itinerants. I don't feel they'd get off on a good footing anyway. Sneezing over someone or forgetting to take the sodden hanky out of your sweaty palm before shaking hands are both definite *faux pas*. Had it been the last moments of the trip I might have pulled myself together and ventured out for some last explorative memory gathering, but I want to guarantee recovery in time for the Perth Test. Consequently, I'm sorry to say, I take the coward's way out and do my cultural research via the TV set at the end of the bed. Notwithstanding the colourful character of the street, the hotel is a pretty decent place to hole up and I could do with giving my liver a rest. Plus it's an opportunity to see how the Australian media approach the world.

I start with the intention of a serious study of journalistic practices, attitudes to sport, and all the career-orientated stuff that will push me forward and get me a press-pass the next time around. Instead, within minutes, I'm hopelessly distracted and puzzling over the viewing habits of this curious nation. I'm not seeking to one-sidedly criticise specks in the eyes of others – British television includes more fatuous dross than you could count in a month of wet Sundays – but Australian TV is utterly bewildering. Why on earth would anyone here want to watch the UK editions of *Escape to the Country* and *Location Location Location*? Haven't the British ex-pats already escaped the country altogether? And who else in Australia has the slightest interest in the British upper-middle-class property market? It's baffling. I know we speak the same language but I didn't think property porn would translate. I watch the Australian equivalents to see if there's any cross-border appeal for me. Nope, they're even more tedious than the originals.

There's a definite trend towards a deification of the old country, usually in a form it no longer or even never existed in. British comedies abound and rainy, green countryside is everywhere. It makes me wistful, but it's undeniably peculiar to be serving it up to a nation that are individually incapable of remarking on Britain without telling me how bloody awful our climate is. Unless their ceaseless attacks on our climate are just a front and deep down they appreciate that it's a lot more pleasant to live in. Next time an Australian starts moaning to me about the weather in Britain, I'll challenge them on this. I now have ammunition: like an alcoholic hiding bottles in the bread bin, they've all got a secret stash of British verdancy on cable.

The Australian perception of the UK appears completely at odds with the view presented in our tabloids; it takes its lead from our own Sunday night TV. They both imagine a happy, tidy, well-mown Great Britain, with only one chav per village, smiling bobbies, whistling postmen, farmhouse teas, and old ladies like Miss Marple (because an unsolved grisly murder a week is a fair price to pay for a decent postal service). It doesn't seem to matter if you live in Wigan and pretend it's not a lie for an hour or two, or live in Wagga Wagga and wish it to be the truth, everyone is equally deluded and nostalgic for a Britain that ceased to exist right about the same time we stopped allowing landowners to impregnate their servants for sport.

Watching it all at 10,000 miles distant, feels like lounging around the Costa Del Sol with a gang of ex-pats, reminiscing over a mythical era when you could safely walk across Hampstead Heath at night with your trousers round your ankles and waving a wallet full of money. Not only was that not a great idea during any decade in living memory, not only have they apparently never heard of Dick Turpin, but since half the expats in Spain are criminals, and half those in Thailand perverts, Hampstead is probably safer in their absence.

Overall, it seems the Australian media view of Britain is even more dewy-eyed than the UKIP's dream of our past, but maybe both have a point. If so many people home and abroad love this cottage garden vision, and cherish natural beauty and picturesque homes built on a human scale, why have our governments spent a 100 years allowing them to be systematically destroyed in the name of 'growth'. And why is every other country doing the same?

What of Australia's view of itself? I've seen some very good Aussie drama over the years – they did a great mini-series on Gallipoli and they made a couple of my favourite ever films – but mostly the home-grown TV doesn't appeal. The comedy is blunt and obvious, and the soaps resemble *Neighbours* and *Home and Away*... oh wait, those are *Neighbours* and *Home and Away*. You get the gist; it's nothing you haven't seen before.

Their news however, is radically different from what I'm used to, and I rather like it. Not the mad crazy Fox outpourings, which would be comical if only they were billed as comedy, but the regular networked national news. Their bulletins have two outstanding features. Firstly, they just don't seem to care about foreign affairs. Now I'm not saying that it's an ideal for living, but it does make a nice change. And why should they report on other countries? They're not part of the EU, not in thrall to the USA, were never threatened by the eastern-bloc, didn't once rule India or half of Africa, and aren't deluded enough to think they won WWII by themselves. Moreover, though they do send troops here and there, they're far less up to their elbows in the Middle-East, Afghanistan, Kosovo and all the other holiday hot-spots that Britain and America are pathologically determined to meddle in. So, shock horror, the Aussies focus on their own country and what a good idea that is, as it makes for much more convivial viewing. I can't watch UK or US news without becoming plunged into gloom or roused to furious anger about the state of the world – it's why I watch sport, to get away from it all – but Aussie news is actually quite relaxing. Secondly, there is little of the endless opinion-tennis that blights British politics; they don't bounce one simplistic sound bite off another and call it balanced reporting. In fact they don't bother with political debate much at all as there doesn't seem to be one. Whereas we in the UK pretend the parties are different for the sake of appearances, straight-up Aussies skip the charade.

The result is something more akin to *John Craven's Newsround*. It's an endless parade of feats of insane athletic endurance, eccentric animals, backyard boffins standing in front of sheds, koalas that have been nursed back to health, women who have put up a fence and want you to know about it, happy whale stories, sad whale stories, plucky outback blokes that have survived a week in the desert after having their arm gnawed off by an angry termite, and all followed by weather forecasts of such ferocity they'll give you nightmares and should have an 18-certificate. And in-between these blokes in vests saying, 'Ah yeah, mate, she'll be right – it's just off at the elbow!' occasionally, just occasionally, up pops a politician of an indeterminate party saying nothing very much about something not very significant. Australian politicians are famously out-spoken against each other when it comes to personal attack, but on the big issues they always appear as if they're on the verge of saying, 'Oh, who bloody cares? It's sunny alright? Just tick any box on the bloody ballot paper and have a beer.' No wonder they had to make voting compulsory Down Under.

News aside, there are other things to like about Aussie TV. For starters you don't need to wait till after 9pm to watch *Family Guy*. I don't know if their kids are less easily corrupted or they want to counterbalance perceptions of domestic life made saccharine by *Neighbours*, but it unquestionably beats *Eastenders* as early evening viewing. Late night TV is reserved for more important things, like the fantastic repeats of old One Day International cricket matches from the 1980s, that kept me happy for my entire trip. Perfect bedtime nostalgia, and presumably shown after the watershed as they're deemed to be a horror film for any watching sports' coaches. The frequent buffoonery of just 30 years ago takes you by surprise, but it confirms my belief that you don't need hard-drilled athletes on mega-salaries risking permanent injury to draw a crowd. Viv Richards' West Indians were pure box-office, even if they mixed occasionally breathtaking athleticism and lashings of sunshine cricket with dopey dropped dollies and crazy run-outs. Tellingly, even then, Australia appeared the least gifted but the most professional team around. In hindsight you can see the empire they were building. But no offence, I'd sooner watch Joel and the Gang any day, they had soul man.

Away from the goggle-box, and back on the google-box: so far on the trip I've been failing in my 21st century duty – and apparently it is compulsory – to keep up with my Twittering. It's hard and expensive to do at the ground without wireless access and only a UK Simcard, so I've scarcely managed more than a few Tweets at the start of play. I take my bed-ridden opportunity to catch up properly with what's been moving and shaking in the Twittersphere, and clearly I've been missing out. The whole network is abuzz with people falling about laughing at the tribulations of an American baby-sitter. Even I understand you require a unique handle on Twitter, and she's chosen the nickname her boyfriend gave her: @theashes. As soon as we reached Brisbane the fans started hitting the twits and she was in for an earful. Much hilarity has already arisen with people, at first accidentally but now entirely deliberately, finding ever more elaborate and absurd ways to Tweet they're enjoying themselves @theashes, all of which are relaying themselves to her phone, which has gone into meltdown. Once she had figured out what on earth was happening and Tweeted: *'I AM NOT A FREAKING CRICKET MATCH!'* the flood-gates opened and she became the pranksters' favourite, and a more popular recipient than Test Match Special.

All of which I feel is missing the point. Who in God's name nicknames their girlfriend the Ashes? It's a bit of a morbid name, jinxing the relationship just a tad – and I use tad in the *Airplane 2* sense of the word. Or is he a sports fan whose exes include the Derby and the Grand National and the FA Cup Third Round Replay? Although being American it would more likely be the Superbowl, which on balance is somewhat worse. Does he refer to them all collectively as the Indianapolis 500?

Opportunely, the star of this saga, Ashley Kerekes (yes, yes, Ashley, I get it, it was either that or Angela), has taken to her new popularity and is engaging with the cricket and trying to learn the rules and terminology. Oh Jeez. 'How to explain cricket to an American in 140 characters or less?' That's got to be the hardest game of all. It takes 150 letters just to name a Sri Lankan wicket-keeper. Not for the first time I reckon I'm not cut out for Twitter and its lack of qualified thought. Regardless, Ashley is enjoying it all, and why not? It's the perfect sport for baby-sitting to, I would have thought almost like a lullaby, with Aggers and Blowers burbling in the background – and there's an expression that must have raised her eyebrows when she first heard it.

It's working out well for her; the whole affair has grown into a world-wide campaign to get @theashes to the Ashes, and to fly her to Sydney for the last match. Why didn't I think of that? I did get 'ashes' into my Twitter name, but also said I was Scottish reporter. What a mistake! I should have pretended to be a Mexican cleaner or a French nurse instead. Or possibly a Swedish supermodel, which might have got me a free ticket a lot quicker. I daresay the whip-round would have been lucrative, I'm just not sure I can manage the whole tour in heels.

PART THREE ~ PERTH

Chapter 20
TO THE ENDS OF THE PERTH
(Sunday 12th Dec)

Some of the England fans have gone to Melbourne with the England team, many intending to stay there until the whole circus returns East in a week's time, or to simply enjoy the city for a few days and then board the plane home. Perth does not figure highly on the travelling fans' agenda. Truth be told the location of the Third Test is as mad as a bag of badgers and a trouserful of ferrets all at once. Going from East to South to West and back to East again, can only be considered a good plan if you have shares in Qantas; it's illogical, expensive and exhausting. So, of course, that's exactly how they do it.

As far as I can see, this sequencing hurts not only England fans, but Australian match receipts, Australian tourism and even the Australian team. Most England fans can only afford to come to two matches, so choose the cheaper option of Brisbane and Adelaide, or the expensive Xmas/New Year package of Melbourne and Sydney. Scheduled after a dead week and right before Christmas, Perth loses out badly. The Christmas and New Year slots of Melbourne and Sydney are unmovable for many good reasons, yet judging by the empty stands in Brisbane, the Gabba needs all the cricketing tourists it can get, and Adelaide (especially with the planned new expansion) wouldn't say no to a few extra bodies either.

My suggestion is that Perth should open the show. The logic

is simple: with the First Test in Perth, followed the next week by Adelaide, it would be easy to see two Tests in a similar climate, hopping West, South, and Home for Christmas; and, if staying for longer, it avoids crossing the country twice. It would also be a gentler introduction for the long-haul Poms, as Perth is three hours closer to the UK and would give them more opportunity to adjust their clocks as they slowly follow the cricket and the sun.

During the week off, the England team could still head to Victoria as they do, before moving onto Brisbane to be greeted by a new wave of fans arriving for the matches on the East coast – three matches that would now be relatively cheap and easy to combine. For those on tighter budgets and with Sydney being so expensive at New Year, a bargain two Test package to Brisbane and Melbourne over Christmas is also very appealing, which would help out the Gabba and assist the MCG in filling that massive ground. The England fans would benefit hugely, and Australia would increase its revenue, both at the venues and in its high streets. It's a clear win-win. The cherry on the cake is that Perth is historically Australia's most successful ground for matches against England, thus giving the home side their best chance of starting with a victory; so it's win-win-win. But Cricket Australia being Cricket Australia, they prefer to shift us all back and forth across the country, like jet-lagged cattle. Did I mention the miserable sods wouldn't give me a press pass?

There are, though, some fans who avoid the jet-lag, if not the cattle analogy. One such is Chas. Five days after our post-match celebrations I see him off for Perth at Adelaide train station. Now, I'm a great aficionado of train travel as a *concept*: with rising oil prices and environmental concerns no longer swept under the carpet, the days of the short haul flight are numbered and I see high-speed train travel (or more precisely 300mph Maglevs) as the future. But my view is not shared by Australia in the present. They prefer nostalgia to vision, and slow, clanking trains to bullets on rails. Out here, passenger trains give way to freight rather than vice versa; they really know how to make a bloke feel small. All in, the trip to Perth takes a shocking *thirty-six* hours, and Chas won't even have a bed; the crazy fool's in a cheap seat the whole way. I'll be interested to see how he fares. But not so interested that I cancel my flight. Leaving later that afternoon, I still beat him to Western Australia by a more than a day.

A short hop through the golden sky later and I'm touching down in the city whose name is the world's most obvious reminder of Scotland's diaspora, after McDonalds. Perth Airport is still a dinky, unglitzy little place; it turns out you *can* get planes in and out of the sky without miles of walkways and shopping facilities. How strange, travelling through Heathrow I'd presumed these were mandatory and in some way crucial to safe transportation. But even without the free market screaming at me, after all my Blackberry issues and the huge cost of using the damn thing abroad, I accept I need an Australian phone as well. In fact, I've hauled a decrepit old dumbphone half-way round the world with the very intention of putting an Aussie simcard in it, but not had the time and since arrival I've realised I need something I can Tweet and Facebook on – oh yes, I'm down with the kids at long last. It's time to bite the bullet and upgrade. I see a little phone-shop kiosk, and am drawn to it like a moth to a flame, or as it transpires, like a lamb to the slaughter.

Short-term phone rental is common in many parts of the world, so I make enquiries with the girl behind the desk. The sales assistant looks pained when I greet her and 'sales assistant' turns out to be a bit of a misnomer; she is neither capable of selling me anything nor assisting me in any way whatsoever. I suspect the big fraud isn't even in pain.

'I can't do anything, the network's down.'

Not a great sales pitch. I appear to have landed in Little Australia. I persevere. 'Well, while we're both waiting, do you rent phones?'

She appears appalled, and not because I used the word rent when I should have said lease. 'Rent?'

It turns out such a practice is unknown here. So unknown that she's fascinated by the concept and makes me explain it twice before she believes me. Fair enough, they don't lease phones in Australia, but I persevere. 'Tell you what, can I buy a cheap phone and a Simcard?'

'I can't do anything, the network's down' Her total immobility, not even glancing at, let alone reaching for, any of the models behind her, makes me wonder if she's voicing a literal truth, and she is in fact entirely mobility dependent on the broken network. Is this some new form of Blade Runner-style Sales-Replicant, designed for only one purpose and paralysed when the matrix fails? Certainly, I've encountered a few Australians with built-in international roaming. But I persevere; today I'm good at persevering. 'I just want to see what the choice is. Have you anything around a $100?'

'No nothing like that'

'Nothing?'

'Um. I don't know really.'

Well turn around, I want to scream. After a bit more wrangling in which she doesn't offer to show me a single phone – refreshing I suppose, the softest cell-phone sell I've ever encountered – I admit defeat and instead produce my elderly dumbphone. 'What about a simcard for this?'

'I can't do anything, the network's down.'

I'm guessing she's an old fashioned trade unionist, one down, all down. I switch from perseverance to distraction and ask her to explain the Australian pay-as-you-go system to me. It's fiendishly complicated, but reassured by this familiar ground she does finally provide me with a simcard, although I can't use it until later that evening, because apparently the network's down. Why didn't she tell me that sooner?

Elation is short-lived, as once ensconced in my digs I unpack to find that I don't have the charger for the dumbphone, and I've only two bars of battery left on it. Possibly it's still at home. There are two sofas in my flat and I have a vague recollection of finding two chargers in the cupboard, and then chucking the spare one on the sofa... twice. However, the network does at least return to operation. (I picture the girl at the airport suddenly animated and buzzing, whizzing through her job.)

First task: check the simcard by calling the Western Australia Cricket Association to see about collecting my tickets. I feel instantly at home, as the WACA greets me with an automated recorded menu and no possibility whatsoever of speaking to flesh and blood. The only difference travelling 10,000 miles has brought to the futile experience of seeking assistance by phone, is that the interminable and mostly useless options have an Australian accent. There is though, one startling surprise, which amuses and appalls in equal measure.

It has already been announced, not unsurprisingly but with poor timing, that Western Australia captain Marcus North has been dropped for his home Test. Yes, North has gone south, just as the rest of the team come west. It's sad for Australia's thirty-something, twenty-something specialist, but a recent batting average lower than your age is scarcely healthy. And it's not half as sad as his new day-job which – do my ears deceive me? – is voicing the option menu of the WACA's call centre. I kid you not, the captain of the Western Warriors, M J North, is there on the end of my phone asking me to Select 1 for Tickets, Select 2 for Forthcoming Events and Select Haddin to bat at 6.

I expect Australia will shortly announce they've replaced him in the team with a call-centre operative from Calcutta. It would be a decent idea for shoring up the Australian middle-order; they need someone obdurate, with the guile and ability to frustrate the English bowlers. He could just stand there and respond to every lbw appeal by saying, 'Yes that is what I am telling you, not-out. Is there anything else I can assist you with?' Or with a recorded message saying, 'Sorry, I do not recognise that option.'

Alas, Marcus is even less use as a menu than as a batsman so I'll have to go there in person. I can handle that. My dumbphone may be basic, but it does have a mapping facility. Or, at least it would if my brand new simcard would connect to the internet. Network up or network down, something is still not working. My, how this technology malarkey simplifies our lives.

Chapter 21
RETAIL THERAPY
(Monday 13th Dec)

Monday morning and, with no podcast to record, I'm officially on holiday. I'm up bright and early and so is the sun. From inside a shady Victorian house it looks marvellous, but when I emerge onto the street at 10am I start to smoulder like a forgetful vampire. A quick run to an air-conditioned train is needed. Perth's suburban rail is very good: it's clean, efficient, regular and an all-round pleasant experience once you come to terms with it. But before you come to terms and while negotiations are still ongoing, it's like every public transport system I have ever encountered: an exclusive club intended only for the city's residents that's as challenging as the crystal maze.

I couldn't understand the company's antiquated website at all, and arrive at the station to find it equally unhelpfully unmanned. True, there are electronic information machines but I suspect they'll just tell me the network's down. Also I don't want to be laughed at; you always are when you start pressing buttons in public. The locals know full well there's no useful information ever to be had from these infernal contraptions, and they enjoy watching you repeatedly re-pressing the same buttons and trying to hear the Dalek voice over the noise of the trains – which, if only you could make it out, is usually saying your train just left. Yes, it starts with the laughing and then moves up to poking you with sticks; except in parts of East Anglia, where having seen you make the magic box talk, they burn you as a witch. I give the information machines a miss.

More usefully, there is a ticket machine, and this at least I can comprehend, but it only takes coins and some weird form of card I've never even heard of. I just have notes, and there's nowhere nearby to get change. I'd use my phone to consult a map, but the simcard still won't connect. Stranded: there's no way to get into town without a train or a lethal eight mile walk in the sun with no map. I gamble on better facilities at the next station and walk up the line beside the tracks, sweating like a hobo; I only wish I'd brought sandwiches in a handkerchief tied to the end of a stick for the full effect. I'm hoping Chas's train from Adelaide will pass by and I'll be able to jump into an open wagon like in the movies; it sounds like it'd be slow enough.

The next station is the same: no staff, no notes, nowhere to get change. Defeated, I reverse back down the tracks to my digs where I look for someone local, with local knowledge of local shops; I don't care if they're for local people, I'm willing to risk it. I'm told that behind the second station is a whole run of shops and banks and everything a man would desire; if I'd pressed on for another hundred yards I'd have seen them. They don't poke me with a stick, but I'm certainly embarrassed.

I've already walked three miles in a circle under merciless sun, but I refill my empty water bottle and head out to the bank. My mind flashes to Bill Bryson. Wasn't it in Perth he found himself walking for miles and getting terribly sunburned? Indeed it was, and I'm presently heading in the same direction, geographically and colourgraphically. In actual fact I'm only about a mile or so from where he started to get into trouble: is this the suburb of death?

But the bank, once found, is cool and welcoming, with no security glass between customer and staff. The young teller is supremely friendly in a way you rarely encounter in the UK, and my sinking opinions of Perth rise once again. These people are good people. As he hands me a large bag of change (unheard of in London without the fat cats taking a cut) he's chatty and wishes me the very best for my stay: 'What do you need the change for?'

'I'm trying to catch a train'

'Don't you have an ESPCC_NPQZ% card?'

'I only have an old fashioned MasterCard'

'Yeah that should work'

'Really?'

'Reckon so'

'Um... You didn't just tell me that, okay? If anyone asks, we never had this conversation.' I have enough change to see me through the next few days and my card is staying in the wallet, untested, for the whole time I'm here. I like to imagine it wouldn't have worked, that it would have been spat out in disgust, and I'm keeping it that way.

Once in town my first port of call is a phone-shop. I wander in and outwardly it's like any of their ilk in the UK: buzzing with activity, lots of people, lots of staff. But appearances can be deceptive, and whereas we tend to employ keyed-in young lads who will give you more technical information that you'll ever understand or require at the entry of a PIN, here in Australia they have a more laidback approach to recruitment: no-one in this shop seems to know anything about phones.

I wait in line behind other England fans queuing up to be told they can't rent phones. Ha! The poor fools. When it's my turn the young girl assesses me warily as if I'm about to use the word 'rent' inappropriately, but no, I am the holder of almost local-like wisdom on that matter. I have even travelled here by train, I'll have you know. I don't waste her time and cut straight to the chase: do you have a cheap phone, good for Twitter and Facebook, for $100 or less? I asked at the airport, but this lovely shop of yours must surely have a meatier selection.

My request is met with a blank denial. Good heavens, who would imagine such a thing? No, no, no, this lovely dumbphone of yours is far superior to anything we'd have in that price range, why would you not want to keep this handsome beast?

I stare at my three-year-old-freebie with newfound respect, and then back at my glamorous assistant with weary disbelief. No phones eh? How about a charger? She slowly examines the phone, turning it over and over in her hands.

'Where does the charger plug in?'

'!!??'

I'm wondering if she really works for the company, or is one of those people that pretend to be doctors. They're always in the papers, medical enthusiasts who just walk into a hospital in a white coat with a stethoscope round their neck, and start doctoring. I read of one who wasn't rumbled for years, despite prescribing creosote for sore throats. My Nosales Unassistant is still turning the phone over in her hands puzzled by its symptoms, but I give her the benefit of the doubt: 'Here, in the side, see?'

'What kind of weeeeird connection is that?'

Uh-oh, I don't like the sound of that. That's the sort of remark that makes the stomach sink, like when the paramedic finds you frothing by the roadside and says, 'Wow, I've never seen a bite like *that* before, what the hell kind of spider was it?'

'It's um... a Sony Ericsson connection.'

'No, it's not. Not here, it's not.'

'Yes it is. They've always been like that. It's what you get when you cross the Japanese with the Swedes,' I add wittily. Or, as it turns out, confusingly. The discussion swings into the surreal: my Unassistant insists Ericsson must be American.

I correct her: 'No, Scandinavian. Like IKEA? And the Vikings? You know – rape, pillage and flat-pack furniture? Spam? Kirk Douglas in leather?' Unsurprisingly, she becomes pensive at this last remark and I worry I've overdone it.

'But wasn't he the first American?'

'Who, Kirk Douglas? Well, yes, he was American, but—'

'No, Leif Ericson, the first man in America.'

'Aah.' Understanding dawns. It's evident I've under-estimated my girl, and the staff here have hidden talents, even if they're more suited to appearing in Two Ronnies sketches than selling phones. But not wanting to let her think she's got one over me, I decide to sow some seeds of education: 'No, the first man to set foot in America was Neil Armstrong, look him up, he was part of Mao's Great Leap Forward. So... *annnnywaayy...* do you have a charger to fit?'

She confers with a colleague and there is much whispering and surreptitious pointing. I'm praying it is phone-related and not concerning rape and pillage; I've repulsed enough Australian youth since my arrival. They need to find the model number – something I thought they might recognise – which will require removing the battery. 'Hey, how do you get the battery off?'

This is the point at which I start to feel I'm on a hidden camera wind-up show and glance nervously at the mirrors, but to save time I wrestle it off myself.

'Oh wait,' says the second assistant when he hands it back to me, 'You can get the model number just pressing this button on the side! Cool.'

My stern look is wasted, but a charger is found in the back-room. Less fortunately it costs a fortune. '$40? But I've already got two at home and I only need it for a month.'

'Doesn't matter if you've got six, it's still $40 mate,' says the colleague, not unfairly nor unkindly; it's just a matter of fact.

Balls. I cough up the cash, and after another consultation my simcard is belatedly connected to the all-seeing Skynet. Inwardly I'm hoping this will trigger the Armageddon, although I expect the Terminators will all grind to a halt when the network goes down. And after some rooting around menus, wonder of wonders, we find that my old-phone does potentially have access to Facebook and Twitter, the apps just need to be downloaded and installed.

'Fine. So let's do that.'

'No, you can't. Not with this simcard'

'What?'

'It's a limited simcard, they should have told you at the airport.'

'Apparently the network was down.'

'Ah right.' She nods, knowingly.

'So, wait... can we put my old simcard in and download them on international rates?'

'No, you can't connect to the server from overseas.'

'So how do I download them?'

'Don't worry; you can do it next time you're home.'

'Next time I'm— what use will they be then!? Why have I even bought an Aussie simcard?'

She is confused, but not at all unfriendly.

'I don't know. Why did you?'

I think it's because I wanted to waste all my time and money going round in circles. Yesterday, Vodafone announced that if @theashes can get to Oz, they'll provide her with match tickets and a free phone so she can Tweet her experience. My idea of disguising myself as a cricket-loving-supermodel definitely sounds like it would have been a better bet. This holiday is not going well.

I leave, clutching my semi-useless 'thing with buttons that lights up', and spot a camera shop just across the road. That's handy, because I'm in need of accessories, but to be honest, I've never felt comfortable in such places. They're always full of slightly sweaty men who wear inappropriate clothes on hot days. When did you last see a man with a professional camera on a sunny day, who wasn't also wearing black trousers and a thick coat with bulging pockets? They say it's to hold the accessories, but I've never needed a coat like that, even when carrying two big Canon DSLRs with all the trimmings – I reckon they're secretly full of sweets. And this looks like one of those shops.

As soon as I enter I recognise it. Cameras have changed markedly in recent years, and many of the cryptic craft skills have become less critical, but you wouldn't realise that in here: this is an old-fashioned place, with dusty boxes full of widgets and thingamajigs. The proprietor looks to be still smarting over the death of film, but I dodge the expected debate on whether my little Panasonic MFT is a 'real' camera or not, and the brief conversation runs roughly thus:

'Do you have a 62mm UV filter?'

'Yes. Here, in this shoebox. $49 please.'

'But that's just a cheap, generic filter.'

'And it's $49.'

'But I have one at home, high quality HOYA, only cost me $7 on ebay. And I only need it for a month.'

'Doesn't matter if you've got six and you need it for a day, it's still $49.'

'You are aware it's sunny outside?'

'Yes?'

'Sure those are the right trousers to be wearing?'

'Yeah? You call that pipsqueak a camera?'

Okay, the conversation doesn't really descend to comparing clothes and camera sizes, and he is perfectly civil, although astonished when I refuse to pay $49 for a piece of junk that cost 50c to make. I mumble thanks and leave, feeling the holiday is still not going well.

Next stop: the WACA. On the map it looks to be practically in the city centre, but Australian scales are large and it's over a mile under the blazing sun. And then there's the weird optical/mental illusion that roads we haven't walked down before somehow *seem* much longer, and sometimes actually *take* much longer even if, as in this case, it's down an almost straight road. No-one has ever explained this for me but we all know it to be true: a 15 minute walk when one is on unfamiliar ground will last at least 30 minutes, unless you're on a first date, in which case it'll be more like 40 minutes with your companion losing enthusiasm every step of the way. Or you're married, in which case, it's a 50 minute argument denying you're lost. I'm not in company so the road shouldn't contain too many invisible hyperspace vortices; nevertheless by the time I get there I'm as hot and bothered as a drugs' mule smuggling heroin wrapped in chillies.

The ticket office, if I recall correctly from when I booked, is at Gate 6. First I find Gate 8, and by the cunning strategy of circling the wall I quickly find Gates 7 and then 6 – which is closed. I prowl round to Gates 5 and 4, and by Gate 4 a temporary sign reassures me that ticket collection is at Gate 6, with a helpful little arrow pointing me back the way I came. Did I miss something? Back we go, and no, it's definitely shut: thou shalt not pass! However, there is a small notice that previously escaped me, informing us that when 6 is closed one should report to Gate 3, with another little helpful arrow back the way I've just walked twice. No problem, I'm good at subtraction, I march round, 5, 4, and find Gate 3 – shut. Not only shut, but no evidence that it ever supplies tickets.

I trudge dejectedly back into town, along a road that, in spite of its familiarity, still takes 35 minutes to reach the end of, and hop the train home. In my distracted state, I board the wrong train: this one will halt two stations before mine and then run non-stop all the way to the sea. I briefly consider staying onboard till the end and then throwing myself in the ocean. But no, I will not be downhearted; I'm on holiday and – like Mitchell – determine to make a Positive out of a Negative. I stride purposefully off the train at the early stop, intent on picking up some supplies and taking a pleasant walk home in the beautiful evening light. It's all a question of attitude, you know.

The most useful thing I've discovered over the last few years is that alchemy is much more fun abroad. You get far better and cheaper potions, unguents and balms overseas, and that's before you even get around to insecticides and the crazy stuff with scary warning labels that say *Best Before it Explodes*. South Africa was a chemistry student's paradise and I carried numerous tins of exotic wonders homeward and all for less than the price of a decent pork pie. These lasted me until I hit Canada, where I replenished my supplies of UV protection and deodorants with bargain protective mists and magical shields. But I'm all out; the last cans are empty, what does Australia have to offer? In the kingdom of skin-cancer, the protected man is king, so I'm expecting a smorgasbord of delights as I wander into the chemist.

'Hi, how you going?' The greeting is as cheery and sincere as the bank-tellers. It's impossible to be grumpy for long in this town, the people are so remorselessly, genuinely nice.

'Good thanks!' I survey the range of sunscreens available and am plunged back into gloom. It's also impossible to be cheerful for long. It's a pitiful selection and all triple the price I'd expected. Surely there must be an economy of scale in selling it to a country that lives on the stuff all year round? Just as super-strength lager is in Glasgow, suncream should be a cheap essential for all the family in Australia. Evidently not. For comparison, I pop into the mini-supermarket next door but it's worse: there's barely a shelf-full and it costs more than *foie gras* from geese fed on caviar. I retreat to the next aisle and hunt down some hair-care for my lengthening locks but a can of mousse is a barely believable £20. Recoiling, I lurch over to the booze and nearly faint: even the sickly cordial that masquerades as wine in this country, costs twice the price the exact same muck does in the UK. £12.50 for a bottle of the cheapest Shit Creek!? How can this be unless they're knocking it out of a vineyard in South London and exporting it here with a fake label? Maybe they are. It would certainly explain the taste. Dispirited, I stock up and I slope back to the chemist.

'Hi! It's you again! How you going?'

'Still good thanks!' I'm trying, I really am. I plonk for the best sunblock and the cheapest hair gel – better to be alive and looking bad than the other way around – and trawl homewards. My pleasant evening stroll is in fact painfully hot and entirely uphill; I should have bought an Ordnance Survey map not a simcard. The thin plastic bags are tearing with the weight of the wine and cutting into my hands so badly I have to keep stopping and putting them down. By the time I reach the house two of my fingers are completely numb and don't recover for over half an hour. But at least I am at last on holiday.

It's fair to say the day has not gone well, and a glass of Australian 'Ribena' is scant consolation. I give it a sip. Yup it's exactly the same muck we get in Sainsburys at half the price – Vin de Peckham as I shall henceforth always call it. But after the third glass it's not so bad. And, who knows? Tomorrow might be my lucky day.

Chapter 22
THE AGE OF THE TRAIN
(Tuesday 14th Dec)

'Well your economy is so bad and ours is so good we thought we'd let you have the Ashes to cheer you up a bit!' quips the barman to the retired couple next to me. He may have a point. To gauge by the many unenthusiastic, resigned faces in the beer garden of the Lucky Shag, one might be forgiven for thinking that England are 2-0 down and the Ashes are in jeopardy. What can have brought about this muted air of doleful contemplation? Are these jet-lagged fresh arrivals, new to Australia and beer at £6 a pint? That I guess to be largely the case: there is a conspicuous lack of sunburn – the complexions still as white as a newborn northerner – and wallets are being painfully examined like a torn hymen. But considering the glorious sunshine, the cooling river breeze and the easy, relaxed atmosphere of the city around us, the pervading mood is incongruous. Could it be they simply feel as I have begun to, a very long way from home?

It's a slightly ironic yearning in my case, as all the indications suggest I am slap bang in the land of my fathers. Here I am in Perth, having recently travelled down the Stirling Highway, through Dalkeith, past a house in Queen's Park called Kilmarnock and then a walk down Aberdeen Street. If you ask for directions round here, it sounds like listening to the Scottish Football results on Final Score. I find myself referring to Hamilton Hill as Hamilton Nil, but nobody gets it.

It's lunchtime and I'm sat in Barmy Army HQ – the afore-mentioned and unfortunately christened Lucky Shag – down on the waterfront. This morning I'd intended to watch the Barmy

Army cricket team play the Fanatics at a club ground over the Swan River, but have once again missed the Barmy bus; the Army are strangely early risers for such mighty drinkers. The game is only a couple of miles away, but after a fruitless forty-five minutes, walking round in circles and puzzling over how, as a pedestrian, to get up and onto the bridge – finding several slip roads but no pavement – I finally give up. Fate has decreed that I'm not to see any of these matches. That is three out of three I've failed on, if this were baseball I'd be back in the pen.

Instead, here I sit, drowning wistful sorrows with the newbies and the rest of the stragglers, waiting to catch up with Chas. The average age is around 50 and the clientele is predominantly male, I reckon my luck is probably out today, in fact I reckon—

'I reckon this place should be done under the Trades Description Act; we'll *never* get a shag in here!' Chas arrives and voices my thoughts before I can think them.

He looks haggard. He couldn't look more haggard if he'd been buried up to his neck in the sand for two days. Head first. Clearly he's been teaching the emus how the ostriches party.

'Looking good,' I say.

Chas needs to vent after his train ride, which has been the sort of purgatory beloved of travel writers and no-one else. He's been stuck for thirty-six hours beside an elderly lady lecturing him on the moral and physical dangers of alcohol. A situation that would drive anyone to drink, but perversely booze is banned on trains. How on earth are they supposed to compete with the airlines with such strictures? A train must be the only place in Australia you can go a day and a half without finding a tipple. Perhaps that's why the old lady is on board, maybe she lives there. Maybe she's a secret millionaire and owns the railway; maybe she's responsible for the policy! I suggest this to Chas.

'Do you know, in thirty-six hours that never occurred to me?'

'You didn't ask?'

'No.'

The only way he has survived was by 'secret toilet drinking', which I take to mean drinking secretly in the toilet, not out of it, although I don't ask.

'Crawling at 40mph, with nothing but a crying baby and a snoring, whistling teetotaller for company.'

'She whistled?'

'Through her nose, as she slept. Like a train.'

'She slept like a train?'

'No, like a baby, she whistled like a train. As she snored. Grunt, whistle. Grunt, whistle.'

'Ah, gotcha. What about the baby?'

'He never seemed to sleep.'

'Any whistling?'

'More like a klaxon than a whistle.'

'Ah, clearly diesel powered, not steam driven like the old lady. The old ways are dying.'

'Do you know, that never occurred to me?'

I'm beginning to wonder what did occur to him in all that time spent, quite literally, under the radar. 'Come on Chas, you must have seen some incredible sights! A close up view of the real Australia, the stuff we poor fly-boys don't get a whiff of.'

And indeed he had: 'One kangaroo and three emus.'

'That's all?'

'That's all.'

'In one and a half thousand miles? They've got more than that in Whipsnade Zoo.'

'Red soil. Just miles and miles of red soil. With a piped commentary from geologists.'

'How was that?' I ask brightly. This is an old land, no doubt full of sedimentary goodness and igneous interest.

'Remember those old Open University programs from the 1970s? Grey studio sets with blackboards and monotoned, bespectacled robots in flares and kipper ties?'

'Yeesss...'

'It was like that, but without the colour of the ties.'

I'd say Chas has had a high old time of it, the sort of adventure denied to those poor souls condemned to a quick flight with free drink and hot stewardesses. While we were in the bleak skies enduring the latest movies, he'd been treated to piped, authentic rail-roaders' music. 'What was that like?'

'Like a sea shanty.'

'Cool. Could you see the sea?'

'No.'

'Ah.'

In seems the only excitement the trip had offered was during the stops in the middle of nowhere. At the ghost town of Cook, heedless of there being at least 5000 flies for each and every person that stepped off to stretch the legs, one young couple had thrown hygiene to the wind and decided to conjoin in one of the abandoned houses.

'Really?'

'Really.'

'Did you watch?'

'A bit. There was nothing else on.'

I picture a fly caught up in the copulation, and the resulting Jeff-Goldblum-like progeny. Such extra-curricular activities had not been mentioned in the tour itinerary; I'd seen no 'Have-it-Away-Days' advertised at Adelaide Train Station. And yet, the towns *en route* clearly knew the effect those rail-shanties and geology lectures could have on the captive male. At the last redneck outpost before Perth, everyone stepping off the train was greeted by the local Madam, with a polite enquiry as to what services they required.

'Really?'

'Really.'

'Did you ask for anything?'

'A helicopter to Perth.'

Within five minutes Chas had counted fourteen drunks lying unconscious by the side of the streets, and decided to return to the train. I postulate that they'd been caught drinking on the last train and thrown off before Perth.

'Do you know that never occurred to me? But I don't blame them.'

'Chas, I salute you, you've had an experience, and now you can dine out on that story for years. I'm actually jealous.'

'Really?'

'No.'

A couple of hours later Chas heads back to his hotel for another nap. I can't face the walk to the WACA for tickets, so head into town to hunt for some food. Wandering down Hay Street I'm enjoying the vibe when I find myself passing another phone-shop. Aha, they're propagating: spreading their seeds like a dandelion; or possibly their spores like a poisonous toadstool. I pause to gaze in the window.

It will sound odd, but yesterday I didn't examine the displays. I'm so used to being immediately set upon by turbo-charged staff intent on making a sale that I don't look anymore; I just let them attack like angry geese, and barrage me with options. It's easier than picking something from the display and being told I can only have it if I sign up for 18 months of kidney dialysis. I blink and look in the window again. And a third time. There, bold as you like, is a row of phones, all $99, two of which proclaim their main selling point in big letters: Twitter and Facebook Apps. More than that, they come with a free cap to keep the sun off. I go into the shop and again – refreshingly it's true – there's no hard sell. But the hunted turns hunter and I track my quarry down. In fact I follow him around the shop and pin him in a corner where he can't escape.

'Phones! $99! What!?'

The sales-assistant stares blankly but seems unperturbed.

'Phones! $99!' I point, to make my point.

He appears sympathetic and about to attempt non-verbal communication with the crazy foreigner when I draw breath and explain. My pursuit has not been in vain and I've trapped someone who is actually familiar with his specialised subject. He's happy to help, and explains at least the first failure in my quest: 'Yeah they're not that bright at the airport mate, it's why we keep them out there.'

At last I've found a man I can do business with. Swapping insults about his fellow employees, he says I can take the charger back for a refund ('no worries') and offers to sell me a phone there and then, reassuring me that his colleagues in Britain will switch it to the UK network for free on my return. Tempting, but I have a better plan.

Chapter 23
A SCOTSMAN ABROAD
(Wednesday 15ᵗʰ Dec)

The next morning I head to the WACA first thing. Another call to Marcus North has established that they close at the early hour of 3pm, which explains my previous failure. I'm clutching a print-out of my online booking form which definitely says that Gate 6 is the gate for me, accept no substitutes. The walk now takes only 20 brisk minutes, and as I near the ground I pass a dozen or more England fans in ones and twos, heading back from the WACA into town. They look as strangely downbeat as the faces in the Lucky Shag, but this is promising. I head to Gate 6 and find it locked and barricaded. It still says to check over at Gate 3. I circle around the wall, 5, 4, 3— oh wait, this isn't gate 3 at all, it's an unnumbered service gate! As with my quest for a bank I'd foolishly stopped just before my target destination. Elated, I run the last yards around the blind corner to find the mythic Gate 3— locked and bolted. Dammit!! I shake the gate and shout. I should have tried this approach sooner as it produces a couple of surprised caretakers, who regard me as they would an escaped lunatic that has been missing his cage and decided the WACAs gates make a rattling good substitute. I give them another shake and they approach warily.

'Where the hell do you collect tickets from?' I demand, politer than I felt.

'Gate 6, mate.'

'No you bloody don't!!' They instinctively jerk backwards, but are reassured by the bars between us.

'Yeah you do mate. Opens at eight tomorrow.'

'Are you telling me, I can't collect them till the day of the game?'

'That's right, mate.'

Don't you think that some kind of sign, one little notice, one sentence on your website, one line on the booking form, one solitary piece of useful information on your bollocks useless phone-line might have sodding told me that?

I don't say any of this, but instead slump over the gate in defeat. The caretakers look puzzled, but the expressions I saw on the other fans' faces are explained.

'Okay. Thanks.'

The walk back to town takes an hour.

With a day to go, and the pre-match blog written, I have a chance to explore a little, and it's well worth it; Perth is a handsome place, if not an outright supermodel, then undeniably a head-turner. Visually, it exists in the late 19th and early 21st centuries, having avoided most of the 20th altogether. The shining skyscrapers, born of mineral wealth, soar above old colonial houses, like rocket ships waiting for launch. The somewhat ramshackle three-room house in which I'm staying – a place without aircon or heating, and what can only be described as a genuine brick-shithouse that needs to be checked for redbacks every morning – is on the market at a snifter over $2 million. Make no mistake; Perth is a very wealthy city. The Western Australia mining interests are the driving force of the Australian economy, the Swan River and the azure ocean are populated with hundreds of gleaming, bobbing yachts, and the supermarkets are filled with denizens who don't wince or cry aloud when buying bread at £4 a loaf. I tell you, they might be city slickers, but they're tough these Western Australians. I've not compared meerkats, but I reckon a shopping trolley of family groceries in Perth would stack up pretty unfavourably against an Arbroath family's mortgage; but when cleaners can make $2000 a week out by the mines, nobody's complaining.

Prices aside, I've been surprised all along by how unalien Australia has felt, not like being abroad at all, everything has a familiarity about it that I can't quite place, and it's not just the street names or the repeats of 'Dad's Army' on TV. And then I realise where Perth reminds me of: it's a sunny love-child of Edinburgh and Glasgow. The main shopping streets of Hay and Murray echo Princes and George Streets in Edinburgh, and are flanked by Alexander Terrace that represents Queen Street. They're linked by indoor shopping arcades reminiscent of Glasgow. The Bell Tower on Riverside Drive provides as recognisable a spike as the Scott Monument, and it sits on the Swan, Perth's very own River Clyde. Overlooking the whole show is Mount Eliza, Perth's mini-Arthur's Seat, which includes Kings Park, its Holyrood equivalent, where you'll find people gathering for the view from the war memorial, not unlike they do from Edinburgh's Napoleonic memorial on Calton Hill.

This may sound tenuous, but I promise you, if you're familiar with Scotland's principal cities and you go stand in Perth, provided you look beyond the very un-Caledonian sunshine, you'll soon start to see what I mean, and more and more similarities will present themselves. I'm staying out in the affluent suburbs of Cottesloe and Mosman Park and their attitude and relation to the city remind me of nowhere more than Edinburgh's Corstorphine and Morningside, especially because there's a touch of fur-coat, no knickers amidst the wealth. But rather than hopping the No.23 Lothian bus through Bruntsfield, they're linked to the centre by a suburban train that puts one in mind of riding Strathclyde Passenger Transport out to Bearsden. And, I later discover, Fremantle even has a touch of Clydeside, and a large dollop of the old, undemolished Leith about it.

Why should we be surprised by this? Scottish cities take their form not only from their topography but from Scottish minds, and there are minds full to bursting with Scottish DNA all around me. And under a sun that more than rivals Africa, the oldest buildings remind me most especially of a neighbourhood of Cape Town I explored, where nearly everything had Scottish names. I'm not dreaming: this is how the Scots rebuild themselves abroad.

What I've enjoyed most in the last two weeks, is that Perth and Adelaide have succeeded in keeping their small businesses in an age of globalisation. I've already seen more bookshops than I could count; real bookshops too, not stationery shops with a couple of bestsellers on a stand, but honest to goodness specialist booksellers, both new and second-hand. Were it not so far away, I'd happily come to Australia for a week just to go browsing. I've been hunting for a copy of Alan Clark's *Barbarossa* for years, and here are five mint copies in the same shop! Tragically, my case already won't shut or I'd be making off with them all, and this beautiful book of Ronald Searle illustrations too! Why do I have to come to Australia to find a book by a British artist who lived in France? Chiz chiz chiz.*

It's not only bookshops; the specialist trader is flourishing here, and the high streets and suburbs are a real experience, not just the dreary line of charity shops that so much of Britain has been reduced to. In my afternoon of exploring I find every kind of individual product represented with a store of its very own – from pen shops and hat shops right down to toy-shops you'd expect to find staffed by long-nosed wooden dolls. Christmas is a-coming, and there's no more magical kingdom to fill your stockings in than the elf-scale shops of Perth.

Who can say why they survive here and not in Britain but I have a pretty persuasive hunch: Australian supermarkets are utterly crap. Nasty, cramped, badly lit, under-staffed, expensive and half-full of nothing you want to buy or eat. They don't even provide you with anything that could sensibly be described as an effective bag, so you leave them looking like a street juggler with a grocery gimmick. They're the antithesis of the shopping cathedrals of Britain and offer no sort of competition to the fresh food sellers that surround them. Most distressing for the skint, nothing is ever on sale, and many of them don't have a licence to sell alcohol so you can't even drown your sorrows. Only in chocolate are they well provisioned. Why Cadburys have so many more varieties here, that they deny to their mother

*a chiz is a swiz or swindle as any fule kno.

country, we can only speculate, but a small child could happily live in the chocolate aisle, and not eat the same thing twice in a month. I may have to myself, and die with a decaying smile on my face, because most startling to a frazzled British brain, is that the microwave meal is a virtually unknown art-form. The usual three or so options are small, uninspiring and wildly over-priced; you can eat out for not much more, so what's the use of them?

Although this is desperately inconvenient for me – rushed, away from home and searching for cheap instant hits, amidst the shopping gloom – after a while I do experience something akin to schadenfreude. I'm glad that the Australians have no access to the lightning fast, super cheap shopping experience; it's nice to be in a country that is not run (indeed over-run) by the billionaire purveyors of plastic-fantastic produce. Sometimes you lose more than you gain from progress. Please God, let Tesco never discover this country; they'd clean up, but I hope they never get the chance. Australians still love real food and shop for it like real people, not drones whose trolleys run on train tracks round the miles of frozen aisles of British Supermarket mainlines. I miserably confess to being one such drone, like everyone else using my busy-worker-bee status as my ready-meal-excuse, but long may the small traders and food markets – these little remnants of Old World cultures – live on in Australia, still preeminent to New World American hyper-marketeering.

Talking of unpleasant shopping experiences, I have an appointment to keep. I head back to my friends in the phone-shop with my unwanted charger and receipt. The $99 dollar phones on display suddenly seem blindingly obvious. In my defence they weren't so obvious to any of the staff either. Sadly I get a different assistant on this occasion and am unable to continue our discourse on American history, but I do at least get my money back.

'Don't you want it mate?'

'No, I'm going to buy one of those phones. One of those, over there. That you don't have. One of them. From a different phone-shop with the same range. But in the colour "visible".'

'No worries.'

Not the reaction I was looking for. I'd hoped for at least a ripple of curiosity, but the facial expression remains entirely neutral. Hmm. I walk to the second shop that I deem more deserving of my custom and pick up a Nokia from my new-found friend of yesterday. It has a Finnish charger and connection we can all recognise and agree on, and he's clued-up enough to avoid any arguments regarding Vikings, voyages of discovery, whether Finland is in Scandinavia, and anything to do with roll-mops, fjords or open sandwiches. Result.

In pursuit of justice I head back to the first shop with my new purchase and take the time to find and buttonhole my original fragrant (or flagrant) Unassistant.

'Hey, remember me?'

'Eh... yeah. Kirk wasn't it?'

'Yup, that's me.'

'What can I do for you?'

'It's about this phone that you didn't sell me.' I produce it from its red bag like a white rabbit from a hat.

'Oh yeah? What's the matter with it?'

'Ah ha! So you can see it?'

'Yeah.'

'Ah.'

She appears equally unflappable, not in the slightest bit surprised by my question, or unnerved by the raving madman before her. I guess be surrounded by so many deadly species toughens you up. Or I've over-reacted to my frustrated labours of the other day. That's always possible.

'Is that all?'

'Yes. S'pose.' I look at my feet.

'Anything else I get you?'

'No. Um... that was it.' I try to look nonchalant.

'Is everyone in England as intense as you?'

'No. Only when they're driving vans.'

Chapter 24
LITTLE SHOP OF HAURITZ
(Wednesday 15th – Thursday 16th Dec)

There's negative thinking and there's positive thinking – and no doubt there are teams of well-paid sports psychologists currently fleecing both sides – and then there is wishful thinking. And after that, last stop on the line before window-licking, there is la-la dreamland. Welcome to the world inhabited by the Aussie fans who were hoping that Shane Warne would play for their team in the Perth Test. It was just too far-fetched, and yet even Brett Lee added his name to the long list of Aussies requesting that the legendary spin bowler return to the team. That is how desperate the Australians became in the aftermath of the Adelaide disaster.

A curious reaction, as Lost 1, Drawn 1 hardly seems like a reason to panic just yet, but in the spin department Australia had been panicking before England even got off the plane. Since Warne retired four years ago they have tried ten spin bowlers with the most recent suggestion being Michael Beer. Most of the Barmies, especially those from 'oop North' who specialise in such things, say England have nothing to fear, as Australia's beer is rubbish. They came 10,000 miles to make that joke and by God they're going to use it. Many will be hoping Beer gets a contract down South for Surrey or Middlesex, so they can get more mileage out of it without having to pay for another flight.

Unhappily for the dreamers, in the week between the Tests, it has been revealed that Shane Warne has more pressing engagements than donning the whites and returning to the Australian team. Shane is almost the last of the old breed, the last that might have fitted into the moustachioed teams of yesteryear, when the only dietary consultants were barmen and the only protein supplements, peanuts. So rather than risk his reputation and submit to the gruelling fitness regime of the Test side, there's tabloid stories that he's been working off the pounds in a South Kensington hotel with Liz Hurley, which enhances his reputation among the fans far more than a mediocre comeback would. Given the choice between Liz and an Australian cap, it would be a tough call for a lot of men, and when you already have more caps that your head will ever need, the hotel option is distinctly the more exciting option.

Meanwhile over in New South Wales, Australia's recently discarded spinner, Nathan Hauritz, was revealing the less glamorous side of professional sport, with an impromptu sale of Australian cricket memorabilia. In a scene both entirely normal and mundane, yet simultaneously completely bizarre, there was Nathan sitting in front of a cardboard box at his Sydney flat, flogging off his unwanted cricket gear like it was broken toys and Russell Brand DVDs (watched once, laughed twice). When asked why he was discarding his national teams' clothing he replied simply, 'I don't play for them anymore.' Some disgruntled players burn their bridges by speaking out, bitterly and unguardedly; Nathan it seemed had decided to sell his bridges to the tourists, à la London.

England players present and future have had a quieter time of it. As I packed up in Adelaide and argued my way across Western Australia, they headed back to Melbourne with many of the Barmy Army in tow, and continued their unbeaten run with a draw against Victoria. The main interest was in whom should come in to replace the injured Stuart Broad, who'd packed up after Adelaide for the even longer trip home with a torn abdominal muscle. He's a grievous loss. Properly managed, bowling first or second change and given time to develop his silky batting as well, I personally feel he could finish with a career record better than Flintoff's, with both ball and bat. But Broad has gone, and England's bowling has narrowed.

None of the three possible replacements absolutely forced themselves into contention in Victoria, so it seems unlikely

England will be going with the five bowler option and only Tremlett will get a chance. It's unambitious. And to my way of thinking, if you're worried the substitute won't be as successful as the injured player, surely you'll need more bowlers?

Only an incurable optimist would write the Aussies off, and optimism isn't in my vocabulary. (Well obviously it is now, but I had to ask Dave what it meant.) If Australia win the toss and bat I'm tipping them for a fight-back against a four man England attack that harbours a seriously jet-lagged Anderson. Oh Jimmy Jimmy, Jimmy Jimmy Jimmy, Jimmy Anderson (as the Barmy Army call to him across the outfield) has used his week off to fly to all the way to England and back to see his new baby, born in his absence; a round trip that makes Chas's train ride seem positively refreshing. But England's selectors are nothing if not stubborn, it's a prerequisite for the job, so I expect to see a bleary-eyed O.J.J.J.J.J Anderson opening the attack like a hero-cop, without having first called for back-up.

I head for bed early on Wednesday night. To sleep, perchance to dream; and, in this case, dreams that are invaded by Leonardo Di Caprio in his Inception guise, coming on to bowl leg-spinners on a dusty fifth day wicket. He seemed a more sensible selection than Warne, but it's easier to pick his wrong 'un. I wake at 5am Thursday, already nine wickets down, with Bell and Anderson at the crease. Disturbingly, a bleary-eyed Jimmy keeps holding up play to change nappies, so I'm glad to be awake. That's the fourth day in a row I've been up with the sun; even the short jump from South Australia takes a bit of getting used to. I take my coffee out into the garden where I'm joined by a flock of friendly grey and pink cockatoos, which nibble the dandelions as I absorb the team news; and absorb the fact that I have a flock of genuine, honest to goodness galahs sharing breakfast with me, an unexpected treat.

After all the sound and fury regarding Warne and Beer (two words that often go together— actually, four words that often go together), by 9am we hear that it signified nothing, and neither will be playing. Australia have recalled the young spinning all-rounder Smith, and sport a refreshed four-and-a-half man pace attack: Bollinger could consider himself unlucky to be dropped, but only because a man of his portly girth might have got stuck in the door when they tried to eject him.

Immediately I'm worried. The Australia I've seen may be rich and prosperous, but Bollinger aside, it's only just begun to consider the temptations of growing soft and decadent. Underneath, Perth remains a hard-rock mining outpost. This is the town that forged Dennis Lillee in fire and blood, and anyone who's had to use a dunny like mine, and seen the spiders, will realise there is venom in Australia still. With their positive selection policy they've made clear their intentions to bite.

Meanwhile England are retaining their basic formation. It's unambitious but, in fairness, Colly took more wickets against Victoria than all England's seamers put together; though that was a slow pitch and even Strauss picked up a wicket with his Mickey Mouse bowling (he might even have been wearing the ears as he did so). But six batsmen it is. If things carry on like this, by the time we reach Sydney, England will be playing eight batsmen and Australia will be fielding a more balanced ten bowler attack.

I ask the galahs their opinion. Loudmouths that they are, they say England should be thankful Brett Lee and Shaun Tait aren't still playing Test cricket, or they'd really be in trouble, mate. I reckon these birds aren't as dumb as they're made out.

Chapter 25
THIRD TEST, DAY ONE
ENTRANCE POLICY
(Thursday 16th Dec)

I arrive in town and follow the sea of England colours pouring eastwards like a Tsunami with intent. Really I should be leading the charge as, strangely enough, I know the way by now, and it only takes twenty minutes to walk there from Perth station. Now to pick up those pesky tickets. Straight away the flaw in the WACA's policy is revealed, when the snakes of people queuing outside the ticket booths present themselves. I'm here fairly early but I doubt I'll see the first ball, as the lines are not moving an inch. With match reports to write, I shamefully part-jump the queue, but it still takes thirty minutes waiting to get to the front, where a cheerful girl is eager to help, if only she could. The problem, I'm told, is that the slow internet connection to the booking site is overloaded. I've not been so astounded since I flew from Singapore. There are 21,000 people here, and they're only printing the tickets now? Even a small theatre would have the tickets pre-printed. But everyone is ever so, ever so, nice; so I wait patiently and chat good-naturedly to the girl.

I want to collect tickets for the first four days, but it takes nearly fifteen minutes to print my ticket for day one, alone, and in that time the queue behind me has doubled in length. I very politely suggest to a supervisor that this is not the best system ever conceived, and she is not so nice, irritably pointing out that they've been open since 8am. At this I want to get angry, very angry. No-one can say I didn't come early: I called twice, I came days in advance – twice – and now you tell me I should have come at 8am? Am I supposed to get up at 5am just so I can get here first and beat the rush? (Okay, I did get up at 5am, but that was an accident.) Besides, there's nothing to do round here: I'd have to walk to the ground, collect tickets, walk back to town, and then back again to the WACA for the 10.30 start – more or less been there, done that. And if we'd *all* come at 8am, we'd still all be standing in a queue for fifteen minutes per printed ticket! We came at 9.30 because we didn't think a world famous venue would have a ticketing service slower than it must have been before the invention of the internet, perhaps even the invention of the phone. The mean stupidity of that response, existing as it does in a world of taxpayer-funded multi-million-dollar redevelopments, very nearly causes my gaskets to blow.

This is what puts people off attending cricket: it's not that the rules of the old game need to be changed, or that they need to provide better facilities and shopping; it's the basic lack of common sense and a decent service at a reasonable price. She and her bosses simply don't care that we've come 10,000 miles for the privilege of standing in a line. But the sun is shining, so no worries, right? And that's what this boiled down to: the usual shrug, what's the matter with you, why do you care so much, what's your problem?

I hold my tongue and say nothing to the supervisor, as I'm keen not to hold up all those behind me. Instead, I warmly thank the lovely, apologetic girl serving me and tell her I'll return later for my other tickets.

'No worries, we'll just put them in an envelope for you to pick up!' Could they not have done that before 21,000 people arrived at their doorstep?

Next I join the ranks waiting for security to search their bags. At least in Oz they don't pretend it's the non-existent threat of terrorism that justifies the intrusion. They want to stop you bringing in strong drink, and that's fair enough. Perth has a bad reputation lingering from past crowd trouble and they understandably want to moderate the threat, whilst cleaning up on the weak beer sales. But here too, trouble is brewing. No-one is being allowed in with opened drinks, which is creating a rebellion among those who have carefully stocked their bags with cheap squashes and refrigerated tap-water. I see both sides:

it's a standard practice – they could be spiked – but as drinks here are life-savers not luxury, can you blame the punters for feeling aggrieved? Fortunately for me my water bottles are unbroached, but there's another regulation awaiting the unwary.

'No, you can't take that in.'

'But it's sunblock.'

'It's an aerosol, no aerosols.'

'It's sunblock. Without it, I die.'

'No aerosols.'

'This is the skin cancer capital of the world, and you won't let me in with sunblock?'

'No aerosols, if you want to go in you'll have to throw it away.' He gestures to the bins, now overflowing with perfectly good bottles of water and juice.

'I'm not throwing it away, it cost $26!!'

'Leave it outside. Might still be there when you come out.'

There's no sensible answer to a comment like that. I'm genuinely speechless, and meekly leave the queue, doing my hungry guppy impression. What exactly do they imagine I'm going to do with this tin? Ignite it, like James Bond, and spray it in someone's face? There are easier weapons to smuggle through. For instance I can make a 'Chelsea Brick' out of a newspaper, and I could probably fashion a stabbing implement from the plastic in my cap-peak; my toe-caps might be steel, and for all they know I'm an expert in Krav Maga – all more lethal than dousing someone with a fine protective mist.

This perfectly illustrates the pointless futility of 99.99% of the modern 'security' that blights our lives: the hoops you must jump through are absolutely no deterrence to, nor prevention against, criminals and undesirables who are expert in subverting them; they serve only to inconvenience and infuriate the honest and law-abiding. And for that matter, no-one's being frisked; I might be carrying hand grenades in my pants.

Ah, that's it! I shove the tin down my trousers, return to a different line and sail calmly through – armed, dangerous, and ready to cause pasty-skinned mayhem. So much for your silly jobsworth entrance policy.

I'm glad of my newfound criminal status as by 10.30 it is warm – very warm – and the tin down the trousers is not only essential but pleasantly cool. The packed and picturesque ground looks a treat and, with the England fans beginning to deck it in their flags of many nations (England, Wales and Scotland) and teams (from Aberdeen to Exeter), it's starting to resemble a medieval jousting tournament. And with two men at either end wearing helmets and armour and clutching wooden staves, the illusion is almost complete, all it needs is—

'What the hell was that!!??'

A loud fanfare from the herald signals the start of Jimmy Anderson's run. We miss the first ball because the crowd near me swivel our heads as one: someone has managed to sneak a full-size Vuvuzela past the guards. So much for security. I guess he has more spare room in his trousers than me. I'm not an out-and-out opponent of the VuVu; an entire army of them sounding endlessly would wear a bit thin, but I find them greatly preferable to West Indian steel drums and infinitely more refined than compressed-air-horns. A skilful African can get a range of tones out of one, and here in the land of didgeridoos and circular breathing I reckon it could be enjoy a renaissance. Sadly, after three quick wickets with accompanying trumpeting it is confiscated by the killjoy stewards. Nobody was complaining, so they are met with a torrent of abuse far louder and more offensive than the occasional toot of the horn.

Back on the pitch, you wonder if the stewards have confiscated the Australians' Factor-30, as they're the ones finding it all too hot to handle. Anderson and Tremlett appear completely unruffled as they lope into bowl and rip the heart out of the Aussies; it's 36/4 already. Everything about the Australian top order today looks out of form and out of the groove, like a scratched record that's skipping and just can't play. The early breakthroughs are as inevitable as a man in flip-flops slipping and spilling his beer – and I soon lose count of how often that happens, each and every time being greeted with wild cheers.

So much for jet-lag; so much for needing five bowlers: these would be the comments I'd normally expect from fellow fans right about now but, unusually, today I'm sat amongst a large contingent of Aussie Fanatics. They're a fun bunch, and are loud, boisterous and very vocal. Or at least they are for about seven minutes before the collapse commences and then they lapse into the uncharacteristic hush that is fast becoming their norm; any more of this treatment and they'll be taking a vow of silence. Their biggest cheer is for an overturned decision, with Watson being given a brief reprieve by the third umpire. Cheering a computer model: sport is not what it was. But even this effort is like a mouse squeaking when compared to the herd of English elephants around the ground, who gleefully trumpet 'Cheerio, cheerio, cheerio!' to Ponting as he trudges off after another failure; no Vuvuzelas required. I swear I saw some spraying beer through their noses.

Credit to Sir Ricky, he turns and stares hard at the chanting England fans, with a defiant Arnie-like 'I'll be back' nod of the head. But will he? Will the real Ricky Ponting show up in this series or is the sun finally setting on a glorious career? Personally I'm hoping the sun would go down at least a little, as even my over-priced protection proves insufficient to soften the ozone-less Western Australia glare. I'm beginning to sizzle and lunchtime can't come soon enough for me or the Aussies.

In spite of my pessimism it would have been a surprise if England hadn't broken through, such is their present confidence; this is reflected in the swagger of their fans – even those in flip-flops – and the 'English waddle' reaches cartoon levels after lunch when Tremlett disposes of new-bug Smith. Smith is a jaunty little character, but in his oversized baggy green cap he looks about twelve years old, and I half expect him to burst into tears and blub for his mum on his way back to the pavilion.

69/5. Not yet a knockout, but surely a standing count of eight. But then, whisper it, the fightback commences, and the locals that stood proud for Advance Australia Fair at the start of play, crank up the shouts of 'Aussie-Oi!' My Fanatic friends are well conducted by a burly fellow with a David Boon tattoo and really raise the volume. This is more like it! Amazingly, travelling fans outnumber the home support today, but numbers are not always required to win the vocal battle and off the pitch at least, the fightback doesn't last. The Fanatics are brought crashing back to earth by just one solitary, fat Yorkshire man behind us, who tunefully bellows, 'Sit down, Shut Up! Sit down, Shut up!' with the power of Big Ben. Le Rosbif - One, Barramundi - Nil.

This is my first time properly among the enemy, (the 'New Enemy', not to be confused with 'The Auld Enemy'), and I'm surprised how little the actual cricket features in their day's activities. I realise they're not on a once-in-a-lifetime trip, but action on the pitch is largely ignored for long periods as they prefer 'singing' and sledging to spectating. In contrast, on the other side of the ground, in between rousing choral recitals, the Barmy Army are downright devoted in their studious attention to the bowling of Graeme Swann, craning forward in their seats, as if they're planning an appearance on Mastermind and don't realise they've all selected the same specialised subject.

Despite the difference in focus, the thirsts are matched and the Swan River noticeably lowers as the breweries struggle to keep up with demand. Today I'm not joining in. I'm laying off the booze for this match in order to better report the cricket, and because with a three hours less helpful time difference my audio deadlines are perilously tight. But I do need fluids, possibly intravenously. I estimate I drink 6 litres of water through the day and yet eject no more than a stubby's worth in the dunny, the rest is simply steaming off me.

There is so little shade at the WACA that at every break in play, any small patch round the back and out of the sun, even a square foot tight against a wall, is instantly filled with a sweltering, sweating Pom. The visual effect is not unlike a large number of peasants being lined up for a Mexican firing squad; it's like one giant Dave Allen sketch. Even without beer, in the heat my brain occasionally simply stops working, and I lose track of my short-hand sentences half-way through... thing... um.

Notably, all the pitch-side stewards are African, not an ethnic grouping you see much of in Perth, or one represented in any of the other jobs at the WACA. The reasoning seems sensible enough, a steward has to stand in the full glare of the sun for seven hours in black clothing and a plastic bib, and only the African lads can handle that. Good on them, as they say round here. Unless that's the only jobs they'll give them, in which case, not so good.

I think I spot bowling legend and commentator supreme, 'Whispering' Michael Holding prowling round the ground, although I may be hallucinating. Such are the conditions that I'm having flashbacks to my childhood and the scorching summer of 1976. That long summer of endless blue skies and England versus the West Indies at a parched and sun-blasted Oval, and there's me, sat inside with the curtains drawn, watching it all on TV. If any trouble breaks out I'm half expecting to see the Sweeney turn up and sort it out with a good old-fashioned punch up. While I'm glad not to be in front of a TV, the dark room is sounding appealing.

What little trouble there is, a spot of exuberant beer-sloshing by the Fanatics, is dealt with by quite the happiest, friendliest police I've ever seen. The WA cops arrive with smiles (and guns it has to be said), and put the rowdies in their place with a couple of matey words, chastising them for the poor quality of their vocal efforts compared to the Barmy Army. Nothing, but nothing, could endear me more to Australia than this display of high-visibility, low-temperature policing. Having seen so much counter-productive, aggressive bullying by police in the UK, it's nice to see proof of how easy it is to keep order if you keep your cool and retain your humanity. The Fanatics are chastened and the rozzers leave them with the laughs ringing, no growling required from Regan and Carter: I feel like applauding.

After the initial adrenalin rush, the near 40 degree temperatures visibly start to drain the England bowlers of energy, and there are only four of them. Three really, as this is a seamer's pitch and Swann is not yet effective. Too late, Collingwood is roped in for an over, but by tea England have wilted and Australia have strolled to 179/6. Don't say I didn't warn you. A cuppa and a cucumber sandwich revives Anderson enough to finally break through Haddin, but then Johnson and Siddle cream the flagging bowlers, and in the blink of an eye the natives have remarkably reached the entirely respectable 268 all-out on what is obviously a low-scoring wicket.

We're only in the 3rd Test, England are only 1-up, but already the bitter and hysterical recriminations in the Australian media over the perceived obsolescence of their team has unrealistically saturated English thinking as well. There is a genuine air of surprise amongst the England fans, a sort of bewildered chatter: How did they score *quite* so many, where did they magic-up all those runs from? Weren't they supposed to collapse for 150? The script has changed, and England now need at least 300 to get it back on course. But the confidence remains among the fans. Thus far they've out-sung, and out-drunk the Australians – and the jovially out-ed the camper ones – so when Strauss and Cook emerge for the nightmare of 12 overs at the end of the day, many expect them to easily knock off 50 before close and put these 'convicts' in their place.

Instead the Australian attack appears genuinely menacing. Harris, Siddle and Johnson are all instantly 10kph faster than the English trio. Having three near 90mph bowlers and a wily 85mph all-rounder as your fifth bowler, seems to be rubbing it in rather. But catches still win matches and Ponting misses an easy chance in the second over. Notwithstanding his good relations with England fans off the pitch, the relentless taunting when he's on it appears to be getting to him. Ricky looks agonised, and England skate on.

The team reach close of play intact, which is more than can be said for some of the fans, among whom there are casualties. On a day that burned through my sunblock by 1pm, for once Jimmy Saville's long-sleeved, long-trousered, top-hatted white 'uniform' was some of the most sensible clothing on display. Three lads topped even Jimmy by dressing up as Bedouins, in the full robes and with obligatory Knightsbridge shades. I might try a few bed sheets myself tomorrow. Even hardened

Australians have been crisping and there are expressions of relief that the 2022 World Cup is going somewhere a bit cooler like Qatar. I've bleated and whined a lot about temperatures, but today I met not one, but two locals sporting seeping bandages from recently cut-out skin cancers, making the 'no aerosols' policy appear even more fatuous. It made me realise this was the real deal, you can actually die from watching cricket here. The closest I'd got to that in the past was watching Chris Tavare bat, and wondering if there was any point in going on.

Emerging from Queen's Gardens where I've been recording my close of play audio, I'm accosted by four scantily clad women punting their wares. It's the first time in my life someone has handed me nude photos of themselves, and still the latest time, though I'm holding out hope it's not the last. It transpires these painted ladies are local strippers who work in a club down the road and the calendar I've just been given features their fleshy charms.

'Which month are you?' asks a bolder punter than I.

'I'm May'

I'd about to add, 'Or she May not,' but she clearly can and does, so I demur. I turn to the fifth page, and pathetically she looks better with her clothes on, which isn't saying a lot. I've seen no shortage of attractive girls in Perth, but none of them are in this calendar. It's the usual collection of implanted, orange hard-faces wearing too much make-up, photographed inexpertly in unsexy poses in harsh light, by the proud possessor of black trousers and bulging pockets. I'm guessing, but unquestionably there is no glamour in 'Glamour'. Even with my little camera I could take a better photograph of these girls; he's made the positively plain look negatively ugly. You have to hate women to take shots like that. I toss the calendar in a bin and walk on. Absurdly, it makes me happier that Perth still has councils that provide and empty waste-bins, than it does to be handed naked photographs. I must be getting old.

Chapter 26
THIRD TEST, DAY TWO
A GREAT DAY FOR BATTING
(Friday 17th Dec)

It's another brilliant morning, but the walk to the ground is quite unlike yesterday's. The first inkling I get of the different mood is the large numbers of fans already ensconced in the bars and cafes I pass. I assume they're fuelling with booze or coffee for the long day ahead, but then I reach a ring of scavengers a few hundred yards from the ground: hordes of English ticket touts. The WACA's ticketing regime that drove us all mad and took us so long to circumnavigate on day 1, has been bypassed within 24 hours. Why do I suspect that when Columbus landed in the Americas there were touts on the beach offering to buy or sell tickets home? Yes, the hyenas are out in force, their accents – Cockney and Scouse – particularly urban and grating.

Who has sold them the tickets? Maybe they bought them legitimately, maybe they used the usual touts' tricks, but I wonder if it's weather dependent. It occurs to me that the sunburned Englishmen I've passed may have no intention of coming to the unshaded ground today, and faced with another blazing day and a miserable exchange rate, have preferred extra beer money and convalescence in air conditioned bars to another three sessions without an ozone layer.

As if in evidence of this theory, outside the ground is like the scene from Lethal Weapon where Mel Gibson shows off his old wounds: Thursday's crowd are flaunting their weirdest and worst sunburn. My prize goes to the bloke who'd dozed off and sunburned the palm of his left hand. Luckily his right was holding a pint and was unharmed or his sex-life might have taken on a masochistic edge. I suggest he cools the burn with a cold beer, while evening up his tan on the right.

I shouldn't mock: I'm burned underneath my thick hair, and even more painfully, on the upper insides of my wrists. 'Cricket watcher's burn,' I've termed it: acquired by sitting with hands loosely clasped in your lap or holding pints. Yesterday I met a hardened ex-pat who raved about this country and told me it was unthinkable he'd return to England. Today he's sat near me again and as I say hello, I notice he's wearing leather gauntlets to cover the injuries. He's in as much pain as me.

Over the radio, from the smug comfort of a refrigerated booth in the shade, Michael Vaughan says it's a glorious day for batting, and he's half right: it's undeniably a glorious day for not fielding. I'm well covered up but there's no place I'd less like to be today than stood in the blazing sunshine for six hours. If England can keep Australia out there till tea, their all pace attack should wilt and become vulnerable. Australia will be gunning for a major breakthrough before the Barmy Army have written a new song about them. Silencing the crowd is extra important in a heat that shortens tempers to the length of a Ponting innings.

That should be easier today as, once I'm through the gates with my sunblock down my trousers, I see a huge difference in the ground. The Barmy hardcore are still there in strength over on the west of the ground, the flags of St. George (and St. Andrew and a Welsh Dragon or two) still in evidence, but the swathes of loud Englishmen with a more football-terrace-like attitude are heavily depleted. Is it the sunburn? Or had more Australians snapped up the tickets already? I fancy the former, as the members stands are still half-empty. I despise touts, but if they can lay their hands on tickets for those permanently empty prime seats, I might revise my opinion. Either way, there is a far deeper sea of yellow and green caps, and consequently the mood is completely different. Thursday was boisterous and loud, with singing galore right from the off; today is more muted and intense, with sporadic roars from the Aussies rather than the continuous noisy background clatter the English provide.

And there are plenty of those sporadic roars, the real Australia show up at last. It all happens so quickly – less than two sessions. After another dropped catch and a frustrating first hour, the humidity rises and suddenly a rejuvenated Johnson swings the ball like a boomerang; the first time I've been able to use that tired old metaphor in a land where at least it's fitting. He's so good the only surprise is that he can't get the ball to do a complete circuit and come back to him by itself, taking out a koala or two on the way. Here is the legend we've heard tales of, but none in England had truly believed in. As he tears through England's batting like it's tissue paper – wet whinging Pommie tissue paper at that – I glance at four lads behind me who have bravely come dressed as St. George. In head-to-toe mock chain-mail they're well protected from the sun, but suddenly here was the mythical dragon all too real. I glance over my shoulder and the knights seem small, hot and unsaintly.

'Will the real Mitchell Johnson please sit back down again?' I mumble to no-one in particular. Viewed at first hand the impression is of an Australian team with their tails not only up, but as high as a troop of baboons. Indeed such is the excitement amongst the Aussie Fanatics that I fear some red bums will be displayed before long. The loudest cheer is for KP's dismissal for a duck, but the Aussies are more generous than the England fans are to Ponting and he's allowed to leave the pitch without jeers. However following the successive dismissals of Trott, KP and Strauss, one local loudly poses the question: 'Your South Africans are all shit, you got any English?'

Fair point, well made. But indeed they do. As in stand-up comedy, confidence and aura in cricket can only really be appreciated from close up and in the flesh, and Ian Bell is the most confident player in the England team at present. Whereas KP and Colly hopped to the crease like nervous kangaroos fearing the Johnson Boomerang, Bell strolls out, as cool as a cucumber ice-cream – he's in completely in the wrong position at number six. When he gets off the mark with a perfectly timed off-drive you feel there's hope for England so long as he doesn't run out of partners. Credit to the Australians: they work him over and he too is hopping by the end of the morning. You can tell a pitch is lively when you expect to see Zebedee come in at number eight. But alongside an impressively stoic Prior, Bell sneaks England through to lunch. Phew!

This morning England have scored 90 for the loss of 5 wickets, something even a Martian with American citizenship would understand is not a good showing. In fact it's downright bad show old boy, is the rough thrust of most lunchtime conversations. Alcohol is being taken liberally in pain-killing quantities, but with my new dry regime there is no palliative for me; I'm watching this surgical dismemberment without anaesthetic. While refilling on coke I get chatting to a couple of mischievous old men out from Cumberland (not Cumbria they insist). They're knocking back the drinks and laughing, and altogether unnaturally happy in the circumstances. I say 'chatting to,' although with the language barrier, at times it feels more like an oral exam.

'What's the celebration?'

'Pete's divorce.'

'Ah. That's nice...'

'Aye, th'art bloody right it is,' interjects Pete through a mouthful of beer that renders his accent only slightly more impenetrable.

'So why are you so happy, Matt?'

'Ah git 'is wife's ticket!'

They cheer and toast one another.

'Ah-ha. Is that why she divorced him?'

The full story is even more outrageous. Pete bought two tickets to Perth, in full knowledge that his marriage was not long for this world. When he split from his partner, his good friend Mathew's wife took pity, and suggested Matt go to Australia to keep Pete company and help him to get over the break-up. It seems to have worked, Pete is looking as happy as the cat that got the cream; or a pig in shit, depending upon how you view these things.

'That was the plan al' along, man. There was naw way Matt's wife wad let 'im ga abroad wee'oot 'er otherwise, an' naw way ah was coomin' oot 'ere with me ex. All cam' thegither nicely.' Pete toasts Matt again.

'Ye cou'd say it was the perfect crime.' Matt toasts Pete.

'Aha. Matt, Pete, I'm in awe. Genius. There's just one thing you boys haven't considered.'

'W'at's that?'

'Ye mean aw the nagging w'en ah git hame? Ah'll cope.'

'No, Matt, what if your wives had a plan too?'

'Girraweh! What plan?'

'W'at ye talkin' aboot, man?'

'What if, even now, your ex and his wife are shacked up together in the honeymoon suite in Las Vegas, spending all Matt's savings?'

'Give ower!'

'Ye cheeky booger...'

Fortunately the lads are too proud of themselves to be annoyed at my leg-pulling and we part on good terms. I leave them deep in happy conversation with two baffled Aussies who look in need of simultaneous translation. If that's how they talk I'm scared to think what they put in their sausages.

An entertaining interlude, but I scurry back to my seat, keen not to miss a ball. We're entering the most crucial session of the match, and I'm hoping England have a similar plan to my lesbian wife fantasy as, figuratively speaking, the tail needs to wag the dog. But it doesn't work out that way. Almost immediately Prior is unlucky when a ball comes off his body and trickles onto the stumps and after that, despite Bell's fifty, the good ship England is holed below the water-line and sinks to the bottom for a thoroughly inadequate 187.

Australia have a convincing lead; a glorious day for batting, my arse. Facing four properly quick bowlers on a fast, bouncy wicket is a challenge in any weather. Today the Australian public turned out in significant numbers to back their team, and in return their team turned up to play. I'm glad they're back and making a fight of it. It's been two of the most magnificent sessions of cricket I'm ever likely to see, and the game needs many strong teams simultaneously to survive as a world sport. And the $20 I treacherously bet on Australia last night is looking like a shrewd investment, but don't grass me up on that one.

Australia have to bat through a session, but the England bowlers are still weary from yesterday; the six batsmen providing them with barely sufficient time to shave before they had to dash out in their pads. And here they are once more, warming up to bowl: it's like Déjà Vu.

The first hour brings no joy, but Finn – the youngest and sprightliest – provides some cheer with a double breakthrough, including a nervous, forlorn Ponting for a miserable 1. I travelled halfway round the world to see one of the most exalted batsmen in history; I might as well have stayed at home and watched Surrey 2nds. As the great man slinks off, I get chatting to a pair of well-spoken English ladies behind me, who are clearly glad to see him go.

'Good. I don't like Ponting, his eyes are shifty.'

I feel I need to stand up for my old mate from my Brisbane days: 'That's a bit harsh, isn't it?'

'Well he just isn't gentlemanly enough for a captain, is he? Not like David Gower or Mike Brearley were.'

I consider reminding her of some of England's less aristocratic skippers – Gatting, Beefy and Freddie spring to mind – but decide against sowing dissension in the ranks in this time of trouble. The hope for England is short-lived. Finn is expensive, Swann is poor, and the England attack look, dare I repeat it, a bowler short? Yes, my scratched record is available from all good retailers.

But true to their principles, as England struggle, the Barmy hardcore get louder and louder. This is how they came into being, born in adversity, they are not fair weather fans and realise support is most needed when your own two legs are failing. Collingwood, Trott and Anderson understand this, and at one point come part-way across the pitch to applaud the Army for its efforts. It's a great touch and well deserved. The noise lifts spirits but it's not enough, Australia gather themselves and finish the day 200 ahead with only 3 wickets down. Uh-oh.

Chapter 27
YOUTH HOSTELLING IS FUN
(Friday 17th Dec - Evening)

As usual I sort through my audio files on the train back to the beaches, but tonight, as soon as they are dispatched I'm packing my bags. I've been staying out in a lovely old colonial house near the sea, and it's all you would expect. Attractive from the outside, dark and shady inside, with beautiful original wood floors, and bathroom facilities a navvy would blush at. Not quite true, there's nothing wrong with the shower, but it's odd to modern eyes to find that a house with three grand rooms has a poky little shower-room and a dunny out the back. A more recent spot of building has at least connected the lavatory to the house via a tatty utility space of bricks and corrugated iron, but heading through the dark kitchen into a semi-outhouse with a two inch gap under the door feels weird. Nevertheless I like it a lot, it has character and charm, and a spot of judicious renovation could make it a palace, even if it sounds over-priced at $2.2 million.

Judicious renovation doesn't appear to be been the previous owner's forte. The same construction work that annexed the loo has added a small room of questionable facility, whose primary purpose seems to be to completely board up one of the bedroom windows and plunge it further into darkness. The other window has already been shaded with canvas, and the porch at the front does for any attempt by the sun to infiltrate the house in that direction. I realise it's hot out there but the way old Australian houses are deliberately kept in perpetual night, requiring ever burning bulbs even at midday, is surely taking things too far. It just makes the shock of stepping out into the blazing day so much more traumatic. And oh boy they like it dingy over here. The ubiquitous old-fashioned tungsten lights are all wrapped in thick dark shades to render them both entirely useless and slightly less energy efficient than a power station that runs on mithril. I'm burning carbon by the ton and I can't even see my face in the mirror at midday. Every morning I have to convince myself that shades, shorts and T-shirt are indeed the right clothing, even if the inside light and temperature screams overcoat, fur boots, and a torch.

But the time has come for pastures new. My original plan had been to have a three day holiday by the beach and then move into a city-centre hostel the night before the match started, but with all my errand running I've not even set foot on the beach and still haven't switched digs. Regardless, there's no time for paddling now, there's work to be done, so I'm moving closer to the action and already I'm dreading it: Australian hostels are notoriously among the worst in the world. There's no question that I've packed very badly and my downsizing proves it to be ever more ridiculous. I'm painfully aware that when I get to the hostel I'll be out of place among the backpackers; how many of them will be carrying a leather laptop case and a dressing gown?

I slug into the city and trundle to my destination just as the inhabitants are emerging for a Friday night of fun. It was a fluke getting this room, as I left it late and it was the last one in town, but the hostel isn't as bad as I thought it would be: it's much, much worse. I won't say it's filthy because it's only slightly dirty; and I won't say it is comfortable, homely, characterful, relaxed, charming, well-appointed, fun, funky or pleasurable in anyway whatsoever, because it isn't. It has free-internet, which is more than you'd get in a hotel, so let's be positive. But in every other way it is the worst place I've ever stayed, anywhere in the world, except possibly the mouldy 'six by eight' room with a damp sofa and no bed that I once took in Shepherd's Bush for three months when I was skint and desperate. But that cost less per week than this place costs per day, and I only shared facilities with two cute girls, not hordes of sun-dried travellers. I appreciate margins can be tight in the hostel game, but the proprietor is keener on lounging around smoking roll-ups than lifting a finger.

I have a room to myself; somewhere I can lock the door and hide in. The idea of spending a night in one of the mini-dorms, with another seven sweating bodies adding to the airless torpor in the windowless rooms, fills me with horror. Although there is quite enough horror, what with the door-less men's toilet directly adjoining the social area. The bed is the most un-comfortable I have ever encountered, including the heather-filled sacking I once slept on in my grandmother's house. The mattress is roughly the shape of a rugby ball and made of scrap metal and live eels; the sheets – too small to even be tucked under at both sides – simply slide off this wondrous shiny creation. The dim bulbs throw a light so fitful that I can barely see my socks without taking them off and lifting them within sniffing range; they aren't even energy-savers so are adding to the equatorial conditions, but as there is no heating they are probably essential warmth in the winter. Other than that, the cluttered, tatty, crumbling kitchen and the murky showers that I later find dispense only cold water for most of the day, there is nothing fundamentally wrong with the place that a bit of elbow grease wouldn't put right, but it isn't forthcoming. Even a couple of days work with a bottle of Cif and a tin of emulsion would make a huge difference to rooms with stained walls and no natural light whatsoever, but I don't see it happening any time soon. If my mum saw this place she'd either have a heart-attack and fall down dead on the spot, or more likely turn Ninja and strangle the owner with the cord of her apron.

I'm not alone in my general revulsion and frustration. It is succinctly summed up by a fellow Brit as 'a f*****g shithole', and the overall demeanour of the other occupants is one of either resigned despondency or prickly suspicion. Possibly suspicion that someone else has a better room than them and they've drawn the short straw, but in this place you wouldn't reach the bottom of the glass with any of them. Not that you'd need to, we're already among the dregs. When money's short I've hostelled in other parts of the world, most recently in Cape Town where the place was so nice I could gladly have lived there and written novels, but I can't ever recall paying so much for so little as this. I realise Australian labour costs more than African, but the fundamental problem is a lazy revelling in the crusty travellers lie: that indolence and squalor are an essential part of the trip. But it doesn't have to be; grow up.

Perhaps in order to stop disillusioned inhabitants drowning their sorrows so deep they get the bends sobering up, like a long-distance train, the hostel is dry: no booze allowed. If only Chas had booked in here, I'd have laughed for a week. But for myself, I've never needed a drink so badly in my life, and flee as soon as my case hits the floor.

It's Friday night and the town is fairly lively, there are throngs of people heading towards the bars. I take a walk around and I like the vibe of this place, but probably I'm a little too old for the area. There are beautiful young girls and not so beautiful young men out in droves. The girls are in standard Perth evening-wear: whereas by day they all wear a vest, denim micro-skirt and gladiator sandals, by night, this has become a vest, micro-dress and high-heeled gladiator sandals. High-heeled gladiators? It's a new one to me but an interesting novelty. They look great – the girls not the shoes – and in fairness the boys have made an sterling effort too.

Shirts and dark designer jeans are the gents' order of the evening. This is a trend I see repeated across Australia; when the temperature is still so high that the pubs of England would be filled with cropped cargo pants and faded old T-shirts, the Australian man dons glad-rags that would make a dingo sweat. It's as if there is a competition for who can wear the thickest, hottest trousers. It's smart, and I do like people making an effort, and with the ubiquitous air-conditioning it will only be sterility-threatening on the walk to and from venues, but the long sweltering queues outside bars are not so tempting to be stood in. Even though my shorts-cooled sperm count is probably a good deal higher than theirs, next to these glitzy young things

I'm completely under-dressed and feeling like an embarrassing dad for the evening.

It's hard not to feel old, because I'd swear there is a missing generation: Perth appears to have a dearth of people in their mid-to-late twenties. Maybe it's an optical illusion, but I suspect it's a similar phenomenon to one depressingly common in British provincial towns. Since the expansion of university places in the UK over the last twenty years, every autumn, swathes of teenagers depart their homes and head to the big cities to secure a degree, and except for Christmas and the occasional weekend, generally they don't return to the counties until their mid-thirties and are seeking to raise families. Areas with good schools are particularly youth depleted by this exodus, explaining the high proportion of tea-shops to nightclubs in, for example, Perthshire, Scotland – what I call the Scone-Beer index of a town. Perth, Australia however, has plenty of places of higher education and there's no shortage of teenagers. Instead the missing generation starts a little older, and I assume is due to the vast numbers of Australians that go travelling and work abroad after university. In Britain alone there are enough young antipodeans to fill a small city, so it's hardly surprising the demographics are a bit skewed. The visual effect is curiously sci-fi, like a dark secret nobody talks about, and you start to wonder if the 20-somethings have all been turned into dog-food.

Ahead of me, not in tins, but squeezed so tightly into their sparkly dresses they may as well be, are two of the most gorgeous girls I've ever seen in my life. They're walking as purposefully as you can in impractical footwear, and come upon a group of English lads walking leisurely in comfortable shoes, so their paces closely match. As soon as they coincide the boys prick up their ears, wag their tails and only refrain from panting by enormous restraint. I give them the once over and wonder if these fellows are ex-pats, as they're dressed in heavy jeans and smart shirts; they know how to blend in and I sense wolves in sheep's clothing. From a standing start the leader of the pack is evidently wise in the right things to say and immediately strikes up a conversation with one of the girls. I take my hat off to him because he's the shortest and ugliest of the blokes, but I guess the Staffie is bolder than the bloodhounds. He's rewarded for his alacrity as our goddess does not shrug him off and the conversation instantly flows. I reckon this puppy has learned a few tricks.

I'm an old dog and I can't watch; after the buskers of Brisbane, I know where this all ends. I detour and wander round searching for a likely watering-hole to cap the night in, but surrounded by teens in glad-rags I soon realise I'm way past this lark and circle back to my lonely host-hell for a sober night spent sliding off the mattress. En route I pass the same bunch of lads. The girls have gone, but our protagonist – who really is as plug-ugly as only an England fan can be – is explaining that it's easy when you know how, and proudly showing off the new addition to his iPhone's contact list. With my luck, if I met a girl like that, she'd give me her number then my phone would pack up.

Chapter 28
THIRD TEST, DAY THREE
A LITTLE FAITH
(Saturday 18th Dec)

Agincourt, Bannockburn, Perth: three legendary underdog wins. The third may be yet to happen; we can but dream. The trouble with citing historical precedent is that on most occasions the underdog is completely walloped, and today may be more of a Culloden. I said before that I don't really believe in momentum in sport. By its very definition, it doesn't stay long in one place, and so you only have it right up to the point that you suddenly lose it without warning. But if it exists it's now in the hands of the Australians. Will the pendulum swing again? Will the guards at the gate confiscate it from Australian bags this morning, or wave them through to victory?

If England can come out firing and skittle the Aussies for less than a 100 runs, they should win in four days, and we can all get to the beach in time for beer and medals. It could happen, the pace of the pitch will mellow, Australia have no recognised spinner and the team batting fourth at the WACA has scored over 300 in the last four matches. That's the view of the incurable optimists, and I really do mean incurable, drugs will not help those people. Much more likely, if Australia bat through two sessions they should level the series tomorrow, and the psychological blow of having been on the ropes at 69/5 and then coming back and winning will be massive. With Christmas homesickness just starting to bite for the tourists, the series will be wide open and we'll be on a seat-edge for weeks yet.

Nonetheless I'm excited. Anything might happen as cricket is a topsy-turvy old game, slightly less predictable than 'Through the Looking Glass' and dictated by a similar logic;

anyone who has ever seen English umpires deciding on when a damp pitch is dry enough – play tomorrow, play yesterday but never play today – will understand what I mean. Alice Down Under would have been a bestseller for sure and, coincidentally, much now depends on a madman in a massive Top Hat. It is no time for shrinking violets: Jimmy and Billy must rally the Army and get on the case early to bring up the same huge groundswell of noise that did the trick on Thursday morning, and hope it works its magic again. Failing that, I've booked one of the strippers I met to streak across the pitch and distract the invincible Mr Cricket. It may not work, but it will have its consolations.

At the ground it's a bit cooler, praise the Lord, and my sun-block in the shorts trick has become second nature. If this carries on I may start to get cocky and attempt to bring a load of cannabis home from Thailand, and spend the rest of my days opening the batting for the Bang Kwang High Security 2nd XI. But once inside, the WACA is looking truly glorious. It's a fine old ground, and I decide to go exploring during the morning's play. The locals are out in force and I join the picnicking groups spending their Saturday on the eastern grass bank. There's a lovely lazy happy atmosphere all around, and you'd never suppose two teams were locked in mortal combat nearby.

These are not original 'hills'. I'm amazed to learn these gentle slopes were only added in 2002 when they stopped playing Aussie rules here and the ground was refurbished. I'm ecstatic to find sympathetic and intelligent development so recently. The icing on the cake would be to erect translucent shade sails – a marvellous idea proposed by one of the families I get chatting too. 'How much could it cost to put up a sheet of canvas on a few poles?' the wife asks me. Gazing across to the sweltering western bank where the Army overspill is stationed, I daresay they'd happily arrange a whip-round and sort it out. Get the small things right and the people will come. Cricket needs placid spots like this if it is to preserve its identity, otherwise we may as well just watch football. And if capacity is an issue, sell tickets to the members' stands, as even on this sunny weekend they've each brought three imaginary friends with them.

Since I was there, I hear permission has been granted for a redevelopment of the WACA, but from a very limited perusal, the plans appear quite imaginative, incorporating residential blocks in order to cover costs when there are no matches on at this (thankfully) cricket only venue. I like the idea of people living at a ground; just so long as they don't ask us to keep the noise down, why not? Anyway, I'm not going to argue politics today; everything is all just too splendid.

The day trundles on and so do the England bowlers. Lunch and tea come and go and the attack starts to sag. Finn loses a full yard of pace as he toils through the heat. Excellent yesterday, today he is ineffective and expensive. When the ever jaunty Collingwood comes on for a spell he provides some much needed energy. Leaving aside whether he's 'good in the dressing room', he's good for the fans too, with his never-say-die, switched on attitude. Anderson looks hugely peeved when Strauss delays the new ball and lets Colly carry on, but he's just taken a wicket and had another dropped, more than Jimmy has managed all day. Sometimes you need a cool head in a crisis, and you could fry an egg on Mr A's glowering forehead.

Impressively, none of this dims the enthusiasm of the fans. My favourite moment comes when one of the professional photographers, replete with inappropriate clothing, small-penis-compensating big lens and suspiciously bulging-pockets, repositions himself in the stands to get some photos from on high. He picks his new angle with care and lines the shot up precisely, only to find three bonny lads from Sunderland jumping up and dancing and singing in front of him every time he raises his camera. Timing is everything off the pitch and on. Where were these boys when I was trying to buy a filter? I'm glad to say the 'tog takes it in good heart; sports snappers are generally a decent bunch with genuine skill, and at least his trousers aren't black. But honestly mate, take your coat off.

Finally, a little after tea, it's all over. This is still a bowler's wicket, and Australia only muster 309, thanks almost entirely to Watson and Hussey. My master plan to distract Hussey with a streaker came too nothing. I hadn't actually arranged it, it was just wishful thinking. Be careful what you wish for: an hour or so into the shaky England reply, a short hairy fan dashes onto the pitch removing clothes as he goes: not so much a streaker as a stripper. I don't know if he was inspired by the girls outside, if it's done for a bet, or if he shares my prejudices and wants to set an example to the sweating photographers, but it's an amusing if unsavoury sight. Unfortunately his tangled trousers impede his attempts to dodge security; he's clearly not thought this through. The show gets even seedier when he's hurled to the ground naked by three large Africans. Watching grown men wrestle has never been my thing, and even less so when one of them is nude. Even so, as our 'in-flight' entertainment is brought crashing down and bundled off the pitch, I briefly consider filming it and submitting it to the website BlackMen–WhiteCocks to see if it's the sort of thing they're after.

Comedy interlude over, attention shifts back to the crisis at hand. An Australian lead of 390 is in the can and England are quivering at 51 for 2. It says much for how far England have come that the radio commentators are talking seriously of England reaching the target. They have memories of South Africa making nearly 450 in the 4th innings on this ground two years ago. But in that game Australia had made the lunatic mistake of playing only three seamers and a spinner who took one wicket for 204. That sounds familiar. What kind of crazy fools would field a team like that? Uh-oh. Australia, at least, have since studied the entrails and won't get fooled again.

England need 391 for the Ashes. It is possible, just not very likely. And by the end of the day they have been blown away and it's as far-fetched as discovering a lost tribe called Malcolm in the Colchester Garden Centre. A point reinforced ten minutes before the close by a disembodied voice in my ear.

'Are you ready mate?' says the voice, and then the body materialises when a meaty paw lands heavily on my shoulder. It belongs to the large Fanatic behind me.

'Ready for what?' I reply in my best prison-warden cool.

'Ready for England to loooooooooose!! Hah hah hah!' he adds with a Sid James cackle.

'Well, I'm from Scotland, it doesn't really bother me,' I lie, not wanting to give an Australian another easy victory.

The cock crows and Strauss whispers in my other ear: 'Stuart, do you deny me again?'

I'm sat back among the Fanatics for the final session, and the truth is I am totally ready for England to lose, and have been certain they would since lunchtime on Friday. I'm a Scot; deep-fried pessimism is in my diet. It's 81 for 4— no— 81 for 5, Collingwood out on the last ball of the day! He shouldn't even have been on strike for heaven's sake. He was distracted and annoyed by Anderson's refusal to take a single off the previous ball, and he's done by the ferocious pace of Harris. After most of the last three days in the field, Oh Jimmy Jimmy looks simply too knackered to run another 20 yards in full armour.

I take the opportunity to reiterate my prediction of a loss for England at the MCG. If you're going to be a harbinger of doom, you have to pick your moments, and I figure the Fanatics will be a receptive audience. Disappointingly, rather than welcome me as a prophet, my Australian companions are completely unconvinced, and their pessimism out-weighs even my own.

'Nah, mate, we're shit really.'

See, I told you there was a lot of Scottish DNA hereabouts; I told you this place reminded me of the land of the smoked sausage supper.

'We need to find five new batsmen for the MCG,' opines another. Down here, if you don't score 400 they want the whole team sacked. I wonder if any Aussie players have considered managing a team in the Premiership; they'd enjoy the relative job security.

Three times I've denied England, but in truth I'm only doing it superstitiously, to fire them back into action. '*The team you cheer for will always lose*' is one of the maxims that has seen me through life with little evidence to the contrary. If you support

Arbroath and Scotland it's a pretty safe bet. So I'm relying on deliberately not cheering for them to bring them back into it.

England have always been great front runners: wonderful when their tails are up, but dismal when it's going against them. They can run right through their opponents or collapse like a domino toppling world record. The principal reason we recall Botham's Ashes so vividly is that fightbacks are such a rarity. But today I've been impressed with their refusal to drop their heads despite being pasted. There's a steeliness about this team and morale still looks strong. Weather permitting I think they can win one of the last two matches, and 2-2 will be enough. No I don't think it, I believe it. At moments like this – when all about you are losing their wicket and blaming it on the review system – a little faith is important.

Chapter 29
THIRD TEST, DAY FOUR
BIG BOYS CAME
(Sunday 19th Dec)

Australia may need to find at least one new batsman for the MCG – Ponting's broken his finger, poor lamb, and he will not be on the field today. Apart that is, from when making a speech and collecting the winner's cheque. Yup, Ricky or no Ricky – and some would say no Ricky is the right call – play is unlikely to last very long, and a fifth day ticket is not worth the paper it's printed on. Happily, I didn't actually buy one; less happily I have an absolutely brilliant seat today and the weather is nice and cool. It's the best seat I've had all tour (and it transpires the best I ever get), I could sit here all day, but with five wickets down the vultures are already circling.

I'm sat to the left of the ever faithful Army, just behind fourth slip, with my camera cocked and ready to take advantage of my stellar view. All I need now is some last minute heroics from the 'lower order'. Wait. I don't like calling them that. I've always wondered if the term was coined when the batsmen were gentleman amateurs, and the bowlers were mostly working class players and thus looked down upon. It wouldn't surprise me. Let's call them the tail instead, and poor Ian Bell is once again going to have his natural game spoiled protecting them. But maybe, just maybe, he and Prior can make a fight of it first.

Play begins and immediately my perfect seat turns out to be the worst in the house, as I'm sat behind Australia's number one fan, who bellows out encouragement between every ball. 'Bring on Hilfenhaus – give them some spin!!' he suggests on about ten occasions. And when Hilfenhaus is bowling, he switches to 'Bring on Siddle – give them some spin!!' In the best Aussie tradition he only has one heckle, and it doesn't even make any sense. Meanwhile the extreme pace of Harris is tossing the English aside like yesterday's news. 'We've got to get Prior out!!! Bring on Siddle – give them some—' I switch off my camera and decide to find a quieter seat.

The moment I do so, Michael Hussey takes the most utterly brilliant catch, right slap bang in front of me. Consequently, I have no permanent record but I do at least get to watch it in real time from only fifty yards away, and I still don't believe it. The ball is nearly past him before he takes off – the next moment he's in mid-air at full stretch and has the ball in his hands. I'm in awe. Mr Cricket has lived up to his namesake Jiminy; he really should be wearing a top hat after the way he's played.

As Prior trudges back, I take a wander myself. This is easily done as today, ironically, I can have my pick of seats; the crowd is disappointingly thin, half full at best. Couldn't the Aussies spare a Sunday morning to see their team win? There's no point redeveloping the stadiums if you can't even sell the smaller capacities you already have.

What I'm looking for, at eight wickets down, is a story, or today will be a short podcast. I'm hoping for a contribution from the locals; more streakers would be most welcome. Yesterday we showed the Australians what we were made of – pies and beer mostly – surely now it's their turn. None oblige on this occasion, but generally, when England are involved, off-pitch entertainment is easy to come by. I feel more use should be made of this resource: an impromptu match between the fancy-dressed fans would get a more attentive audience than the usual displays of kids' knockabout that nobody takes the slightest notice of. Hand the outfield over to a game between the Spice Girls Irregulars and the Durham Babies XI and you have the perfect lunchtime-filler. People have paid good money and they deserve a show; where's the harm I say?

While I'm musing on sideshows, blink and you missed it, England are vanquished. It's a little anti-climatic. We're all finished in less than an hour, before the cucumber for lunch has even been sliced. So with nothing else to write about, for once I try to pay close attention to speeches. Strauss, in keeping with England's long line of batsmen-captains, blames a lack of runs. I think he's misguided on that, but I admire the willingness to point the finger at oneself for coming up short. He felt they should have got 391, and that they had been in a good position on day two until Johnson bowled so well, and ... the words blur and all I seem to hear is, 'Big boys came... big boys came...'

Our Andrew is, physically, a pretty good double for Harry Enfield, and certainly 'Kevin and friends' have looked rather spotty and pubescent in this match, but whether through humility or over-confidence, my instinct says that he has missed the point. In contrast, Sir Ricky gets it spot on: 'To get 270 on the board on that first day was probably the difference in the end.' And that's the truth of it.

England badly misjudged their selection and strategy in this match. Coming into the game, Australia were in disarray, the media were on their case, their players injured or out of form, and it was the perfect chance to 'make them grovel'. But Australia scored 577 runs on a bowlers' wicket, because England didn't heed the lessons of history, left the horses for the course in the stable and went into battle with too few weapons. And the WACA cemented its reputation as England's bogey ground. Prior has been hinting strongly that Bresnan hits the gloves hardest of all the England quicks, and his addition might have formed an interesting pace foursome, and crucially have allowed the pivotal Anderson a little more respite from his punishing workload. Ironically, Collingwood, who might have made way (16 insufficient runs), ended with the tidiest figures – 1 wicket (and a drop) for 6 runs – suggesting his inclusion made *some* sense; yet he was given only 8 overs, which clearly didn't.

True, hindsight is a great selector, there's a touch too much automatic pilot coming from the England camp; some-times that gets you to the airport, but in a storm you have to fly the plane yourself. Sending in an exhausted Anderson as night-watchman, when he's too dopey to even run a quick single, was a pre-prepared response to the time of day, rather than a well-considered decision taken on the merit of the match situation.

Choosing to field first was another doubtful call, as it rendered Swann superfluous. He might have been useful on a damp fifth day but the match was over in three. Had they batted, Australia's bowlers would have had to toil through the heat, while Anderson had a nap, leaving England to bowl last in overcast conditions. I checked the forecast – didn't they?

This match is gone and now England's biggest fear is that Ponting won't play in Melbourne. What if, God forbid, the Australians pick a batsman in good form and appoint a tactically astute captain? This would suddenly get a whole lot harder.

'Of all the 110 fingers in the Australian team, why did it have to belong to Ponting?' wailed one distraught Englishman when I told him the news, 'why not Hussey or Haddin!?'

Were I Australian I'd be tempted to give him the finger for that remark, but he's right: it's one of the less crucial digits at present. Personally I've always hated injuries in sport. They're so unfair, so contrary to the idea that hard-work and talent are the root of success. Derek Redmond's hamstring tear in the 1992 Olympics moves my bottom lip to tremble every time, and where would Simon Jones be now, but for the terrible series of injuries he's suffered? Taking precious wickets here no doubt and how England could have used him on that first afternoon. Sadly, sporting glory so often relies on your opponents being crocked. I swear Scotland would have finished fourth in the '78 World Cup if their two best defenders, Gordon McQueen and Danny McGrain, hadn't been injured.

Happier thoughts present themselves when I get chatting to some lads dressed as convicts in the old black and white stripes kit, and collar them for a precious interview. They tell me they'll be sneaking out of town under cover of darkness, and heading to Melbourne hanging on the underside of a slow freight train. It's a good gag, but I'm sure Chas could persuade them it's better to turn yourself in and do the time.

Yes, spirits are still high, and outside the ground I find a gang of people taking photos, and Jimmy and Adge in the middle of it all, clutching a replica urn. Adge is upbeat: 'If you'd offered us 1-1 at Christmas before we came out, we'd have taken that!'

It's a great way to see it, and it's also great to see Aussies smiling, and posing for photographs with England's most distinctive duo. Hands are being shaken all over Perth, dignity is restored to Australia, and we fly to Victoria with honours even. Or at least I fly; I suspect Chas is planning on cycling.

Meanwhile, I have two free days; Perth is my oyster. I've not walked more than a hundred yards when, with perfect timing, the thickening clouds start to spit out rain. With the weather closing in, if England had put up half a fight they might have saved the game. But only might And they've saved me from a soggy day in the uncovered stands watching the umpires soothsay, so every cloud has a silver lining after all.

There's five shopping days to Christmas, and on the way back to my hovel, on a non-descript street corner well off the main drag, I come across a Salvation Army brass band playing carols. There's also a choir and a man talking incomprehensibly through a megaphone (is there any other way). The choir and the ringmaster are all wearing Santa hats, one is wearing the full Claus rig, which takes me by surprise as they're the first Santas I've seen since I've been here, and even on the coolest day so far it seems wildly incongruous. As I get closer, I realise there's something else that's nagging at the back of my mind— ah yes, the choir are all Chinese.

I'm aware that thanks to the missionary work of the likes of Eric Liddell there are quite a lot of Chinese Christians, but the addition of the Santa hat combined with the Australian weather creates the impression I'm watching one of those bad translation 'funnies' that are the stock in trade of any office email, like a sign on a low ceiling saying 'Carefully bump head please.' I love it as I loved the Chinese advent calendar I was once given. (It was the only one I ever had with real surprises behind the doors: dragons and spring rolls to name but two.) And as the band plays I take the time to sit through two old favourites, played perfectly in tune but sung on a different scale. For the first time in my life, I hear 'We Three Kings of Orient Are' the way nature intended.

Chapter 30
PAYING MY RESPECTS
(Monday 20th Dec)

It should be day five of the match, but instead I'm at a loose end and the weather, as forecast, is grey, chilly and spitting with rain. After all the sunburn it would be hypocritical to complain, so I wrap up warm and head out to Fremantle.

I've heard great things about Freo, which is always a worry, as it now has a reputation to maintain. And sure enough it entirely fails to live up to expectations. It isn't bad, in truth it's nice, but it isn't great, it's just... there. Or, here, to be precise. Architecturally I stand by my earlier Scottish comparison, but I suppose you could add a touch of Brighton libertarianism to the mix, but only a touch. I'll come clean and say that on a grey day I find it rather dull. There are a decent number of well-preserved old buildings, but they don't appear to be doing much with most of them. The whole place just lacks any atmosphere or focus, and while a dampish Monday before Christmas may not be peak season, it seems empty and lifeless.

Searching for a bit of interest I wander into the Maritime Museum. There are a few pieces to raise an eyebrow, but scarcely worth $10. I fear that I've become rather spoiled living in London and within a short walk of so many treasures. And then I spot something the Big Smoke cannot hope to rival, something well worth the trip and then some. In a rather innocuous out-of-the-way spot by the railway lines, facing nowhere in particular and with his back to nothing very much, as if he's been here a thousand years and is all that remains of a vanished empire, is a bronze statue of a man perched on top of a Marshall amplifier.

I walk over and say hello to the memorial to the late lamented Bon Scott, original lead singer of AC/DC. For a moment I stand in reverential silence. An inappropriate thing to do I realise, I should have screamed and leapt about, or produced a sound system and turned it to 11, but it's not really my style. I want to take a photo, but it takes at least twenty minutes to get a clear one, as anyone that passes decides they have to jump in front of it and get their own photos. Why does everyone need to be *in* their own photos? It's not about you; just take a picture and piss off. But while I'm standing there waiting for the families to move out the way, I notice something pleasing: even children know who he is. Twelve year olds don't just stand there for the camera; they adopt metal poses and make devil-horns gestures with their fingers. What are they doing listening to *Highway to Hell* at their age? I know I was, but it had just come out when I was their age; shouldn't they be listening to the Pussycat Dolls? On reflection, no they shouldn't. Bon's gritty, lyrical masterpieces of drink, sex, sin and debauchery are far less corrupting than the drivelling, sexually-submissive vanity of that claptrap.

My faith in the next generation restored, I head back into town on the trail of another icon. Subiaco is known as being quite a hip area, but it's something of a Mecca to me, as it is the land from whence Dennis Lillee sprang. I jump off the train expectantly, keeping a wary eye out for cricket balls aimed at my head by budding Lillee Jrs., but as I walk up Rokeby Road, it's turns out to not be at all as I imagined it.

This is another very nice area; a fine place to while away some time, but it's far, far too timid. I'd hoped for Dante's inferno, open volcanoes, blazing furnaces spewing rivers of molten steel along the ground, the distant sound of ominous heavy machinery, and a slow but insistent hammering assaulting the senses. Instead I get a leafy little run of twee shops and eateries. It doesn't sit right that this genteel little suburb gave us the fiery demon that was the young Dennis. I suppose he did at times resemble an angry extravagant hairdresser who's just been asked for a short-back and sides, but it's shattered another myth.

Was this once a tough neighbourhood, in days of yore? Alas, I suspect that if Lillee were born here now he'd wind up as no more than the baddest-ass Barista on the planet, cooking up espressos to knock your head off and bring an Englishman to his knees. Times have changed.

The wind is starting to whip up, the clouds darkening again, but having met one legend and walked in the footsteps of another, the time has come to pay my respects to some less famous names. As I leave Subiaco heading south, my mobile internet connection cuts out, so I'm map-less again, but that's as it should be. I'm not exactly sure of where I'm going, but technology won't be required this time.

I enter Kings Park through the backdoor (another similarity with Calton Hill at night). Walking up Saw Avenue then onto May Drive, it's tranquil, but not at all sterile like most contemporary civic amenities. The trees are tall and mature, there are lawns but there is also scrub, there are roads, but also rough, narrow paths between the roads, hinting at hidden treats. The combined atmosphere is pleasant but with the ever so slight tinge of wild darkness that any 'tamed nature' should have. Just as the most interesting moggies have a touch of wildcat, and the best dogs a suggestion of wolf, Kings Park has tiny echoes of unforgiving wilderness, and much more than a whisper of death.

Death is all around me. Here is one of the world's great tributes to the casualties of the Great War. There are numerous memorials to various battles scattered through the park, but more touchingly all along May and Lovekin Drives are planted eucalyptus trees, each with a plaque commemorating one or more of the dead. Those that mark more than one loss are the saddest, for they mourn brothers. A few trees have had to be replanted, but many have been here ninety years, slowly stretching up out of the sandy soil on their way to heaven. By one recently replanted tree are named two brothers, the younger dying first, the elder making it to within six weeks of the end before falling at the last. Just behind their plaques a solitary red poppy is poking up through the leaf litter and fallen bark. Surely it must be deliberate, yet its backward off-centre placing seems accidental or even supernatural. Was this the child of a seed planted decades ago, suddenly flourishing in the newly disturbed earth, as the poppies bloomed among the shell turned earth of Flanders?

I walk slowly, taking the time to read the old fashioned names and to note the young ages. There are well over a thousand trees, which do not in any way count all the dead, only those whose families could pay the ten shillings, but for the modern eye to whom the names mean nothing, it is enough. Enough to create a sobering, saddening and yet comradely effect; you feel among friends amid the trees, as if an unseen battalion surrounds you. There are any number of emotive war memorials in Britain, those of the First always the most tragic, but to read the names ten thousand miles from the scene of the crime, ironically brings it home all the more powerfully. None of these men needed to leave their factories or farms, their fishing boats or offices, to die in the mud or sand at the behest of generals who considered the Anzacs expendable. They could have remained quartered safe out here, and let Europe's leaders burn the maps themselves. Instead they sailed from Fremantle bound for the Menin Road and Gallipoli, something that those of us who are descended from Tommies who lived through it all, would do well to remember.

You can drive through the park, but thankfully I'm only disturbed by a couple of cars in the hour I spend wandering, the most flustered activity belonging to the ants. You've not seen ants till you've come to Western Australia; here they come in all sizes and colours, although only one anty shape obviously. They are the original settlers of Mount Eliza, and they easily predate the original naming of it *Mooro Katta* by the Nyoongar aborigines. They will own this town and this whole continent when man has long gone. I pause by a commemorative gum tree and watch a system of trench excavations being carried out with military precision by a company of hardy sappers. The grains of sand carried on the shoulders like sandbags, the burdens heavy, the action hurried and nervous of sudden attack, and staccato like an old film reel; it's all wonderfully appropriate. I've always admired ants above all others, their engineering endlessly fascinating, and all carried out in a brisk, cheerful manner. I can think of no more suitable companion for the fallen of that innocent era.

Then something strange. I'm used to seeing ants carry eggs and larvae, but these fellows are collecting what looks like little, tiny sea-shells and putting them aside in a separate pile from the excavated soil. They seem to have a curious agenda, something beyond food and reproduction, but it's beyond my powers of geology and entomology to divine. It's as if they're mining for precious gems; do ants have a sense of the aesthetic? Or is it money, and do they trade these shiny baubles for greenfly cattle and captured slaves from rival hills? Soldiers have always carried trophies home, have they not?

I leave them to their hoarding and head to the cheaply titled 'State War Memorial Precinct'. (They may as well have named it the Anzac Arcade, or the Remember Them Retail Park.) Names aside it is well worth it: an area of simple, elegant monuments that overlooks the city and the Swan River basin. There are a fair few tourists around, but the behaviour is calm and dignified, there's not the horrendous squabble for photographs that ruins many memorials in Europe. Uniformed Japanese sailors mix with Italian teenagers, a family of locals are having a quiet picnic and a game of soft-balled cricket nearby, but all are restrained in their behaviour, being so close to something of such significance. The Pool of Reflection and Flame of Remembrance were only opened in 2000, but they work well, notwithstanding their excess of concrete. This actually creates a similarity to the dismantled remains of a gun-emplacement, which I'm sure is accidental, but not entirely out of place. Thankfully I don't yet know their ugly official titles and am able to savour their contemplative quality without distraction. In fact, forget I told you, just go there when it's quiet, stand by the pool, watch awhile the flickering of the eternal flame that burns in the middle, then turn and gaze past the Cenotaph and out over broad Perth Water and remember those that have gone before: fuel for the soul and brain.

Some Health and Safety box-ticker has ringed off the area in front of the Cenotaph with barriers while they replace the permanent fencing. Placed as it is, next to a tribute to those that faced mortal danger, day-in day-out for years, I find this nanny-nonsense even more preposterous than usual. A few other tourists are hovering behind them, but I think to hell with it and just climb over; if I fall over the edge they can prosecute me in hospital. I'm rewarded with an unobstructed view of the city and some pleasant isolation in which to reflect.

The wind is whipping up the hillside and aggressively shaking the trees above me, there's that wildness again, that hint of something not entirely under man's control. Despite the deliberate planting in the park, one can still sit here and unimagine the sky-scrapers, and see the river valley as the native peoples would have seen it less than 200 years ago. Now flick back to the present, and it's not a particularly attractive skyline: the buildings are dully generic, the bridge pig-ugly, and it's not in any way famous like New York or London. And that's a real shame, because as a natural vista it easily beats both. But I'm thinking, what it really needs to complete the scene – and all that's missing for a homesick Scot – over at the south end of the bridge, across the way from the new town, is a nice big castle.

Chapter 31
UPRIVER AND DOWNRIVER
(Tuesday 21ˢᵗ Dec)

It's my last day in Perth and the forecast predicted 31C, but instead it's raining and 16C. It's all feast or famine round these parts. I've decided to go upriver, but having peeked at the weather and poked around in my wallet, I'm going by train. River cruises are fun but they also cost an arm and a leg, so I'm going as far as I can usefully go on the Transperth rail line, then joining the riverbank on foot to see what I can see.

In my old travelling days such missions were an adventure, as I'd likely only have a mini-map from a town guide that ran out as soon as one stepped beyond the city centre. It made for some long and interesting excursions, but usually meant I never saw a whisker of what I'd intended to visit. These days though such urban goose-chases are declining, as we have online-mapping. Ah, map-apps, the travellers friend, except when they're completely and totally wrong. For those planning to visit and drive around Britain, my first advice would be to get a proper SatNav, as relying on an online map will lead to a great deal of public humiliation as you reverse back out of dead-ends. On foot they're even worse: like the time one took me up a South African hill-path in the midday sun, and then left me at the top staring at a high electric fence and no trace of the promised path down the other side. Nevertheless, as a rough guide to where the hell you're going, they do the job. Or would do, if my phone was working. Oh heavens, here we go again.

The network might be down – it does happen I'm told – but I wonder if I'm simply out of credit. With no way to connect, I can't check this myself so I make a pit-stop into the mini-phone-shop in Perth station on my way to the train. In point of fact, the pit-stop analogy is a poor one, as it implies speed and efficiency, Formula 1 style über-mechanics returning my phone to race winning glory, when what I actually get is another of their employees of the month, kicking the tyres and unable to tell my big end from my carburettor.

'Hi, I've got a signal, but my phone's not connecting. I don't know if there's a problem – or am I out just of credit?'

'That's usually a good sign.'

'A good sign?'

'Probably.'

"*Probably,*" I should have paid attention to that word, but am distracted by his incomprehension of my questioning that this is in any way "*a good sign.*"

'But I've only been Tweeting, I've barely even made a call, it can't have used $25 credit in five days?' Careless: I shouldn't even have mentioned credit; I've put the idea into an otherwise empty head.

'No, it probably is, it can use quite a bit.' That word "*probably*" again.

My train leaves in a couple of minutes and I don't want to waste any more of the day, so I let him sell me $49 airtime to see me through to the rest of the series and rush for the platform without crediting the phone and checking. Once on board, it becomes clear the damn thing is still as dead as a Dodo with a MySpace account. Bugger.

The train ride is interesting, these suburbs are not as glamorous as the Fremantle line and I like to see all sides of a city, so I peer out the windows nosily. The day is brightening up, but I can't for the life of me remember which station I'd planned to jump off at and find myself at the end of the line by mistake. But it's a big river, how hard can it be to find? I wander back the way I've come, safe in the knowledge that it's definitely this side of the tracks... maybe... if I came out the station on the right side. Now if only I could remember the name of the road that leads to the river...

I'm not completely stupid (honest), but I'm convinced I have a silicon-based brain like one of Terry Pratchett's trolls; it works best in cold temperatures. Once it's over 25C I revert to primary school level; by the time it's 35C I'm a dribbling goon and in serious danger of being thrown out the remedial class. It turns out the forecast wasn't quite so wrong after all, as now the clouds have burned off, the temperature has soared over 30C and the jumper over my shoulders seems ludicrous. But by following my sweat-dripping nose I stumble across the right road and have only been wandering in circles for fifteen minutes, it just felt like forty-five. It felt like forty-five to my neck as well; the second dose of sunblock goes on thick.

The first surprise is that the river is little more than a swollen stream. By the time it's wound its way to the town centre it's a huge lagoon, but here you imagine you could practically wade across it. Nonetheless, it is lovely to be out of the city, and I head upriver, casting a wary eye on the signs warning me of lethal snakes in the area: *Here be Dugites and Western Tiger Snakes!* I cast an even warier eye at the ground and any shady piles of stones. A cruiser potters past and deposits tourists at a vineyard across the river, provoking a pang of jealousy, but I'm happy to be stretching the legs and seeing snake signs, I bet those pansies haven't seen a snake sign. I don't want to see the actual snakes, I'm not *that* interested in lethal wildlife, but it's nice to see the signs. I photograph one to show off at home, and start inventing a tale of risking life and limb in the outback. In truth, I'm not even vaguely in the wild, the nearest streets are still within a hefty stone throw, but you would scarcely realise it, all is tranquil and beautiful. And hot: it's now at least 35C.

'Warming up, I reckon.' A local in neatly ironed green shirt and shorts, solid boots and socks, and with a handsome green leather Stetson, strides past me at twice my pace. Blimey, I hope he's just Aussie weather-worn and not really in his sixties or I'm even more pathetic that I thought.

'Certainly is.'

'Over 40 tomorrow they say.'

'Yup. Warming up.'

We've reached a consensus and he disappears into the

distance in a trail of dust. I could walk like that if I had a leather hat, I bet you. Although my head might explode. Not that I have any usable brains left to lose, but I do have a problem. The river is not as sheltered as I'd expected, the trees are fewer than hoped for and I have no idea where I'm heading. Upriver is all very well, but I don't know if in another hour I'm going to happen upon a way back to the road or if I'm going to end up in real wilderness and collapse of heat-stroke where I won't be found for a week. Plus my Factor-15+ is just not enough with so little shade. If I keep going with the sun behind me my neck will be in serious trouble: it's time to head back.

'Heading back, ay.'

'Yup, heading back.'

The 'Green Man' steams past me again. He's seen enough too. The ironed creases on his shorts and shirt sleeves are still as straight and crisp as a guardsman's trousers and there's not a bead of sweat on him. I'm wearing a sweat-drenched T-shirt, an old, tatty cap that's faded and wet-through, and crumbling walking shoes with holes in the side. I'm ashamed. But if further upriver is too much for him, I've made the right decision.

I'm just about back at the road when I check my phone, it's now working; there was nothing wrong with it, it was just that the network was down. How foolish of me to expect a phone-shop operative to recognise whether or not it was actually operational. I find myself recalling the insistent girl at the airport with a touch of nostalgia; she had her priorities right, she'd have given it to me straight, that one. So that means I wasn't out of funds but – I wade through menus and check my balance, $49 – they've cancelled my previous credit. This is how it works in Oz; you don't top-up, you get fixed lump sums. I sit in a shady spot and call India. It wasn't my intention to call India, but whether in Plymouth or Perth, all lines lead to Dehli.

'Hello, you are through to technical support, my name is Sheila, how can I help you?'

'Hello, "Sheila," Can I speak to Marcus North please?'

'Sorry, there is no-one here with that name.'

'Just checking.'

"Sheila" is confused but does her best to help, and confirms that I'd had $18 of my $25 credit remaining. I'm told there's no way to refund my $49, it's been bought and added and that's that, but after some wrangling she sorts me out with a grand total $67 credit. It's a result of a sort, but will I use it all?

Fast forward twenty days to the night before I leave for home, after Tweeting and Googlemapping from dawn to dusk just to burn it all up. At five minutes to midnight, I call and check my balance: the automated voice comes back: 'You have $49 of credit.'

But that's a month and ten sunburns away. Now I trundle back into town and stop by the sado-masochism club that is the phone-shop.

'Remember me?'

'No'

'That doesn't surprise me. Did you know your network was down this morning?'

'Probably. It happens.'

'Signal was showing, but nothing would connect.'

'It's a good sign.'

'You'll go a long way in this job.'

'Probably.'

Tragically, I was forced to agree; the signs were good.

Five minutes later I am on a train again, heading back to old haunts. One thing I must do on this trip is at least stand in the ocean on three coasts (the north will have to wait) and it is time to get the toes wet. Perth's coastline is simply awesome, with near white sand, the water just pleasantly cool and a variety of brilliant colours – blues and greens and in places crystal clear – and astonishingly in most places the beaches are nearly empty. I start at Cottesloe and wander northwards. Burdened as I am with a camera and surplus clothing, I only go in a couple of feet, which is perhaps just as well, as the water washes my sunblock off and in minutes I'm burned behind my knees. By the time I've retraced my steps back to where I started to wash the sand off, I've burned my feet as well. Forty-five minutes of paddling and broiling, but well worth it.

There's no time to seriously injure the rest of my body, as I want to get across to Rottnest Island twelve miles offshore, which I hear is an unspoiled place of wonder, and a lot more pleasant than it sounds. I train it the short distance to Fremantle and grab the fast red and white ferry that zips me across the Indian Ocean. It's not cheap, but it's certainly travelling in style. There's even a bar on board but I don't have a drink, just marvel at the beauty of the water on what has turned out a sparkling calm day. And I've seen nothing yet. At the island itself, the limestone rock leaches into the sea, and patches of the water become an almost luminous aquamarine, and yet so pure you can see the bottom. The effect is absolutely breathtaking. What a wonderful place. There are some marvellous eateries by the dock, and even a few houses you can stay in overnight if you book decades in advance, but once away from this little settlement the rest of the island is what it claims to be, a series of unspoiled white-sand beaches surrounded by crystal clear warm water. Everywhere I look there are beautiful people wearing not many clothes, they do like to let it hang out over here. I ask a local about numbers and am told that this is peak season, but in winter the trade falls off dramatically.

'Really? What's the weather like here in winter?'

'It's like your summer.'

'Blimey, that bad?'

'No mate, like a hot August day in England.'

I weigh it up: 25C, with clean soft sand, warm water, and yet no queues or crushes or sunburned whales in bucket hats; just a few lithe tanned bodies decoratively draped on the rocks like resting mermaids.

'I'll be back.'

I sincerely hope I do come back one day. I want to hire a bike and pootle around aimlessly till sunset, but I only have time for a taster and 35C is too much. It's time to head home, to cool down, clean up and enjoy one last evening walk through Perth.

Chapter 32
NATIVITY STORIES
(Monday 20th & Tuesday 21st Dec)

Christmas is nearly here, and soon I'll be flying with Santa to Melbourne; no presents required as checked luggage, I'm assured by Western Australians that there are no good children in Melbourne. Incredibly, this is the first year of my life I've gone through the run-up to Christmas without once hearing anyone remark, 'the nights are fair drawing in' – normally a mantra as constant as 'Hail Mary's and 'Our Father's the day after a race meeting at the Curragh. I wondered before I came how it would feel to be out in the sunshine at this time, when normally I'd expect to be battening down the hatches and booby-trapping the chimney, and so far it has been as unexpected as my Chinese Advent Calendar.

This is not solely due to the heat, but also to the rather lovely way Perth marks the passage of advent. There are plenty of decorations in the street, there are coloured lights a-hanging, but the imagery is exclusively traditional Christian; there's not a fat Santa or red-nosed reindeer in sight. I realise not everyone may be of that particular religious inclination, and I myself haven't set foot in a church in years, but to see Christmas celebrated in a way that isn't a bloated combination of kitsch and corporate greed is a delight. The decorations aren't hectoring or preaching; they're tasteful and understated and remind you that the spirit of Christmas wasn't always chocolate-flavoured Vodka. Wandering the quiet streets in the late evening is as pleasant a festive experience as I've had for many a year. Ever since the lights on Regent Street became a promotional event for movies, I've refused to go near the place from November till

January, yet I can linger in Hay Street quite contentedly.

But something grander is stirring. During the last few days Forest Place has been the scene of much clanging and banging and hanging; it looks like the circus is coming to town. Yesterday, dancers arrived – warming up, stretching their hamstrings and honing their moves – and I began wondering what form the show would take. My curiosity was answered without feline casualties. Even in Australia I'd be as surprised to see a kangaroo in a town as I would a cow in Berkley Square, so my eyebrows shot up past my ears as I rounded the corner and met three fully-grown camels. About a nanosecond later my eyebrows plummeted downwards and my nostrils desperately attempted to close themselves, but that's camels for you. Of course, the nativity, I should have guessed.

If you can't love a camel, at least from a safe distance, what's wrong with you? They are the great characters of the animal kingdom, the French of the fauna world. Funny looking, grumpy, long nosed, shrugging, shambling, malodorous, irascible clowns. Unfortunate hump-backs born into servitude with the weight of the world already on their shoulders, they are the ultimate beast of burden, an animal that when freed of professional portering duties finds even the unforgiving outback a place of plenty to its satisfaction. There are over a million feral camels in Australia, and if they could write their own mythology, I'm sure it would tell of their eons wandering in the desert till they found their promised land – in another desert. Yup, you've got to love a camel. But preferably from at least ten yards away.

I'm drawn to the camel handler as much as I am to her charges. As a youth I had a crush on the glorious girl-with-attitude that was a young Jodi Foster. No, not in her *Taxi-Driver* days, but in the happy-sad films that showed up late at night on *BBC2*, like *Stealing Home* and *Carny*. And here she is right in front of me, a dirty-blonde tomboy who has run away with the circus and finds herself in charge of three camels. Bright but tired sleepy eyes, tanned arms and no make-up or artifice whatsoever, just an old T-shirt and jeans, and a camel on a rope.

What more could my 19 year old self have desired? Unhappily age has run away with me, but I can still be charmed, and I love watching this girl as she requests her petulant charges sit down. But they're camels, not servile dogs, so while two drop to their knees in prayer, one fellow refuses to oblige.

'F*** you, I'm French, I do what I like!' he says, rolling an invisible filterless Gitane around his comedy-lipped mouth.

Jodi remonstrates with him, but in an entirely personal way. It's not, 'Sit down you stupid Camel'; these two are well acquainted, they're on first name terms, and it's more, 'Oh give me a break Jean-Paul! You sat down yesterday. Now you have an audience you're showing off for the tourists and showing me up. Sit down, or I won't let you watch Mr Bean later.'

'*Sacre-Bleu*! Mr Bean is a comedy genius; you are too cruel Jodi, too too cruel. *D'accord*. I shall sit down, but only to write poetry. You have not won this.'

'*Mon Dieu*, Jean-Paul, you are such a baby!'

He sits down grudgingly, and I want to leap the barriers and propose marriage (to the girl, not the camel), only two things stop me: the twenty year age difference, and the fact that I can't think where to suggest we run away to. Where can you go when you're already in the circus, but back to the mines or, in my case, the fishing boats? I reluctantly pull myself away before I am arrested for voyeurism, or locked up for talking to myself in a French accent.

That was Monday when I was on my way to catch the train to Fremantle, but incredibly they cancelled the show that night due to 'inclement weather': three spots of rain and temperatures plunging as low as 16C. To me that's sunbathable, but in Perth they send out the gritting lorries.

Tonight though, as I wander around the advent decorated streets of Perth one last time, I swing by Forest Place and catch the show in full swing. The cast are absolutely putting their hearts into it. Their hearts, several sheep, three camels, a donkey and the kitchen sink. And, strangest of all, an owl. I don't remember an owl in the Christmas story? But there, behind the soberly dressed narrator (in suit and tie), and looking as surprised as me, is an owl the size of a barn door; although whether it is a barn owl, a barn-door owl, or a brick-shithouse owl, I couldn't tell you.

The donkey enjoys its cameo, the sheep do what sheep do – which is not a lot – and the camels do their bit carrying wise men from the East, or in this case 100 yards from the corner of Murray Street. It seems like a lot of effort to go to just for that, but that's the magic of showbiz. Under the ever more startled gaze of the owl, and disappointingly, Jean-Paul is behaving himself. I was hoping at least for a dirty protest and a chorus of *'Non, je ne regrette rien'*; I do so love a bit of animal-initiated chaos. Jodi Foster is (equally lamentably) wrapped head to toe in Bedouin robes – I favoured the slave girl option personally – as she guides the three kings on their way to meet the messiah. I reckon those wise men must have got lost; Bedouins live to the south and west of Bethlehem, not the east.

The whole show is a spellbinding mix of standard nativity fare, perennial favourite carols, incongruous dance routines, Christmas pop songs, and scenes so out of place I wonder if someone's spiked me with acid. When a troop of small boys come on dressed as Napoleonic infantry and march to 'Little Drummer Boy' I have to screw my eyes back in. Is this what it's like to be a parent? Do they have to watch stuff like this every year?

I'd say the director is aware of this annual penance and has added a few unexpected sixpences to the pudding. I am suddenly presented with the sight of the athletic chorus line, arms akimbo, frenetically jiggling their breasts from side to side, right in the faces of the audience, while singing 'I love it! I love it! I love it!' From my safe distance of eighty yards it is eye-opening, in row one it must be eye-endangering. I swear they deliberately put these bits in to keep the bored dads quiet.

Titillation aside, the whole thing is unbelievably, granduesquely, awful in conception, but just about saved by the great skill and enthusiasm of the dancers and singers, who belt through their numbers with infectious and unrelenting gusto. I'm almost won over by the 1970s-style innocence and exuberance of the production; it only needs the Two Ronnies to come on in drag to complete my enjoyment. But no such luck, it ends not with a bang but with a clanger. They wrap up the show with an all-singing, all-dancing rendition of 'Rocking around the Christmas Tree' – surely the worst song ever written. I run and hide after two bars. I'm not sure if I'm glad I've seen this surreal spectacle or if it has spoiled the purity of my Christmas thus far, but it certainly beat the Christmas edition of Strictly Come Dancing.

I take a walk and sit in McDonalds, munching a burger and feeling left out. Perhaps I'll become a camel handler too. Is there much demand for performance-trained camels I wonder? Surely it's a very seasonal business. After pantomime season it's a buyer's market for dwarves, and I reckon the camel season must be even shorter. Owls, I imagine, get year round gigs. So long as they don't eat your guinea pigs, an owl is a versatile and always welcome guest. Put an owl in a show and nobody bats an eyelid – and nobody did tonight (except the owl). But who'd book a camel in February? I guess the sheep have it toughest. They'll be getting ready to sign on in January, not realising they'll be chops and sweaters by this time next year, and some younger, prettier ewes with stars in their eyes will be getting their gigs. That's show-business kids.

After a mournful meander along the riverside, I pass back along the elevated walkway above Murray Street, as below me the show packs up. Jodi has donned the Perth uniform of cut-off demins and vest, and been joined by two young lads who help load the camels in the trailer. One has big feet and a white man's afro – genuine clown hair – and the other has that Robbie Robertson cool. He's either Jodi's boyfriend or brother, as the two of them are at one with each other and with the camels. They roll up the heavy smelly mats and load them aboard, keen to move on, as if they know they don't belong here. It's a routine they're all familiar with, and they have that wiry strength of the travelling performer; Jodi would probably beat me stone dead in an arm wrestle. Finally it's all stowed and I watch wistfully as they walk beside the truck as it progresses slowly down the precinct and away from me. The camels in the trailer behind stare back. As the lorry pauses to allow the kids to climb in and the circus gets back on the road, Jean-Paul looks up and gives me a slow sagacious nod. I know exactly what he means. *Ça ne fait rien.*

There's a short, unfinished, half-built street near the hostel, it's free from street lights and a perfect place to pause and gaze at the night sky. Somehow the heavens seem nearer in Australia, and one absolutely brilliant planet is giving us its very best Star of Bethlehem impression. Even with a bright full moon the stars are sparkling, glistening as bright as I've ever seen, dazzling in the desert sky. When we look at the constellations, in effect, we're travelling back through the ages, seeing them as they were thousands of years ago. Australia always feels a little stuck in the past, and tonight I am too; and we're both a little closer to the stars.

PART FOUR ~ MELBOURNE

Chapter 33
CULTURAL CAPITAL OF AUSTRALIA
(Wednesday 22nd – Thursday 23rd Dec)

I'm truly sorry to say goodbye to Perth. The people have been warm, friendly and, phone-shops aside, helpful at every turn. Even when asking about packaging in a post office, a mundane chore turned into a pleasant exchange. As I've never enjoyed a pleasant experience in a post office in Britain my life, in spite of all the hassles, I'd definitely like to return and make up for the time lost fighting with technology. In the spring though, when it's a little less lethal. The 'Green Man' by the river was right, Perth was warming up and it goes on getting hotter; by February there are bush fires destroying homes. But right now at the airport I'm happy to be on my way and continuing the adventure. So is the large contingent of Barmy Army recruits necking pints of lager at eleven in the morning, hardly a dignified manner in which to prepare for arrival at the most sophisticated city in Australia.

I've been looking forward to Melbourne most of all. To the outside world it's known as Australia's sporting and comedy capital – two of my primary interests right there – and this place is the capital of them, excellent. Apparently it's considered to be Australia's overall cultural champion, and as I'm also an aficionado of art and classical music I feel we'll get on well together. Plus I'm particularly fond of trams, and Melbourne has more than anywhere else in the world, it just gets better and better. I'm told they even have real weather, and that sometimes in the winter you need a coat. Good, good, because nothing interesting ever came from year round sunshine. But there's another reason I've been keenly anticipating Melbourne: everyone but everyone I've ever met who has been to Australia, raves about Sydney but shrugs off Melbourne. They drag out a thousand photos of the Harbour Bridge and the bloody Opera House, they swoon over the beaches, they call it Syders and act like it's the only place in Australia worth a damn, but when quizzed about its rival just say, 'Yeah, Melbourne's alright.'

We have a word in Scotland you may not know: 'thrawn'. It means to be stubbornly obtuse, to be difficult for the sheer hell of being difficult. It can be applied to people, animals, even objects with moving parts, and my mother uses it a lot, but especially around me and mostly in my direction. She may have a point, because after all I've heard about how bloody amazing Sydney is, I feel Melbourne is almost bound to be better.

It all starts so well. We bounce in, from out of the sky, and we really do bounce: despite the sunshine it is one of the roughest flights I've had in a long while. I don't care, I'm excited to meet the four million people below me and by now it's all second nature, as is the diazepam and a large glass of wine combo. Funny how soon you adapt to other ways of being; Australia has begun to seem quite small. The first thrill is at baggage claim, where I'm joined by Mitchell Johnson. Sharing facilities with the Australian team is old hat for me, as you know, but it's nice of him to ride shotgun and check I got here safely. I scan the conveyer belt for bat-shaped luggage to see if I can be of assistance, but sadly he doesn't stick around long, whisked away by a lackey-cum-handler. But just a moment later up pops Brad Haddin. Shucks fellas, you shouldn't have gone to so much trouble. Brad takes plenty of time to sign people's caps and shirts, even England caps which are all some tourists have on them, and he does it with a smile. I consider buttonholing him for a sound bite, but then he's pounced on by the big boys of the media, and I'd feel bad holding him up any longer. Nice lads. England didn't give me an escort, the miserable sods.

As it's pleasantly warm rather than murderously hot, I decide to walk the short distance to the hotel, and miraculously I don't get lost; though I am a little thrown by the motorists, who are so courteous it confuses the hell out of me. Every time I even think about crossing a road, happy to let the cars go by and find myself a gap where I can, the cars all stop and usher me across like a VIP. How absolutely bizarre and yet cheering. And this remained the case for the whole week: drivers who weren't indifferent psychopaths using their cars as potential murder weapons. Uncanny. Is this usual behaviour? Are they naturally considerate, or is there a death penalty for aggressive driving I've not heard about. Either way, I'm seriously impressed.

When I reach my hotel the greeting is the warmest I've had anywhere, the staff welcoming me to Melbourne with open arms. They want to hear all about me and where I've come from, and when I tell them that my digs in Perth were on the unsavoury side, they're appalled. They take it very personally: Perth has let Australia down and Melbourne intends to put that right. I'm provided with a map of the city, given directions to useful shops, instructed in the best ticket to buy for the tram and where to get it; the contrast couldn't be greater to my logistical cock-ups of the previous week. And when I gratefully step into my room I'm delighted to find it a veritable little palace, considering it's the cheapest actual hotel of the entire trip. I'm so happy to have my first hot shower in five days that, aside for a quick run to the shops for wine and biscuits, I don't leave the room all day, just savour the clean linen and sleep the sleep of the just. Melbourne gets 10 out of 10 so far.

The next day I'm up first thing, no time to waste, spraying on the sunblock and out onto the streets under a bright blue sky. It's perfect, like a bright May morning back home. I hit Victoria markets, explore the town centre, cross the Yarra, stroll the South Bank, and wander aimlessly, till winding up at the Melbourne Museum entirely by accident. I even manage to fit in the Docklands on a loopy way home.

I don't do it all at once though. First, there's what I came in time to refer to as the 'Sunblock Dance'. Within forty minutes of leaving the hotel the clear blue sky has become solid heavy cloud, the temperature plummets and the rain comes down. Before I can make it back to the hotel I'm soaked through and absolutely freezing. I have a shower to warm up and flop on the bed. Forty minutes later I'm considering which protective clothing to wear, peek out through the curtains, and it's horizon to horizon blue sky again; is this some sort of a trick? It's back on with the sunblock and out in the sun again. I'm used to showers, I'm used to changeable weather – I positively enjoy it – I'm just not used to switching entire weather systems every forty minutes. This was going to present a whole new challenge.

My first discovery is fantastic, in the precise sense of the word. Some bright spark has put a complete 19th century factory in a shopping centre. Years ago, when they were tearing down an old foundry in Edinburgh to put up a retail park, I was disappointed that they only kept a small piece of wall, when they could have left some of the old plant and works as reminders of what had gone before, as they do with cranes next to riverside warehouse conversions. They'd have made far nicer sculptures for the car-park than the usual abstract dross, and they'd have been free. Melbourne has understood my design philosophy and run the ball all the way into touch: they've built a modern indoor shopping centre and left the entire lead-pipe and shot factory that stood on the site, bang in the middle of it, with a soaring glass roof to keep the rain off the huge old tower. It's an absolutely incredible feature, a total surprise, and it livens up an otherwise miserable modern arcade no end. It's now a museum, but it works even as an art installation. Let's be honest, we all prefer the walls of Tate Modern to the stuff they hang on them.

I carry on my exploration, but I fear I may already have seen the day's highlight. Something is nagging. It's a combination of things I can't yet put my finger on, but I just don't think I like this place very much. When I go back through my photos it all looks quite nice, but at this point in time, after the glam elegance of Perth, the ambience of Melbourne is grungy and aggressive, the townscape brutal and unsympathetic. Downtown Melbourne is pretty darn hideous. The best of it, the acclaimed South Bank, sits on the muddy, ugly Yarra River and is a botched job. For out and out close-up horror it's not nearly as bad as London's I concede, but it's a missed opportunity. It's cramped and unsure of itself, it's trying too hard to be a 'famous river bank' and consequently is a second rate copy of everything that's gone before; there's nothing recognisably Australian about any of it, it could be Manchester canal-side. And if you can't build 'Australian', because you haven't figured out what that is yet, at least build pretty, but everything is so drab.

Much of the CBD is tatty and cheap, dull modern sludge or a few – too few – old buildings neglected and under a mile of grime. Disappointingly little of the past has been preserved in any of the areas I see. All that's left is the ultimate horror of 'Heritage': tacky horse-drawn carriages pulling gauche tourists past shining steel and concrete buildings. They're celebrating a past they've already erased. What exactly are they trying to say? This is how it used to be before all the horrendous new construction work? It's not real at all; it's the worst kind of plastic history. You'd get a more authentic and slightly more pleasurable historical experience if you contracted pleurisy. There is nothing to be seen from the back of the cart but miles and miles of the worst modernity or a horse's arse, and it's a tough choice.

With a bit of imagination new can be good, and I've found one building that I really like and which is bang up to date. The Eureka Tower on the South Bank is one of the great pieces of modern architecture on this planet. There, I said it. A towering blue oasis of hope among a desert of dreariness, it achieves something that has become so very scarce in the last 70 years: it looks great from any angle, and in any weather and at any time of the day. That's the measure of a building but nowadays it's as rare as a dinosaur steak. Contemporary buildings are generally designed with only a couple of flattering angles that look good in the brochure, one of which is invariably from way up in the air, and what use is that to anyone who doesn't have a helicopter? But the Eureka cheers me up whenever I see it, morning, noon or night. I'm also interested to go inside, as it is home to Skydeck 88, which is a viewing platform on the 88th floor – the highest in the Southern Hemisphere – and not an 80s themed disco as I originally imagined (they may want to consider rebranding that one). As if that wasn't enough they've added an 'Edge', a three metre all-glass cube that projects from the Tower, leaving you suspended 300m above the South Bank as if floating on air. I've no head for heights, but I'm willing to give it a go, even if I'm a little worried that they close it in high winds. If it's liable to blow off, it doesn't sound like it's strong enough to stand on in the first place.

If you look hard enough there are a few diamonds in the coal seam. One such is the Royal Exhibition Building. It stands next to the Melbourne Museum, with tasteful old gardens alongside, and beside it a water-eroded sandstone fountain of fantastic sculpted design. The fountain alone is a precious gem, my favourite in the entire world, but even without that it's a majestic old pile, and one of the last of its kind. Opened in 1880 and missing a couple of parts due to fire, it survives as one of the few remaining Exhibition Halls from the century that invented the idea. A slumbering beauty from an age of elegance, now alone in the city with only its memories for company, like the oldest resident of a care-home. I walk round it, and yes, from any angle it's just great.

Shamefully the same can't be said about the accompanying Museum, which from the outside is a dog's dinner. It has its colourful moments, but again it's 80% 'death-grey', the pallor of someone with lead poisoning. How ironic that the dead lead factory looks so healthy and everything living looks so ill. It's obviously not a cheap building, just conceived by an impoverished imagination. I've absolutely no idea what's inside it; it is 5.02pm and so closed for the day. It was the same story in Perth and I missed all the galleries there; it's such back to front thinking. Whether a tourist or a resident on their day off, in the morning you want to be out running errands or exploring, and it's not till the day starts to ebb that you're ready for some relaxed culture, but by then the museums are all bloody shut. I can't single out Australia here, nearly every gallery in the world is open but empty at nine, and then closed by five, when millions are finished with work and seeking distraction. Small wonder everyone ends up slumped in front of the TV watching documentaries about museum's collections instead. Do they have to be so stuck in the past? Would it kill them to open 12-8 instead?

Mostly though, Melbourne is as grey, grey, grey as a Norman Foster theme-park. I already thought it was drab, but when I hit the recently redeveloped docks I'm appalled, it's one of the most repugnant areas imaginable. They are not short-of-cash bad, or we've-let-it-rot bad – both of which are ostensibly worse – they're pots-of-cash-but-we-built-this-already-outdated-dreary-pile-of-junk bad. Imagine an unbroken sea of all the blandest, harshest modernism, altogether in a heap and completely dead by six o' clock; right, you've got it: welcome to Melbourne Docklands. I'm hugely disappointed. I thought this was the cultural capital? I thought it was once Australia's first city? Where the hell has it gone?

I wander rather mournfully back into town and finally find some bright vitality in the streets, courtesy of Chinatown. It hardly screams Australia but Melbourne's Chinatown is one of the biggest in the world and apparently does some of the best food you can get, so I'll be keen to come back here at least. But the legs are getting sore, so I speed my journey home by hopping a tram along Elizabeth Street for a few blocks. As you know, I'm no tram-spotter but I like trams a lot; they have a charm to them. Yet when this one draws up I have to question my loyalty. It's a rickety, crumbling old boneshaker that only a Melbournian could be proud of and not only has it not been painted this century, but it comes in this season's colour: grey sky grey. They sure know how to sell themselves in this town.

Chapter 34
PARKS
(Friday 24th Dec)

On December 24th I'm usually on a train to Scotland, or running round Oxford Street like a headless chicken trying to find something, anything, my girlfriend will approve of as a present. Either women are hard to please, or I'm rubbish at presents, but if you're not happy with an illustrated history of the Scottish Premier League, what's the matter with you? This year I'm spared the ordeal of both a packed train and a shopping-frenzy, as I'm heading out to meet up with an old friend from London, who doesn't expect anything more from life than a slap in the face: Scottish Dave. 'Scottish Dave' is a nickname his American ex-girlfriend gave him; I'm hoping affectionately, and not to differentiate him from her other boyfriends called Dave. Really he should be called Dissatisfied Dave or Furious Dave, as he must be the most permanently irritable man presently in Australia. Nothing is ever good enough for him anywhere he goes, and as I wait outside his hotel, I'm certain he'll have complaints about that too.

'Cheer up Stuart, you must be the grumpiest man in Australia!'

'Me? What about you?'

'I'm an optimist, I believe things can always be better. You're just miserable.'

'Thanks Dave, Merry Christmas to you too.'

'Oh yeah. Merry Christmas. Forgot about that.'

'How's the hotel?'

'Excellent.'

'Really?'

'Yeah. Except for the corpse of an enormous spider in the light fitting casting a huge bat-signal-like shadow over the bed, that's a bit creepy.'

'Really?'

'Yup'

'Are you sure it's dead?'

'Well the bugger didn't move for an hour with the light on, and I'm sure as hell not going to unscrew it and find out.'

'What if it's gone when you come home?'

'Then I'm moving home.'

'What if hides in your suitcase?'

'Don't scare me on this beautiful day.'

'Beautiful? ... Are you feeling okay?'

Dave's unexpected light mood is because he's planned the itinerary, and he has a special treat in store for me. He's a great fan of Formula 1, whereas I prefer sport. A multiple fantasy-league winner, he hasn't missed a race in years, whereas I still prefer sport. I try to convey this to him but he's sadistically determined to convert me, so our first stop is Albert Park, home of the Australian Grand Prix. We jump the tram southwards, with me nudging him all the way.

'Look, Dave, there's a man driving a tram! Let's see who wins, him or the tram behind.'

'They can't pass, Stuart.'

'I know! Exactly! Come on, let's watch this for two hours.'

'There's a lot of subtleties involved in Formula 1—'

'Yes, some of them are painted red, some of them are painted blue—'

'Some of the cars are very different, there can be a couple of tenths of a second per lap between them.'

'That much!? Dave, there's a new shiny tram, do you reckon he'll be two-tenths faster to the park than this one?'

I manage to keep this up for at least ten minutes before we jump off our tatty grey steed at the bottom of Elizabeth Street and switch to a Ferrari-Tram for the run over the Yarra and down the St. Kilda Road to the venue. Venue is perhaps not the right word, as it's just a regular old park, albeit a nice one with a lake and some great views of the city skyline.

'Dave, where's the track?'

'Um... it's... it's here somewhere...'

'Where?'

'I think we're standing on it.'

'What?'

'I'm not sure, it looks different on the TV'

'Is this it?'

'Maybe over this way...'

We end up on a dirt track beside the lake.

'I don't think they come this way Dave'

'Yes, yes, but over that way...'

After another fifteen minutes of this we find a bit of kerb and a run off area and establish that yes, we have indeed been walking the track all this time. I'm delighted.

'How many times have you watched this race?'

'One or two...'

'What's the name of that corner?'

'Um... it's er... it's not quite like I imagined it, Stuart.'

'Funny. It's exactly as I imagined it. It's a bit of road.'

'Yeah, just picture it Stu, just picture two cars coming down here wheel to wheel at 180mph—'

'Spoil a nice park probably. I thought Melbourne was meant to be one of the really glamorous venues, one of ones the drivers loved because it's chic and not stuck in the middle of a forest?'

'Well, I guess they dress her up a bit. You can do a lot with lights and make-up. Just look at Kylie.'

'Kylie's gorgeous.'

'Alright, look at Danni.'

'She's very pretty too, I certainly would—'

'She's not bad for a bloke, I grant you, but the camera always lies.'

'—be proud... Can we go now?'

'Okay.'

'Quack!' The contribution from the duck was the smartest thing anyone had said all day.

We head back the way we came on foot and stop off at the Shrine of Remembrance that stands in Kings Domain. Kings Domain is a pretty grand name for a park and Melbourne's war memorial is pretty grand. It's another spectacular tribute to the fallen, a huge ziggurat that towers over you. It took seven long years to build, and tragically only five years after it was finished Australia was back in another war. Imposing, but suitably solemn from the outside, the shrine inside is a moving place of contemplation. I take off my cap and straighten my trousers before going past the gent at the door to pay my respects. It's saddening to see the obligatory brash Spaniards in front of me, wandering in chewing gum and chattering and flash photographing that which really should not be photographed. While I do generally like the Spanish, as they're a lot more fun and less judgemental than the British, they can take crass to a new level when it comes to tourism: the Japanese don't know; the Spanish don't seem to care.

I escape to the crypt for a moment's reflection; the lists of units and hanging colours seem from a far more distant age, but the sense of permanence is deeply touching; nothing is forgotten down here. Up for some air, I join Dave on the roof, and though hardly the point, the view from the top of the monument over the ornamental garden and back to the city is one of the best urban panoramas in Australia. Go, pay your respects and savour the experience. If I have one complaint it's that, while perfectly maintained, it's been left behind by the city beside it. Having constructed something so majestic it's shameful that Melbourne's town planners have let the neighbouring district do what the hell it likes. The busy road and ugly, unsympathetic developments that run alongside do the memorial no justice at all. But then that's partly a tribute to its magnificence. The constant traffic that streams past the puny little Cenotaph in Whitehall are hardly ideal either, and who notices? London swallowed St. Paul's whole, but with so much space and a clean slate I had expected Australia to do better, but it's too much to hope for; the fault is not Melbourne's it is man's.

Back outside and there's a host of excellent statues scattered around the surrounding grounds. If there's one thing Australia does well it is sculptures. There are dozens of them throughout the cities, and they're mostly very original and attractive, and add greatly to the street scenes. Perth was outstanding in that regard and had the most incredible collection, they were everywhere and I lost count. Melbourne is no slouch either, and those by the war memorial don't let us down: they're splendid and run the gamut from stirring to poignant. If you see only one thing in this town, the shrine and its surrounding sculpture should be it.

We retreat from the noise of the St. Kilda Road and Dave drags me over to the Royal Botanical Gardens, something of which he professes to be a connoisseur. My grasp of botany is non-existent, so I ask his expert opinion.

'Oh I haven't a bloody clue, Stuart, I just like green stuff.'

'I thought you said your sister and brother-in-law were botanists?'

'They mostly studied mould. This lot's a bit big for them; wouldn't fit under the microscope.'

'I thought your mother knew every plant in Scotland?'

'Yes, but it never really features in the conversation.'

'Don't you know anything about this stuff?'

'Bits and pieces; I've picked a little up over the years.'

'Okay, what's this?'

'That's a tree, Stuart.'

'I know it's a tree; what kind of tree?'

'It's a big tree, Stuart, a very big tree. Nice isn't it?'

He had a point. I may not be able to tell a dahlia from an azalea, but the Botanic gardens are a leafy, flowery, bee-buzzy haven with plenty of interest even to the uneducated flora-palate. Just as I'm thinking this we pass a large sign saying '*Caution, bees are active in this area*'.

'Bloody hell, how dangerous are the bees in Australia? I thought it was the spiders we had to watch out for?'

'Some people are allergic, Dave.'

'Some people are thick if they don't expect bees on flowers.'

'Health and safety? Maybe they can be held legally responsible for the bees?'

'It's not that dangerous; it's not like they're working overhead.'

It's a sad indictment of a city if bees are such a rarity, and certainly I didn't see any more in my week here. We leave the gardens and walk up to Linlithgow Avenue, one of the unnecessary roads running through the small park. For a city that shouts about its trams, Melbournians are way too addicted to their cars. With so little greenery around, it's perverse to hand it over to the gas-guzzlers; what are these roads even serving? In answer, we pass the Sidney Myer Music Bowl, which opened in 1959, when car ownership started to boom. It's a great facility to have, but Australia is hardly short of land; surely if you want an open air music venue (and who doesn't?) you build one somewhere else, and plant some new trees around it; don't dump it in the middle of the city's most precious organ – its old wheezing lungs – and trample the precious parkland to dust.

'I suppose it helps keep the bees down,' remarks Dave, a die-hard opponent of gigs in city parks, 'You can't be too careful.' Dave's mood is darkening in tandem with his skin, as his cheap sunblock has rubbed off in places and he's managed to burn himself for the fourth time since he arrived in Australia. 'Where are the signs warning me the sun's active in this area Stuart? I've a good mind to sue.'

'Who? The park authorities or the suncream manufacturers?'

My spirits are sinking as well; I've got a problem too. I'm limping quite badly because the tendons or ligaments or some other stringy bits in my ankles, which have been hurting like hell these last two days, have suddenly and dramatically got worse; much worse. In fact I'm in absolute agony. We pause by a handsome and convenient statue of Queen Victoria – there's always one around in Australia when you need it – and I take some painkillers, but there's no way I can go on. I'd been enjoying today, but enough's enough; so Dave goes to hide from the Celt-hating-sun and I hobble uncomfortably homewards.

On the way, another side of Melbourne re-presents itself. While exploring yesterday, my own feelings towards the city may have been adversely coloured because I'd inexplicably felt myself to be in a somewhat hostile environment. It wasn't just the buildings I found unsympathetic, my view was being prejudiced by the people. Wonderful hotel staff excluded, everyone seemed so physically confrontational and prickly; even their hair was uniformly spiky. When you walk through a town, rather than simply drive to a destination, you get an awareness of the mind-set of a place, and my spider-senses were telling me that Melbourne was thinking distinctly chippy thoughts. This was reinforced when some loudmouth shouted aggressively at me in the street for no reason whatsoever, but at the time I had shrugged it off. Today though, things just get worse.

First I ride the tram back. It's a brand new tram, gleaming in the sun, and at this time of day filled with office workers on their way home. There are smart suits and shirts-sleeves, and me, and next to me, six teenagers, swigging booze hidden in paper bags. Classy. One casually produces a large drill-bit and begins carving his name into the middle door post. What the hell? I've lived in London for twenty years and have never seen a 16 year old vandalise a bus or a train filled with people at 6pm. But nobody bats an eyelid, nobody does a thing, and Michelangelo goes on with his masterwork. He's two feet away from me and I reckon one unexpected blow to his face might alter the game, but there are six of them and he's holding a sharp implement. Admittedly two of them are girls, but they actually look meaner than the boys. None of them are exactly tough – they're not 6'3" with six-packs like some of the adolescents in Brixton – they're just little Nintendo pricks with the Melbourne mullet and sagging jeans. Maybe I should just punch him and see if anyone joins in. I don't. My excuse for my cowardice is that my legs are in a bad way, and it's not my city to defend; but really I'm scared of trying four plus two against one; I'm just a scrawny little writer. What's the excuse of the large muscled Aussie Rules aficionados around me?

I get off the tram in a foul mood and reckon I can just about make it to the shop for an over-priced bottle of wine to kill the pain and wash the experience away. But within yards two blokes in their twenties take it upon themselves to follow me up the street. They start laughing and shouting at my limping steps.

'Call that a bloody walk mate? What's f*****g wrong with you?'

I'm not dressed in anything that would identify me as an England fan. I'm in old clothes, and even my little camera is hidden in a tatty old bag I brought deliberately to not stand out, so I look as untouristy as possible; there's no reason I should be considered 'the enemy'. Nor is there any reason to assume that my limp is not a permanent affliction, but these boys don't care, they just want their little lives to feel big and the disabled are an easy target.

'Jesus, look at you mate, your f*****g leg's wonky!'

I give up on the wine and head straight to the hotel.

'We're f*****g talking to you mate!'

They're larger than the kids on the tram and I don't fancy my chances in a confrontation, albeit neither would last two seconds with any of the people of my acquaintance that I consider to be hard. The difference is that none of those people would ever act like this, who the hell does? Thankfully I've reached the hotel so I abandon the wine-run and leave them to their pea-brained entertainment of imitated limps and ape-like gesturing. Then the penny drops and I realise what's been troubling me all along.

Melbourne is a large city of nearly four million people, but it has the mentality and manners of a parochial little town. The nice people are especially well-mannered, but they live alongside the louts and the thugs. I'd expect courteous drivers in the countryside, and be unsurprised by random abuse from yokels after the village fete, or threats in the streets of post-industrial ghost towns. I'm just totally unprepared for it anywhere that might be called cosmopolitan, and has things to do after dark other than glue-sniff.

The inhabitants seem defensive and their style is small-town too: boys with spiky mini-mullets and heavy metal T-shirts, girls with postures like tortoises.   Even the middle-class office workers look brittle: women with severe short hair cuts and shoes so bad they're trying too hard from both ends; men who dress like players, who want to be in the *Financial Times*, but somehow it comes out like the *Lowestoft Gazette*. Nobody is at ease with themselves. Everyone and everything in this city is trying to compete with an unseen opponent and getting it wrong – it's like they're speaking a language they've learned from a book but refusing any native who corrects them – and then pretending they're not even trying.

There's no doubt about it, so far I'm very disappointed. Every time there's an up it's followed by a down. I thought Melbourne was going to be the highlight of the trip, but so far it's not working out between us.

Chapter 35
CHRISTMAS
(Friday 24th – Saturday 25th Dec)

In my early teens I embarked on a crusade against one of the most powerful companies on the planet. It wasn't much of a campaign, all I did was write one angry letter, but that's a lot of effort for someone who's asleep sixteen hours a day. My letter was to the Walt Disney Corporation and accused them of blatant racism. The specific cause of my ire was one of their lesser-known creations: Scrooge McDuck. Throughout my upbringing I had enjoyed and sometimes endured their various cartoons, from Goofy to Huey, Dewey and Louie, I'd run the gamut of emotion, but at no time did Donald Duck speak with a Scottish accent. Admittedly his elocution bore more than a passing resemblance to a Glaswegian leaving the bar on a Saturday night, but the diction was ultimately unCaledonian.

Furthermore, even at 13, I was familiar enough with Dickens to have sussed that Ebenezer Scrooge was not intended to be a Scot either, any more than the Ghost of Marley was meant to be a Rastafarian. So my question was straightforward: when two non-Scottish fictional characters collide why does he have a Scottish accent unless you're seeking to stereotype us as a bunch of skinflints? Clearly the Walt Disney Corporation was racist and I was going to voice my displeasure. I received no reply, just a stony corporate silence. This may be because I finished the letter with a cheeky attempt at international diplomacy, assuring them I wouldn't take my concerns to the United Nations if they provided me with an all-expenses holiday to Disney World. Or more likely they never even received it as I didn't put enough stamps on to cover the postage to California.

Looking back, in early middle-age, I may have been a little premature in my outrage. Not because I think we're a miserly nation of cheapskates, but because these days I'd rather like a role-model to aspire to. I used to love Christmas in the 70s, it was the decade that perfectly merged the innocence and devotion of the past, with just enough proto-consumerism and TV specials to keep a teenager happy. But these days it's all run to seed and there is so much to dislike I lose count: the Christmas shopping starts in September, everyone expects presents and no-one's happy with an orange or a tangerine, spoilt screaming kids screaming for ever more and receiving ever more without even a 'waste not want not' cliché attached, fat people getting fatter, drinkers getting drunker, the joy of Christmas cards replaced with the irritation of round-robin emails in the inbox, office parties full of fat slags and lecherous married men, family get-togethers full of … well… families, and everyone but everyone enforcing jollility with the inevitable, 'Come on!! It's Chriiiiiiiiisssssstmaaaaas.' As far as I'm concerned, only Noddy Holder should be allowed to utter those two words, and even then I wish he'd put a sock in it two years out of every three. With all that unnecessary stress and pressure, it's no surprise the suicide rate intensifies over the festive season. As far as celebrations go it's only slightly less lethal than the old Aztec festival of the dead.

But thus far, I've felt Australians do Christmas properly. I greatly preferred Perth's approach to anywhere I've seen in Britain. Melbourne appears to have an altogether different, but equally effective approach – it completely ignores it. Walking around town these last few days, apart from a couple of window displays here, a scruffy tree there, and a dab of tinsel in Bourke Street, you'd be hard pressed to notice anything much was happening. Christmas just doesn't seem to be that big of a deal. My hotel has not marked the occasion in any way, there's not even a free mince pie to be had. In one sense I like this, as I don't feel that I'm missing out on anything by being here among strangers. Whether it's because Jack Frost isn't nipping at their noses or their chestnuts aren't roasting on an open fire, yuletide celebrations in Victoria are as low-key as the North of Scotland Stony-Face Championships.

There's no midnight mass or final fling for me on Christmas Eve, instead, I am in my hotel room watching a re-run of the 1984 Australian Rules football Grand Final between Essendon and Hawthorn. When I play Scrooge, I take it to a new level. Essendon won that thrilling match, and as exciting as Aussie Rules is, it is equally enthralling for me to see the MCG as it once was. The stadium looks very old-fashioned and puts me in mind of my trips to Hampden in the 80s, where you were so crammed in you spent as much time making sure you weren't being urinated on as watching the action on the pitch. Both have been extensively developed since then, but whereas Hampden's capacity was decimated to 55,000 and the Hampden roar was never heard so fully again, the MCG fell from 125,000 to 97,000, which is still formidable number of spectators. I already can't wait to take my seat.

I channel flick with the sound down till I doze off, awakening early on Christmas Day to see the Queen staring at me disapprovingly. Or maybe she always looks like that. Hang on, that can't be right, is she giving out her favourite recipe for fruit cake? No: I flick the volume up and she is delivering her annual address to the Commonwealth. It's not even Christmas Day yet in Britain, they're still hanging their stockings and lying to their children, and here she is letting the Aussies into the secrets first. I have a good mind to phone my Dad in Arbroath and tell him what she says. It would spoil it for him, but at least the rest of the family would finally get to watch the Simpsons this year, instead of another account of 'That Was The Royal Year That Was'. Ultimately, like Ebenezer, I'm too mean to make the call, and leave him with his cherished illusion that the Queen is speaking personally to him, live on the big day.

Normally by noon on Christmas I'd have eaten an entire box of Black Magic and be finding a new excuse for not doing a jigsaw with my relatives. I shouldn't need an excuse, other than an aversion to counting down the seconds till my death, puzzling over small pieces of cardboard sky, but still they harass me. Thankfully no justifications are needed today, as I'm meeting Dave for lunch and I highly doubt he packed a jigsaw of Edinburgh Castle in his luggage. We've arranged to meet at Flinders Street Train Station, which apparently is a cliché as old as Melbourne, but who are we to break with convention? The Station is an impressive structure, built in a time when the railways were critical to a city's development. This is Melbourne's restored King's Cross if not quite its St. Pancras; it can't reach that level of grandeur, but it's a good effort. Bookended by domes, with a clock tower in the middle, the red brick and golden cream stucco facade stretches two city blocks; so it's unfortunate I didn't say where exactly by the station I'd meet him. Five minutes wandering is rewarded; I just follow the stream of invective to its source.

'Is it just me Stuart, or is this place reminiscent of a film set?'

'It's just you, it's always just you.'

'I'm serious. Look at the scale of the facade, it's magnificent, but there's nothing behind it, it's like cut-out of a train station.' I can see what he means. It's half Victorian, half wild-west. 'I keep expecting to step out onto Flinders Street and see a bunch of cowboys coming down it, ready to draw their guns.'

'Alright, Wyatt Earp, let's find a saloon.'

We leave the station then wander ever more listlessly round the neighbouring streets. Offices and shops are all shut, people are sparse, and without apparent signs of Christmas it's all for no obvious reason. The resultant atmosphere is more like a summer Bank Holiday Monday in a provincial backwater, or possibly the aftermath of a Triffid attack. There's so little buzz my usual cynicism is completely out of place and rather affected; you can't resent Christmas when there's no Christmas to resent. After twenty minutes of this we accept defeat and head for another old Melbourne institution. It's into Subway for 6" subs and a crap coffee for Christmas lunch. Here at least the season of goodwill is in the air, but I'm still determined to resist.

'Hello Sir, do you want a free cookie?'

'No.'

'Yes.'

'Free cookie sir! Special for Christmas!'

'No, thank you'

'Yes, please.'

'You don't want one, Sir?'

'No.'

'Yes, he does.'

'No, I really don't.'

'Yes, he really does!' Dave settles matters by taking and eating my cookie as well as his own.

'There! Merry Christmas. Don't say I never get you anything.'

'Best present I've had this year, Stuart.'

Cookies aside, I have a dilemma. I've been invited by text for a Chinese meal '*tonight*' by the two ladies whom I'd met in Perth. Typically weirdly, their Brit-phone hadn't been able to connect in any way to my new Aussie mobile, so they've sent the message – not to the seed-jammed and only intermittently functioning Blackberry – but to my old dumbphone that's not been charged since Perth. I've been keeping it switched off and only checking occasionally for messages. But what with the difference in time-zones, taking the battery on and off, and swapping different simcards in and out, the clock has gone haywire and shows 'middle of the ocean' time. The message is bewilderingly time-stamped '4:37am', but I can't tell if that's when it was sent or when it arrived today, whether it relates to UK or Oz time, or to the phone's 4:37am – which by my calculations would make it tomorrow, but I may be wrong on that. How best to respond? If I accept and it was for yesterday, apart from looking foolish, I'll embarrass my prospective hosts by forcing them to uninvite me on Christmas Day; if I don't reply or decline, I appear rude and miss a nice dinner with interesting people whom I really want to interview.

'What should I do Dave?'

'It's a problem'

'That's why I asked you.'

'Don't ask me.'

'I'm asking you, who else can I ask in here?'

We both glance around at the assembled faces, all (save ourselves) inscrutable members of the local Chinese community, each equipped with a free cookie.

'Wise men, Stuart, have come from the east; it's a sign.'

'I don't suppose my fortune was written in those cookies you ate?'

'Not unless your fortune lies in chocolate chips.'

In any case I take it as an omen and accept the invitation, and we head out to find a pub – some place more interesting than another dull hotel bar. We try our luck in the town centre. Nothing doing. Round and round and round we go, till at last we find one that's open. There's a queue outside, even though we can see through the windows that inside it's only just half full.

'They must be waiting for something else, Stuart'

'Is this the…?'

'That's the queue, mate!'

'You're kidding?'

'Do I look like I'm kidding?'

'How many guesses do we get?'

I'd love to say we got a witty reply, something about only good boys and girls getting in, but this is Australia; they don't do wit, and Dave's comment is too subtle for a bouncer.

'I'm not bloody kidding, mate.'

'No worries, mate' I reply, in an effort to blend in. We beat a retreat, unwilling to stand in line in the cold, while the staff figure out that people brushing shoulders inside might not be life-threatening.

What now? The Barmy Army have a Christmas bash on, but we didn't get tickets as neither of us were in the mood for Christmas classics and total excess. Plus we wanted a break from the cricket conversation and blogging. A nice laid back day-off, free from responsibility and hype, and with a few innocent hi-jinks thrown in; is that so much to ask? The Melbourne tradition is to hit St. Kilda, but it's already 3pm and the weather is closing in. It's grey and miserable and starting to rain, I can't imagine there are many having barbies on the beach today. Worse, all the walking of the last two weeks has been too much for me. I'm still hobbling badly and when I take my shoe off I find my two pairs of socks (for added padding) are soaked through with blood. Anywhere in the world, if but two Scotsmen are gathered together they shall bring gloom and bad-luck upon one another. Since I'm nearly back at my hotel and I might be going out for a Chinese later, we agree to call it quits for the day and head to our respective homes.

The shops are shutting, off-sales are off-limits. How crucial was my decision to abandon the quest for wine yesterday, when I was assailed in the street? Oh to be in London with its the illegal under the counter booze sales, 365 days a year. I'm missing a proper White Christmas back in Scotland, with deep, deep snow all around and fresh snow falling – the heaviest since 1962. My best friend later tells me it's the most beautiful Christmas he's ever seen in his life, and he ends up snowbound for three days, trapped inside with a mountain of food and wine. Whereas after a shower and applying some plasters, I'm back in bed with the curtains drawn against the rain, watching the all-day Simpsons' special with nothing but a cup of tea and a biscuit to kill the pain. It's not exactly the antipodean idyll I imagined. My dumbphone beeps, now on its last unchargeable bar of battery; the Chinese invitation was on UK time, it was for last night. I'm high and dry for the evening, with only a loaf of bread and some Tasty* cheese in the fridge. Merry Christmas. Or as Scrooge McDuck might put it, 'Bah Humbug, Jimmy.'

---

* The Australian name for their nasty version of cheddar, and a bigger lie than pretending it's from Somerset.

Chapter 36
FOURTH TEST, DAY ONE
BOXING DAY
(Sunday 26th Dec)

This is it. I'm finally here. Whatever happened, with or without limps and assaults, fair weather or foul, I was not going to miss today. The Boxing Day Test match at the MCG, one of the most iconic sports events on the planet. To think, the number of times I've watched this match on TV at the end of a Christmas Day in freezing cold Arbroath and said, 'I wish I was there.' Who says wishes don't come true?

'I wish I had bionic eyes. I could be the third umpire, I could come to every match and they could refer decisions to me.' The bloke behind me might be out of luck on that one, but it took me 35 years of waiting, so you never know what the future holds.

'Most blokes your age are wishing for a bionic penis...' opines his neighbour. Stop spoiling it! Listen, the important thing is that I'm finally here. A world record crowd is predicted to be heading to the ground, the standing room is all sold and even with the cooler weather of Victoria, things are coming to the boil. It's make or break for both teams in front of the biggest crowd of them all, and there's nowhere to hide.

Actually there are plenty of places to hide; while rather grotty, the MCG has quite extensive internal areas out of the arena where you can squirrel away from the sun and crowds, but that's no good for the man next to me, he has a scorecard to keep and has to watch every single ball; he's glued to that seat for the next seven hours. Yes, I'm back with my old mucker from Adelaide, Lionel, but this morning he does not seem happy.

'What's up?' I ask genially, my previous woes all forgotten with the excitement.

'I don't like crowds.'

Here we are, 89,999 excited cricket fans in a densely packed concrete bowl, and 1 cricket fan who doesn't like crowds.

'I hate to break this to you... I'm not sure you've chosen the right match.'

'Yeah, yeah.'

'Have you ever considered watching Arbroath?'

'I'm fine when I'm sat down, I just don't like moving in crowds.'

'So stage-diving into the mosh-pit at a rock gig?'

'No!'

'What about the Toyko underground? The people aren't moving... relative to each other...'

'Can you stop talking about crowds?'

'Sorry. I'll just sit here... and count bodies... one... two...'

'Tis the morning after Christmas, and all through the MCG not a soul is dozing that's for sure. Nor are we wearing our new Christmas jumpers, although it's none too toasty, so for once I wouldn't have minded getting one. As Lionel and I settle ourselves and open the crisps, the big news is that Bresnan is playing in place of the exhausted, top-wicket taker, Finn. It's a grievous loss but perhaps he wouldn't be so tired if he'd had a fifth bowler to share his labours... just saying. But cometh the hour, cometh the man, and the stage is set for Swann to bowl a full day on a pitch that should suit him. The MCG curator (groundsman to you and I) has said the most successful teams here have always had variety in their attack. Unquestionably Swann's performance of the Sprinkler belongs on the Royal Variety Show, but I'm not convinced that's what he meant.

Australia are revitalised but unchanged: Ponting is passed fit to play after all and their Perth pace attack is retained despite its homogeneity and the slow pitch. They'll have to wait their turn as England have won the toss and are bowling first in overcast conditions: the selfsame gamble as at Perth. It's brave stuff, but they're determined to polish the Aussies off this time. Will the Baggy Greens try to force the pace and slip up? First day over-ambition has been the downfall of many a team at the MCG.

Australia are unchanged in more ways than one. Not only is their team identical, but as soon as play gets underway they begin to collapse in the same old manner. Again, Tremlett strikes first, but here at the MCG the Aussie roar to greet Ponting's arrival is absolutely immense, no English boos could possibly be heard above it. Only one cricket ground in the world sounds like this. Will 70,000 on-side voices lift the skipper?

Tremlett leaves the field, and a frisson of worry ripples through the England faithful. Have the selectors blundered and left England short of bowlers again? Reassuringly, Bresnan demonstrates why he should have played in the last match, bowling fast and grabbing a wicket almost immediately. Ponting responds confidently, blasting Anderson for some meaty boundaries. And then relief all-round, Tremlett returns. It was clearly just a loo-break and it did him good: he takes the ball and sends Sir Ricky packing. Better out than in, I say.

It's obvious that the rain is coming and it will give Australia time to regroup, but their hearts must sink when Mike Hussey is out just two balls before it starts to fall. Australia are 58 for 4, and with Boy Scout Smith at the wicket and Mr. Cricket toasting muffins in the pavilion, their batting is looking desperately thin. When the drops start to pitter-patter down, the players slope off, and I start collecting clichés for the lunchtime blog: 'It's the Boxing Day Test, England have the Aussies on the ropes and are hoping to deliver a knockout punch...' Come on, what do you expect at short notice, Proust?

England's bowlers seem to be more than enough so far, but we've been here before, ten days ago Australia were 68 for 5. However, there are crucial differences: Anderson will be over his jet-lag, Bresnan has fresh legs and, most importantly, the conditions are more or less English. It's cool and breezy, less than half the temperature it was in Perth, perfect for the seamers and far easier to play in all day without wilting. Even so, it might yet play out the same; I'm counting no fowl of any kind.

The rain continues and it gets windier and colder, all we need is a vague smell of smoked fish and I'd be back in Arbroath. Right now, I'd sooner be at home in the snow, haddock and all, at least it's pretty, whereas this is solely bleak. Whenever I've watched this match over the years it has always been played against a backdrop of glorious conditions; what's going on? It's like ordering your weather online, and then finding it doesn't look like it did in the catalogue. The irony of being out-doors in the rain, when normally I'm indoors watching sunshine on TV, is not lost on me.

I've arranged to meet Dave at lunchtime, which is unlikely to brighten things up and will further reinforce the similarity with home. Anticipating that we'd be amongst 90,000 or so others, I've specified we meet by one of the fine bronze statues of legendary cricketers and 'Rules footballers that dot the outer pedestrian concourse surrounding the MCG: I've chosen Keith Miller to be precise. I'm there as planned but there is no sign of Dave, which is unusual as he is normally as punctual as Mr Seiko. After ten minutes I receive a phone call.

'Where the hell are you? It's bloody Baltic out here!'

'I'm leaning against the Keith Miller statue!'

'So am I.'

'I can't see you…'

'Oh— wait—'

The phone goes dead. A minute later Dave joins me. He's been leaning against Don Bradman. Dave unquestionably knows a thing or two about the game, and yet here he is mistaking the greatest batsman of all-time for a statue of a fast bowler. 'Miller, Bradman, what's the difference? They both looked like they were bloody cold to me. Not a brass bollock on any of them'

I allow him the mistake as he has been caught off-guard by the climatic shift and is standing shivering in a vest and shorts. 'Don't you have a jumper?'

'I thought it would get warmer through the day, you know, mad-dogs and all that?'

'It's not a tour of India.'

'You've not seen the toilets yet.'

We head back inside, out of the weather and into the milling crowds, to wander around the bowels of the MCG, sharing our opinions on it. Having also misjudged the distance to the ground, Dave was late in and missed the first wickets, consequently he's in a characteristically charitable mood. I think it is an undeniably impressive venue with great views of the action, being here has lifted my spirits, but the C in the title is a little misleading: it's not a cricket ground, it's just a sports stadium. If anything it's an Australian Rules football ground more than a cricket ground.

'Well I think it's a crap-hole.' Grumpy is in fine form. 'If Albert Speer had batted at three, this is the stadium he'd have designed...' Notwithstanding Dave's more forthright views on concrete as a building medium, neither of us can deny our delight at being here for the Boxing Day match, it's something to remember in the years to come. We vow to keep our tickets as mementoes. 'Stuart, it'll remind me of the day I paid to freeze my tits off in a half-finished 1960's tower-block. It just needs some dog turds on the outfield to complete the effect.'

I accept it's not the prettiest, but the flood of people is bringing it to life: like London's South Bank on a Sunday (and with weather to match). By now we're standing by a merchandise stand and Dave is gazing wistfully at extra clothing. He's still talking, but this time to keep himself warm; like Tam O' Shanter's wife, he is great at nursing his wrath to provide extra heat.

'The question is Stuart, do I show loyalty while we're here and buy Barmy Army gear, even though it's all u—'

'Well—'

'... Do I buy Australian gear as a souvenir, even though it's all g—'

'Well—'

'Or do I tell the jackals to shove it and go home for a top?'

'Why don't you buy Barmy Army gear as a souvenir?'

'But I'll never wear it again.'

'Why not?'

'You can't wear England kit in England!'

'Can't you?'

'Everyone will think I'm English.'

'Good point.'

We agree that genuinely would be beyond the pale.

'Only place I could wear that would be in Old Compton Street after dark.' As usual Dave's line of conversation is beyond most people's pale. 'No, what I really want would be a nice bit of West Indian kit; I like maroon, it's a gentleman's colour. And the kit of choice for a man of my physique.'

'What? Small, scrawny and pasty white?'

'I was referring to the trouser region.'

'Aha.'

The rain has abated, but in other regards the weather continues to get worse. The temperature drops to only 12C, colder than England ever is in its equivalent June; this is like early March in Grimsby. With play scheduled to resume shortly, Dave makes his mind up and regretfully heads back to his hotel for the free clothing option. 'I've got a fleece in South African green, they can't argue with that.'

He'll need it by the time he returns, as there will soon be one at the crease. Foolish, foolish boy, he left the decision too long and misses the first thrilling hour of play after it resumes. England come out of the traps like greyhounds: mean greyhounds, intent on kicking hell out of the rabbits that ran them ragged last time. They'd already disposed of their chief tormentor Hussey, and more quick wickets ensure that the other thorns in their paws from Perth – Haddin, Johnson and Siddle – are all back in the pavilion before Hussey's muffins are even buttered. When Johnson lands a four ball duck the Barmy Army, out-gunned four to one, roar with a ferocity that practically rivals the Australians.

In only 17 overs after lunch, the last 6 wickets fall, and it's all over before the kettle's boiled. England dropped two catches and lost both their umpire referrals, but the Aussies have resembled headless turkeys all day. When the last of the leftovers, Hilfenhaus, trudges back to the tunnel the Australian total stands at 98; their lowest ever score against England at the MCG. 98; which apart from a disaster in Manchester in the 1950s, is their worst Ashes score in 98 years. And Dave managed to miss most of it for want of an extra layer, which does little to lift his spirits.

He's not the only one in the doldrums. At the start of the innings the atmosphere had been sensational, the Australian crowd deafening, but as the wickets tumbled the Aussie fans fell quiet and clearer and clearer we heard Billy the Trumpet bugling England onwards; like their batsmen the Aussie fans had no answer to the onslaught. They're now feeling their hangovers and are sitting quietly chastened, like schoolboys told off for running in the corridors.

The official attendance is announced at 84,344; we've just missed the world record and I won't make it into Guinness after all. Looking across the ground it's plain to see that every corner is completely jam-packed, except one barren area. Once again the members haven't shown up and the best seats in the house remain empty. If a crucial Ashes encounter on a national holiday isn't enough to bring them out, they need shooting.

But on the bright side, at last the sun comes out; making a mockery of Dave's newly sported fleece, and driving him into further paroxysms of irony-driven fury. In suddenly perfect batting conditions England sail on without a care in the world, and yet more Australians stream out the gates. This time there's been no psychological blow of an Australian fight back, and on a less bouncy pitch they cruise past Australia's total and reach 157 without loss. After one rain-interrupted day at the MCG, only feathery ashes remain of that WACA phoenix. As long as England don't gift-wrap their wickets tomorrow, the trophy is practically theirs to parade as they see fit.

My predictions for the series have been pretty good, and it could still theoretically finish 2-2, but my belief that Australia would win at either the Gabba or the MCG is woefully wide of the mark. In the circumstances I'm happy to concede my error. I have achieved my dream of attending the Boxing Day Test match at the MCG, and on a day when England made history; it's one to always remember. By the time I get back to the hotel the news is breaking that Hugh Hefner is to marry again at the age of 84. That's only a marginally better result in my book.

Chapter 37
FOURTH TEST, DAY TWO
WIRELESS REPORTING
(Monday 27ᵗʰ Dec)

I wake up to find the Australian papers are once again laying into their team. One headline splashes, '*A Sadly Remarkable Day*' whereas *The Herald Sun* describes their first day efforts simply as a '*DISGRACE.*' For once, it's hardly overstating it; their best performance yesterday came from the actor Hugh Jackman. In a tea-time contest in the nets for Channel 9, he launched Shane Warne for several huge hits. Proof also, if it were needed, that Warney is a spent force.

The TV has an altogether more subtle approach to their team's plight, politely turning their back, with breakfast news concentrating on the Sydney to Hobart yacht race instead. For a sport crazy country to just ignore the Ashes because they're losing is a bit much. They were happy gloating as they levelled the series in Perth, so I want some humble pie to go with my turkey sandwiches, dammit! Instead I get commentators oo-ing and ah-ing over a spectacle that's only slightly more interesting than watching someone trying to hang out their washing on a windy day. I can't understand why a bunch of millionaires poncing around on dinghies and accidentally urinating on themselves is considered a sport. I think Chas's train ride was probably more worthy of televising. Certainly by the end of the journey the 'heads' must have looked much the same. If it carries on like this, when the Sydney test is on we'll be treated to coverage of the All-Tasmania ping-pong finals.

I turn off the TV in disgust and get ready; I have a cricket massacre to watch.

Australian town planners seem to have a penchant for regimented districts; they like to keep like with like. Thus the MCG is located in the Melbourne Sports and Entertainment Precinct, that comprises Melbourne Park, Olympic Park and Yarra Park, which together house an array of arenas and venues that can cover just about any sport you care to mention, except (thank god) round-the-world yachting. There's also a conference centre – no doubt used by businessmen who like the conferences on sport best of all. There is still a bit of greenery around, but with such a mountainous range of concrete, the effect is distinctly none too parky. Being in the land of the literal, they might want a rethink on those names, unless they refer to the car parks that now fill what was once green space. Altogether it claims to be Australia's premier sports precinct; which is hardly worth shouting about, as they only really have Sydney for competition on that one. It's like Glasgow boasting it has more neds, schemies and junkies than Edinburgh; it's no great achievement. But the precinct and all these facilities are within a short walk of the CB so today I'm not complaining.

Weather-wise it's another parky day in Yarra Park, but this time we've all come prepared. Yesterday I saw a group of Australians wearing nothing but shorts, flip-flops and body-paint – initially green and yellow, but slowly changing to turquoise and green as their skin turned blue – they were evidently hardier or drunker souls than Dave. Today however, we're all in what I realise is the Melbourne optimum: warm coats and sunblock. It's an odd combo, but very effective, and it sees me through the chilly morning and into the brighter afternoon.

England's brilliant performance yesterday once again gave the lie to the doubtful concept of momentum. It's switched again: it's no more likely to stay with the same team than a roulette ball is to stick on red. Never bet on momentum; never bet on red except in the Premiership. And it's probably unwise to bet on redhead Peter Siddle as well; as with Mitch, you never know when he will show up.

Siddle is a decent bowler with a big heart, and I'm going to attempt to coin a new nickname for the lad: he should be called the Bus. He's big, he's red, and with Peter it's always nothing for ages then two or three at once; plus he's dangerous to stand in front of when he's in a hurry. This morning he unexpectedly takes two quick wickets, giving the Aussies a brief flicker of hope. But with the openers gone, Trott and KP simply pick up where they left off, and after that the only uplifting moment for Australia is when a game of pat-a-cake with a beach ball knocks Billy's trumpet out his hands – something the Fanatics have been longing to do for weeks.

It all gets livelier in the afternoon, and though there are 'only' 67,000 in the ground today, the atmosphere ignites when Haddin vociferously appeals for an edge off Pietersen's bat but Aleem Dar, who's been absolutely outstanding since his two errors at Brisbane, gives it not-out. Haddin's convinced he heard something and they call for a referral, but it merely backs up the umpire and 'Not Out' comes up on the big screen to loud cheers and jeers from the Army.

As if it was somehow Dar's fault, Sir Ricky goes ape. Absolute spiked-orangutan crazy, I've seen nothing like it for 23 years. After yesterday's performance and this morning's press reaction it's amazing Ponting has any gaskets left, but those he has he blows big-time, shouting at Dar and wagging his finger in true Mike Gatting style. Siddle, ever the team man, joins in. But whereas Gatting was unquestionably in the right in '87, Ponting and Peter haven't got a leg to stand on. Hot-spot appears to show a trace near the bottom of KP's bat, but it's nowhere near where the ball passed, so presumably shows a small scuff off the pad: a feint mark more than a faint one.

Only much later do we hear whispers that Ponting had actually asked our Kevin if he hit it, and in ever mischievous mood, KP had said yes, and pointed to the bottom of his bat. It was the wind-up of the series and Ponting fell for it.

The crowd are getting restless, some Australians are embarrassed, and the Barmies join in:

'Same old Ponting, always cheating!'
'You're getting sacked in the morning!'

And this time they may be right. However, the joke is briefly back on England as with the atmosphere in the ground now as charged as a thundercloud, a still rumbling Siddle is brought on. He steams in, and dismisses Pietersen fair and square. Johnson joins in the action and Australia rally to reduce England to 266 for 5. If the home crowd had shown loyalty and stuck around yesterday to get behind their team, we might have seen this sort of fire when Australia most needed it.

At last there's a gladiatorial mood in the air, finally this is the renowned MCG as I've wanted to see it. You almost feel the game's back on when Johnson takes his third wicket and Prior starts to walk back to the pavilion. Then, just to drive Ponting even further to the brink of a stroke, Aleem Dar stops Prior, checks with the third umpire and recalls him. There's a moment's confusion then Dar signals no-ball. Unbelievable! None of us have ever seen anything like it. An umpire reversing their own decision after calling for a replay on the front foot, is this a first?

No-balling is a pet bug-bear of mine, but I can do nothing, Ponting can do nothing, and nor can Australia. The wind is removed from their sails, they deflate in front of our eyes and they've no hope of reaching Hobart now.

The Barmy Army's current favourite song rings out at full volume with arm swaying accompaniment:

'He bowls to the left... he bowls to the riiight...
That Mitchell Johnson – his bowling is shite!!'

To add comical effect, what breeze there is blows inflated 'plastic bags' across the ground like tumbleweeds. Being sat only yards away from their launch site, I can exclusively reveal that what the radio commentators primly call bags, are in fact inflated condoms. Either the lads responsible are fans of Porterhouse Blue, or they've given up hope of conquering in Melbourne. I think they're Australian, so they're probably right.

In an inspired moment, when Trott hits his hundred the Barmy Army chime in with the chant of:

'He's got more runs than you!'

They might have been planning it a while, but it's the best of the tour and puts us all into fits of giggles as England plough on remorselessly. Prior and Trott finish the day unbeaten, giving England a lead of 346 already. The retention of the Ashes is, if not the merest of formalities, then a very close neighbour that's popped round to borrow a cup of sugar.

I hurry home this evening, as I'm due to feature on Mark Pougatch's *Radio 5 Live* phone-in show and I want to get back ASAP. I'm still hobbling badly so though it's not far to the hotel I decide to grab the tram on Wellington Parade and save ten minutes. I see one waiting at the stand and all commuters will be familiar with my dilemma: do I run for it and risk looking like an idiot when it speeds off before I get there, or walk and definitely miss it, then wait an unspecified time for the next one. Standing still hurts more than walking so I run for it, but then pull up after three steps in blinding agony. Bugger: running hurts most of all. A few seconds later the tram, only ten yards away now, pulls out.

A kindly Melbournian behind me offers his advice: 'You'd have got that if you'd f*****g run for it, mate!'

I turn and glare at him, and he sneers and laughs. Is shouting at people in the street the Australian national hobby? What is wrong with everyone? You have to love the people in this town; they make it very easy for a Scotsman to support England.

My affiliation continues to raise eyebrows. On the radio this evening I'm again introduced as a mythical creature, weirder than the cross between a griffin and a duck-billed platypus: a Scottish England fan. Not half as uncommon as an English Scotland fan I think, but keep schtum; I'm on to talk cricket not conflict. The obvious discussion point is Ponting's show of dissent and its effect on the supporters, both home and away. Plainly, having immersed myself in all Australian culture – beer, Vegemite and Aussie Rules – I'm now considered an expert on local issues. My feeling is that Ricky's hissy fit was ultimately counter-productive. At first it raised the Australian's intensity and they got the breakthroughs, but many of their fans were unimpressed by such behaviour from the skipper which will add to the pressure upon him. More importantly, it fired up the Barmy Army, who although outnumbered will always beat the locals for stamina. They kept on the case for hours, right until close of play. I finish by recounting my favourite chant – 'he's got more runs than you' – and despite semi-fluffing it, I hear Simon Hughes laugh. So another highlight to add to my trip, the great broadcaster and writer of some of the best cricket books published, actually laughs at something I said.

'What, were you talking about your love-life again?' says Dave who has rejoined me in the hotel bar.

'No, I was talking about the Barmy Army.'

'You were talking about 10,000 men, away from their partners, drinking every night but never going past the wine and song stage?'

'Yes...'

'So you were talking about your love life.'

Just for a change, Dave is not happy. He's had another weather disaster and is badly sunburned on his arms and back. It's no ordinary sunburn, this one took real skill to obtain. Thinking the thick clouds of the morning would offer some protection, he decided to save money by not putting sunblock on his already brown arms till the sun came out.

'What's wrong with this country Stuart? How the hell can you get burned through a suntan and clouds as thick as an Irish bank-holiday?'

'They look pretty bad; didn't you feel it?'

'Not a thing, they didn't even feel warm, it only just started to hurt an hour ago. But that's nothing...' He shows me the already scarlet top of his back and neck.

'Ouch!! How the hell did you do that!?'

'When the sun came out, I took my shirt off, slapped on the Factor-30 and sat down for a couple of hour's tanning.'

'So how'd you burn your back?'

'I only did my arms and front, and the bloody sun was bouncing off all the glass and concrete behind me. The bastard thing snuck up and mugged me.' I'd heard of shade tanning before but not seen the proof till this moment. It seemed incredible, as it hadn't been any warmer than a late spring day in Britain, but there was the evidence before me, and behind Dave. 'Lovely country this, needs a roof.'

Neither of us can afford the extortionate internet prices at our hotels, so once again, once the podcast is complete, we trudge to Mickey D's to upload files. We try three separate branches, our cholesterol levels nudging upwards into the red, but for whatever reason the old trick just does not work in Melbourne; the free wireless can barely handle the text files, let alone the audio. Then Dave has a brilliant idea.

'Come with me Stuart. No, don't close the computer...' We walk out onto the South Bank and Dave wanders back and forth in front of eateries and offices. With an iPad it might have been cool; with an open laptop in the hands of the scruffiest man in Australia it looks bonkers. 'Come on, one of you buggers must have left your signal open...'

He strikes gold outside a restaurant. The trick is to get in close enough to the building without being asked to sit down and buy something, but Dave has found one with a row of small hedges to shelter diners from the river breeze. Soon, he's on the laptop, crouching down behind a bush, looking like a badly dressed paparazzo with a chronic Facebook habit. But it only takes five minutes of dodging waiters and soaking up curious stares from diners and passers-by for the day's work to be on its way to Blighty. Who said there's no such thing as a free lunch?

Chapter 38
ALL IRELAND
(Monday 27th Dec - Evening)

There were some important files to send that evening. In addition to Dave's usual bragging rights about predicting events better than me, we'd been discussing the Irish question. Not the complex issue that has dogged politicians for centuries – although after a couple of pints we'd absolutely give it a go – instead we again considering our fellow Celts attitude to supporting the England cricket team. It had all begun the night before when I met a Dubliner called Gerald who bore an uncanny resemblance to Charlie Watts of the Rolling Stones. Once we got past his likelihood of appearing on Stars in Their Eyes ('Tonight Matthew, I'm going to sit behind a drum kit looking bored') we chatted over his 'National Service' living in New York and New Jersey; he wasn't in the army, it's just compulsory to go for two years if you're Irish. Finally, like two mating birds, we stopped fannying around and got down to the serious business of sport.

First up was Aussie Rules and Gaelic football, and much like the annual Shinty-Hurling match, Gerald informs me there is a silly hybrid version where Australia play Ireland in a free-for-all bloodbath that winds up like the film Rollerball. This I have to see.

'That's part of the reason why I love watching England play cricket, it's international. Only the Irish know who the all-Ireland champions are, only the Aussies know who won their Grand Final and only you Scots know who the tossing the caber champion is.'

I laugh at the very suggestion that anyone in Scotland cares about who's got the longest caber. I'm also affronted, because I'm well aware that Collingwood had won the Grand Final, I don't waste my life, oh no sir.

But Gerald continues: 'It's healthy for your outlook and your demeanour to support an internationally played game and support a team that's not your own. Sometimes patriotism and sport can get the jingoistic juices flowing too much and this can lead to a more dangerous nationalism; but how can it, when I am supporting England wearing my Cricket Ireland shirt?'

His attitude resembles my own, and exactly the sort of thing I want to say to the SNP activists that would take cricket off Scottish screens, only he's expressed it more eloquently. Damn these silver-tongued Paddies with the gift of the gab. I quiz him on Ireland's own team. He doesn't see a conflict: in the same way one might have two football teams. A good point I think, many people have a big team and a small team that will only ever meet in a cup-tie once in a blue moon, but then he proposes an Irish Test team playing a two match series against England in Dublin and Belfast. 'How great for the island would that be?'

I agree that it would, though it rather spoils the idea of having two teams you support that never meet. And the Irish team are unlikely to ever be up to scratch at Test level, because the best Irish cricketers will still want to play for England to have access to the biggest games. That is the crux of the issue for Irish and Scottish cricketers: cricket is going the way of football and the very best players will always seek to leave for bigger sides with bigger pay-cheques. Nevertheless, I'm reassured that if fans from the Republic of Ireland are happy supporting England, then it shouldn't be so hard for us Scots.

And Ireland is currently a more relevant nation to consider than Scotland, as with Collingwood failing again, Dubliner Eoin Morgan might yet get a game. He's not the first from the Emerald Isle to take the England colours, but if it is strange for a Scot, it must be virtually treason for an Irishman. And Morgan is a hundered percent Irish, no English parents, grandparents, old sheepdogs, or English links of any kind.

Those that claim sport and politics shouldn't mix or are even separable should study the Irish revolution and the role of sport in the Republic's ultimate independence. Gaelic games proudly took their place in the vanguard of a new brand of Irish resistance to English and British culture. More than a century ago, the Scots had happily taken to football and the Welsh to rugby, but Irish Nationalist politicians regarded football, rugby and cricket as an extension of English imperialism. And if you've ever been to a public school rugby match you can see their point.

But they weren't the only ones; the church too, took sides. In the 1880s, Archbishop Croke spoke out claiming 'the ugly and irritating fact that we are daily importing from England, not only her manufactured goods ... but her fashions, her accents, her literature, her music and her games and pastimes is to the utter discredit of our own grand national sports.'

It was a bit rich coming from him, as in his former role as Bishop of Auckland, he'd been exporting his own religious brand of imperialism for some time. What did the Catholic Church carry abroad if not language, literature, music and all the rest? Maybe it was the Maori's skill at rugby that made him realise Ireland were on to a loser and needed to find some sports that Polynesian islanders didn't play. Regardless of such hypocrisy, Croke and the Catholic Church, the Fenians and the home-rulers, all came together in 1884 to lend their support to the newly-created Gaelic Athletic Association with the Archbishop as its first patron. It was an act every bit as important to Ireland as the selection of Hebrew as the official language of Israel: the GAA helped define the country and breathed life into dying ideas. Plus increased participation in some pretty rugged Irish-only team sports had the useful by-product of generating fit and healthy men for any paramilitary resistance battles that might occur in the future – the battles would be won and lost on the playing fields of Croke Park.

The GAA is probably the best example of politics shaping sport and then, in turn, sport shaping politics. But not content with the promotion of their own games, the GAA proceeded to ban any members from playing British sports; a ban that was only lifted in 1970! If you were Irish and played rugby, football or cricket you were effectively a traitor to the cause and were not welcome, so out you went.

Advance to Eoin Morgan and his place in the England squad. He straddles two stools: as a youngster he played most sports, nationalist and unionist, and he attributes his trademark reverse sweep to his hurling days, but even then he wanted a larger stage. Famously he once said, 'From the age of 13, I wanted to play cricket for England. I've never felt any shame in saying this is what I wanted to do.' But he was also a decent rugby player, and in the same interview he admitted to having dreamt of scoring a winning try for Ireland, and it was always against England. So is the England flag simply one of convenience to compete at the highest level, or does the name on the badge on the shirt no longer have such painful significance as it had to Morgan's ancestors?

'I know just the man to ask.' Dave has the bright idea to interview, John, an Ulsterman who is over here with Living with the Lions. The North sits in its own half-way house: British but providing players for Ireland. Just to make things even more complicated, John may be here with lions, but surprisingly he's a wallaby – he's supporting Australia. 'I came out for the Perth Test and thought I was their lucky talisman, but not looking so good now, is it?'

Lucky charm or not, he's not short of guts and he can't be accused of being a Merino sheep in lion's clothing; he's permanently clad from head to toe in green and gold Australian colours, and has been since the day he arrived. I'm not certain he had any clothes on him when he left home, it's possible he got on and off the plane naked and only dressed after he'd hit the souvenir stand. Admittedly he's not in the heart of the Barmy Army hordes, but he's still setting himself up for daily jousts with England fans, he can't be afraid of a rigorous debate.

'What do you actually do, John?'

'I'm a religious studies teacher.'

'Aaahhhh'

Had I been there I would have leapt on this and taken the conversation onto the Protestant settlement of Ulster and their sports of choice, but Dave gets to the real nub of the issue, and with Paxman like skill extracts the ancient and deep-rooted socio-political reason for John's allegiance:

'All my family support England at the cricket. But when I was playing against my brother in the back garden he always wanted to be England so I had to be someone else—'

And thus ladies and gentlemen, the artifice inherent in loyalty to the nation state is exposed.

'—and that country was Australia and my support for the Baggy Greens started then. When I was bowling I was Jeff Thomson or Dennis Lillee, and when batting I was one of the Chappells.'

Dave admires Lillee and Thommo above all others except legendary Scottish Sea-Captain Thomas Cochrane and a young Farah Fawcett, so they proceed to share memories and he asks absolutely nothing whatsoever about cricket's role in imperialism or nationalism. Useless.

'But you've come all this way and they're losing, John.'

'Yes, but only to a Rest of the World XI. And let's face it I've done alright supporting them over the decades!'

Back at the hotel bar I have a question of my own, for Dave.

'What happened to asking about differences in the popularity of cricket between Protestants and Catholics, and whether Morgan has sold out? What happened to comparisons between Ireland and Scotland? What happened to everything we discussed?'

'No-one wants to hear all *that*, Stuart – leave it for the PhD.'

Chapter 39
FOURTH TEST, DAY THREE
FAMILY GUY
(Tuesday 28th Dec)

A sunny morning in Melbourne, and for the first time it may resemble summer by the time we take our seats. Another warm reception surely awaits Ricky Ponting following yesterday's outburst; odd how that expression can have two completely opposite meanings. Last night the under-pressure captain was fined $5,400 for his petulant finger pointing, a bit of a let-off really. If he'd only used his broken pinky he could have claimed he was showing it to the umpire to elicit sympathy. As it is, there's precious little for him in today's papers. *The Age* claims that his outburst '*betrayed the agitated state of mind of a man for whom cricket has turned sour.*'

While the press don't always reflect the mood of a nation, he has only muted public sympathy. He's a victim of success, having won more matches than Border, Waugh or Taylor but lasting long enough to become the face of the team's eventual decline. As I take my seat I still believe he will have a major say in this game, but with the bat, not the mouth: I'm positive he will score big in the 2nd innings. So positive that I have a bet on with Dave who doesn't agree. (Obviously, because if he agreed there would little point in betting.) We do, however, concur that regardless of Ponting's performance it won't be enough to scramble a draw, the Australian ship has sunk.

The morning session brings more woe for them when Harris, their best bowler in this series, pulls up in pain. He's no spring chicken and if most of us had barely heard of him before Adelaide, it's due to a career already blighted by a continual series of injuries. Harris consistently bowls at around 90mph, the sort of speed that did for Shaun Tait's Test career at an early stage, and which saw the super-quicks like Shoaib, Thomson, and Bishop miss so many games. It seems constantly eking out the very last few mph are what shatters the body. It's later confirmed he's suffered a stress fracture, one of the worst injuries of all, and will be out for months. He's a grievous loss for the Sydney game and it's a tragedy for a player finally getting his time on the big stage.

In his absence, Bus Siddle is again the pick of the bowlers and the spearhead of the attack. It may all be in vain but both sides enjoy his spirited performance. However, the majority of the crowd, both singing English and occasionally roaring Australian, are just waiting to see how far ahead England will be before the real excitement of the Aussie rearguard action begins. It's a great position to be in but the anticipation is killing some of us. It's certainly killing me, as I don't want to miss a shot but I'm needing to strain the potatoes; which is not such a great position to be in. Isn't it about time Strauss declared?

Just before lunch, Siddle, an unfortunate rhyme in the circumstances, puts me out of my misery and takes a well-deserved sixth wicket. Yes, the Bus finally stops and I can have a wee-wee. It's a bitter-sweet victory for him, as England have made 513. Trott has run out of partners but is not unpleased; He's missed a double ton but his Test-average is now over 70! So, a lead of 415, the battle is really on – in the same way the Battle of Culloden was really on: it should be a foregone conclusion and my money is on her Imperial Majesty's men.

At lunch I meet Dave and ask what he thought of the morning's play. He launches into his usual monologue, before signing off in his usual way: '—and that's why I should be chairman of selectors, Stuart! Why, how did you see it?'

'Mostly from behind a huge green and gold foam hand with *"Go Aussie"* printed on it.' Yes, my analysis is limited today as I have had the great pleasure of sitting in the family stand. And to multiply the torment, today children are allowed in for free if accompanied by an adult – so there are thousands of the buggers.

'I wondered why you were dressed like Wee Jimmy Krankie, which adult did you sneak in with?'

'Very funny.'

'If only I'd come as Steven Smith, I could have joined you.'

Not true: even with funds running low I wouldn't stoop to that for the dubious honour of being surrounded by more sticky faces than I've seen since they cancelled Tiswas and before I got the internet. Besides, I've never felt family stands were fair on the children. When I started watching Arbroath FC in the early 1970s, its old ground didn't have a family section; just a single mob of kids, teenagers, drunks, fishermen, cutthroats and assorted desperadoes. And that's how it should be. Part of the fun was mingling with the adults, getting a different perspective on life, over-hearing the profanities, listening to the streams of abuse, and hoping for a sly drink from a stranger. That was part of the event, part of the spectacle – if watching Arbroath play football could ever be called a spectacle – now they sanitise it to the point of sterility.

I definitely won't be making this mistake ever again, as the other downside of this stand is that no alcohol is allowed. The only time I need a drink more than when I'm surrounded by my family, is when I'm surrounded by someone else's. Plus the only scrap of off-field entertainment I get all day is listening to the fathers holding back the expletives – the sentences suddenly curtail, or odd words are substituted. My favourite comes when a volley of abuse leads to a stumble for an appropriate finale, which climaxes in the memorable line 'Collingwood you... Collingwood!!' That's telling him.

On the field, for the rest of the day England dominate, and those expecting a spirited comeback are left bewildered by another lacklustre, bordering on incompetent, display by the Baggy Greens. They need a Boycottesque performance from one of their openers and they get it from Shane Watson: not a patient defensive innings but an inept display of bad calling that runs out his opening partner, Phil Hughes. But the Aussie fans accept their fate stoically and continue to enjoy themselves; it's

Family Day and there's a calmer spirit of bonhomie than usual. As Ponting walks out, this time there are warm cheers all round, as much from England fans embarrassed by some of his previous harsh treatment.

Ricky digs deep, but after a bolstering cup of tea, Bresnan puts on a show. The big Yorkshireman looks like a chap who enjoys a happy hour or two down his local pub, but surely none happier than this. First he bags Watson lbw, and then Ponting chops on for only 20. When he snares Hussey for an unaccustomed duck the writing is on a wall the size of Pink Floyd's. I'm guessing it was a proper Pontefract cuppa, none of your poncy Twinings, lad. By close, England are in an unassailable position, still 246 ahead and Australia 6 wickets down. Even a Botham and Dilley style batting spectacular from Haddin and Johnson won't save this one. One phlegmatic Melbournian near me opines that Cricket Australia need to follow England's example. I'm expecting him to say something practical about central contracts or less Twenty/20 cricket, but instead his big idea is to 'pick more bloody South Africans.'

Ponting's dismissal means I have lost another bet to Dave; three in a row since he started this game. He was so sure the Melbourne Test wouldn't go the distance he pre-booked his flight to Sydney for the fifth day to miss the crowds. Or so he says. As I hand over another fiver, I like to think he just got his dates wrong. This time he wagers that play will be over in an hour tomorrow, with Siddle last man out. That's a bold prediction and I have in my favour the law of averages: Dave has to be wrong eventually. He's certainly been over-confident as he doesn't even have a ticket for tomorrow, so will have to get to the gates early and hope it's not Perth-style queuing fiasco all over again.

I've been laying low on the social scene since Adelaide, but after a whole day spent surrounded by children, I drag Dave out for a beer. The official Barmy Army pub, PJ O'Brien's, is jammed, so we walk up town hoping to do better than we did on Christmas Day. With so many England fans in Melbourne, there's a second 'official' pub, the Turf Bar on Queen Street. From the outside it looks something like an old Irish bar, but that's about as much as I can say. I'd love to give a *Beer in the Evening* style review of the bar and facilities, or regale you with drunken tales that'd put hairs on your dog, but I haven't got any, and with good reason. As we approach the door there's a few people standing outside. They're not smoking so for a moment we think they're queuing, but then they give us knowing looks and stand aside to let us in. What they know that we don't they're not letting on, but it only takes us one glance to find out: the pub is quite literally packed solid. A huge homogenous mass of exclusively male bodies in England shirts, are linked together, arms round shoulders, swaying and singing as one:

'Swwaaaaaaannnn!!!!!! Swann will tear you apaaaaaaart...'

'Oh, not that one again,' says Dave, who is a serious Joy Division fan, as if we couldn't guess by his ever sunny demeanour.

I'm not feeling a hundred percent today, and the thought of fighting through that lot to get to the bar does not appeal. We turn around and walk out again, exchanging more knowing looks with the others outside, and shooting a few of our own at any new arrivals who roll up. Halfway back down the road we're approached by two small, minxy English girls with short skirts and mischievous expressions – always a good start to any encounter – and they ask us the way to the Turf Bar.

'It's up there on the left, follow the singing... but, you know, I'm not sure...'

'Is it really good?' says one twitching her nose witchily.

'Well...'

'You'll love it, you'll fit right in!' cuts in Dave across me.

'Well, they're on for the night of their lives,' I say when they're out of earshot.

'I think that's their plan.'

The rueful sighs come simultaneously. Tonight, half a dozen lucky men are going to find out what it's like to be an off-duty Premiership footballer.

We head back south of the Yarra River and back to lighter

and brighter PJ O'Brien's. It has cleared out a bit and is a lot more genteel than the Turf Bar, although that's hardly an appropriate word and not saying much; the Lower-West-Bottom-in-the-Marsh cider drinking and cheese-rolling festival is more genteel than the Turf Bar. We fight through the crush and bump into Barmy legend, Adge Walton. He is showing no sign of letting up on his on-going celebrations, but he admits an unexpected tinge of disappointment in the situation.

'Maybe it's just me getting old but I think I enjoyed cheering on a losing side a bit more. There was a real bond in adversity.'

'But you've waited for this for twenty years!'

'Oh it's still great to thrash the Aussies, but I just miss the backs to the wall stuff.'

At this point we're joined by Chas, who's accompanied by his new friend, the first Welshman to join the gang, Leo. Chas has just taken Leo up the Eureka, but both were disappointed. Leo tells us it wasn't worth the money.

'I had to wait for ages and then I only got a few minutes in the box. You can't even take photos of each other; you have to buy the one they take of you!'

'They take photos of you? While you're up there?'

'Yes, so you can say, "Been there, done that".'

'It's not something I'd want to broadcast,' opines Dave. He refuses to be in photos, especially his own, and having been up the Sears Tower when it was still the tallest building in the world he already has the metaphorical T-shirt; although not a real one as he doesn't want the publicity.

We all get drinks and settle in. The major talking point in the bar is whether the MCG authorities will allow the England fans to all sit together for the victory tomorrow. Adge has intimated that the Barmy Army hierarchy have been lobbying for it, which sounds both reasonable to request and smart to organise it in advance; better than everyone pfaffing around switching seats. I can't envisage many Australians coming, so there should be plenty available. If the locals don't show up on a fourth day when they're winning, there's no chance they'll be there to see the last rites of their Ashes campaign. But the England fans will be out in force; after twenty-five years of hurt on Australian soil, the inevitable can't come quickly enough.

My phone goes, duty calls, who could this be at this time? Have I made it to Radio 4 yet? I leave the noise and clamour for a couple of minutes and return with good news but speechless.

'Who was it?'

'What is it, Stuart?'

'He can't speak—'

'...'

'He's just doesn't want to offer to get a round in.'

'You're obsessed with rounds, Chas.'

'—he's struck dumb!'

'...'

'I'll have a VB if you're offering...'

'Of course he can speak. Stop being so bloody melodramatic. Was it the police? What have you done this time?'

Dave snaps me out of it. I bear the glad tidings that our podcast has reached number one in the iTunes sports charts. It's unlikely I'll be recognised in the street, gain groupies or be followed by the paparazzi, but it still feels like an achievement. Neither of us had a clue what we were doing when we started but here we are competing with the best podcasts from *Talksport* and the mighty *BBC*. All the more mind-blowing as we've done it on a broken, knotted shoestring with no resources or access whatsoever; we'd even had to borrow a voice recorder and a laptop to hide behind a hedge with. Considering we've never even been on a cricket tour before and have been plagued by illness, injuries, mishaps, telecommunication breakdowns, and our own outright incompetence, it's a bloody miracle mate.

To celebrate the news, I buy Chas a drink, and Dave loses the prescription sunglasses he bought especially for the trip. You could probably hear him cheering in Scotland.

Chapter 40
FOURTH TEST, DAY FOUR
STORMING THE MCG
(Wednesday 29th Dec)

Attending a sporting event that is a foregone conclusion feels strange to me. I suppose fans of the largest football clubs must have been doing it for years, but it's not something I'm accustomed to. The idea of buying tickets simply to watch a face-rubbing display seems peculiar, but as an Arbroath fan it's a rare novelty, and I reckon I'll enjoy it.

Yes, for me the morning is as pleasurable as it is straight-forward. I arrive early at the ground and wander in, taking the time to savour the air. As expected, only the English hordes are out in strength, though it's good to see at least a few Aussies in fancy dress and determined to get the most out of their tickets. Whether in clothes or costume, all is sunny and gay as we wait for the English matadors to come into the ring, followed by the Australian bulls and the inevitable finish.

All the while I'm blissfully unaware that I've arrived just before outright chaos erupts at the gates, and Dave and the boys are still right in the middle of it. Only about 12,000 English fans have tickets already in their hands, the rest have either booked and need to collect them, or are still hoping to buy one. And apparently the MCG, the world's premier cricket venue, couldn't organise a piss-up in the VB brewery. It should be a quick ten bucks down and in through the gates, or it could even be free as they sometimes do in England. Instead, when Dave rolls up there are already 5000 people in queues hundreds long, as the MCG laboriously prints off meaningless slips of paper. They haven't laid on nearly enough staff to cope, so even those who are only collecting pre-purchased tickets can't get their hands on them. All around, irate tourists are berating any officials they can find. To fuel the flames, because they weren't expecting high numbers, the venue has only opened up a few gates, making the obligatory bag-search even slower and more annoying. What in the hell do they think will happen? Play is only going to last an hour or two and there's nobody spoiling for a fight, so just let them all in with their opened bottles of water and grow up. It's pettifogging madness.

Meanwhile, I'm sat happily awaiting the start of play, next to the most pessimistic England fan I've ever met. The battle for the Ashes is all over bar the shouting, and shouting isn't barred in Australia, just girlie drinks with umbrellas in them, so really it's all over. The shouting will soon be ones of victorious delight from the England team and supporters, assuming they can get in. But there's no convincing Grant; he's not counting his chickens, not yet. After four once-in-a-lifetime trips to the Ashes, where he has witnessed more English pummellings than a Saturday night in Gateshead, so you can understand why he urges caution. Perversely, he's claiming optimism, glad that the injury to Ryan Harris leaves Australia a bowler short, when only an unreconstructed pessimist would expect England to need to bat again. They've got so many runs they could almost afford to sit out the first innings in Sydney (that'll confuse the Martians). The rest of us expect this to be over before lunch, and even the Australians must be hoping for a mercifully quick end.

But regardless of inevitability, in cricket as in constipation and coprology, you still have to go through the motions. Play begins with an almighty roar from the Barmy Army, and in only the second over Tremlett administers the syrup; Johnson is sent on his way to the sea-side. Always delighted to wind up Super-Mitch, another huge cheer erupts in the ground, which triggers a revolt at the barricades. While we applaud, Dave is witness to the storming of the Bastille.

'Unbelievable Stuart, Unbelievable!'

'What happened?'

'John gave me his ticket, said he couldn't bear the sight of so many smug Englishmen.'

'That was nice of him.'

'Yeah, he's top man that boy. Un-believable!'

'It's not that unbelievable, the English can be very smug.'

'No, not that, the MCG. What a bunch of half-brained clowns. I take it all back, there is absolutely nothing Nazi about this building; the Germans can bloody organise things.'

Apparently Dave had just given up hope of ever getting in, and was heading home when he met a phlegmatic John, who'd decided on a morning's sightseeing in preference to watching the last night of the Proms. Re-armed with a premium Living with the Lions' ticket, he was able to skirt around all the queues to another gate and get in. But as he'd passed by the crowds, the cheers had gone up for Johnson's dismissal. With two large roars in quick succession signalling that play would shortly be over, the irate England fans waiting for security checks lost patience and simply started vaulting the turnstiles. Once that started, everyone joined in. As Dave came through his quieter gate the security were getting a flood of emergency calls on their walkie-talkies to head over and help. For a moment they were unsure – like security everywhere they only want the miserable low-pay-check, and don't like risking their necks for it – so Dave had generously helped make up their minds for them:

'Don't go over there; it's like a bloody war-zone!! There's thousands of them, they'll tear you to pieces!'

Dave is still laughing about it now.

'It was great, Stu, they all started staring really intently into the bottom of people's bags and pretending their walkie-talkies were talking to someone else.'

'Disgraceful.'

'I like to do my bit for the cause.'

'Unbelieeeeeeevable!!' We're joined by Leo and bringing up his rear, Chas.

'Yeah, Dave just said. What happened, Chas?'

'Unbelievable, Stuart, unbelievable.'

'He's right you know!'

'I gathered.'

'Can you believe it?'

'Probably not.'

'After keeping us out there for an hour, they've now decided to let everyone in free.'

Bang on cue, there's a broadcast through the tannoy confirming Leo's words: admittance had suddenly become free for the day. Pretty optimistic to expect a day out of it, I wonder if they're in league with Grant. The proclamation of peace is greeted with a three-part harmony cheer. Part one is from happy England fans who already had tickets and think it's a nice gesture, part two is an ironic cheer from those who have just vaulted their way in; part three is more of a miserable groan from those who queued for an hour and paid $20 or more, only to miss out on the freebie that was announced five minutes later.

'This is how the French revolution started, Stuart.'

'What, over a game of French cricket at the Stade De Paris?'

Dave ignores my question, he's the happiest he's been.

'Shame John couldn't be here.'

This is now more of a home game than a home game; there are pretty much only England fans left. The official attendance is 18,899 tickets sold, but there must be at least another 3,000 on top of that; any Brit in the city who could get off work is here. Pleasingly for the masses, we get a little bit of entertainment when Haddin and the Bus give it a go and land some hefty blows. It takes some doing to reach the MCG boundary, but they're up for it. Again I recollect the glory days of Botham and Dilley, and see Grant's face etched with anxiety. But when Siddle holes out to Pietersen on the boundary in front of the bouncing Barmy Army, the game is up. Poor Harris is on crutches so can't even pretend to bat and Hilfenhaus (German for 'house of the rabbit') can't keep Haddin company for more than a couple of minutes; so that, ladies and gentlemen, is that.

The Ashes are retained with a day and a match to go, the crowd erupt and there's a virulent out-break of man-hugging. Such is the joy that even the Yorkshiremen are forgetting the compulsory 15-inch separation between belt-buckles. Here the difference between British cultures becomes obvious; the English are far more liberal and continental with the skin.

Neither Dave nor I will allow ourselves to be touched with bargepoles, unless there's a non-related attractive female at the far end. We stand apart from the crowd, like cactuses at a balloon party, waiting for them to settle down so we can relax and remove the poker.

'It's a fairytale ending!' says Chas.

'And we're all at the ball!' adds Leo.

'With 20,000 ugly sisters,' suggests Dave.

I'm not sure I'd use the word fairytale but Chas is adamant – although thank God, he doesn't start singing 'Prince Charming'.

'Come on boys, I remember staying up all night as a kid, hiding under the blankets so you wouldn't get caught—'

'I remember that.'

'—listening to the cricket—'

'No I don't remember that.'

'—all the disappointments of the 80s and 90s and Noughties—'

'I certainly remember those...'

'—and now finally I'm here and we've won!'

'What's this story about, again?'

We eventually shut Dave up and enjoy the moment. Such is the scale of the victory there isn't much gloating, and Ponting receives a good reception as he walks out to accept his wooden spoon, a real walk of shame in the circumstances. There are the usual interviews to ignore, Ponting is gracious, Strauss says something or other, Trott says something else, and the Barmies are largely quiet but really just want to get back to the cheering and singing. There's nothing said immediately after an event that couldn't be said better the next day after some reflection.

Finally the teams are set free and England do a lap of honour, or rather, run over to where all the expectant fans have been waiting patiently. They're shaking hands with fans and waving, and accepting flags, and waving them too, when suddenly Sgt. Major Collingwood marshals the troops, and the team assembles in lines as if about to do the Haka. But no, with principal dancer Swann at the helm the whole group launches into a rendition of the Sprinkler right in front of the fans, and we shower in its sparkling waters. Brilliant. I'm convinced they perform it in an anti-clockwise direction as homage to being in the southern hemisphere. Cook shows a particular flair, I sense he fancies himself as the next Ramprakash on Strictly Come Dancing.

It's the most momentous day for the England Test cricket team in a quarter of a century and conceivably the most glorious in the history of the Barmy Army as well. I accept that's debatable: some die-hards will argue that anyone can support a winning team, and real character is forged singing when you're losing. I take their point, but the celebrations and singing in the ground are absolutely unbelievable. Long, long after Bresnan wrapped up the show there are still more than 15,000 England fans, running through their repertoire of songs. It's incredible how Jimmy, Billy and a couple of 'lead singers', orchestrate thousands of untrained voices so quickly and effectively.

The number which sends shivers up the spine today, is 'Take the Urn Home', sung to the tune of Sloop John B. The original song was repopularised by the Beach Boys, but I reckon the Barmy Army – who do their version with wonderful accompanying mimes – could give them a run for their money if they're ever allowed to play Glastonbury. Notwithstanding the dodgy scansion, I reckon it would take a Welsh Rugby crowd to match them; and the way it is sung today will last in my mind longest of all memories from this tour.

> We came over from old Blighty,
> The Barmy Army and me,
> Around Melbourne town we did roam,
> 6 quid for a pint (drinking all night),
> A grand for the flight!
> With Strauss our captain, we'll take the urn home.
> (chorus):
> So hoist up the John B sail,
> See how the mainsail sails,
> Call for the captain ashore
> Take the urn home (take the urn home)
> We'll take the urn home, we'll take the urn home;
> With Strauss our captain, we'll take the urn home.

The timing of the victory is spot on as it coincides with the opening hours of Melbourne's bars; I love it when a plan comes together. When you're the home side, what you lose on the field you gain in the cash registers. Let the sack of Melbourne commence! We follow the crowds over to the South Bank, but we won't be storming the breach ourselves just yet, we still have work to do. There's time for a couple of quick pints in PJs, but we can't linger long, there's a match report to write, and audio to transmit. Plus I have to stay reasonably sober as I'm scheduled to be on *BBC London* at 3pm to talk about the victory scenes. After we've downed our drinks and Perfectionist Dave has tweaked the blog and sent the files via the hedge-telegraph, he heads off for a last wander around town and leaves me to it, saying he'll catch me on his way back for a final drink. It all feels very anticlimactic, but the day is young and maybe once the interview is done I'll get a second wind.

Maybe it's all this hanging around windswept hedges, but I start sneezing again. With ninety minutes to wait before the call from the Beeb, I go back to the hotel for some anti-histamine, to head it off at the pass and avoid another attack of lurgy. Anti-hists on top of sunshine and beers – big, big mistake. As soon as I sit on the bed I pass out, and sleep on and on. The *BBC* ring and ring and ring again, but I've left my phone on vibrate and I sleep right on through. I sleep through dreams of Australia playing 5 wicket-keepers and winning in Sydney by 2 innings, 7 wickets and 146 runs. I'm still asleep when Dave rings me at 5pm and I sleep through that.

I finally come round at 8pm wondering what day it is. Dave is now packing and getting ready for bed before his early morning flight, and everyone at my hotel has already hit the town. I call a couple of numbers but no-one is answering their phone; presumably they can't hear them due to the noise of celebrations. England have retained the Ashes on foreign soil, and I'm left solo with the TV remote for company; only my liver is in a good mood.

Chapter 41
DOWN BY THE SEA
(Thursday 30th Dec)

In the hotel foyer this morning I bump into Grant. He is much less pessimistic than yesterday, but it doesn't seem to suit him. He's sporting a rash of stubble, a pale yellow complexion and eyes so bloodshot they could be mistaken for liver. I diagnose a spectacular hangover. Grant speaks slowly as though he fears speaking quickly will induce vomiting. His drawn out words tell of a great night at the Leveson, where the celebrating England fans were joined by some of the victorious team; if Grant's recollections haven't been clouded by alcohol the highlight was Swann leading the singing of Champagne Supernova. As he says, memories that will last a lifetime, albeit by the look of him that might not be that long. I'm immediately jealous and am rueing the hayfever and pills that put me out of action yesterday.

I leave Grant to his breakfast and head into the Melbourne sunshine. The options for the day are plentiful but time is short. On the plus side, at least I'm up and at 'em when most are still nursing throbbing heads. Coincidentally I immediately bump into Chas and Leo, who were either up with the lark, or they've been at it all night. In fact they've been out for a while, and now they're heading back to the MCG for the full tour and a visit to the Sports Museum. This sounds good to me, and it turns out to be the ideal 'tourist' experience for the sports geek – guilty as charged. It's great to see behind the scenes and really experience the scale of the place when, best of all, we walk out onto the famous pitch that I've admired for so long. The museum doesn't let us down either and merely re-confirms my desire to return to Australia when the Aussie Rules season is in full flow.

Being in its spiritual home I'm getting a taste for a game I've only ever seen on TV. So that's one tick in the box for the day.

Next I decide on St. Kilda, as Dave has recommended it highly. Chas had gone down solo on Christmas Day, but due to the wind and rain, had to content himself with no more than getting drunk and guzzling a T-Bone in a strange bar by way of celebration. He doesn't want to repeat the experience, so I leave the boys to their mischief, and hop on a tram and head there alone, to see it as it should be, in the bright sunshine.

I can't explain why tram travel is more fun that bus travel, but it just is, and it's rarely more fun than when it's taking you to the seaside. I jump off early and stroll past the cafes; there's a nice air to the place, this is how I imagined Fremantle would be but wasn't. Considering there's four million people in Melbourne I'm surprised by how small it all is, but that's no bad thing, it makes it feel more like a shared secret.

The beach itself is something of a letdown. I'm not sure what I was expecting, but the sand is muddy and the waters likewise, there's a lot of seaweed and sea coal around and there's a freezing cold wind blowing. As soon as I step away from the concrete promenade I have to wrap myself in fleece. Fleece and sunblock, here we go again; it's like being in the Alps. In spite of the conditions there are still girls parading in bikinis. I catch their accents – North West English – well that explains it. Trained in miniskirts on the Friday night streets of Lancashire, they've come a long way for this tan and they aren't going to bottle it now. When the breeze gets up you could hang a coat off their goosebumps, never mind anything else.

There are hardier people out among the breakers. I dabble a toe in the unappetisingly murky waters, and it's decidedly not warm. I reckon they must be Russians, accustomed to plunging into holes in frozen lakes to sober themselves up; only vodka can explain it. The Aussies are better wrapped: the waves full of kite-surfers in wet-suits, and well-muffled dog walkers are out in strength. I like dogs, but if there are more people taking their pooches for a poo than there are swimming, it's a sure indication that this is not a bathers' beach. I'll give it a miss.

I return to the esplanade and promenade myself, although not in a two-piece, and the entrance to Luna Park gawps at me maniacally. Luna Park, or Parks as there's another in Sydney, are an Aussie legend. Melbourne's is the oldest (I later discover), and both have a large mad face as a gate, so you enter through the open mouth with vast teeth hanging above you like the sword of Damocles. I first heard of them twenty-five years ago through Colin Hay, singing about the view from 'Upstairs in [his] House'. I suppose its Melbourne's Coney Island, equally iconic and outdated; the grinning face a distinctive piece of branding from before the term was coined. But by myself I have not the slightest desire to go in.

There's nothing more depressing than going to a funfair by yourself. If you aren't already feeling friendless and hard done-by, the expressions of pity and contempt you attract will soon make you reconsider, and decide, that yes, you are the most pathetic creature on God's green earth and sadder than a clown. And that's just the looks you get from the cutthroats that strap you into the seats. The happy couples and gangs of cool-kids that surround you, shrieking with incoherent joy, will watch you and think: Not only does he not have a girlfriend, but he's never had a girlfriend and never will; or worse, that you're a serial killer prowling the fair for victims. I stay clear of Luna Park.

In truth, iconic or not, like sea-fronts around the world, there's something tacky and garish about it all, and it contrasts badly with the elegance of the kite-surfers, the bobbing boats off-shore, and the calm of the fishermen, dangling their rods off the pier. That's when I realise why St. Kilda is not sitting right. I was expecting a beach like Australian beaches are supposed to be – beautiful sand and warm water, both full of bodies – when really it's a British seaside; it's more Carnoustie than Malibu. Once I realise that, I shed my preconceptions and start to enjoy it much more, watching the sun twinkling off the water and taking in the fresh mellow air. It's a picturesque view down the beach, the surfers skimming their chariots over the water, their multi-coloured horses dancing in the air above them. There's plenty to like here. Yes, it's a nice place St. Kilda, in its way.

And so is Melbourne. I've not been entirely fair to a city I've hardly explored. If I haven't always enjoyed the place, perhaps it's because I don't know anyone who belongs here and didn't get to see the suburbs and the inside story. If your only impression of Manchester is the city centre on a Saturday night after a derby match, you'll find little to love and plenty of aggressive Scallies oozing hostility. But the different areas hide a fantastic night-life among wonderful people, many that only the locals can show you. And Melbourne is Manchester-by-the-Sea in a lot of ways. It has the cloudy skies, the sports mad fans that define themselves around footballing pre-eminence, the dress-down grungy kids, the trams, and the proud history that it is determined to bulldoze and replace with anything brutalist and grey. This last is driven by the same desperate, ill-conceived and ultimately hopeless rush to keep up with a bigger brother to the east, and for once Australia is ahead of the old country: there's sadly no real sense of its heritage or cultural inheritance left in the city centre. Melbourne was Australia's principal city for a long while but there's little sign of that, much of it could be anywhere. It's not just the buildings that have gone, it's the unique identity: Manchester should see Melbourne as a warning. Nonetheless, I hope to come back someday and see the city through a local's eyes, I'm in no doubt there is much good that I missed. Preferably, I'd like to see it through the eyes of some very large locals, who can thump the living daylights out of all these belligerent bastards I keep running into.

When I next see Dave in Sydney, I take him to task on his misleading recommendation. 'You told me St. Kilda was like Baywatch on a bank holiday! It's nothing like that.'

'No, I know. It's like the North Sea with good PR.'

'So why didn't you say so?'

'To give you something controversial to say in conversations, make you more interesting at parties.'

'Yeah, thanks.'

'Well if I'd said it was like Arbroath you wouldn't have gone, would you?'

PART FIVE ~ SYDNEY

Chapter 42
NEW YEAR'S EVE
(Friday 31ˢᵗ Dec)

We're cutting it fine: flying to Sydney for the largest party on earth with only hours to spare. It only adds to the air of anticipation. The city is sparkling in the sun, and with the first glimpse I catch from the sky I understand why it has so many acolytes and inspires love in a way Melbourne seldom appears to. Captain Cook didn't set eyes on this place, leaving Botany Bay and then sailing on up the coast in poor weather and straight past one of the world's great natural harbours. He must have kicked himself black and blue when he heard the news. But it's a nice touch that Sydney International Airport is in Botany; I feel it's the appropriate place to arrive.

The flight is a short one but fun, as the *BBC*'s cricket correspondent Jonathan Agnew is on board. Aggers is held in enormous regard and is something of a cult figure to the England fans. I always felt he should have played for England more, but the affection he inspires as a journalist far exceeds anything his creditable playing career provoked. I can now confirm that oft made Test Match Special jibe; that his wife is far too attractive for him and he's batting well above his lowly average. And I don't mean that anymore than anyone else; he is charm personified and exudes warmth. When a fellow passenger intrudes and asks him to sign a copy of his book, Aggers does so instantly and graciously, and then asks if he is enjoying it. Before the chap can answer he undercuts himself: 'I should have asked that before I signed it, really.' A plane full of laughing cricket fans slips gracefully along the Sydney tarmac and we've reached our final destination.

Melbourne may boast the iconic stadium and match, but when it comes to the iconic night out, you won't top Sydney; not even New York has managed that. The spectacular fireworks display as the clock chimes midnight to mark the New Year is shown throughout the world, and anyone, anywhere else, who likes a knees-up, can't help but wonder if their party is second best. Conversely, I have enjoyed New Year festivities as far afield as London, Edinburgh and my Gran's house in Angus, but there is always the nagging doubt that the curmudgeons ensconced in front of their television enjoy proceedings more than the curmudgeons, like me, who are actually at the event. (Odd that Gran's house was on the telly; Grampian TV was scraping the barrel that year.) Will Sydney silence my doubts? I may not have chosen the best partner in crime for the evening, as Dave, by his own admission, has only ever enjoyed one Hogmanay in his whole life, when he unexpectedly found himself in a Bristol hospital and snogged one of the nurses. I'm expecting the complaints to drown out the explosives.

I'm sitting in the lobby of my hotel, just yards from George Street – arguably the most important thoroughfare in the country. A street that never sleeps and with more skyscrapers than any other in Australia, it connects Central station to the south with the Rocks in the north, where Sydney Harbour Bridge towers above. And tonight that's the destination for hundreds of thousands of revellers. Dave is coming from his apartment near the SCG but arrives early, having been in the city for a day and already mastered the public transport system. To me this is a piece of navigation as impressive as any by Captain Cook, and the best either of us has managed all tour. My record of travelling within cities is usually limited to plaintive cries of 'Stop the bus, please, I need to get off,' even, as we've seen, when I'm on a train. I usually find myself visiting the attractions at the end of lines, regardless of my original targets. I figure at least you know where you're starting from.

Dave is in a mood. The terms 'good mood' and 'bad mood' don't really apply with him, it's hard to tell them apart. But he's definitely in a mood. Yesterday, he successfully got into his new apartment, flicked a switch and blew every fuse in the house. He spent his spare day in Sydney waiting in for an electrician. We're both flabbergasted that an electrician came out on Friday 31st, and even Grumpy was willing to chalk it up as a relative victory. Except for one small problem.

'Stuart, I think I'm dying.'

'What?'

'I shook hands with the electrician, and he could barely breathe with some god awful lurgy, and the bastard's given it to me.' I don't shake his hand in greeting, it's not the Scottish way. Dave has travelled Australia, coating his hands and face in anti-viral foam every time he set foot on a plane, and unlike me had escaped scot-free from the usual recycled bugs that plague the air traveller, but on the cusp of the big event he's been struck down in the safety of his own apartment. 'I was so happy to get it all working, I was congratulating him. I knew the moment I did it, it was a mistake. Damn it. Damn it. Damn it to hell.'

'You might not have caught anything, wait and see.'

'My throat already feels like it's been slit with a rusty knife, that's always how it starts.'

'Well, we'll never find an open chemist at this time.'

'Who asked for a chemist? Let's find a pub.'

For once we've done some research, and the bad news is that the best views go hours before the main event, and many of them are alcohol free zones. When we get to the Rocks at 7.30, it's clear we might be able to elbow our way to a good view, but no way are we going to stand for over four hours without a drink. Sod that for a game of soldiers. We may have travelled halfway round the planet, we may be within touching distance of the world's most famous party, but to patiently stand guard with aching legs in an alcohol free area is too much of an ask; we could never show our faces in Scotland again.

Chas and Leo are somewhere nearby seeking a vantage point, but the chances of us successfully rendezvousing among a million people are near zero. It's no good saying you're 'by a big building' or 'near a tall bloke with a beard'; as a helpful hint that's not going to cut it. Plus Chas isn't answering his phone. Either he can't hear it amid the crush or he's been mugged by a sailor on shore leave. Maybe, right now, he's having his organs eaten in an *Angel Heart* style satanic ritual. Possibly I've taken that idea too far, but unquestionably the mobs of happy people bring Victory celebrations to mind. I'm just not sure if anyone knows what we've won or who we've beaten, all we know is that we've reached the end of something.

Why do we have this fascination with finality? It's been mankind's excuse for a party since the dawn of time. I'm guessing it began with celebrating the conclusion of a hunt by eating what you'd just caught, and that led in time to harvest festivals, and then we all just went utterly mental. Nowadays we mark the end of years, the end of school, the end of university, the end of theatre runs, the end of jobs, the end of working lives, the end of the pier, the end of a bit of rope; even a decent funeral is a celebration. Presumably with marriage – the one exception where we rejoice at the beginning – we're really marking the cosy belief that it's supposed to be for life and is therefore the end of a quest. The bizarre thing is that, unlike a tasty mammoth steak you've just risked your life for, most of these endings are quite saddening, yet we choose to enter the succeeding period of uncertainty with a blinding hangover.

Talking of which, there's still half a view to be had on George Street a little way back from the Bridge, but why be a street urchin when Sydney's oldest pub, the Fortune of War, is just yards away? Considering the tons of gunpowder set to blow on all sides of us, the pub is aptly named. The first surprise is that there's no admittance fee, the second is that we get bar-stools and breathing space. It is quickly becoming apparent that Sydney is a wonderful place to spend New Year.

That may not sound like much of a revelation, but our reasoning is not the stuff that makes the headlines. Out in the street the police presence is small, friendly and inclusive, with nothing like the heavy hand of London, which corrals and herds you humourlessly, needlessly closing off roads and views. There are a few small road blocks to the paying areas, but the miles and miles of metal fencing that is dumped in British cities every time someone opens an envelope or sets off a banger, are entirely absent. This is how it can work if you don't treat people as animals. Before we hit the pub we'd had a good wander around, and nobody was pushing or crushing, the handful of police we saw were having no problems and, allowed to freely mingle, the atmosphere was entirely without threat or danger. Dave, who was in Edinburgh in 1996 when people were crushed and seriously injured against roadside barriers, is particularly impressed: 'I saw it coming Stuart, and got out just in time. But this is how it should be: Hogmanay with seating.'

One of the big problems then was that near midnight they closed all the pubs, and thousands who had just necked far too many drinks, far too quickly, hit the streets all at once. That's not an issue in Sydney as most of the bars are free to get in, they stay open through the night, and are busy without being crowded. Such civilization needs to spread to the UK quickly; the Aussies have us beat 3-0 on this one. Around us the drinking is unhurried, everyone is coming and going at their leisure, and there's only an open bar to be squeezed against. Admittedly, working on New Year's Eve may not be a great deal for the working man or woman, but judging by the enormous quantity of festive free gins our inept and staggering barmaid is getting through it has its perks.

Suddenly there's a terrific explosion and we jump off our stools. Only metaphorically, we're not going to give them up that easily. Hang on it's nowhere near midnight, has some joker snuck onto the bridge with a match? No, it's the nine o'clock family firework display: sympathetic to the sleep patterns of families and children, the City provides an earlier performance.

'What a great idea Stuart.'

'It is; it's nice for the kids to see the fireworks.'

'More importantly, it gets all the selfish bastards with prams out the way and makes some bloody room.'

'You're a hard man, Dave.'

'Sod them, they push past everyone, ramming their buggies into your ankles till you jump out the way, and all so some self-righteous middle-class muppet can claim they're providing an eclectic upbringing for their kid.'

'Maybe they want to see the fireworks themselves but can't get a baby-sitter?'

'I don't care, they take up three spaces each and normally their kid is either sound asleep or wakes up at midnight and shits itself – they're probably scarred for life. I'd have them all arrested for child abuse.'

We both agree Sydney's idea is a lot better. Oh yes, they can teach us much about how to stage New Years Eve, if only they could do something about the vuvuzelas. I defended them in Perth, one occasional toot on the horn never did any harm, but this year they are the must-have accessory for dimwit Italian tourists. How completely mentally vacant must you be to think that honking tunelessly and almost continuously for five hours is entertaining? Outside, it sounds as if all the legions of Rome are preparing to march again, and one of the principal reasons we choose pub over street is that we know that neither of us can last till midnight without shoving a vuvuzela where the tomatoes never sun dry. But anyone who has ever watched Italian TV won't be in the slightest surprised that they're so easily diverted.

The pub is getting busier. In Melbourne they'd have locked the door three hours ago, but it's still no worse than a hectic Friday night in Soho or Bigg Market or Deansgate Locks – places many here will be familiar with because they're nearly all English. Once they reach critical mass some decide to spoil the atmosphere by firing off a few fanfares of their own: cricket songs break out in the pub. One valiant buck retorts with his best 'Aussie Aussie Aussie' response, but with no allies to hand he is soon shouted down. Nevertheless, he's done enough for the songs to fade away and non-tribalism to return. Good.

The wait at the bar is lengthening in direct correlation to how hammered the staff are getting, and Dave's been trying to get served for half an hour. He's only four feet away, but we can't talk while he waits, because if at any point he takes his eyes off the barmaids they're likely to serve a lost dog or a pillar before him. There's an iffy moment when one successively serves queue-jumpers no less than ten times in a row (yes, he counted), but the general conviviality brings forgiveness from the punters. He finally returns with booty: 'Bloody hell, she couldn't have been more clueless if you'd hidden Colonel Mustard and the candlestick and asked her whodunit?'

'Half an hour is about usual for you.'

'Oh look Stuart, I got three pints for me and one for you.'

'Funny.'

He hasn't wasted his time, and in-between counting queue jumpers he's made peace with an Italian, and successfully negotiated a bilingual conversation about cricket, promising to organise an England tour of Italy. Perhaps then we can wean the Barmies onto chanting, 'Are you *Italy* in disguise?' in future matches. But I'm not one to harbour a grudge as you know...

Chas makes contact around eleven, and unless Mickey Rourke is texting on his phone, he has not been sacrificed and has a good spot down by the shore. It sounds perfect, but as it took him and Leo a couple of hours to prise their way in, squeezing themselves into the tightest cracks, we don't reckon it is worth the wild goose chase and carry on drinking. But we're not complete alcoholics, so approaching midnight we pop outside for a little peak at the Bridge and the show. Someone starts a countdown, someone else starts one at a slightly different speed, numbers cross over and synchronise, midnight arrives, Cinderella's coach turns into an exploding munitions dump and the mice dressed as footmen are launched squealing into the air.

The entire performance is spectacular. So we're told. In truth, we've left it a little too late, and the few hundred yards from our earlier spot is now crammed with bodies and this proves crucial. We see a few fireworks – the ones that fly highest – and plenty of flashes and bangs, but on the whole it's not a great deal more exciting than my Gran's, and at least in Angus they don't have vuvuzelas blasting and drowning out the bangs and booms. Can't these Italians Ooo and Aah like normal retarded human beings? Again I suspect the bores and curmudgeons ensconced in front of their television sets have enjoyed the firework display much more than many of those, like us, who are here in the flesh.

Even so, it's been a good night, and Dave pronounces it his second favourite Hogmanay ever. 'The disappointment was only slight this time, rather than the usual "crushing".'

'Don't you ever enjoy it?'

'I quite like New Year's Day, with the Church Bells ringing and so on, but the 31st is my least favourite day of the year.'

'But you're a Scot.'

'Yes, and it's the great Scottish lie. A charmless alcoholic over-indulgence without redeeming features. A celebration based on drowning loneliness in alcohol and reflecting on all your past failures; maudlinly wishing everyone's next year won't be as miserable as this one was, followed by an absurd list of self-improving promises you'll never keep. If you're already having a good holiday you don't need it, if you're isolated it only emphasises it.'

He's always more eloquent when he's hammered.

'It's not always that bad, Dave.'

'Starter for ten: what's the defining image of every New Year's Eve in London?'

I pause for a moment's reflection, before hitting upon the obvious answer: 'Sand-covered pools of vomit at the Tube stations?'

'Go it in one.'

Yup, Sydney does it better on every score.

I head back to the hotel, and Dave decides to walk home even though the buses are still running. He either wants to clear his head and avoid the crush, or if it's part of some masochistic desire to suffer on Hogmanay. Either way, the next day he says he didn't see a policeman all the way back to Randwick, nor any need for one, which says much. Although he does nearly get run-over when he accidentally walks down an express bus lane. Knowing Dave, if he had been killed, he'd have died struggling with the irony that another New Year's Eve had been spoiled, but this time by good public transport running through the night.

Chapter 43
BARMIES v FANATICS
(Saturday 1ˢᵗ Jan)

It's 2011. I have my first hangover of the year, but it's not so bad; a day under the duvet will not be required. This is good news as the last game of the Fans' Ashes, between the Barmy Army and the Fanatics, is being played this morning down by the seaside at the Coogee Oval. I've missed four matches so far, but I'm determined to make it for the fifth.

I am feeling a *little* fragile, and every action will have to be performed painstakingly, but when I reel across the road to Wynyard Station I'm delighted to discover that the buses are running on New Year's Day. Less delighting, all the ticket counters are shut. No worries, there are ticket machines – every one of which is showing *'NOT IN USE'*. Not to worry, newsagents sell tickets, and there are two on this very street. The nearest one is closed (no worrying, I'm getting closer), and at the other my request for a ticket is denied: 'Sorry we're out of tickets. We'll have more tomorrow.'

Out of tickets? More tomorrow? Worry. I've gone from naturalised Australian back to British in two minutes flat. And how is a ticket tomorrow going to help me now? I'm going to miss this game, five out of five, what a record. I text Dave: he reckons it'll take me 90 minutes to walk it; I'll miss the start but I'll make it. In the shameful absence of available Irn Bru, I pick up a sugary bottle of Coke, and lurch onto the streets of Sydney.

I have a pretty good idea where I'm heading, and it gives me the chance to get a handle on the character of the city. The first thing you notice is the names: Kings Cross, Paddington, Liverpool Street – was Sydney founded by a group of trainspotters? When I reach Oxford Street, like you, I see another pattern, and for a while I expect every corner to offer me free parking or direct me back to Jail. More than just patterns emerge in Oxford Street, as this is the cornerstone of Sydney's gay district, and even though it is mid-morning there are plenty of parties continuing from last night in the bars and clubs.

John Inman once said he was invited to reprise his role of Mr. Humphries in the Australian version of *Are You Being Served?* because the producers said there were no gay men in Australia. Either they'd not taken a cruise down Oxford Street or these blokes are part of some elaborate practical joke. It's a colourful area with a good sense of humour, and not far from the turning which leads to the SCG, is a gay sauna called Bodyline. A 1930's sporting scandal that almost led to the breakup of the Empire has spawned a venue where no sports clothes are allowed. But you're probably just as likely to be caught at leg-slip fending off a bouncer. Give those men a round of applause ... or a warm hand upon their entrance.

The walk down Anzac Parade is whisper quiet; the SCG and the Sydney Football Stadium lie eerily silent. Don't be fooled by the names: the Cricket Ground hosts the football (Aussie) and the Football Stadium hosts rugby. Why they named the newer SFS the way they did, I don't know. Possibly the literal-minded Australians think Rugby League Football should be given its full title, or it could be because here in NSW they consider Rugby to be the game of men, and Aussie Rules to be a devilish Victorian practice fit only for the despised Melbournians, and so pinched the word to spite them. I suspect they were just being thrawn, and it's a fiendish plan to wrong foot the tourist.

Further on there is sporting life in action: I turn into Allison Road and find the very impressive Royal Randwick Racecourse hosting its New Year's Day meeting. I hadn't anticipated finding a racecourse in the middle of a city. It's quite a surprise – as is the dress code. I know in the UK, many like to stand in muddy fields in their finery, but prejudice dictates that it is always more unexpected to find Australians in dark suits on a blazing sunny day. As with the nocturnal dress sense of Perth,

I'm struck once again, that the casual no-worries culture Australia is famous for, is a manifold misrepresentation. The rather more formal mores have lingered here long after they have almost vanished from the homeland. Gazing at the sweltering black and navy mass, my mind wanders back to colonial administrators in full-rig watching parades and polo matches, with thick jackets and their stiff collars tightly buttoned-up. But someone should take a punt on opening a shop selling light-coloured linen suits – it'd surely be worth a flutter.

In spite of the gambling temptation of the racecourse I must stick to my mission and continue uphill then sharp downhill to Coogee and the sea. Of course, with the law of unfamiliar routes holding sway, it was never going to take 90 minutes. Two hours would have been a safer bet, but even then I must have either made a mistake or crossed the Randwick Triangle. I finally roll into the lovely Coogee Oval 150 minutes after I set out, and the match is just about over. I don't realise this until Dave, whose flat is opposite the Racecourse and who has been here from the start, points out that the Aussies innings has been and gone. Oh well. More infuriatingly, I've also missed the Aussie bowling legend, Glenn McGrath. Glenn had come down before the game in recognition of the many thousands of dollars raised by the Barmy Army for the *McGrath Foundation* breast cancer charity, over the course of the tour. I'm relying on Dave for the scoop.

'How was he?'

'Couldn't have been nicer.'

'Did you get an interview?'

'Er... not as such, no.'

'How long was he here for?'

'Oh, ages. At least an hour. He was posing for photos and shaking hands and talking to the media, couldn't have been more obliging.'

'So did you speak to him?'

'Er... no, not as such.'

'Why not?'

'I wasn't sure he'd like my opening question.'

'Which was?'

'Well, it was going to be, "Are you having an affair with Shane Warne?", but I chickened out, he's a big lad in the flesh.'

'So you didn't get anything?'

'I got some photos. But he was doing so much for the cause I felt bad for him; I didn't want to make him work.'

'Not even a sound-bite?'

'It's not about the stars Stuart, it's about the fans. We're here to talk about the fans.'

'Useless.'

'I was expecting you to be here for moral support. I'm hungover.'

'So am I.'

'Yes, but I had an hour's walk home. I nearly died under that bus you know?'

'You'd be as much use under a bus.'

'I certainly feel like I was hit by one – I stayed up till five, drinking red wine and watching TV.'

'Why?'

'Couldn't sleep, I'm still on Melbourne time.'

'Melbourne's in the same time-zone.'

'Someone should tell them that.'

Celebrities aside, the Fanatics had started the match like a greyhound from the traps, blasting boundaries, but then some great fielding from the Barmies quickly removed their top order in a rush and saw them reined in for a low score. Sounds familiar: sport mirrors sport. In response the Barmy team progress in stately fashion, and meanwhile Dave and I grab an interview with Paul Burnham, head honcho of the Barmy Army.

Under Paul the Barmies have become much more than a loose band of supporters following the team around the world. Ten years on from its beginnings, it is now a thriving business that does much for charity, organises tour packages for its members, and coordinates activities overseas. Paul has been with the Army since its first muster during England's tour of Australia in autumn 1994. He and the other founders met in Sydney, '... singing songs about the Aussies. The name came from the Aussie media. We were losing badly, yet still we'd sing. Their press loved us and called us barmy, but the British press hated us. We got some replica shirts made and sold them to the fans.' The shirts went on sale just as England finally won a match, and sold out.

After the tour, Paul and co-founders, Dave Peacock and Gareth Evans, trademarked the name and established the Barmy Army as the brand it is today. And as anyone who has toured with England can confirm, they've gone from strength to strength; witness the fact that both myself and Dave are members. In the sixteen years of their existence, Paul says he's never noticed any division or bad blood between English and Celts and delights me when he reveals the crucial role played by Scots in establishing the initial flavour of the Army.

'There were a group of fans from Poloc Cricket Club in Glasgow who really started a lot of the singing and chanting – as well as the drinking, naturally! Their enthusiasm for having a good time *in addition* to watching the cricket rubbed off on a lot of other England fans.'

I knew it; I knew I was not alone. Sure I'd met many Scots on my travels, but this was like being brought up by a bear, and then finding there's a whole wolf-pack of man-cubs having a rare old time in the very next jungle.

The interview is interrupted as Paul is also in charge of the Barmy Army's batting line-up and is obviously keen for a win. And win they do, the match and the series, with only three wickets down. It's their first ever series triumph Down Under, and is naturally celebrated with a choreographed team display of the Sprinkler. Swannie would be proud.

As the celebrations get under way I chat with Mr. B. Cooper, a.k.a. Billy the Trumpet. Billy regales me with the tale of his travails trying to enter grounds with a musical instrument; true to form he's endured a litany of hassle from security. Lucky he's not Billy the Double-Bass I reckon. But after a lot of paperwork, permission was finally granted for the trumpet to be admitted to all five Test grounds, provided it was carried in a case with only one zip. (Okay, I made that last bit up, but I do wonder.) I'm surprised to hear they have specific forms for such eventualities – makes you wonder what other official documents are lurking under the desk. Next time, I'm going to apply for permission to bring in a giraffe, just to see.

When Billy confirms that, once through the gates in possession of a lethal trumpet, he does *not* play along to 'Are you Scotland in Disguise' I want to go English and man-hug him. 'It's a football song and doesn't really belong in a cricket ground. And anyway how can you sing that song alongside Rule Britannia which, of course, was written by a Scotsman.'

I'm naively impressed by his musical trivia, and much to Dave's ears' relief I finally let bygones be bygones on that one. But our interview comes to an abrupt end when Billy's talents are called upon to accompany the fans' team's celebratory songs. Let's hope it's an omen for the real thing.

Chapter 44
HOLY COWS
(Sunday 2nd Jan – Morning)

When I first started travelling I didn't care for obvious sight-seeing. The last thing I wanted was to come across to the locals as a tourist. That was the lowest of the low as far as I was concerned. Perhaps it was insulting portrayals of tourists on TV, or possibly it was living in Edinburgh and London, where life is lived in constant exasperation with slow-moving foreigners possessing no peripheral vision and getting in the way of our already frustrating day-to-day existence. It's not that I had any street-cred to lose, but nor did I want to associate with the fat-checked-arses of the American vacationers that once roamed the world in brigades. Lockerbie and then 9/11 changed all that, and Americans were soon afraid even to go to the Kwik-E-Mart on the corner, and as their numbers dropped so I slowly came round to the idea. There's still absolutely no cool to be had surrounded by Germans wrapped in pink Gore-Tex, but these days I care less what people think. And there's safety in numbers, something I could have done with in Melbourne. So my new approach is to accept that it is not my fault the locals are grumpy – they're just wishing they were on holiday too – and recognise that sometimes the way of the tourist is the path of the righteous.

First, I have to inspect Australia's most famous landmark, the Sydney Opera House. This is obligatory: you have to have a picture taken of yourself stood in front of it, it's the law. When you arrive in the country, they frisk you for drugs and smuggled fruit and veg, warn you about carrying brass or woodwind into cricket games, and then direct you to the Opera House for a mug-shot, from which you can be identified as a mug.

Seriously, don't bother. I've nothing against it, it's a nice enough building and maybe it was revolutionary when it was first proposed. It's a pleasant place to stand and gaze over the water, and it has a great bar running down the side of it, which is a dramatic place for an evening drink. But in the flesh, or rather cement, it's surprisingly small and rather ordinary; it is completely without wow factor. The 'shells' are interesting, but like so much modern architecture, you'd never understand their point unless you're told: they can theoretically be assembled into a complete sphere. Who cares? They're not in a sphere. They're immovable lumps and they're sticking up like wafers poking out of an ugly ice-cream tub of dull chocolate concrete.

It's not entirely unembellished, it actually has millions of little stones embedded in it, but from more than two yards away, it may just as well be plain concrete with added food colouring. It reminds me of nothing so much of my Alma Mater, the University of Stirling. When Stirling Uni was built in the 1960s (you can picture it I'm sure), they went to great expense pebble-dashing the boxy horror with granite chips quarried in Skye. Up close, they sparkle slightly on the annual summer's day (and there's usually one at the end of May), but from any vantage point from which you can see the buildings as a whole – stones or no stones – they appear to be bare dirty concrete, and are considered among the ugliest halls of residence in Scotland. So what was the point?

And what is the point here? It's a gimmick to garnish an architect's presentation, but it inflates costs and adds nothing to the final effect. And cost is important: the Opera House wasn't properly finished because they ran out of dough. So the architect got the chop, and his crazily overambitious vision was fudged. Unfortunate, but it's hard to have sympathy with those whose follies come at eye-watering public expense, and his original plans would have provided a mere two thousand seats for privileged bums. Yes, the Sydney Opera House is not really much to sing about. It's in a better location, but in of itself it's not a great deal more impressive than the Royal Festival Hall, which is deliberately not saying much.

Speaking as a tourist, and indeed on behalf of tourists, I only want the 'been there – done that' photo. None of the mob of people milling around me are planning to see any concerts any time soon, so you could replace the whole thing with a cheap plastic facsimile, and nobody would know any different. In fact, maybe they already have and we've all been duped.

However, the ice-cream tub does have a lot to answer for. Its iconic status has been hailed as an example of how to put a city on the map. It's why, when the year 2000 rolled around, the huge sums of money stockpiled in the British millennium fund were largely wasted on vacuous nonsense – symbols of a confident Britain that apparently had nothing left to say. There would have been no stupid Millennium Dome without the stupid Opera House. London could still have built itself a new multi-use space – they could have usefully put one in Battersea Power Station and killed two birds – without recourse to a £789 million vanity project. But they wanted the icon by the quays to match.

The Opera House's fame merely hides the painful truth: construction over-ran by ten years, and on completion the acoustics were rubbish, the stage was too small, the orchestra pit dangerous and the facilities for performers inadequate. And this grandiose failure came in *fourteen times* – $95 million (at 1973 prices!) – over budget. As an iconic precursor of the Dome, it was bang on the money, so to speak.

Over the other side of the water is the Harbour Bridge. It at least is a commercial and aesthetic success. It's indubitably a jolly nice bridge: all old stone, steel girders and satisfyingly large rivets; and catching little peeks of it as you wander around town never fails to give a warm feeling. But it's not very big and if you're used to the grandeur of the Forth Bridge, your first words will probably be, 'Is that it?' That's no fault of the bridge, that's unfortunately the truth about so many famous attractions that photographers have flattered with careful use of light, perspective, and retouching. Take a tourist to see shabby old Piccadilly Circus at night and their first words are usually, 'Is this it?' or, 'Umm... Okay, can we go now?' or more often, 'Where's my wallet!? Who took my phone!?' However, at least

Sydney keeps its bridge in good condition and puts it to plenty of use; it carries both trains and cars, making it a sensible investment. Long after Scotland's dull-red icon has been allowed to rust into the sea by the vandals who run our railways, Australia's bold iron icon will still be carrying people to and fro.

Holiday snaps taken, I set off in search of the obligatory T-shirt. Those of you who have read *The Game* by Neil Strauss (no relation, and about chasing ladies, not runs) will know the old chat-up chestnut of always carrying some carefully chosen photos about your person. The idea is to pre-select pictures of yourself in interesting and exciting places and poses, and then put them all in a packet as if you've just got them back from the chemist. (The book was written in the days of film obviously, so you may have to pretend to be a hi-brow art student and wear silly clothes in garish colours for this to still work.) Supposedly, if you leave said photos conspicuously sticking out of your pocket, any girl you're speaking to will be irresistibly drawn to them, and at some point request a peek; they're nosey that way. You then casually produce your cunning portfolio designed literally to show you in your best light – surfing, snowboarding, skydiving... standing in front of a fake plastic Opera House – and she's so impressed by your exciting life that she offers herself to you then and there.

Ladies, you may mock, but I do actually know someone who does something very similar to this and it undoubtedly works: his little black book would give me a hernia just picking it up. Gentlemen, if you try it, just remember not to include any photos of whatever it is you really do with your time, e.g. train-spotting, lying around in your pants or recreating the Civil War.

The holiday T-shirt is the less subtle version of this gambit: it says been there, done that, it's not enough to bore you with my photos, I have to flaunt it on my chest. Look at me! I've been somewhere, look upon my chest ye mighty and consider shagging me. I'm not entirely immune I confess, and I've come a long way for this, so let's see what they have. I'm hoping for something better than *'Aussies Do It Down Under'*.

Dotted about the quay are a dozen or so tourist-trap shops, all selling the same sort of stuff— except no, wait— they're selling *precisely* the same stuff. Not only do they all have the same range as each other, but it's the selfsame tat they had in Perth, over 2000 miles away! Exactly. Down to the whiskers on the kangaroo's nose. Either it says *'Australia'* and is identical, or it says *'Sydney'* but might as well have *'Perth'* crossed out beside it. Okay, there's a few extra Opera House and Bondi pieces, but the sweets, the hand-creams, the calendars, the pencils, pens and writing tools of other bygone eras, the tea-towels, the key-rings, the drink holders, the hats with corks, the wind-up things that go ping, the noisy things you give to children and later regret (or give to other people's children as a malicious prank), and even the boomerangs and didgeridoos, all appear to have come from the same supplier. Only the cityscape snow-globes are different, although just as fruit-loop mental. Snow!? What is this, Melbourne?

And it follows you around. I later find the famous (and tawdry) Paddy's Market filled with stalls selling the same twenty T-shirts I didn't want before, on the same 'Buy Two, Get Another One You Don't Want Free,' deal. And they turn up again at the airport – it's like being stalked by a Chinese sweat-shop. This vast land appears to have one price, one sales strategy, and only one factory in Asia supplying tourists the length and breadth of it. Which rather raises the question: why go 10,000 miles to buy the stuff? Why not just ship it straight to Europe and sell it there? It would be just as authentic. Perhaps we should all wear T-shirts that simply say *'Made in China'*, and then we can pretend to have been anywhere we fancy.

I make one last desperate jumble-run for something wearable, something that will at least provoke a little envy without making me look like a penis. But ultimately it's a dead end and I give it a miss. I guess it will just be that little bit easier for the women of the world to continue to resist me.

Chapter 45
TOURIST TRAIL
(Sunday 2nd Jan – Afternoon)

Call me a miserable nit-picker, and many often do, but Circular Quay sounds as inauthentic as the bush-hats with plastic mini-corks. It's not circular, it's semi-circular; they've completely let down the side as far as Australian nomenclature goes – were the Snowy Mountains named in vain? Admittedly, a circular quay wouldn't be much use, that would be a boating pond, but that's not the point.

I'm still loitering around the Quay because I've decided that if I'm going to be a holidaymaker, I should go the whole hog. Box-ticking photos are all very well, but I'm here to catch a bus. Yes, the way the tourist demands it; I'm taking a ride on an open top, hop on, hop off, guided tour. All aboard!

Now imagine my delight when no sooner am I welcomed on deck that the pedant in me is silenced by the information that it was originally christened 'Semi-Circular Quay' and only later abbreviated as a convenience. Yup, when it comes to dull literalism, I knew Australia wouldn't let me down.

The tour is well worth it and I spend the next few hours jumping off at likely-looking spots. Despite my assault on the holy cows, the fact remains that Sydney is still a darn nice place to be. The natural harbours and bays are an inspiring setting to build a city, the streets have a happy buzzy ambience, and compared to Melbourne it has retained far more of its architectural heritage (with a small h, not the dreaded capital H).

For some, the Rocks are a bit of a kitsch area, but I feel they pull it off alright. As with Covent Garden, it's an area that may have completely lost its original working class purpose and be a twee place over-run by souvenir hunters, but it is still pretty and a better result than the traditional post-war bull-dozing would have been. I learn that this was the fate of the Tram Depot that once stood on the site of the Opera House. The depot – built to resemble a castle in homage to its predecessor Fort Macquarie – sounds utterly extraordinary and well worth standing in front of for a photo. I reckon I'd have preferred it to its replacement.

The old Queen Victoria building that we pass and where I meet Dave later, is as beautiful a shopping mall outside and in, as any you'll find on the planet. The fact that the accompanying statue to her Maj' originally stood in Dublin and was a gift from the Irish in 1947, is a strange combination of funny, charming and tragic. It's a nice statue, and it saved it from the fate that met Dublin's statue of Nelson (ka-boom!), but am I alone in thinking that's a bit like getting a birthday present from your mate, then finding a tag on it written in unfamiliar hand-writing, saying: *'Happy Christmas 1986, love Aunt Dottie'*.

You can't help noticing that the name Macquarie appears a lot. The Fort and trams may be gone, but there are still Macquaries everywhere in Sydney. It's a name repeated so incessantly you start to wonder if there is a serious genetic bottleneck or possible incest problem. However, thanks to my old friend Vladimir MacTavish, I already knew who this name referred to: Lachlan Macquarie, the Governor of New South Wales 1810-1821, and the de facto Father of Australia. Victimised for his inclusive and progressive views on former convicts' place in society, he was eventually, shamefully, driven out by jealous rivals. But before then he did more than anyone to set this country on its way. And this 'father' was born (and later buried) in the Inner Hebrides of Scotland. As Vlad says in his book *The Top 50 Greatest Scots of All Time Ever*: 'It seems particularly apt that a nation of aggressively anglophobic binge-drinkers should consider a Scotsman to be their father.'

In truth, Lachlan himself was more of a staunch Presbyterian-type who preferred tea. He loved his wives dearly, and though he didn't entirely get over the death of his first, it was the second, Elizabeth, after whom Mrs Macquarie's Road is named.

For a road, it doesn't really go anywhere. It was a curiously unconstructive construction project, intended to keep convicts busy, but it does at least take you up to some more great views, with Mrs Macquarie's Chair – a seat carved into the sandstone – at the far end of it. Greater love hath no man than he should build his wife a road; why say it with flowers when you can say it with Tarmacadam? Having already built Elizabeth St. in her honour, he was clearly a man who once he had an idea, wouldn't let go of it. They thought big in the 19th century, but I bet that was an anniversary present that he never heard the end of.

'Darling, I've got you this—'

'Is it—?'

'Yes!'

'Oh, how sweet. Another road. You shouldn't have.'

'Anything for you my beloved.'

'No. Really. You shouldn't have...'

In comparison my Christmas shopping efforts are looking pretty flimsy, but at least I'll be able to get them on the plane.

Mrs Mac's Road skirts round the Botanic Gardens, which are a fabulous place to eat your sandwiches and I've no doubt Dave will soon be here pointing out trees. These gardens are entirely unlike, and complementary to, Melbourne's. They're more of a park than a tropical garden, and are home to some extraordinary 'bird-life'. The birds are everywhere, and I stand for a while in the overhanging branches of a tree, with a flock of lorikeets feeding on blossom around and above me, occasionally bravely snatching proffered flowers from a tourist's hand.

The most impressive though, are not real birds, but bats. Giant fruit bats are common around here. Until you've seen a flock of small-fox-sized bats take off at twilight, you haven't experienced a true vampire nightmare. Now they're trying to drive them away from the Gardens as they're killing irreplaceable trees. But their funky bat-aggravating radio antennae don't seem to be working, as there are still thousands of the furry devils, hanging upside down like hooded, grungy skate-boarders trying a new extreme sport. I suggest they play them freeform Jazz – that should do the trick.

If he was to return to his old city I'm sure Lachlan Macquarie would be impressed on how it has developed, and he'd no doubt recognise much of it. Many of the buildings he planned are still standing, albeit with new uses. The Sydney Conservatorium of Music is definitely the most unusual one, it has battlements. A feature that is even more curious when you discover it used to be stables. The Victorians really were absolutely wonderfully way-out bonkers in a way that modern architects with their silly spectacles will never comprehend. These days they think they're being *avant-garde* if they build anything that isn't square, but I'd say Macquarie was in the vanguard of an army that was already besieging other planets.

That's not to say the modern town-planners haven't tried to funk things up a bit, there are plenty of contemporary and wannabe-futuristic touches around; some excellent, some vaguely comical, some useless. The Sydney Tower is fantastic. It's one of those indulgences from the days of the Space Race, when everyone got carried away constructing ever higher towers to satisfy Man's temporarily fashionable craving for the skies. A fun time it was and still is, as it's left behind all these silly needles for us to climb up and look out from, like pirates in the crow's nest. Its viewing deck might not be as high as the Eureka, but the 360 degree spectacle would take some beating. And the fact that the view of Circular Quay is obscured by the ugliest building in Sydney only makes you appreciate the rest of the wonderful vista all the more. Without an Opera House to obsess over you realise how much else there is to enjoy.

In sharp contrast, the elevated monorail is a silly superfluity with no useful purpose. Opened as recently as 1988, it's already as dated as a 1960's vision of the year 2000. And it's an unfinished idea: it currently runs slowly in a little loop from nowhere to nowhere. Granted, it'll glide you from town out to Harbourside half a mile away, but once you factor in climbing up to the station and waiting for it to arrive and depart, it is genuinely quicker to walk. And because it's run by a private company, it's not included in a weekly travel pass – always a sure sign of an expensive tourist trap rather than a useful utility.

Public buildings and whatnot are all very well, but there's only so many a city needs and unless it gets its houses right it will still be a pig. Sydney is not only home to over four million people, but it is truly vast: larger than greater London and more than twice the size of New York, so I won't pretend I've studied it all, but many of the areas I did see were terrific. The beautiful old houses of Paddington, although a bit dilapidated and ramshackle in places, are as characterful as any to be found in Europe and suggest a hundred stories behind every door.

Nearby Kings Cross is an exotic land of gracefully decaying youth hostels and late night revelry. Never have I seen such a concentrated collection of excited and weary teenagers. The excited ones are starting their adventures; the weary travellers have come full circle and are at journey's end. They lie in torpor in their campervans outside the hostels, hoping to sell them on to those inside. Having spent five nights in one, I doubt there's much to choose between them in the comfort stakes. The licence plates tell stories of their own: Western Australia and Northern Territories predominate, these wheels have come a long way and are probably on their third or fourth circuit. Three young Frenchmen gather round the open carcass of an autopsied vacuum cleaner as I pass; one reaches inside and gingerly removes the cadaver of an enormous spider, holding it up for inspection before casting it aside. I nearly jump out my skin.

The dead spiders society aside, what most troubles me this afternoon, is the one question I wanted to ask the tour guide because the bus commentary certainly didn't cover it, and it is this: 'Where did you hide all your homeless over New Year?' I didn't see a single beggar on December 31st, but a couple of days on there are hundreds of them roaming the streets. It's one of the most extraordinary facets of Western civilisation that it's very richest rub shoulders with those without even a roof over their heads at night, and the fact that this is true of pretty much every major city on Earth and no-one bats an eye-lid, says much about selective vision and the myths we choose to tell ourselves of progress and opportunity.

I wonder how the great social reformer L. Macquarie Esq. would view it. Some in the 19th century thought the poor would always be with us and saw them as an imposed burden, rather than an indictment of their supposed progressive society. Others, and this is still number 1 in the US charts, thought all poverty was a self-inflicted. But you fancy other worthy Victorians – the sort that successfully fought for the abolition of slavery and stopped children from working in sweatshops – you fancy they imagined we'd have had this one licked by now.

More than anyone, radical social reformers like Macquarie and his peers invented (or most recently reinvented) the vision and belief in the continual forward progression of Man. Would he have been happy with the multi-million-dollar meaningless-mono-rail and the over-budget Opera House, or pissed off that Sydney still has an underclass unwelcome in polite society? I shouldn't have expected anything different, it's the same the world over, but it's sad that even with a practically blank canvas to start from, and a new and unique identity to forge for themselves, Australia manages no better in this regard than the mother country does with its unwanted progeny.

And something else is either missing or at least inconspicuous. There's no doubt this is a wonderful country, a unique place with great people, but as an outsider you can't help notice the contradictions and curiosities. Australia is clearly proud of their military history and the human sacrifices they made in the conflicts of the 20th century, their beautiful war memorials are testament to this and I hope I get a chance to visit Sydney's as well, but there is a conspicuous absence of memorials to the battles on their own land. Aside from one installation in the botanic gardens, I've not seen a single reminder of the bloody conflicts with the indigenous people. I'll put my hand up and admit I've not explored thoroughly, and I'll keep my eyes open over the coming days, but it emphatically wasn't a pit-stop on the bus route.

Chapter 46
RANCID ALUMINIUM
(Sunday 2ⁿᵈ Jan – Evening)

It's time to meet another man with a question I'm certain no tour guide could answer.

'Stuart, does every city have a minimum annual aluminium allocation it has to use up?'

I've hooked up with Dave at the Queen Victoria building, and he remains undisputed king of the unexpected opening line. As long as I, or anyone else, have known him, he's never begun a conversation with anything as simple as 'hello'; instead you're always given the impression you've come in half-way through an unceasing indignant monologue of outrage, and this one is right up there with his best.

'Look at this, look at this! I said look, Stuart.'

'I'm looking, I'm looking!'

He wants to show me his day's photographs, but I can't tear my eyes away from his latest sunburn. Combined with the zinc cream streaming off his face in the waterfalls of sweat cascading down his forehead, it's as if he's the victim of some hideous flesh eating virus. He looks like Michael Jackson in the Thriller video. Or any time after that video, for that matter. Dave concedes it's not a look that's likely to be a hit with the girls.

'I peeled off the sunburned skin yesterday, but there was more sunburn underneath.'

'You look like a patchwork quilt.'

'Well, I can assure you it's not as comfy and reassuring.'

'What would your mother make of you?'

'If I know her she'd just say "That'll l'arn you." She's a tough customer my mum.'

Dave has been attempting to take photos on foot, and he's not happy with his efforts. Like me he was delighted by the lack of crowd control barriers at New Year, but whereas the UK goes for the fencing option, Dave has noticed that Sydney is intent on getting through just as much metal but finding other pointless uses for it. He has a point. Every shot he's taken in the town centre is completely ruined by the hundreds of ugly, double-pronged lampposts that litter the CBD. They're ludicrously numerous and resemble giant galvanised sleepwalking stick-insects, or perhaps ten metre tall anorexic Cybermen. And these horrors are jammed incongruously in front of even the oldest and noblest buildings.

Worse still, to clutter the streetscape further, each is hung with the same tacky banner: this week's effort is proclaiming that it's New Year's Eve in Sydney. Well fancy that. New Year's Eve? In Sydney? Who'd have guessed? There was me thinking a million people had gathered here from every corner of the globe entirely by coincidence. Come on, if you're still living by an ancient lunar calendar and didn't know what the date in the West is, chances are you're not currently in Sydney to see the banners, so what's the bloody point of them? It's not even a tasteful or attractive design. They're cheap and garish but the design team will have pocketed a fat fistful of taxpayers' cash and all in the name of branding. And as Dave is now pointing out, dragging me by the arm along the road and gesticulating with wild fist-waving fury, they spoil every street-scene, every vista and every tourist photograph of the city, mine included.

I'm not quite as angry as Dave, nobody is, but he's doing his best to convert me and sometimes it's easiest to join in. As usual, he has a theory and something of a point. It's not restricted to the CBD. He's been exploring within a few of miles of his adopted 'hood, and has noticed that metal usage is district dependent, as if some councils got a job-lot off the back of a lorry from a bloke named Bruce, and are trying to find ways of dumping it before the cops come calling. Away from the city centre, some areas have almost no street furniture whatsoever; they flag up things via the low-key method of a bit of paint on the road. Whereas other suburbs have gone signposting bonkers. They have them for everything, even marking the start and end of every parking bay, be it only one car long. On a quaint little street corner, Dave attempted to photograph all fourteen unnecessary metal poles he could see within a twenty yard radius.

'I couldn't fit them all in Stuart, the camera has not been designed to encompass that much urban vandalism within one shot. I'd need NASA to do it from space.'

'NASA? Are you're not exaggerating a little?'

'No I'm bloody not! In fact what are rockets made of? You don't suppose Cape Canaveral is just an excuse to burn up aluminium?'

'No, I don't.' Nevertheless, the staggering waste, not to mention the environmental disaster of all the required smelting, has to be seen to be believed. The hard-rock miners of Australia will not be going out of business any day soon.

There is only one option to cheer Dave up (aside from sedation) and so we head for a pint in Jackson's Bar in George Street. This happens to be the pub where the Sydney branch of the Rangers Supporters Club congregates to watch their team's games, and around midnight they will be showing the Old Firm match live. With the Rangers fans' little UEFA Cup riot in Manchester still fresh in our minds, I hope the big screen TV doesn't break down or this nice bar could be overturned. Although they must be used to a few rowdy souls, as they have a Beer Drinkers Hall of fame, with brass plaques displaying the names of all those who have successfully drunk all 101 beers the pub sells. 101? No wonder David Boon was so well trained.

Should we hang around all night to watch the biggest Scottish club game and see how crazy it all gets? I can't imagine a more ridiculous thing to do having come this far, I can see pissed Rangers fans any day of the week, but I would like to study the clientele. Are they ex-pat Scots or true born Australians clinging to an ancestor's dream? And since some Rangers fans wear England football strips to matches just to wind up tonight's opponents, who are they supporting in the cricket? Alternatively, if it's fierce rivalry we're after, Dave tells me of another bar where, after midnight, taxi drivers and drag queens go head to head in a big karaoke sing-off. I do hope that becomes a tradition that lasts a hundred years.

A tough choice but ultimately we decide on two quick beers and 'none of the above'. It's the start of the final Test in the morning and I'll probably be at the match alone – or at least without technical back-up, I can't be the only ticket holder – as Dave is definitely dying. His prediction of life-threatening illness has proven as astute as his sports punditry and his lungs are starting to bubble, just as the storm clouds are beginning to pile up outside. We're discussing the team news when the first rumbles of thunder break out; then I realise it's just Dave coughing.

'Are you alright?'

'Aluminium poisoning; it's the new lead they say.'

'Are you sure you've not swallowed your own zinc cream?'

'Nonsense, zinc's not poisonous. And it's the primary component of Viagra, I'd be bound to know by now... and so would the barmaid'

'Well let's have one more before the grave. It's your round.'

Dave's coughing gets markedly worse and he falls off his stool melodramatically. I reach for my wallet and order us liquid sustenance while we preview the match.

Australia are lining up an adventurous selection. It was announced a couple of days ago that Ricky Ponting is not fit to play, proving what we all suspected, that he wasn't fit to play in Melbourne and was retained as a gesture to an illustrious past. His jaded captaincy has defined his team's performance, and had they dropped him at the MCG the scoreline might be different. This time, with nothing to lose, they're going for it: Clarke has the captaincy and Australia's first Muslim player, Usman Khawaja will get his opportunity to bat. That's a whole can of discursive worms waiting to be opened right there, but more excitingly in pure cricketing terms, Michael Beer, a spinner with only seven first class games behind him, will almost definitely take over from the injured Harris. It's the most inexperienced debut since Eve handed Adam a shiny red apple and said, 'You're opening the bowling, sunshine'. Beer is a wonderfully engaging lad, and his youthful enthusiasm will be a valuable addition if he gets the nod ahead of Bollinger. Certainly, like policemen, the Australians are getting younger: with Hughes, Khawaja, Smith and Beer playing, the team is collectively 37 years younger than the one in Brisbane.

Dave heads back to Randwick and I take the shorter walk to the hotel. I'm already lounging on my bed, watching TV, when Marco Polo texts to say he got on the wrong bus and is now walking through Centennial Park in the middle of a thunderstorm that's right over his head: *'Have sunblock in eyes and wet-through. Don't know whether to pray for rain to stop, or a direct lightning strike to end the misery.'* This is more like it, Dave has returned to form; he was letting the side down with his expert navigation on the first two days. I tell him to watch out for bats. Centennial Park is full of them, and with the thunder and lightning it just needs a smattering of wolves to complete the Transylvania theme. He texts to say he's taken a wrong turn adding fifteen minutes to the soggy walk: *'Not funny anymore.'*

How wrong he is, there's far more humour and drama in his sodden misfortune than anything on Australian TV. I text back: *'When you left the pub you should have said, "I'm going through the park, I may be some time."'* If he never makes it back he might go down in history as the 'Scot of the Antipodes' and get a statue and a docudrama about his fateful trip. Regardless, as I channel flip searching for something that isn't a *BBC* repeat, I'm certain that with or without Dave, Sydney will be up early this Monday morning. It's the decider: will England win 3-1, 2-1 or 2-2? One for the Martians to argue over, I'm having an early night.

Chapter 47
FIFTH TEST, DAY ONE
GRASS ROOTS
(Monday 3rd Jan)

Monday morning and the team news is out: England are going into the last match with an unchanged side. Isn't that the mistake Australia made at the MCG, fielding the side that won at Perth? An enforced freshening up has worked well twice already, but in spite of me writing '*FIVE bowlers – Go for the WIN!*' seventeen times in purple ink on Qantas napkins, and slipping them under Andy Flower's door in the dead of night, they're going with the same four bowlers and Collingwood. With the Ashes secured it's a timid choice and scarcely justifiable on current form. I'm starting to wonder if 'good in the dressing room' is a euphemism. Unlike batsmen, bowlers are ruthlessly cast aside even when in top nick, and despite missing a game, the now rested Finn could have finished the series as top wicket-taker, but he won't get his chance.

As I leave the hotel, Sydney is under heavy cloud. Those who move to Australia for the weather are out of their minds. It's either hideously humid, raining like a warning from God, as lethal as the Sahara, freezing at midday in midsummer, or drab drab drab; it doesn't seem to do pleasant. At least the city is showing off and running free buses to the ground, so we all zip on down Anzac Parade in great spirits. There's no doubt about it, as you approach across Moore Park the SCG is a wonderful sight even under grey skies, a welcome contrast to the relentless concrete of the MCG. It's a curate's egg like the rest of them, most of the old stands with matching roofs have long gone, but crucially enough remains for it to lift the spirits as you head in. There's something about roofs in that particular shade of copper green to instantly take you back to a bygone age, even if most of it is only paint.

Admittance is fairly painless; there are no perverse regulations, or restrictions on bags with buckles or trousers with two legs or men under four foot eleven tall. And then we see the signs: *'No readmittance to the ground'*. What? Is this some cunning trick to guarantee we spend each lunchtime in miserable queues for over-priced food? Or are they too lazy to pointlessly check bags again? Whatever the reason, my midday quest for wireless is going to be easy this time around: I simply won't have any – we're locked in for the day. Usefully, Dave finally arrived home and didn't die in the night, so is sat grumbling on a sofa, and I can call him with an account of what's happening – like an old fashioned reporter ringing the story in. Judging by the sky, I wish I had the raincoat and hat to match.

Once inside I must say the old ground retains a charm. It's a full house, but all fall silent to listen to the address from the Indigenous Australian Elder that prefixes the matches. I've seen this a few times, and it seems a nice touch at inclusion, although some Australians have voiced the opinion to me that it's either window dressing or 'a load of crap'. I've not studied the issue enough to have any opinion on the matter, but it always gains the respectful hush of the crowd, whatever their true thoughts. This time, however, the high volume of the microphone surprises the fellow giving the speech, and he recoils and exclaims clear as bell, 'Oh Bugger!' Large portions of the ground dissolve into innocent fits of laughter, which sit well next to the Elder himself finding it funny and pulling an expert clown face. I thought it was particularly appropriate that a welcome to the land should be expressed in this manner, as I've no doubt something very similar escaped a few Aboriginal lips not long after the very first greeting, and once the novelty of the beads and mirrors had worn off.

Strauss loses the toss and is consigned to the field but the overcast conditions look good for England. The downside is that after the rain overnight Anderson is slip-sliding around and threatening to twist his ankle at any moment. An injury at this stage would herald a certain defeat and there are worried faces among the English. For 118 minutes the Aussies chip runs at under two an over, and the crowd's opening roar becomes a quite murmur as we become absorbed in the tense battles being fought. This is Test cricket for connoisseurs; it's not all non-stop action, you know. I text Dave: '*God this is boring.*'

He admonishes me: '*It's Test cricket for connoisseurs, it can't all be non-stop action, you know.*' I'm not sure leaving him to write the blog unsupervised was a good idea. The phone beeps again, he always likes to have the last word twice: '*It's a good old fashioned battle of nerves, there's pride at stake.*'

I make a mental note never to allow Dave to edit anything I write ever again. But it's a battle of nerves and there's pride at stake. If Australia win here, England will not be able to claim full bragging rights over this series; you can't respond to a chant of '5-0' with a retort of '2-2'. As the sun breaks through at last, Jimmy Saville gets to his feet and by sheer force of will (and lager) gets the Army going. The voices soar, the Barmies are on their feet, sunshine and song combine, and with only four balls left till the safety of lunch, Tremlett breaks through. One down; we're on our way.

Lunch is spent in Stalag-luft SCG. For us the war is not over, and release is not an option. If it looked more like the MCG, Dave would say the illusion of prison camp would be complete. In many regards the SCG is decidedly fan-unfriendly. The separate stands are all self-contained and there are limited walkways between them, making chatting to friends in other stands a right old hoo-haa. Obviously with no re-entry allowed you can't meet in a nearby pub, so you're left with the SCG's own paltry efforts and a mooch around the back. Even the bars are as welcoming as Skegness in February. They won't sell alcohol to anyone wearing sunglasses or a peaked cap, which considering the clouds have parted and we're sitting in the midday sun in the middle of summer, is pretty much their entire clientele. I check, but I don't see any signs saying motorbike helmets aren't allowed, and if I had one to hand I've give it a go. It's all pretty poor stuff, as if the crowd are an inconvenience, and the SCG is added to the growing list of venues getting it wrong. The Aussies should try whinging a bit more; they might get some better customer service.

After lunch, a little moment of history: Usman Khawaja walks out to bat. If there were any doubts about how he'd be greeted, I'm delighted to say the cricket fans make their thoughts plain and cheer him to the rafters, many giving him a standing ovation. It has not escaped our notice how many non-white faces one sees in Australia – downtown they're often in the majority – yet they scarcely feature in the cricket teams. Aborigines are common in Aussie Rules, but one eighth of Jason Gillespie aside they've not made the Test side yet. The Boxing Day match at the MCG in 1866, was the MCC versus a completely Indigenous Australian side; things seem to have gone backwards since then.

The same issue is largely true of England in recent years. Once upon a time England drew on naturalised Caribbean quicks like Cowans, Lawrence, De Frietas, Lewis, Small and Malcolm, but that trend has dried up and the team is less ethnically diverse now than it was twenty years ago. A fair bit has been written about the inability to bring on board the legions of Asian lads playing cricket in the English northern leagues. Those that have made it through haven't cemented a place and have even met with hostility from their own community for playing for England, but they are surely a better long-term bet for fresh blood than depending upon emigrating South Africans.

Cricket Australia is in the same boat, the white man's game at Test level has remained steadfastly white. Will Khawaja's debut open the door to a new sub-continental flavour being added to future Aussie teams? Time will tell, but Khawaja looks like a class act, walking to the wicket calmly, and confidently belting his second ball to the boundary. We will see plenty more of him in the future. With the sad decline of the West Indies team and their youth heading towards basketball, Test cricket is in real danger of becoming Indians versus Anglo-Saxons unless the gospel is spread.

Another wicket falls and out steps local boy and new skipper Michael Clarke. His fellow New South Welshmen give him a very ambivalent greeting, and the Barmy Army welcome him to the captaincy with a chant of: 'You're just a shit Ricky Ponting'

Clarke was already under fire, but now he's over the flames, in the frying pan and on the menu. The pup fares no better than the old dog, he returns another poor score, the skies return to grey and the crowd remains muted. It was probably too much to expect more fireworks so soon after New Year's Eve, and today is all about the gritty Test cricket we'd expected before the start of the tour. If you believe Dave at home on the sofa, the relatively low-key response from the fans is explained by an absorption in the mental battles being fought; if you believe me it's because the kiddie-beer is even more watered down than usual as the clouds open and top up our glasses. Hands up everyone who packed an umbrella for Australia? Yup, thought not, me neither. But every time it rains it rains pennies from heaven, and even at the current exchange rate we'll soon be able to afford another round.

An early tea is taken, but it takes a little bit of comedy to get there: the umpires dancing the players into the pavilion while the lights warm up, then back out briefly, then in again with the score at 111. The late David Shepherd would be superstitiously shaking it all about were he still with us; we're just shaking the raindrops off. There are plenty of fans already wearing the bright pink colours of the *McGrath Foundation*, as part of that charity's fund-raising drive through this match, but they're beginning to resemble wilted flowers. The lads with cut-out watermelons on their heads are probably the most sensibly attired. Some of these are of the most intricate design, with visors and all sorts, but the danger is that in these favourable conditions their heads might start to grow. Then again, I hear watermelons actually grow in manure, giving the melon-heads as they're called, another potential nickname at their disposal.

The funniest moment of the day comes when an Aussie sitting in the front row of the Barmy Army section – foolhardy in itself – responds to the provocative chant of, 'Does your boyfriend know you're here?' with a series of hand gestures and insults. Warned by the police for this, which is a trifle harsh in the circumstances, he ignores their order to cease and desist and continues with primeval responses until he is finally thrown out. As he is led away Billy the Trumpet spontaneously bursts into the opening bars of *'Another One Bites the Dust.'*

And another one's gone! With just a little play after tea and Khawaja on an excellent 37, Swann grabs his wicket just as the rain starts falling again. His agony is compounded when both teams walk off the pitch with him and play is washed out for the day, leaving affairs at 131/4. Losing a wicket just before a break is a feature of the whole series for the Baggy Greens.

And so after a quiet day I trudge through the rain to the nearby Doncaster Hotel for a much anticipated meeting with a man called Mark, or as he's better known on Twitter, @White_Ox. Mark has become a regular fixture of the podcast with his entertaining take on the affairs from an Australian viewpoint. Making home recordings after play in deepest darkest NSW, he's been sending these through to our enormous background staff of editors (er… that would be Tim… although he is a big lad). Mark's professionalism has put us all to shame and really made the whole thing work, sparring at a distance with an Englishman called Archie who has been giving the other side from the comfort of his sofa back in England. He's definitely something of a radio natural, recording long sections with barely a slip of the tongue, which anyone who's heard Dave's efforts after he's had less than 35 but more than 100 fluid ounces of beer will know is tricky.

I join him and his father and friends and they are a charming bunch. Friendly but slightly reserved, and scrupulously polite, when Dave staggers in from his nearby sickbed to join us for a medicinal pint or two, he refers to it as, 'old-fashioned country manners.' Whether Mark lives in 'the country' or he just had a better upbringing than the kids of Melbourne I can't say, but I feel when we talk cricket that I'm part of that timeless conversation that has been running since the inception of Ashes.

Far better than my Bus Siddle effort, Mark has coined a new nickname for Tremlett: 'Dad and I, we call him Peter Pan. Not because he's the lad who never grew up, he's a mountain of a man, but he's got batsmen in Never Never Land.'

Perfect, and in fact I love the idea of the whole Australian team as pirates. But for Dave and me, it throws up the question of who should play Captain Hook and Tinkerbell.

'Captain "Pull" Ponting and Anderson, perhaps?'

'Maybe Johnson and Ian "Tinker" Bell?'

'Maybe, maybe. Who looks most like they're being pursued by a crocodile, Stuart?'

'Dunno. Who's the lightest on their toes?'

Dave for once is stumped: 'Don't ask me, I'm useless at these things. If only Chas and Leo were here...'

On more serious issues Mark is definitely on our wavelength. He's disappointed and appalled by the concrete monstrosity of the Victor Trumper Stand – the largest and worst in the SCG – that has replaced his beloved Doug Walters stand. I understand Mark's frustration; in yet another example of unsympathetic development, the new stand was dumped smack on top of both Doug's stand and what remained of the old Hill. As I explained in Adelaide, this was the traditional area for the grass-roots fan; in fact I've always wondered if that's where the term came from. And it was from the legendary SCG Hill, the most famous of them all, that sledger supreme Yabba taunted a fly-swatting Scottish England captain with the immortal line, 'Leave our flies alone, Jardine. They're the only friends you've got here.'

I'm glad to say, that though the Hill may be gone, the grass-roots fan is alive in well in the shape of Mark. But though he recognises the importance of tradition he's no backward thinker, and his views on the future are interesting. Here's a man who's as Aussie as they're cut, saying it did his heart proud and is one of his highlights of the series to hear the ovation that greeted Khawaja. 'It was a real cultural shift, a wonderful story. Not since 1992 have we had a debutant at number three. The reception that he got was unlike anything I've heard for an Australian cricketer in a very long time.'

That pretty much silenced any doubts I had about Australian attitudes to a multiracial team. Not that we got into deep discussion on socio-political issues, there was far too much bonhomie and clinking glass for all that. This is evidenced when we turn to the issue of the crowd jeering Clarke as he came out to bat. Mark confirms that Australians around him were just as guilty, but opinions vary on the reasons behind this. I wonder aloud if a number of his countrymen don't care for Clarke because his squeaky-clean, metrosexual image is so far away from the tough guy heroes of old. Mark only very tentatively agrees: 'It *could* be that; they *may* not think he's strong enough...'

He sensibly appears about to 'take the fifth' while the tapes are running but, before I can draw him further on the matter, Dave cuts across us both and ruins the interview with a spirited defence of Clarke in the names of international brotherhood and alcohol mixed with Night Nurse. Like me he's prone to switching sides in the name of conviviality but sometimes it is like working with a scrawny Oliver Reed.

@White_Ox has one more bombshell to drop. His father is with us, but when he steps out for a moment Mark relays the tale of his honest surprise when earlier he'd asked his dad how long it had been since he'd been in the SCG? 'When I was 19, about 35 years ago,' came the reply. It'll have changed a bit since then Mark warned him. When they walk out into the ground his father scanned the scene, took it all in and said, 'Yeah son, sure has changed since I played here.'

The penny drops and the full significance of the ragged, dusty baggy NSW cap that takes pride of place in the shed back home sinks in. There were only five teams in the Sheffield Shield back then, and they don't hand those caps out for free at the door. We're in rare company, and with breeding like that is it any wonder Mark's a thoroughbred cricket commentator?

Chapter 48
FIFTH TEST, DAY TWO
FAIRY-TALE CHILDHOOD
(Tuesday 4ᵗʰ Jan)

It is without doubt, the most compelling breakfast television in history. Competition in this genre is not stiff, but listening to the brilliant Syd Waddell and John Gwynne commentating on a pulsating World Darts Final is the perfect start to any day. They're also talking the most sense of anyone on television. Again, not hard when you consider the competition, but at least the numbers the darts commentators work in are absolute, whereas the weather forecasters on the breakfast news are only predicting 'the possibility' of rain. So not really a forecast then, just the sort of guess we could all make by looking out the window at the gusty and overcast conditions and having a wild stab. Unfairly they're the only ones that get paid. With Dave's psychic ability for making accurate predictions, I reckon he should diversify and have a bash at the weather.

It's another sell-out crowd, but the day starts badly for Australia with England removing the dangerous brothers quickly: Haddin goes first and then, to shush the doubters (me and Dave) Collingwood clean bowls Hussey with a brilliant in-swinger. I wonder if Colly's considered an alternate career: he's a bit old to start out as a bowler but he'd make a fine magician. @White_Ox, texts me stating that with Hussey out and the longest batting tail in Australian history, his side won't make 200. Whatever happened to the Australian cockiness? But then again whatever happened to Australian batting? When Smith and Siddle fall and Australia are reeling at 187 for 6, Mark is sounding like a guru. Ultimately though, his prediction is as wayward as Johnson's bowling, and all thanks to Mitch himself. The Superhero of Perth enters the arena and throws the bat in grand style, ably assisted by his Boy-Wonder Hilfenhaus.

What to make of all these dramatic shifts? The perfect ones to ask, if only I could reach them, would be the group of twenty blokes I see in the next stand who have all come dressed as Richie Benaud, complete with comb-over wigs and Channel 9 branded microphones. They're so realistic I actually I start to wonder if there's been a cloning experiment in a Coogee laboratory that has got loose, and fled back to its natural habitat, the SCG. I can't see what they're saying, but if they're anything like the real thing they'll all be moaning about the front foot law.

There is little more exciting in Test cricket than the bowlers giving their opposing numbers some stick and the crowd are loving it. It could be the preponderance of dead-pan Benauds, but so far the atmosphere has been as subdued but intense as a chess match between tranquilised schizophrenics. For the first three and a half sessions of the match the biggest buzz around the stadium was the noise of the bats and birds inhabiting the nearby parks. Sydney is the crowd of connoisseurs they say, and compared to the other matches they've all had their mouths full. Now thanks to the exploits of Johnson and Hilfenhaus the Aussies now have something to cheer about, and cheer they do. The SCG has come alive and Australia are back in this game.

Johnson is batting brilliantly for a bowler, but you'd think he was Viv Richards in his pomp, as Strauss begins setting fields so defensive the Germans would go through Belgium to avoid them. We presume he's trying to get the 'rabbit' on strike: a questionable tactic at the best of times, and even more so when you're keeping one bowler off strike to target another. When Hilfenhaus trots down the wicket and blasts Bresnan for a huge six, the flaw in the plan is exposed; the rabbit has become the greyhound. Finally, eleven overs past lunch, the assault is over, after Johnson departs and Hilfenhaus attempts a tennis forehand against Anderson. 280 all out. England must be padding up with memories of Perth fresh in their minds. And once again Dave is closest in the betting stakes, how does he do it?

Strauss showed Johnson's batting far more respect than the Barmies show his bowling but it was an impressive display by the tail. @White_Ox texts once again, claiming he always thought the tail would post a decent score. There hasn't been a more dramatic change of tune since the Marx Brothers invaded the orchestra pit in *A Night at the Opera*.

Tunes are in shorter supply at this match: so far the England portion of the crowd is playing a smaller part in affairs than usual. The open acoustics of the SCG provide little amplification, and there seems to be considerably less drinking going on. Possibly all bolts were shot over Christmas and New Year, perhaps the funds of the tourists are running low, or maybe we're all weary after weeks of sun, singing, and sledging. There's no shortage of England fans in attendance, but there appear fewer of the hardcore Barmy Army, and the killjoy regulations of the MCG and SCG regarding hanging banners have made it harder to raise the flag and concentrate resistance around the ground. You'd think it was a deliberate tactic, a little bit of anti-England psychological warfare, but really they don't want you obscuring their precious advertising hoardings. Money wins over personality again.

The Aussie fans find their voices in a very unmusical way after lunch, turning their ire on Tremlett, fielding at deep square leg. A couple of kids are waiting by the hoardings hoping he'll sign their miniature bats and hats, but he is steadfastly ignoring their requests. Soon, shouts of, 'Sign the bat!' head in his direction. These then turn to 'Sign the bat, you [insert obscenity of choice],' which in time becomes a series of probing questions in a form that really children shouldn't be exposed to. Finally we reach, 'Hey Tremlett [obscenity] [obscenity] [obscenity] [repeat until effective].' I've not seen many people change their minds when insulted, and Tremlett continues to concentrate on his fielding, which is well within his rights, if a little cold. But still the children wait and you can't help but feel for them. At the end of the innings he has the perfect opportunity to do the decent thing and sign a couple of bats and make everyone happy, safe in the knowledge he'll be off the ground before it becomes a flood of requests. But instead, with all the hauteur of Douglas Jardine, he walks off without a backward glance.

The good news for Australia, is that if Mitchell Johnson bats well then he bowls well – or so the Aussie fans say and hope. The last time he did, England barely had time to locate a wall, let alone get their back to it. But not on this occasion. On a far more placid pitch, and without Harris to join the barrage, the England openers look secure, with Strauss racing to a half-century. By tea they're 73 for 0 and the Barmies are singing at Hilfenhaus: 'Are you Johnson in disguise?'

The Australian fans are equally unimpressed with the Hilf'. The tail-hero of just an hour ago, he is now fielding in Tremlett's shoes, and he won't sign the children's bats either. Although not quite so expletive ridden, he also comes in for a verbal pounding; cricket fans are very even-handed like that.

Things take a turn for the surreal when the Hilf' is joined by the Hoff': David Hasselhoff arrives in the ground escorted by Glenn McGrath and Shane Warne; neither of whom really match up to Pamela Anderson or Erika Eleniak it must be said. Play carries on but we're all craning our necks to see what on earth they're up to. Just beyond the boundary, the Hoff takes guard against Warne – who apparently only bowls at actors now – and not for the first time I think Australian sports coverage is barmier than the Army. It must be even more baffling for Strauss and Cook, who are hearing cheers that don't coincide with their shots. We in the ground don't hear the post-game interview, but I imagine it went something like:

'David, blah blah blah'
'Shane, blah blah blah, fantastic spectacle, I love cricket!'
'Blah blah blah, understand the lbw law?'
Laughter
'No. Blah, blah blah, Crocodile Dundee, AC/DC!'
'Blah blah @theashes?'
'Blah, blah, incredible story, fantastic spectacle...'
'Blah blah...'
'... and buy my new album!!'
Laughter

After tea Strauss is dismissed, Trott follows for a duck and hearts are fluttering, as Kevin Pietersen hops out to the wicket to a chorus of boos. Despite his double-ton at Adelaide, he's seemed nervous and fidgety all tour. One career-best swallow doesn't make an Ashes summer and I'm convinced all is not well in his head. How will it go for him here? He effortlessly clips his first delivery from Johnson to the boundary. Ah. Right. Probably would have been a six if he weren't so nervous.

I'm sat next to Lionel again and we're just agreeing that KP looks jolly confident when, at last, it's the moment we've all been waiting for: 'Ay, ay, it's Beer o'clock!' It was beer o' clock hours ago for most fans, but Lionel's right, this time it's official: Michael Beer is coming onto bowl. This is a fairytale. Beer is 27 years old and has never *even been* to the SCG before, but he's been pulled from obscurity onto the biggest stage. How he must have wished for a debut in Perth, in a winning team on a ground he knew, just to settle the jitters. The metaphorical wood-cutter's son trots in and the evil Baron Pietersen disdainfully thumps his opening delivery to the boundary like he's swatting a fly.

'Welcome to Test cricket,' says Lionel and all the radio commentators in perfect sync. The words are coming out of every pair of lips in the SCG; that old joke never goes out of fashion. But he's a well-pulled pint this lad and he keeps his head. With Cook on 46, Hilfenhaus holds onto the catch that gives Beer his first Test victim. He skips in joy! The crowd erupts! But wait! No! I tell you it's pantomime and exclamation marks all round the ground today. Mouths are open, there are disappointed Ohs and sympathetic Awws, all the peaks and troughs of the day coalesce into one delivery: the umpire Billy Bowden is asking the third umpire to check whether the ball is legitimate. Unbelievably, almost unheard of, a dead slow spinner has over-stepped the mark and no-balled. Cook survives again. Even above the clamour, I'm sure I can make-out twenty Richie Benauds going into over-drive: the back-foot law shouldn't have been scrapped, it would never have happened in my day, you could still get change out of a googly— those boys certainly picked the right day to commentate on. Cook has had all the luck of both teams put together in this series, he's more Irish than Morgan, and poor crestfallen Beer must fancy something stronger.

Not the fairytale he'd hoped for then, but at least he plays the handsome Prince for the crowd and takes the time to sign a couple of the waiting children's bats. For this he receives a huge cheer from English and Aussie fans alike, but that only alerts killjoy-Clarke who gives him the bullet for doing so, and not moving squarer as the skipper had been requesting. The poor lad. And poor lad also, the child who'd been the very first to the boundary, who'd waited *four long hours* for an autograph from Tremlett or Hilfenhaus, and who had given up his vigil just minutes earlier. When he sees the others getting autographs he runs back to pitch side, but tragically it is too late: Beer has moved away, and the boy goes home unrewarded. It's tough being a kid. I don't know if he cried, but I nearly did.

Michael must have been close to tears himself when he realized he'd blown the chance to dismiss the England run-machine and turn the game around, but he still has a card to play. The move squarer does the trick, and when he catches a mishit Pietersen pull shot he gets the biggest cheer of the day. And with that wicket the Australians are just about back in the match.

So the weather has stayed fair and we couldn't have been given a better show if one of the Opera House sopranos had popped in to give us an aria. The fat lady shouldn't be singing for another two or three days but we can't tell yet if the Australian score is a good one or not. The locals at the bar I'm in, think not. It is two hours after the close of play, and I'm out for a pub-crawl around the Rocks with Chas and Leo. It's not much of a crawl; we don't even manage sloth speed. Truth be told, slowly spreading lichen would overtake us as we only get as far as the first bar. Here we find a U2 tribute band playing and reckon that will do us for the rest of the night; ironically we'd found exactly what we were looking for. Fortunately Dave isn't here or he'd find a way to pull the plugs, cut the leads or set fire to the building; he's not a worshiper at the Church of Bono. My view is that as sanctimonious, hypocritical tax-dodgers go, he's got some of the best tunes, so why worry about it? Clearly I'm going native.

'A Scotsman, an Englishman and a Welshman walk into a bar—'

'Heard it!'

'You don't know what I'm going to say.'

'I've heard every Welsh joke going.'

'It might not be a Welsh joke—'

For the first time I have a proper chance to talk to Leo without Chas sticking his oar in. And there are sensitive issues to discuss, I want to ask him about a personal matter.

'Leo, you're not like us—'

'What do you mean?'

'You're Welsh'

'Yes, Stuart, have you just noticed?'

'No listen—' Regardless of the shakiness of my mental processes at this late hour, I'm genuinely interested in Leo's opinion as a Swansea lad. As a Scot, I'm an obvious outsider, and as an Englishman, Chas is an obvious insider, but what is Leo, if not an inside-outsider? 'How do you see it, where do the Welsh fit in?'

'We're next to England, Stuart.'

'I know you're next to England, but in what way?'

'If East Anglia is the arse, and Devon and Cornwall are the legs, then we're are sitting on England's lap.'

I drunkenly make my point clearer. The Welsh have been completely captured by the English. Never mind the luxuries of separate Parliaments and legal and education systems, where it really matters, in international cricket, Wales has been wholly swallowed up by the perfidious English. Scotland and Ireland have one-day international sides, but the English and Wales Cricket Board's only concession to Cymru is a few games in Cardiff. Bad enough to call themselves the ECB, but they've put three bloody lions on the shirt without any sign of the Welsh

Dragon. 'No-one shouts and sings "Come on England and Wales," do they?'

'It's a bit of a mouthful, Stuart.'

'I would be bothered by that.'

'I'm not that bothered really. I'm from *South* Wales and Glamorgan kind of act as the Welsh team.'

Glamorgan's status as a first class team is often used as an argument against Wales having their own international team, and to their credit, they do play across the principality, including Colwyn Bay on the north coast. However, going by that unreliable barometer of public opinion the *BBC* message-boards, some Welsh fans remain annoyed. Having said that, going by the number of Barmy Army Welsh Brigade T-shirts I've noticed on tour there are plenty that couldn't give a monkey's.

'It must have cost you a fortune to come here, why have you spent so much money and time following England to Australia, when you could have followed Wales to New Zealand for next year's Rugby World Cup?'

'Oh I don't like rugby.'

'You don't like rugby?'

'No'

'Really?

'Lots of men rolling around together, no, not my thing at all.'

'Oh.' See, just when you think you know someone they surprise you. 'Are you sure you're from Swansea?'

Chapter 49
FIFTH TEST, DAY THREE
JANE MCGRATH DAY
(Wednesday 5th Jan)

The SCG is a magnificent vision this morning: bathed in golden sun at last, it is gift-wrapped in pink. All round the ground the fans are marking Jane McGrath Day in aid of the *McGrath Foundation* by dressing for the occasion. It's a marvellous sight, with the players emerging from the pavilion onto a pink carpet, and the beautiful 19th century Ladies Pavilion rebranded as the Jane McGrath Stand. It's a charity that crosses borders, as Jane was the English girl who married Australia's fast bowling King; the sort of deal that once secured peace between countries for a generation. Even without it being for a good cause, I doubt spectators have been so attractively dressed since the 1960s, when everyone arrived in a shirt and tie (and a heavy overcoat and NHS specs if it was in Britain). It's just a shame Brian from the Brisbane and Adelaide leg of the tour isn't here; he could have worn his pink shirts without anyone batting an eyelid.

The clothes may have changed, but some things remain constant, Alastair Cook keeps scoring. Today he picks up his 700th run of the series. Any luck going around tends to be his preserve: the edges never quite carry, every near miss is as good as a mile, every review in his favour. 'Out' yesterday off an inexplicable no-ball, this morning he's reached nervous 99 when again Beer appears to have his man, with a catch low down by Hughes at short-leg. The Australians are ecstatic and carry on lengthy celebrations, congratulating Beer on his maiden Test wicket, without even glancing at the impassive umpire, who has not raised an eyebrow let alone a finger. Cook is having none of it and stands his ground, and only Australia's persistent backslapping leads umpire Bowden to request a review: *Not Out.* Hughes and Haddin had known this too. The replay shows Hughes shrugging at Haddin in uncertainty, before the jubilation of his unsighted team mates convince the fresh-faced twenty-two year old to join in. Once more the Beer goes flat.

So Cook survives for his century by an inch, but the Australians don't applaud. He has now scored 8 million runs in 3 years at the crease at an average of 100,007.23 – no mean feat for a guy the Aussies had thought a soft touch. This summer has belonged to him, he's milked his purple patch like it was Ermintrude from the Magic Roundabout; the darker pink variety of the *McGrath Foundation* T-shirts worn today is an approximately appropriate colour. Only Walter Hammond C.B.E is beyond him in the English Ashes stats.

Impressive as that is, Dave is unconvinced: 'Meh. Michael Vaughan scored over 600 in a losing team facing McGrath, Warne, Gillespie and Lee, that's a different league from this.'

It's true Vaughan made a couple of ducks and had more innings to reach his mark, but @White_Ox made a similar point: do they prove he's a great batsman or that this is a mediocre attack? Most of the Aussies are more convinced of the latter.

'Stuart, you're not wearing pink!'

Chas and Leo arrive.

'How do you know I'm not wearing any pink?'

'Ahhh, that old one.'

'What about you, are you wearing pink, Dave?'

'Oh jeez!'

Dave has revealed a peeled piece of skin, still as pink as a pink grapefruit underneath.

'Did you do that for charity?'

'I think you'd better make a contribution to the *McGrath Foundation*, you'll be needing their services.'

'It's a breast cancer charity you dufus.'

'Men get breast cancer too.'

Dave is ever knowledgeable.

'Really?'

'Really?'

'Shit.'

'Yup.'

We're all chastened into reflective silence, it might be a pretty sight in the stands but it's a serious matter. We respond like men and clam up and stare hard at the cricket.

Lunchtime rolls around and I have another request for a radio interview, this time from the *Melbourne Sports Network*. Once more I am impressed by the Australian host's humility in defeat. There is no brash confidence that this series is just a blip, there is a genuine concern about the future of Australian cricket.

It all makes me wonder if we're seeing the downside of Australia's sporting obsession. Here sport is life: in terms of importance, it is their sport, art, music and literature rolled into one; so when they fail, they have nothing left with which to console themselves. In every city I've been, I've seen hundreds of people playing sport, knock-around matches between families are common outside cricket grounds, and tennis courts are in every park and always filled. Yet as a country they're being whipped in the cricket and have only one aging old battler in the ATP top 100. If you bet your entire culture on sport and then lose, your whole national identity is thrown into question. Maybe that's why the Brisbanites so hate Andy Murray, he's from a country where tennis is a game for girls at public school and courts are as rare as sunny days, but their only decent player of recent years, Lleyton Hewitt, can't hold a candle to him.

I say very little of this – you want to keep these things light – and the interview moves on to the issue of singing at Australian sporting events. They simply don't. Every Aussie Rules team has its 'song' but it's only sung in celebration, not during the game when mouths are occupied in maintaining the barrage of abuse – it is football after all. Nevertheless, to turn the tide against the mighty Barmies, a competition has been launched on Australian radio for the best home fans' effort, with a prize of $10,000 at stake.

'Did you tell them about my master plan?'

'No.'

'Awww, Stuart!'

Dave's grand scheme is to infiltrate the Fanatics and join the ranks of Scotland's great Australian song writers by donating them a ditty. He's been working on the idea for some time. The one drawback is that he's never written a song in his life.

'I'm credited as a writer on a music CD.'

'You didn't actually write any of the tunes though.'

'Nor did the Barmy Army, unless Ian Curtis has come back to life and joined up. Besides, I told you, I have a winning strategy.'

'Which is?'

'To set it to the tune of "Flower of Scotland." That'll wind up the English.'

'And make them sing "Are you absolutely certain you're not Scotland in disguise?"'

'That will only prove its efficacy.'

In fairness, having heard the hopeless level of competition, if Dave can muster a choir he must be a shoe-in for the prize. I put it to the boys that the Fanatics absence of a repertoire is all the more bewildering when you consider that it was Australians who gave the world the most famous cricket song of them all.

'Did they?' asks Chas.

'Yes.'

'Surely "Dreadlock Holiday" by 10CC is the best cricket song?'

'Right era, wrong band.'

'"Meeting Mr Miandad", by the Duckworth Lewis Method?'

'Good song, but wrong era, wrong band.'

'"N-n-nineteen (not out)" by Rory Bremner?'

'Oh god no. Wrong everything.'

'"Snooker Loopy" by Chas N Dave?'

'No and I don't fancy your chances in that competition, after all. You're all wrong. Everyone knows the best cricket song ever written is "Howzat!?" by Sherbet.' There are groans around me. I accept that it's not strictly a cricket song – it's about a straight-up Aussie bloke catching his Sheila cheating – but I guarantee every man of a certain age is singing it right now.

'Howzat!? You messed around – I caught you out – Howzat!? ...'

See, told you. In spite of arguably the worst band-name in history (which I'd have thought must have got them into a few punch-ups over the years), 'Howzat!?' not only took Sherbet up the charts in Britain and Oz, but even reached number 61 in the United States.

'Now that I've foouund where you're at – it's goodbye. Well HowZat!? It's goodbyeee!'

'Shut up, Dave.'

With a catchy lyric like that, clearly these were the lads you'd nominate to take the Americans aside, and have that awkward conversation about cricket you've been putting off.

After lunch, much rests on Australia's most consistent bowler of the series, Siddle, and their occasional match-winner, Johnson, but on a nice flat pitch with a ball that won't swing they're as limply ineffectual as... well, Hilfenhaus. Some commentators wanted Doug Bollinger to play in this game at his home ground, but the Sydneysiders aren't convinced the 12th man would make a difference. As Doug bounces around the boundary rope with drinks, he cops some serious flak from home supporters suggesting he must be absolutely hopeless if he can't even get a game in this team. 'The Rug' responds admirably, and gives them the Olde Agincourt two fingers; though it would have had more weight if he'd got a single arrow on target in Adelaide.

Smith eventually gets a bowl, and though the two spinners may have future, at present they don't strike terror into their enemy. Their warm goofy grins lack Warney's big burger bite, and there's a similar gulf between their best deliveries. On a day that is flooded with pink, all Australia is suddenly harmless and gentle. Is this the country that brought us more deadly fauna and fast bowlers than you could count? If so England have found themselves a team of Steve Irwins who know no fear.

Together with Ian Bell, Cook takes England to tea and the

match begins to look safe already. When he's finally dismissed for 189 by Shane Watson the Aussie team are not keen on applauding him off the field – let's be charitable and assume from sheer exhaustion – but the crowd give him a standing ovation. It's a shame he didn't make the end of play as Dave had been working on another song:

'He bats through the day, he bats through the night... Stuart, what rhymes with night?'

'You know very well, and it's hardly appropriate. In any sense of the word.'

'What, even in the sense of "to appropriate something"?'

'Now you're just talking night.'

'Okay, how about this? He bats through the niiiiight, he bats through the daaaaay... Chaz, what rhymes with day?'

Almost immediately after Cook departs, Bell is given out, caught off a possible fine edge. He calls for a review, and with the 'hot-spot' technology showing nothing Aleem Dar rightly reverses his decision. It's relayed to us by the radio commentary that the Snickometer suggests Bell has nicked it, but as it's considered unreliable technology it plays no part in the review process. He might have been a lucky boy, we'll never be sure, but that should be the end of it. Instead it turns into a heated debate.

Tony Greig, not often short of an opinion, believes that despite no admissible technological evidence that Bell actually touched the ball, Aleem Dar should have upheld his original decision of 'out'. But he behaved absolutely correctly. As the rules stand the batsman has a right to say, 'Prove I hit that.' Only if there is incontrovertible evidence to the contrary can the on field umpires decision be over-turned by the third umpire. Greigy reckons there isn't proof he *didn't* hit it, so Dar should stick to his guns. But that's a logical absurdity akin to a witch trial; essentially, 'If there's a hotspot he's guilty, if there's not we dismiss it as "fallible" and the batsman is burned either way.' Aleem Dar understands what others do not: that if technology designed to prove a positive is called upon and comes up blank, he is morally obliged to pardon Bell – innocent until proven guilty. Otherwise it's like arresting people on suspicion and convicting them because they can't produce conclusive evidence they didn't do it.

The debate rages in the stands too, there is outrage that Dar didn't have the 'guts' to uphold his original decision. But you *cannot prove the negative*, only observe the absence of the positive, and either you accept the technology as incontrovertible evidence or you don't use it at all. It would be oxymoronic to believe it only when you *choose* to believe it. Maybe Snicko should be utilised, or like the Indians you believe that no gizmos should be allowed at all – these are other arguments altogether. While each side in a match has the right to call upon hot-spot, Bell was 'not out', and Aleem Dar realised that. He has once again been flawless in this match; he was probably right to give Bell 'out' on instinct and absolutely right to over-turn it, however unfair that sounds.

Salt is rubbed in the wound when Bell is dropped by Smith off his own bowling, and he sails on to his first century of the series. It was a bit jammy, but you can't deny he deserved one for the way he's batted this summer.

With Matt Prior already past 50 in 50 balls, the teams are taken off for bad light. England follow grudgingly, having not looked in the slightest danger and now over 200 ahead. Leaving the pitch is solely the umpires' decision, but if the batsmen had a say in the matter these two would have happily carried on batting by moonlight, heedless of any risk of talking dogs.

England are in the pink and so are all their fans, and for once it's not first degree burns. Vodafone promised $1000 to the *McGrath Foundation* for every six hit and every wicket taken today, and unfortunately we didn't get many of either, just a solid wall of runs. Considering how I feel about phone networks these days, nothing would have given me greater pleasure than to see Vodafone take a massive hammering, but they'll barely have to cough up the price of a plane ticket. On a day that showed Australia's caring heart, Cook revealed he doesn't have one when it comes to batting against Australia.

Chapter 50
FIFTH TEST, DAY FOUR
A TALE OF TWO COLLYS
(Thursday 6th Jan)

It's a sunny sunny day in Sydney. Once again Chas is sitting next to me and he's on a mission. The tour is nearing its end and he's getting worried about his average. How can he return home with his head held high if his mean daily beer intake is still in single figures?

'This is the first time I've started before midday, I'm making one last push.'

'How many have you had?'

'This is my fifth,' he says taking a long pull on a pint.

'That's not bad...'

I check my watch, it's still twenty-five minutes till lunch; he is definitely on his way to his highest score of the series.

'I've got to acclimatise myself.'

'It's a bit late for that isn't it? You're going home in three days.' I realise the ever changeable weather over here keeps you on your toes, but Chas has made the classic holiday mistake of holding back, going too tentatively, and only really letting go and enjoying the trip right at the very end. Or so I thought, but I couldn't be more wrong.

'Yeah, but I'm coming back.' He reveals his vision of a new life. While the rest have been partying and I've been slaving over a hot blog, Chas has decided to emigrate to Australia, and incredibly has already applied for jobs and a work visa. Amazing. One of us has gone native.

'I suggest you apply for a liver transplant now, it'll save waiting later.'

Even more amazingly, he says that Melbourne was his

favourite city. I'm very surprised, but Dave is stunned: 'Maybe it was just a bit English for us, Stu.'

'No, Melbourne was my favourite too,' chips in John, 'It had the most European atmosphere.'

'I like my Australian cities Australian,' I insist stubbornly.

'What about Brisbane?'

'Er... not that Australian. How about Adelaide?'

'Perth, I liked Perth,' says Dave.

'I thought you said Adelaide was like England and Perth was like Scotland?' chimes in Leo.

I need to settle this once and for all, 'Can we all at least agree that we're very happy in Sydney?'

'Agreed.'

'Agreed.'

'Agreed.'

'We've not seen Hobart yet.'

Dave aside, we've reached consensus. So there we have it. If we all do this again, next time around, Chas will likely be a full-on Australian citizen and batting for the other side. And Sydney is definitely a good place to start: from Lady Bay beach to the bright lights of Oxford Street it's got it all. But we wish Chas well, because if resettling Down Under was good enough for bodyline legend Harold Larwood, it's good enough for one of this shower.

There's going to be plenty of unacclimatised casualties today, it's the first early day scorcher we've had here. But the agony of the sunburnt Barmy Army in the stands will scarcely match the agony of the Australian cricketers on the pitch. Matt Prior has just left the field, out for chanceless 118, having scored the fastest Ashes ton by an Englishman in thirty years. Not since Ian Botham in 1981 has anyone given them such a kicking, and that was on foreign soil, not in their own backyard. Bresnan has put in a handy 35, England are past 600 again and Australia are already 329 behind.

The numbers cease to have relevance; they're screwed, completely screwed. Prior's dismissal off so-very-nearly-a-no-ball (but you're allowed to skid forward with your front foot – a new one to me), is the only thing stopping more records being broken today.

Lunchtime arrives and it's time to digest the news, and for Chas, his sixth pint. Earlier today it was announced that this is officially Collingwood's swansong. The battler supreme has gracefully jumped before he is pushed, and retired from Test cricket. There's not a dry eye in the house. Irrespective of Dave and me believing he should have been dropped, what cricket fan, can fail to be sad to see the end of his career? Never has a player given more through five days, than Colly gave through every match he ever played in. I've remarked on how comical fielding and running between the wickets often used to be, and that's changed because of men like Paul Collingwood who added masses of hard work and constant effort to a natural agility and good eye. I'd rate Collingwood as just about the greatest all-round fielder I have ever seen.

I was dumbstruck when I read Simon Hughes book *A Lot of Hard Yakka* and learned how little hard yakka there actually was in the life of a county cricketer in the 80s. Playing cricket for a living wasn't reward enough it seemed, for young men who often just batted between cigarettes and trips to the bookies or the bar. I maintain those days had charm, but if we must have this new age of professionalism then only the fittest will survive; in this series that's been England, and again, some credit for that must go to Collingwood who has always led by example.

He's enjoyed the ecstasy of Ashes wins, and the agony of the 5-0 drubbing through which he played extremely well. There will have been no-one on the plane here who was more determined to turn that around. The sadness is that he wasn't able to provide one last good score. But the lad who has said he can't believe he ever got ten Test centuries won't lose much sleep over that. He's a team man and his team are winning, that's the memory he'll keep. He's chipped in on the field with some blinding catches, and dismissing Hussey may be the moment that turned this match into a series winner. Let's hope for one last glorious run-out before England wrap this up, to bring the crowd to its feet. Colly we salute you.

After lunch England emerge, not as fielders, but inexplicably still fancy-dressed in pads. They only last another two overs. It was scarcely worth Anderson and Tremlett putting the gloves on when they could have been warming up and focussing on the real job in hand. With a lead of 361 already, they've wasted 20 minutes for just 3 runs, and rain is threatened tomorrow. Part of me feels a washed-out final day would serve them right, but then I have joined Chas on the booze.

But no matter how dull England's decision making, Australia will find a way to blow it. This time, Shane Watson, who has been Australia's second best batsman, once again throws away a promising start. He races to 38 at a run a ball, then races down to Phil Hughes's end, without first checking if Hughes was leaving it vacant for him. Two disastrous run-outs in two games, both Watson's fault. Bad enough to be run out by a full twenty yards, but when the issue is time at the crease, what's the point? To win this match Australia would need to bat like demons for four sessions, and then bowl like the devil to dismiss England in a session, and all assuming no rain falls; it's not going to happen, and that suicidal second run wasn't going to swing it. I'm laughing, but Dave, typically, is genuinely cross:

'It's bloody Laurel and Hardy. I always hated Laurel and Hardy.'

'Come on, Dave, it's funny.'

'No! It's too easy. We've come all this way to watch slapstick.' I can see what he means; it's hard to tell the difference between this and the children playing kwik-cricket at lunchtime. 'Exactly Stu, The only difference is the kids were wearing stupid green hats.'

'Actually they're both wearing stupid green hats, Dave.'

'Good point, Chas.'

'I'd love one of those hats,' comes an interjection from the other side.

'John, you needed to practise a lot harder in the back garden to earn one of those.'

I head for the bar to escape the clowns, only to find myself in a queue behind a huge Aussie in a pink tutu. From the circus to the ballet. Some England lads are explaining that wearing pink for charity was yesterday, but he doesn't appear to understand what they're talking about – this is his preferred mode of dress. By the time I'm back in my seat with a drink, Dave is returning from the toilets.

'Stuart, there's an enormous bloody ballerina in the bogs.'

'Is that a problem?'

'I've never seen a ballerina pee standing up.'

Chas and I look at each other and wonder which of us will ask Dave when he last saw a ballerina pee sitting down, but think better of it; some things are better left unknown.

The day trundles on under the hot sun, and the crowd get more and more animated; extroversion is definitely weather and thirst related. After tea the wickets begin to tumble, but by then the off-pitch entertainment has taken precedence, and the new game in the stands involves huge snakes of empty plastic beer 'glasses'. First you make your snake by stacking them together, then – when you reach critical mass (usually over 30 feet long) – you throw the whole lot into the air like slightly more concussive confetti. It's a risky game to play, because the stewards and police are throwing out anyone involved, miserable killjoys that they are. It's a totally harmless pastime, aside from a few splashes of shandy on an innocent T-shirt or two, but the Aussies in the Victor Trumper Stand are deemed to have taken it too far. Once their snake has reached a Guinness-worthy anaconda size it is thrown towards the England fans, and the culprits are swiftly removed without much protest. With great timing, as they are led out of the stadium, the England fans raise the placards we've all been provided with for the day, showing *'OUT'* to the departing Aussies.

We're also treated to the best – or worst – health and safety announcement of all time. The stark warning flashes up on the big screen: *'Can spectators please be careful as the seats are flip-up seats and when you stand up they will spring back up.'*

We've been sitting on these seats all day – most of us for four days – do they think we've not noticed this before? We must have all come and gone half a dozen times to the bar or the loo. Who would be baffled and endangered by a flip seat? Who on earth would try to sit back down on a seat that has flipped up? Then it strikes me. The man on the plane to Brisbane. He must be here; they must have heard that he was in the ground! I jump up and gawp around in a momentary panic, then slump slowly back into my seat, wisely remembering to put it down before doing so. If he's here then my journey has come full circle; I realise with a sinking heart it is almost time to go home.

Things are drawing to a close with Australia still over 150 behind and seven wickets down, so with Smith and Siddle at the wicket England are granted the extra half-hour to try and finish matters off. You can't but feel that if Strauss had declared before lunch when Prior was out, we would have been carrying straight onto the victory party tonight, but the breakthrough doesn't come and, anti-climatically, celebrations will have to wait till tomorrow.

Dave and I leave the ground under gathering storm clouds and finish our podcast recordings in the empty car-park. The Australians have all long since driven home, only the English queuing for buses remain. He's been predicting rain for a while, and Weatherman Dave is a wiser sage than the vacillating blokes on TV; within thirty minutes it comes down like the wrath of god. We stand sheltering under an awning outside the member's entrance, but this time we both have warm enough clothing and it doesn't bother us; after all these weeks we've finally learned to come prepared.

'Were you ever a boy-scout Stuart?'

'No.'

'No, me neither, they wouldn't have me.'

'Just think what we might have learned.'

'Just think how different our lives might have been.'

'You might have come prepared and not spent the entire trip sunburned or cold.'

'Yup, and I still can't tie a decent knot.'

'Have you ever helped an old lady across the street?'

'I don't think I have, not that I can remember.'

'That's where you went wrong then, you should have been a scout.'

'On the plus side, I never had to give evidence to the police about the scout master.'

At this point we are treated to the free show of a sartorially unprepared, topless, drunk Australian lad challenging seven England fans to some sort of a fight. He's doing his best Liam Gallagher posturing, and either he's a secret martial arts expert or he wants to empathise with how his cricket team are feeling tonight and share their pain. In fairness he is pretty game for it but, ominously for him, so are they.

'You don't normally see that at cricket.'

'Look Stuart, look what he's wearing...'

On his head, is a Collingwood (Aussie Rules) cap – he's an escaped Melbournian!

'Aaaah... of course...'

'He must need to get his day's shouting quota out of his system.'

Ultimately the England boys decide that enough candy has been taken from babies today and leave him to his rain-sodden rage. Dave is giving running commentary into the voice recorder when we're accosted by three better dressed and better behaved Australians who are courtesy itself, and pay glowing tribute to the England team's performance, and admit they've been on the ropes since day two at Brisbane. I have to say, it would be atypical to hear any such sporting magnanimity from a defeated England fan. When they're not shouting at you in the street, they're a jolly nice bunch the Aussies.

For the Barmy Army the party will probably be starting tonight regardless, but not wanting to be late for the morning session I have decided to take it easy. And there's an event this evening I don't want to miss at my hotel, a Q&A session with former England wicket-keeper Paul Nixon. I'd love to share his secrets with you, but it would be wrong to pinch his gags or publish some of the hilarious and scurrilous things he told us. Suffice to say it was a top evening of tales of cricket tours, players, and the skill of the wicket-keeping sledge, from a man with the 'big personality' you expect from a glove man. A career in the world of media and after-dinner speaking surely awaits now he has finally called time on his county career. His forthright views on cricket past and present were pretty eye-opening to say the least, but again off the record, so when it was over I collared him for an exclusive I could actually broadcast.

I grill him on his England experiences: not his part in the successful one-day squad, but the fact that he was kept out the Test team by Geraint Jones, who was born in Papua New Guinea and therefore an ex-pat Aussie. (Having given up on Caribbean-born players, England then turned to Australians like Jones, Craig White and Darren Pattinson, before they figured out that the future was bright, the future was the Orange Free State.) What's his opinion on the present rainbow nation team?

Paul is honest and says that having toured as the number two glove-man on several occasions, it's a disappointment not to have got a game at Test level. But he holds no grudge against Jones as the England selectors picked who they thought was the best wicketkeeper available to them. If the rules stated Geraint could play for England then he is English. And so far as the current squad goes, if England are winning and picking players within the eligibility rules then nobody should complain.

It's a magnanimous reply, and I can't help think the selectors had never watched Jones play in that case, as he'd be struggling to be considered even the third best English keeper at the time, and was surely selected for the extra runs he so rarely provided. To me it was an inherent and defeatist belief in overseas superiority, something this tour has surely laid to rest.

Paul, or Nico as he insisted I call him, wishes me well and says he'll be out for a drink the following evening if I fancy a chat. Seems like a bloody good bloke to me.

Chapter 51
FIFTH TEST, DAY FIVE
VIEW FROM THE HILL
(Friday 7th Jan)

Once again the England fans are attending a day's cricket with the result not in doubt, and once again the Australian fans are not here. If cricket wishes to address its attendance issues, then first asking why that is, would be a better start than dressing them in pyjamas and playing music between overs. At least the SCG have had the good sense to announce *last night* that the fifth day will be free so, in spite of the hangovers, a good few are with me to watch the tour wrap up. The atmosphere in the last session yesterday was one of the most extraordinary I've ever experienced but in a way it's nice that it didn't end there. Today feels like a school reunion, as we meet old faces one last time and reminisce over the tour.

The turnout is almost exclusively British and so is the weather: gusting cumulous with showers likely. But not enough to save Australia or to dampen the England celebrations. I take the time to walk around the ground one last time and up the fantastically named Errol Flynn Boulevard, before heading into a corner of Australia that is today, England.

We fill the Victor Trumper and Churchill Stands and then some, the Barmy Army turning what was once the famous Hill into a magnificent showground for away support. Whatever the establishment think of them, the Army is keeping Test cricket alive. Series across the globe are being decided in front of empty stands, and without the England fans here the Ashes would have been the same. There may be those who prefer supporting a losing team, but after decades of hurt even the grumpiest Barmy will enjoy today. There are certainly plenty of bears with sore heads. Yesterday, all the beer was drunk but Bus Siddle and Munchkin Smith kept the English champagne on ice. It was like going to a stag night, getting hammered, and then being told the strippers would perform the following morning. Well the money's in the garter and we're here to see the final disrobing.

'Stop talking about strippers, where are we going to sit?'

I'm roaming round the ground behind a cantankerous Scotsman. Seating is unreserved and I was bright and early, but by the time Dave had dragged himself out of bed, our chance to grab good seats amidst the hurly burly was long gone. We want to get near the Barmies to enjoy the singing, but there's no way. I suggest we sit up above them, but finding two seats together proves impossible; short of asking 10,000 people to budge along a bit, it's not going to happen. We finally get a seat in the gods but Dave is not happy, he feels he's too far from the action.

'It was your idea to come up here!'

'I know, but it looked closer from down there, now I can't see a damn thing.'

I think the view is good, but it lacks atmosphere. We've found ourselves among a rather dull crowd of casual tourists and ex-pats who have snuck along for the day. Most have obviously not been on the tour, some have even brought babies. I'm happy with my seat, but I'm not happy with the babies. 'I don't like these people Dave, it's like being trapped in a Residents Committee meeting of a gated community.'

'And some of them look like the gates are to keep them in.'

I can see what he means, there's a definite touch of One Flew Over the Cuckoo's Nest and at least one Nurse Ratched. We wander across to only slightly less heavenly seats, but soon realise why they were available: Dave has a view of nothing but a hand-rail. Other free spaces are scattered around, but none of the miserable sandal wearers near us seem inclined to offer us seats together. This lot are a cricket crowd but I'm guessing are part of some rather sniffy tour party.

'I think Dave, these are their *actual* seats that they paid for and they don't like free-loaders.'

'I think they can bugger off back to England with that attitude, Stuart.'

We head down to the pitch side, but with all the pfaffing our only options are way over to the left in the Brewongle Stand. We're like shy kids on the edge of the dance floor watching the rest of the school get off with each other. It'll have to do. At least we get a close up view of the action. And wet.

Yes, even today the rain arrives suddenly. They say Scotland has four seasons in one day, but Sydney manages that in an hour. The only time I've seen such dramatic weather changes was playing golf on the Wii. The SCG might have let us in free, but they haven't opened the O' Reilly Stand that is covered, and there's a large number of stewards in place with the sole job of keeping people out, rather than letting them in and policing them there. It's Australia's practical joke on the England fans, to force us to sit out in the downpour, or hide inside in a crush and then return to the prospect of wet bums. I'm surprised there isn't a notice on the big screen warning us that '*Seats may be slippery when wet.*'

We have tried to breech security a couple of times without success, but possibly we weren't persistent enough, as there are a few fans over in the prime Ladies' Pavilion who look distinctly unladylike. Also lots of forbidden flags have been hung in the prohibited areas, although notably with no-one sat behind them. Typical British behaviour: jump the fence, hang the colours, and then scarper before the gardener catches you.

So far we've had less than six overs play, half of which we missed while trudging up and down endless stairs like an M.C. Escher lithograph. But after thirty minutes of 'changeable conditions' Smith and Siddle resume the entertainment. Siddle falls for 43, but Smith just reaches his deserved maiden fifty before running out of partners. With perfect timing, Billy the Trumpet gives us an affecting rendition of the Last Post (is there any other kind?) and the very next delivery Tremlett wraps up the series win. Uncanny.

The singing has barely stopped all morning but now gives way to cheering and more man-hugging. Suddenly I'm quite glad not to be buried in the throng of bodies. The England players embrace quietly at the striker's end and savour their achievement in a tight team huddle, as if offering up a prayer of thanks. Last man out, Beer starts to walk off before remembering it is traditional to wait for your partner and shake hands with the umpire. Perhaps the disappointed debutant fancied he was on for a match-saving 100.

There are a couple of fans dressed as Grenadiers with red uniforms and huge Busby hats and the sight of them brings home that we've just witnessed the changing of the guard. This was as one-sided a 3-1 win as you could imagine. It is the first time in their history that Australia have suffered three innings defeats in a series, and it leaves nobody in any doubt where the balance of power lies between the two old enemies. More importantly, the aura of Australian invincibility that they used to psychologically dominate has been shattered.

The awards ceremony follows, and for one last time the authorities and venue let the fans down badly. There are 19,274 fans here (allegedly) to see the presentation of the urn, and 99% of us are in the East of the ground in the stands that were opened free. So the SCG decide to hold the presentation in front of the empty stands to the West. It's like a calculated insult, a deliberate move to stop anyone that made the effort to show up from getting souvenir photos.

'That's not true Stuart, the members have got a great view.'

We gaze across at the little members' pavilion.

'Half-empty. That's their best turn out on this whole tour.'

In fairness, I'm amazed any Australians wanted to see this, and that stand has been full throughout this Test, but then it only holds slightly more than a phone-box cramming record attempt. The much larger members only M. A. Noble Stand next to it, is as empty as a politician's promise. The SCG website claims it opens the stand to the public for events with low attendance – did they hell.

Anyone with a heart or a brain would have shifted the presentations and interviews across in front of the Trumper Stand, giving the fans a close-up view and with the beautiful old

Pavilions providing a backdrop for TV. But this is Oz and hearts and brains are in short supply. Instead, while the live show plays to no-one, the thousands in the ground watch it all on the big screen at a lower resolution than my tele back home.

We resort to making our own entertainment. When Alastair Cook is presented with the 'Man of the Series' award, former Aussie captain Mark Taylor asks him how, unlike in previous Ashes campaigns, he has managed to score so many runs in this series? Bang on cue, while Cook and Taylor try not to corpse, the crowd bursts into a swaying rendition of:

'He bowls to the left, he bowls to the right,
That Mitchell Johnson his bowling is shite!'

20,000 people spontaneously making the same joke. Magic

As the ceremony closes Jonathan Agnew gives us a brief performance of the sprinkler dance, as he promised he would, and finally the sponsored part of the event is over. The confetti explodes anti-climatically to empty seats, and at last the England players can come over to greet their adoring public. There's no dance from them this time, it's less about jubilation and more about reflection and thanks for the unrelenting support they've received ten thousand miles from home.

Fittingly Paul Collingwood is the main event, doing a second lap of honour by himself to say goodbye, and shaking hands with those wishing him well. The only odd thing about all the farewells is that in the very next fixture he will captain England for a Twenty/20 match. I can but wonder if he'd be better calling a complete international halt here, as he'll never top this moment. The crowd's darling on a victorious Ashes tour, it's the pinnacle of cricket.

The official Barmy Army 'end of tour' party starts tonight but the carousing is already well under way. Not for us old lags. Dave heads off to upload the audio and I go back for a nap, before a trip to Darling Harbour in the evening. It's an opportunity to say goodbye to a few old faces. Lionel and John come out for a drink and, true to his word, there is Paul Nixon in full entertainer mode telling stories from a cricketer's life. The beer is flowing freely when there's another call from the *BBC*, wanting me to chat about the Ashes victory on *Five Live*. It's a bit of a struggle to straighten up, so to find headspace and relative quiet I sit by the dock outside, listening in on the show while waiting to go on air. True to form, it immediately starts raining. I've said it before: if you're considering moving to Oz for the weather, forget it; just stand under a cold shower with a large fan and a sun-lamp pointed at you and you'll get the same effect.

Thankfully it's only baby rain and there's a handy bit of overhang nearby, so I shelter and wait for my turn to babble to the nation, and babble I surely will. Again the queer sensation of talking to people who are tuning in for breakfast banter, while I'm three-quarters cut in the twilight, but it's an amusing little exchange. I'm asked about my highlight, and because of the almost disappointing inevitability of the last two matches, or maybe in tribute to Adge and those with Barmy Army long-service medals, I choose the defeat in Perth. It couldn't top the euphoria of Adelaide, but the way the fans stuck together and kept spirits up when England were losing was magnificent, that's what coming to the live event was all about.

I don't think they quite know what to say to this. I suspect they were expecting a stock answer about Cook scoring runs or smashing the Aussies to pulp. Live media doesn't like it when you actually improvise on your feet; they prefer it when you stick to the clichés. I'm then engaged in debate with another caller, a spirited gentleman from the Caribbean via Birmingham, who is outraged at the hype over England's performance.

'None of these bowlers,' he rages, 'none of them are the equal of Michael Holding!!'

It's my turn to not have a reply, other than an honest one. 'Well who is the equal of Michael Holding? He was one of the greatest of them all.' I'm satisfied that this pips his squeak; he'd come on the phone spoiling for a fight, and all he'd found was consensus. The poor staff of *Five Live* must have been wondering what was going on, no-one was glorying in victory and no-one was arguing, this wasn't the plan at all. Just when

I'm starting to enjoy myself the non-debate is over; they call a halt before we form a new brotherhood of man and sort the economy out between us, and it's time to head back inside.

Easier said than done. It's a common feature of Australian venues that you're allowed in wearing shorts only before a certain hour. There's a clear switch between the day and evening clientele, and while you're not exactly hurled out, they like to herd the scruffier ones into the conservatory and away from the glamorous bar; which doesn't really work as we still need to get drinks, but we've been sending the two best dressed members of our group to get them out of courtesy. Now I'm outside in shorts and it's also time to pay at the door. Were I sober at this point I might have had an issue, but I brazenly say I'm with the England player Paul Nixon and have just been speaking live on the *BBC* and am ushered inside without a problem. If I said that sort of thing more often I'd get into a lot of interesting places, but I can only pull it off when it's true. And when I'm pissed.

I'm sorry to say it's all been a bit too much. The glamourpusses of Sydney have come out of their lairs, and the bar has become a dance floor filled with gorgeous, scantily clad women. I'm no groover and I'm not exactly dressed to compete with the twenty-something gym-dudes that surround the gyrating girls in a predatory ring. If I want to escape the atmosphere of sexual competition, nearby is the official Barmy Army party, where all will be male and united in the common cause of singing, but honestly I'm shattered and I've drunk too much too quickly on a half-empty stomach. Dave doesn't seem keen either, although that could be because he wants to stay and watch the dance floor. He's stood with his eyes wide open, simultaneously salivating and weeping for lost youth; there are fluids escaping every orifice. I don't fancy his chances as he's only saved from being the worst dressed man in the bar by dint of standing next to John, who is wearing a Ryder Cup polo shirt.

That's it, if John has forsaken his full Australian colours, it's definitely the end of the tour, it must be time to go home.

Chapter 52
UP HILL AND DOWN DALE
(Saturday 8th Jan)

'Did you talk to any of the girls?'

'Of course not, I didn't have the nerve. Or the money. And what do I have to talk about?'

'Cricket?'

'I don't think it's a go-er.'

'The weather?'

'Is this the secret of your success? All these winning ideas?'

'Tell them you're a stranger in town—'

'—who's fallen on hard times, and if they're willing to lower their standards can they spare the taxi fare back to mine for a night of sin and debauchery? Now why didn't I think of that?'

'So what did you do?'

'John and I held our heads high, got crying drunk, and then I went home to my monastic cell and a bottle of red.'

'That showed them.'

It's Saturday 8th January 2011 and I'm on a train to the Blue Mountains with God's gift to Australian girls; the gift is, he leaves them alone. I have to remind myself of the date. The days and weeks have flowed into each other like watercolours, and without having had a winter I can't quite believe we're into the New Year. In fact I'm struggling to remember what decade it is but for good reasons not bad. There is little doubt that in a thousand small ways, Australia lags behind its parent country and is forever playing catch-up. It's an old-fashioned place that reminds Dave and me of where we grew up, and one thing we've both been enjoying is that so many of the good things that are virtually extinct in Britain, still flourish Down Under.

I've already spoken of specialist shops and an absence of supermarket supremacy, add to that the courteous drivers and the clean, well-kept parks. Topping it all off, and much more than compensating for many of the foibles, are the reliable, well-funded public transport systems – a relic of a bygone age we feared lost forever from the English speaking world. I'm not talking only of Melbourne's trams, although they are a fine thing indeed, I refer also to the notion that buses and trains should run even on those routes that aren't the most profitable, that they should be easily affordable, and they should run regularly and for most of the 24 hours.

A huge place like Oz is always going to tend towards car-centrism, and yet Sydney's public transport is quite simply fantastic. No doubt the locals have plenty to moan about, and Dave's grumbled about none for ages then three at once, but as an integrated affordable solution to urban transportation it leaves most places for dead. There's no better example of this than a trip to the mountains then back to the beach.

Dave has bussed it up from Randwick and meets me at the station. On our return from a two hour train-ride deep into the countryside we will hop the underground round to the Quay and pick up a ferry to Manly. Back on and off the ferry, Dave will bus it home and all on the same relatively cheap travelcard for absolutely no extra-cost. It would already be deal of the century, but the ferry will carry us across one of the most beautiful harbours on earth, and the train operates to tiny picture-perfect little towns deep into the night: the whole thing is almost too far-fetched. No wonder so many Sydneysiders commute by train and boat and leave the car at home.

The train is perfectly comfy without being plush. Here again, the Australians have it all sussed, just as we once did in Britain but a little bit more intelligently. You don't need luxury that would push the costs' needle into the unaffordable red, you just need reasonable comfort and enough leg-room to not cause blood clots. To double the money without doubling the train numbers and requiring a new multi-million dollar signalling system that probably won't work anyway, they've made the trains double-deckers. And everyone gets to face the right way, because the seatbacks flip round at the other end of the line – genius, and almost certainly illegal under British safety laws. Britain has yet to understand that trains don't need to be completely invulnerable in the event of a crash, they just need not to bloody crash. Which is something that tends to happen when too many low-capacity trains run on consequently over-capacity lines through over-stressed signal systems, and on tracks that haven't been properly maintained, because they were 'saving money'. The money gets spent anyway, generally on this week's latest rebranding and plush new trains that don't even have enough room for your bags, so you have to drive instead. No such worries here, all is grand grand grand. Aside from the air-con the ride is like a trip back in time, an illusion reinforced when we get off in Leura.

Leura is a little garden village with a population under 4000 but a regular train service, rare enough in itself, and its slumbering station sets the scene for what is to come. There are green painted wooden benches, a waiting room with an old ticking clock and an information board that was probably new in the 1930s. It even has its own honour-code lending library. People leave their unwanted books in the cases for you to borrow and read on the daily commute, on the understanding that you'll put them back when you've finished them. How perfect is that?

We have a coffee in the main street, where a conversation starts about micro-four-thirds cameras. Our friendly interrogator is wearing casual clothes entirely suitable to the weather, no jacket and no black trousers, clearly marking him as friend not foe. With best wishes for the day from the proprietor and waitress ringing in our ears, we toddle out and round the village. There's nothing to do, that's not the point. The thing is to be; and being in Leura is as fine as you could wish. The arts and craft shops are tasteful and somehow untouristy, the gardens are all immaculate and in bloom. What could possibly go wrong?

'Shit, shit, shit!'

'What?'

'Oooooooooow, ooooow!'

Dave has something in his eye, something that is intent on mischief. He's clutching his face and rubbing his eye and hopping from foot to foot. Sometimes it seems you can't go ten minutes in this country without finding yourself in pain. Whatever has just flown in there is not sitting easily, and after five minutes of agony and panic, with tears pouring down one side of his face, we head back to the main street to find a chemist. Close investigation with a mirror shows nothing, whatever was there is gone, and a helpful old chemist, a real one not a surly teenager, shows him some trick that immediately stops the pain. I thought I must remember that, that's brilliant – and equally immediately forget what it was. Damn. Dave insists on buying little sterilised water bottles, partly as a future flushing remedy against malicious bugs, partly to ring some money through their tills in thanks.

'This country has it in for me, Stuart'

'Evidently.'

The unprovoked attack is slightly worrying, as we intend to wander east along mountain pathways to look across the valley in one direction, then back west and along to Katoomba. It's been raining heavily over previous days, and some of the paths are waterlogged. Neither of us has hiking boots, and Dave is scaring me silly with tales of spiders. 'The Blue Mountain Funnel Web, Stu. It's a sub-species of the most venomous and aggressive spider on earth.'

'Don't tell me, I don't want to know.'

'It says here, the really dangerous time is after heavy rain, when they come out of their flooded burrows.'

We pause and look down at the squelching muddy track we're standing on, about nine inches wide at its broadest. Heading east first must be a rarity, as this is literally off the beaten path and it's all heavily overgrown. On both sides are dripping rocks and dense foliage that could hide a legion of fanged monsters. Aside from one grass-smoking hippy by a waterfall there's not a soul to be seen, and consequently we'll be the first to happen upon and disturb any bad guys that are lurking. It's like walking down a back-street in Brixton, you're never sure what nefarious activities may be going down around the next corner.

'Shall we go back?'

'I don't know what you're worried about, I'm the spider fodder; I'm their favourite food.'

Dave has a long and turbulent history with spiders. Despite the scientists' claim that British spiders don't bite people, Dave knows otherwise; he's been bitten by more spiders than he cares to remember, sometimes in quite hair-rising circumstances and with quite startling results.

'You're living proof that the British zoologists are wrong.'

'And if we meet a Funnel-Web I'll be dead proof that Australian zoologists are right.'

'They have antidotes don't they?'

'I'll probably be allergic. Besides, I don't fancy the days of agony lying in a hospital bed when I could be lying on a beach—'

'You'd only sunburn, you'd still be in agony.'

'Okay, come on, thump your feet down so they hear us coming and get out the way.'

'Isn't that what you're supposed to do with snakes, won't it just provoke the spiders?'

'Shit, good point. Tread lightly. You go first...'

Needless to say, we survive; perhaps by virtue of finding a good vantage point, then quickly heading back to the road and along the cliffs to the usual tourist haunts. We gaze down on the Three Sisters, another Aboriginal holy site reduced to a box to tick but still a breathtaking view, take the Prince Henry cliff walk where fatter Americans fear to tread, skip the overpriced tourist rides and head up through Katoomba to the station. Katoomba is actually contiguous with Leura, but it too has its own stop on the line. It would be nice to have a look around, as it seems quite bohemian and entirely different from its twee sister village, but we're hurrying back to try and get across to Manly at a reasonable hour.

Once on the train and remembering how the sun sets earlier here, it's obvious the beaches are better left till tomorrow and we needn't have rushed. A foolish error, but instead we ride the underground to its end at Bondi Junction, and then walk in an explorative zig-zag northwards to catch a boat.

The first nugget of gold we spot is a sign outside a pub:

'Big Screen LIVE Sport. Ashes AUSTRALIA v ENGlANG.'

'That's been up there six days and still no-one has noticed.'

'Well it's better than Eng-ger-land, you can see the confusion.'

A little further on is a cafe, with a sign saying *'Vary good coffee,'* it gets better and better. I've not had so much fun since I saw the newsstand outside Melbourne station offering *'Spirit of the Ashes Cricket Book – save $30, now only $9.95'* within an hour of the defeat.

'Look Stuart, it's actually real. Isn't it incredible?'

Dave is trying to take surreptitious photos, and we're not even on a beach. It is incredible, and no it's not a film set, it's a genuine old fashioned grocer's. All it appears to stock is newspapers, tea-bags, instant coffee, white bread, cereal, chewing gum, chocolate, and unrefrigerated cans of Coke and Fanta on half-empty shelves. I can't see the water-pistols, Frisbees and balsa-wood planes powered by rubber-band driven propellers but they're bound to be in there somewhere. And that's it. Nothing else. This place has never seen a fresh croissant or a sesame bagel in its life. And it even has a Union Jack sign outside saying *'Best of British Gourmet and Confectionary.'* Perfection.

'It's like the first place I ever shop-lifted,' rhapsodises Dave.

'Before you acquired some morals?'

'Exactly, before I acquired morals and realised I should be targeting the supermarkets.'

'I'm appalled.'

'I was keeping the shelf-stackers in a job.'

It's hard to get a photo of our magical shop, on account of the windows being boarded up and denying entry to all light. This too is familiar. Outside the boards display newspaper headlines, inside the shelves sit against them in classic 'slam it all in anyhow' style. There's absolutely no light and Dave doesn't want a thump from the owners who may not take kindly to the publicity, they obviously like to keep things low key. Or they may not even have seen a digital camera and still be flogging 110 film, we don't want to scare them. Once again we're back in the 1970s. Not so long ago we passed a genuine old-fashioned baker, and a greengrocer's with potatoes still covered in mud, none of your pansy pre-washed stuff there. It's hard not to be mentally transported to an earlier age; this country is like an episode of Life on Mars, and yet all this sits quite happily alongside the contemporary Sydney CBD.

Sydney is definitely a city at ease with itself, and with the little self-contained districts, you can't help but be put in mind of the London of forty or more years ago, when it was still an obvious collection of villages. The original 'Big Smoke' (and only one really worthy of that title) is the easiest comparison all round. The ubiquity of names Dickens would be familiar with aside, whether by intent, subconscious genetic memory, pure coincidence or alien mind-control, having now seen them side by side I'm confirmed in my belief that Sydney plays London to Melbourne's Manchester. It's far more than underground trains and a river up the middle, its attitude and ambition have parallels. It's the pervading sense of being the fullest expression of the country's civilisation in the pure sense of that word. Yet despite its drive to the future. Sydney does a much better job of preserving its past while continuing to develop alongside. It's not perfect (where is?) but you can sense history in Sydney in a way that is impossible in Melbourne, and I fear will be impossible in Manchester soon.

However, it's just so darn sure of itself, I'd be willing to place an outside bet that Melbourne has a greater creative output than happy sunny Sydney. As Dave says, nothing truly lasting ever came from somewhere sunny, although I must say I feel the Pyramids somewhat shoot holes in that argument.

'But where are the Ancient Egyptians now, Stuart? Eh? Shakespeare will be read when the Sphinx is long gone.'

'Do you read Shakespeare?'

'Not if I can help it.'

'Ever seen the Sphinx?'

'Oh it's probably worn away by now.'

The fact remains Sydney is vulnerable to the usual danger implicit in being at the top of the tree; you have nothing to escape, nothing to aspire to, and the furthest to fall. London imports most of its creativity, originally from the provinces and today from the whole world, but it has precious little of its own. Innovation springs from dissatisfaction, depravation or simple boredom; the worthwhile musical output of the poor estates of Manchester, Glasgow and Birmingham dwarf London's home-grown efforts, that themselves were historically more likely to come from Kentish Town than Kensington. Its best years came in the 60s, from the kids who had grown up in a poor, blitz-wrecked city a world away from the flaccid prosperity it presently enjoys and which gives birth to so little that is new.

If Manchester should see Melbourne as an example of a future it must avoid, Sydney should look to London as a warning of the perils of being an unchallenged top-dog: content supremacy that parasitically feeds on the fruits of empire, breeds laziness, decadence and eventual decline.

But today, Sydney lies back on its warm sand and sings to itself. The week after New Year is a dismal time in a lot of places, undeniably once the Catherine Wheels have spun in Edinburgh and London, there's nothing buzzing for a few weeks there, but Sydney still feels alive and has that distant hum of busy bees.

'You've got to watch those bees, Stuart.'

'You do. I'm surprised there aren't warning signs.'

When we reach the shore we spend the early evening pottering about on ferries to and from the various bays. There's nothing more likely to leave you with a positive impression of a place than messing about in its boats, especially when it's all for free. Painted in attractive Aussie green and yellow, you can ride these fine beasts back and forth across the harbour with the commuters, taking in all the best views to be had at sundown.

The Bridge is still a fine spectacle and, in the dimming light, I see at the north end of that steel leviathan the other Luna Park. A fellow ferry passenger fills me in on some of its history, and I'm amazed to find that I've unwittingly got the complete set. Melbourne's was the first and only one in continuous operation, but Sydney's original rides were shipped here all the way from Glenelg beach after complaints from the residents about the noise! So I was right, Glenelg isn't the sort of place to embrace the tourist dollar. The relocation proved somewhat in vain, as residents complained in Sydney too, and this place has closed and reopened more times than a politician's mouth, but at the moment it's still in business.

'So St. Kilda was first, then Glenelg which moved to Sydney, where was the fourth one you mentioned?'

'Oh, it only lasted about twenty years, but it was in Redcliffe, Queensland. Outside Brisbane.'

Well, I'll be darned, Uncle Bill's. No wonder the BeeGees were all teeth, they grew up playing behind that famous grinning face. Once again I take it as an omen that I've come full circle, it's nearly time to go home.

Chapter 53
A LAND DOWN UNDER
(Sunday 9th Jan)

It's my last day and we're walking along the cliff-top walk that runs between the southern beaches and stretches up towards the South Head. It's spectacular stuff, the beaches, the cliffs, the water – Sydney is unfairly blessed with natural beauty. It's astounding to think that Bondi was once considered a lonely far off spot with only one tragically scarred, reclusive inhabitant, when in fact it's only a sturdy walk from the city centre. This morning, only one inhabitant would be preferable, as it's mobbed with the weekend crowds. Neither of us is much impressed with this famous beach.

'It's a bit crowded.'

'It's a bit tatty.'

'I thought it would be a lot flasher.'

'It's certainly not what it thinks it is.'

'No, there's a lot of poseurs.'

'Yeah. But that's not the word I was thinking of.'

The streets around Bondi all have a slightly seedy air, and it all seems unduly hyped, but no matter, there are plenty more beaches, plenty, plenty more. They all have their acolytes, Tamarama, Bronte, Clovelly, Coogee the list goes on, each with its own particular character and charms, and all more or less connected by a well maintained pathway that alternates between beach and spectacular plunging cliff, with golden rocks softly sculpted by the crashing waves.

While the dramatic walk between them is better in the south, the beaches are better in the north. Manly is rightly famous, and locals' favourite Freshwater is busy, but even on a summer weekend, Curl Curl, Dee Why, Collaroy/Narrabean are big enough to be more than half empty. The sand slopes gently into the cool but not cold water, and on Curl Curl I complete my West, South, East coast ocean trilogy.

Maybe I'm just ignorant, beach holidays are not my thing, but I'm amazed to discover that the famed Australian life-guards only patrol a tiny bit of each. They put their flags up in a narrow little channel, and if you're outside that area, you're on your own mate. Consequently, the swimming areas are packed, but if you're only interested in standing up to your waist and watching the waves you can find plenty of peace and quiet away from the hurly burly. There are advantages to being out of sight of the lifeguards; they do have a tendency to machismo and smugness. Ask Dave: while braving the waters near his flat, and knocked off his feet by an unexpectedly large wave, the lifeguards not only laughed, but played a comical jingle over the loud speakers.

'What did you do?'

'Walked up to the biggest one and punched him so hard he cried like a baby.'

'Oh yes, and what did the others do, when you did that?'

'I don't know, my day-dream never got that far, I got hit by another wave.'

Yes, they're a funny bunch the lifeguards. Most are volunteers, which is certainly admirable, although I daresay the kudos and associated sex suffice as payment.

'Do you reckon he's saved anyone recently, Stuart?'

My eyes follow where Dave is pointing to an older chap, no doubt the voice of experience among the guards. He's probably in his 40s – with the 60 year old wizened face to match – but he still looks the part in red shorts and yellow sun-top, with the floppy red hat. But something is not quite right.

'Bloody hell!!'

'A stomach like that must take some serious maintenance.'

'Jesus Dave, how do you swim with a bowling ball up your shirt?' Our man has the worst pot-belly we've ever seen. I've seen larger stomachs on fatter people, but never have I seen a pregnant protrusion like this on such slim legs.

'He's living off vanished glories that lad.'

'There must actually be something wrong with him, we shouldn't mock the afflicted.'

He doesn't seem afflicted, he looks otherwise healthy, I guess he may still have what it takes – and if he does, I know where he's hiding it. I'll give him the benefit of the doubt; he's unquestionably acting like a life-guard: soaking up the admiration and keeping a safety conscious eye on the young girls, some of whom are even in the water.

'Maybe they use him as a marker buoy, he's got the figure.'

Lifeguards aside the beaches are tremendous, and the sand, if not as perfect as Perth, is nevertheless a fine light gold. The only fly in the ointment of all this beauty is the pollution. Sydney's beaches have cleaned up a lot in the last twenty years I'm told, which means that twenty years ago people must have been swimming in utter filth. Even today you're advised to stay out of the water for at least 24 hours after heavy rainfall due to the muck washed down through the city's storm drains. If your face is your fortune, you'd think you'd try to avoid smearing it with dung. But incredibly there are sewage outlets not far away, and even storm drains that empty right onto the beaches themselves. Walking along the beautiful sands of Manly we're confronted with one that has left a large oily black patch in the middle of one of the world's most famous beaches. How much would it cost them to run that pipe another 500 yards into the sea? I pause to grab a photo; the result resembles a cover of *New Scientist* warning of the catastrophe of oil-spills.

One shouldn't be dumping raw sewage into the sea at any distance, and in this regard there have been improvements since the 1980s when 30% of 'suspended solids' (or 45,700 tonnes of turd to you and me), were dumped straight into the surf by the overflow drains. And that's a drop in the ocean, literally, compared to the hundreds of thousands of tonnes of grease from commercial activities that heads out to sea and then comes straight back wrapped around faeces and coats the beach.

Reading about all this and looking at the warning signs all around us, takes the shine off it a tad. We thought we'd found the best discovery ever, the warm lagoons at Curl Curl and Dee Why, whose gentle rivers run across the beaches into the cooler sea. And there were people in them, some floating, some kids playing, but surprisingly few considering the glory of the waters. It's likely they were the ignorant few, because then we encounter wiser locals stopping their children from going in, saying they won't be safe today, the tides haven't been high enough to wash them out overnight. The fields that lie alongside these picturesque semi-poisonous ponds were once marshes, and were reclaimed in the 1960s by dumping domestic rubbish into the swampy land. This doesn't sound like the sagest piece of town planning either. Truly Australia is the son of Britain.

You can't single out Sydney for the self-same environmental practices that are common the world over, it just comes as a surprise when it sets such store by its beaches and watersports, and the travelling Australians one meets are usually so environmentally concerned. But I guess those are the idealistic children of the responsible middle-classes, and don't reflect the politicians, big businesses and general louts that are the movers, shakers and majority voters; just as green activists in Brighton called Forest and Whimsy don't reflect the broader swathe of British indifference. Ignorance is bliss, and if you're not aware of any of this and don't read the signs, the beaches of Sydney and the walkways and cliffs that run between them have to be among the finest city limits on earth.

Dave and I take a moment out to gaze down upon the tanning bodies; semi-nudity and firm flesh are everywhere, except out to sea where the surfers are wisely covered up.

'What do you see?'

'Lots of bad haircuts.'

'No kidding.'

Mullets, spikes, tangles: neither of us are Vidal Sassoon, but Australians don't do good hair. Before arrival in Sydney I'd assumed it was part of the attitude: city spikes were bold statements on brassy girls, mullets are an anti-fashion comment the world over. But the issue may be the water. A life spent in and out of the sea does nobody's hair any good, but even without that, the stuff that comes through the taps is bizarre.

'Stuart, I don't wish to sound like a girl—'

'Well stop moaning then.'

'—but if I stay in this country much longer I'm going to be bald. My hair is coming out in handfuls.'

'You sound like a girl.'

'It's true. Every time I step out the shower I'm a comb-over short of a toupee.'

'A sausage short of a barbie more like.'

Dave's right though; no wonder cosmetics cost so much, they've got you over a barrel. Suncream and hair products are a licence to print money in this country and Australia's dubious hair styles are the consequence of an unmanageable situation, so to speak. If you don't want to look like a bedraggled surfer – and trust me you don't, in the flesh they look like salted kippers labelled 'Best before 1958' – you have to cut your hair short, and spiky is as good as it'll get.

The hair is not the only indication of ex-Europeans evolving to meet the challenges of this environment. For example, the way they walk. No matter how physically attractive the person, and my goodness there are some lookers, they don't do grace very well in Australia. It's not a genetic deficiency: the kids are straight-backed, sporty and firm of foot, but by early adulthood all have the same ghastly splay-footed ten-to-two waddle, symptomatic of a lifetime spent trying to keep your flip-flops on. I'm not saying it's any worse than a stout England fan in white trainers and his silly side-to-side swagger. But it's seemingly near universal, and so ingrained that even when not in the offending shoes, the Aussie posture retains the hollow back and extended stomach that is so unbecoming of male and female alike. Either that or it's some bizarre piece of neo-Darwinistic sexual selection, where thrusting out your groin leads to more progeny. In any case, I wish the buggers would hurry up and evolve some lower body metrosexuality.

Uncut, dirty, fungal infected middle-aged male toe-nails being shown in public are a worldwide concern that the World Health Organisation has thus far failed to address, but in the land of the flip-flop it's an epidemic, and they need to act fast. Down Under you daren't drop your gaze to ground level for a moment. Male jewellery, moisturiser and even the occasional emotion have all broken cover, but the pedicure got left on the boat. I'm tempted to call for international legislation to make the sale of sandals illegal unless the buyer can prove they don't have toe-nails as lethal as that KGB agent in *From Russia with Love*.

The disease appears contagious, and it's not only the men or just the Aussies; as soon as British girls get off the plane and see the sand, they consider it an open license to let everything go to hell. I'm no foot-fetishist, indeed the less displayed on that score the better – give me a girl in riding boots and I'm happy – but this I've never understood: how can a woman spend hours on her hair and fingernails, apply make-up perfectly, and then emerge dressed to the nines from head to ankle, but in cheap flip-flops with skanky calloused feet?

I was once taken to task by an old-hippy for this view, who insisted that it was, 'Real, man'. Alright, she didn't actually say, 'man.' But the nub of her argument was that as feet are your connection to Mother Earth, it would be artificial to fuss over them too much; they are functional and must be left to look as such. To which I asked: would it be appropriate for builders to have their hands forever coated in mud and cement, mechanics to leave their mitts covered in oil, or vets to have paws smeared always in dry blood and cow faeces? No. So shut up, wash your feet and buy some nail scissors.

But there are many things to applaud, and the most laudable feature of the people of Australia, is probably the easiest to overlook. It does nothing whatsoever to draw attention to itself and unless you're alert you might miss it altogether. But the inhabitants are quite unlike those in Miami or LA, or Blackpool or Bognor, or any other similar glamour-spot. Contrary to myth, there are not legions of fit, tanned skinny bodies; there are far more bronzed, slim, girls in London, Madrid or Milan than you'll ever see in Oz, and more gym-fanatic men too. Emotionally that's probably all to the good, but better yet, there are virtually no fat people in any of the cities. Many are what would once have been termed chubby – before that term was appropriated by blubber-butts who can't admit they're fat – and there are portly gentlemen, not least our bizarre life-guard. But out and out fat is rare and obese is almost invisible.

Three years ago there was a nonsense tabloid story based on suspicious statistics, claiming that Australia had overtaken the USA as the fattest nation on Earth. I thought it was dubious at the time, and unless they've all been hiding indoors for seven weeks, I can now confirm it to be bollocks. I didn't see small town Australia but I crossed this country twice and I'm willing to bet there are more properly fat people in Leicester than in this whole continent. To their great credit, and I attribute this to their fresh food and dreadful supermarkets, everyone here is just a robust, healthy average.

Average: that's the word I've been searching for all trip. Australians are average. Their country is a land of impossible beauty and homicidal extremes in weather and wildlife, but the people are a homogenous bunch. Nobody is very fat, nobody is very skinny, nobody is very sad, nobody is very happy. When we stop to watch a game of bowls on top of the cliff at Clovelly, it's as perfect a moment as you could wish for. The members are chatting as they play, nearby a wedding party are enjoying a barbie and few drinks, but something is missing: nobody, but nobody is laughing. They're visibly content, the faces show none of the stress, anger and unhappiness so common in Britain on a Saturday evening (even when 'enjoying' family days out) but neither is anybody overtly excited or joyous; it's the most subdued wedding I've ever seen.

Consider the contrast: in world terms, despite what people say, Britain has some of the best weather going. Granted it's unpredictable and you don't know whether it will rain in August or be hot in October, but overall it's a temperate, fertile land. It only lacks water in the over-populated poorly plumbed south-east and real droughts are unheard of. Deaths from heat and cold are scarce except among those that climb Ben Nevis in shirt-sleeves in winter, skin-cancer is mostly confined to the sun-bed addicts, and nobody should talk of floods until they've seen what real ones did to New Orleans or in China (or indeed are starting to do in Queensland as I sit by the sunny NSW coast).

When it comes to fauna, forget it: nothing in the UK will eat you and you have to be pretty small and unlucky to die from the shy viper's bite. Yet the people of the British Isles are clearly head-cases. No-one expresses a half-way balanced opinion on anything, misery and mania abound, the anorexic and obese rub shoulders, and both suicidal depression and delirious ecstatic ribaldry are commonplace. It's said the most common sound in the British trenches of the First World War was laughter – which tells you all you need to know about the sort of people a gentle land produces. Humanity must have its excesses somehow.

'The Antipodes' are the geographic opposite in every regard, they are God's own extravagant moment. Everything about this land was naturally already bonkers before Europeans first set foot on it, and consequently it has produced a placid, unexcitable population that have to import their laughter from the *BBC*. Since I've been here I've never been more than a few yards from laughing Brits at the matches, but as soon as I've gone native it's been replaced with ... nothing. There's just a constant, even, burble – like an episode of *Neighbours* where a cat goes missing – while over in the England camp it's like a cross between *Mock the Week* and a screaming argument on *Eastenders*. We're mental, they're boring and that's all there is to it. Yes, I'm aware this is all a broad, and rather extreme, brush-stroke. What do you expect? I'm British. If you want a more level-headed analysis and a duller book, ask an Australian to write one.

'There's a problem with all that.'

'Oh yes?'

'What about the Aborigines? They seem like they're pretty extreme fellows; they hitch-hike the outback without bothering with the lifts, doesn't that shatter the "average" analysis?'

'Yes. Well, all the best theories have holes; I call it the "*havering principle*".'

In Manly's main tourist drag is our answer. Astonishingly aside from the elders at the matches, I've seen only a small handful of Australian Aborigines on this trip; a small sad doleful group in Perth, left behind by life and time, and a didgeridoo player in Circular Quay who was just part of the universal busker fraternity. But standing in the middle of Victoria Parade is a fellow who looks as if he's just parachuted in from another time. It's not his clothes – which are crisp, new, regulation issue jeans and T-shirt – it's his face, which is alive like none of the white ones around him. He soaks up the world through sparkling yellow cats eyes, the most astonishing I've ever seen, and they're drinking in the unfamiliar scenes around him.

At once I believe the old tales of Aborigines recruited by the British ships as look-outs because their sight was sharper than the poor quality telescopes of the time. This boy could out-stare Samuel L Jackson in Pulp Fiction, and probably has a wallet to match. He drags on his cigarette like it's the first he's ever tasted and he's just discovered the fountain of youth. In one mighty draw a quarter of the fag glows red and vanishes. Yup, he's a pretty extreme looking bloke, anyway you shake it, there's not a lot of placid or average in that face.

'Maybe, they're not shaped by the land, Stuart.'

'But they've been here 50,000 years.'

'Exactly. So they're not reacting to it, they're integral to it.'

'Well, they brought fire, I guess, mankind always has an impact.'

'That's not what I mean, I'm talking mystically. What if they actually *are* the land? What if, without them, without the Dreamtime, there is no Australia, no southern land?'

'Hmmm. Could be, Dave, could be. Mmmm. Yes.'

'Do you have any idea what I'm talking about?'

'Actually, no. As usual I have no idea what you're talking about.'

'Doesn't matter, Stu. Just a thought.'

'So; you reckon that bloke's any good at cricket?'

EPILOGUE
ALL ENGLAND

The calendar that most of us live by has seen a lot of shoogling around over the centuries and for the majority of people in Europe, New Year's Day used to be in March. It was Julius Caesar who had the bright idea of creating January and February, and shifting the event from the spring equinox to near the winter solstice. But even among those that liked this swanky new twelve month year, moving the end of it never really caught on; most were still arguing about when exactly spring started, not having wet bank holidays and hose-pipe bans to guide them on the matter. The British were having none of this new-fangled January 1st rubbish and for our big day we stuck steadfastly to March 25th for another 1800 years, long after most of the continent had made the switch. The Tudor and Stuart Euro-sceptics were clearly a feisty bunch, who no doubt chanted *'One Armada and the 100 years war!'* at international archery tournaments ('foteball' still being banned by royal decree).

Only when we finally gave up on the old Julian calendar in 1752 did we all accept the inevitable change. (Although the City of London refused even then, and dodged eleven days tax by settling on April 5th for its new year; so again, not unlike it is today.) I suspect this is why the Scots imbibe so much on Hogmanay; there's obviously still a folk memory among the common man of getting drunk on New Year's Eve and sobering up on the first day of spring, and we're still aiming for that result. And wouldn't you if you lived in Fort William? Academics who study these weighty matters are apparently still divided as to whether this is also why Easter eggs appear in the shops on January 2nd.

Personally I've often thought January was all a terrible mistake and we should shift celebrations back to March, pronto. Bundling Christmas and New Year into one long festive period has many downsides: for your wallet, for your liver, for your sanity, and especially if you have to go to work on those dead, distracted days between the two, when all you're likely to achieve are a lot of paper-clip sculptures and fantasy-football transfers. I'd avoided that, but I'm staring down the barrel of downside number five: after the champagne corks have popped and the last of the turkey is in the cat, there is absolutely nothing to look forward to for the rest of the British winter. Unless you're lucky enough to get a cheering snowfall, January, February and March stretch before you like an endless muddy field of stubble, with not a feast day in sight. Don't try to console me with talk of Valentine's Day; that's fine if you're a lucky lady, but for the lovelorn it's a lonely experience, and for the taken man it's a minefield of expensive relationship booby-traps all waiting to blow up in your face.

Worse, we masochistically choose these bleak months to start new fitness regimes and self-inflicted abstinence; is everyone mental? Getting out for a brisk walk and back to a cup of tea on a fresh April morning is a treat, but February is surely the month to get fat and hit the bottle if ever there was one. But as ever, no-one listens to my pleas for a return to the old traditions. January 1st retains the crown, and with it the air of the beginning of a three month prison term. And this year, while still jet-lagged and in inappropriately thin clothing, I am to be parachuted back into the jail, complete with its drying-out drunks in newly issued track-suits, jogging around the yard. As we fly in through the clouds covering the North Sea, I consider hiding on the plane and riding the free food and drink back and forth to Hong Kong for a month.

Terminal 3 at Heathrow Airport must be one of the grimmest places on earth. It's as grey and grotty as a run-down VD clinic, and it's not the sort of place to which you want to return when your last memory was standing on the cliffs of New South

Wales watching the sun set on a golden day. In truth it's not the sort of place you ever want to return to, unless you're planning to write a sequel to Kafka's, the Trial. Honestly, they should withhold the free booze on the plane and instead give you a bottle of whisky when you step off it, you'll need it to console yourself and see you through immigration. Heathrow's uniformed officials are as happy to see us as ever, not a smiling face among them. You can't blame them, locals always hate tourists, we've covered that, so imagine how it must feel to be trapped in this monumental hell-hole all year, with nothing but streams of happy holiday-makers and tanned, half-pissed returning residents for company. It's a wonder they don't go postal and shoot everyone. It brings me down, but secretly I'm on their side. Never mind Heathrow expansion, how about Heathrow jollification, a bit of colour and a fresh coat of paint wouldn't go amiss for starters.

It's not all bad though, I know my way around, and enjoy as always the thrill of appearing sophisticated and metropolitan among the swarms of dopey wasps, simply by knowing my way to the Tube. Befuddled tourists and various huddled masses wander aimlessly in circles and puzzle over arcane ticket machines and unfamiliar money, but as I smoothly touch in with my oyster card and the gates magically part, it's like being greeted with open arms by an old friend I've not seen in years. I knew you wouldn't have forgotten me.

The Piccadilly train clickity-clacks into the city on an overcast day, and then something wonderful: people are laughing and joking. I swap trains at Hammersmith, and the District Line is positively homely. A young girl whose clothes are trying too hard – clearly an out-of-towner dressed up for her trip to the capital – nearly misses her stop at South Kensington and has a panic getting her bags out the doors in time; amused passengers catch each other's eyes and smirk, but withhold conspicuous amusement till she's off and away from potential embarrassment. By the time I reach Victoria I've heard more home-grown laughter than reached my ears on Australian transport in seven weeks. We might be a difficult lot at times, but even hectic, hurried London enjoys a joke. It's truly good to be home. Now I just need to make it through to spring.

An email in my inbox one morning reawakens me to memories of the adventure. Jetlag always leaves one in a fugue for a day or two, and you start to wonder if you ever really went away or only dreamt it, but here's a cheery greeting from the indefatigable Adge Walton. He's sent me photos and links to videos of shared good times, reminding me of my hopelessly poor prediction of 2-2. It wasn't that bad, I only got one match back to front, but sometimes it does you good to be wrong. It's great to hear from Adge but he's suffering the deflation of the return worse than I. Unenthused by the forthcoming World Cup, like the England team he gave the Ashes his all, and sees the limited overs stuff as a side-show to the main event.

I'm not a multi-tour veteran like him, so I'm still carrying the excitement of having been in the midst of it all, and try to keep the momentum up. If this England team want to achieve the same aura of the great Australian and West Indian teams they're going to need to dominate all forms of the game. The Ashes shouldn't be the pinnacle, they need to go on, take the number one status and keep cricket as an all year, every year, sport in the public's mind, not a semi-annual grudge match alone.

Unfortunately it was already becoming clear in Australia that the ECB are following the money, and their marketing boss Steve Elworthy has justified moving the next series Down Under forward by a year to separate it from the World Cup and 'protect the Ashes brand.' For them it means a nice lucrative series, another in a seeming never-ending sequence scheduled against the big guns of Australia and India. Bad news Steve-O, there is nothing more likely to make me go off cricket and give it a miss than describing it as a 'brand'. The mere mention of the word is enough. Alongside freeze-dried mimed music performances, 'reality' TV, and unrestricted consumerism, branding is in my biscuit tin of modern hates. Or should that be post-modern? (No it bloody shouldn't, that's another one.) True I'm not a fan of the Charters and Caldicott world of old school ties and no-professional-players-allowed-in-the-gentleman's-lavatory, but that doesn't mean cricket should automatically allow itself to be entirely subsumed by the chrome-plated world of executive boxes, corporate hospitality, and going to be seen rather than going to watch. Besides, if they really understood branding, rather than lamely and pathetically following football, they'd realise that's not cricket's Unique Selling Point.

A month later I meet with a man in a pub to discuss the England brand and other matters of national importance. He's newly arrived in the country, bronzed, blonde, and with straggly hair in want of either serious attention or a paper bag over it.

'Stuart, I think I've got skin cancer.'

'Shut up and drink your beer.' Mother knows best. Yes, Dave has returned, and we're discussing a new problem. We both went out to Australia as England fans, and both returned as such, but Dave is less convinced than I. There was some ribbing, a touch of suspicion here and there, and neither of us could join in with chants of 'Eng-ger-lund,' (not least because we had the benefit of a proper education system) but generally we were welcomed as England supporters. I had a wobble around the 'Are you Scotland in disguise?' era, but that's not what concerns my companion.

'It's not so easy, Stuart, they're not the underdog anymore.'

'They're not favourites for the World Cup.'

'No, but cheering for England when they were losing was almost like cheering for them to lose. It made an odd kind of sense. But supporting them now is like supporting Michael Schumacher in his heyday.'

'I see what you mean. And let's face it, cheering for a losing team is second nature to us, we've had more practice than the Faroe Isles.'

'It's just not the done thing, that's all; it's not how I was brought up.' Dave has unearthed a paradox worthy of a Greek. Unlike me, he is a more recent convert to the England cause, only crossing the Rubicon in the late 80s, and I can tell he's wavering when faced with this new dilemma. The truth is there's something oxymoronically unBritish about supporting a supreme England. There is historical precedent for this: touring M.C.C. teams of the late 19th century were actively encouraged to lose for the good of Empirical harmony. Dave was reared the old way: you cheer for the underdog and pray for England to lose. Helped for years by an arrogant, dominant Australia with few likable characters, he was able to let one of those mantras slip and join the England cause, but now he's being asked to renounce his British heritage as well as his Scottish one.

'It's fine against Australia, Stuart, and I hate Vettori so that's New Zealand covered, but what happens when they play the West Indies? I might swap sides.'

'If the ECB get their way, they won't be playing the West Indies, so don't worry about it.'

Dave pulls lovingly on his real ale, and then grimaces. 'It takes a bit of getting used to again.'

Many things take a bit of getting used to, and for a Scot, supporting England is one of them. I've had 37 years to get my brain around it, but even then sometimes you're thrown a curve ball, as even an American would understand. The cricket World Cup is just around the corner, and fortunately for Dave, Scotland haven't qualified, or they might have been drawn against England. Ireland have been and Dubliner Ed Joyce, who opened the batting for England at the last one, has crossed the floor again and is now captaining Ireland. If only he could call upon Eoin Morgan, who was playing for Ireland last time around, they'd have a squad capable of inflicting serious damage.

Strangely, no-one in the world of cricket is unduly bothered by this blatant wife-swapping selection policy, it's a wonder all the players don't just chuck their car-keys in a bowl and let the captains pick an eleven out of that. Call me Éamon de Valera, but if I was Irish and came home to find Brian O' Driscoll in bed with the England rugby team, I'd be howling like a banshee and calling for a change in the archaic divorce laws. And despite the obvious benefit of acquiring such a good player I think even the English of Englandshire would feel something was amiss. This just goes to prove, cricket is somehow different. It is not like other sports and should not be treated as such, now someone please explain this to the ECB and the wreckers of Australian cricket grounds.

'All this branding crap makes me sick, Dave.'

'I know, when I supported England against Pakistan I was supporting fair-play over foul. Now they want me to support a shirt with three lions and a hefty price-tag. They're killing it.'

'But you're still an England fan, aren't you?'

'Suppose.'

'There are no bloody lions in England anyway.'

'I know, three imaginary lions and a Vodafone logo, how can you cheer for that?'

'Just close your eyes and—'

'—pretend the network's down?'

'—think of England.'

'What you want Stuart, is for the Celtic nations to unite.'

'What? In cricket?'

'No, after Bannockburn. If the Irish had got behind Robert the Bruce's brother Edward after he was crowned High King of Ireland, and if the Welsh had come on board we could have kicked the crap out of the English— Of course, in bloody cricket!'

'So Scotland, Ireland and Wales?'

'And the Cornish. There's got to be some authentic Trescothicks out there. And Bretons, of course. And especially... most important of all—'

'The Galicians?'

'No, South Africans with Celtic parents.'

'Craig Kieswetter?'

'For one. He's the new Geraint Jones'

'Is that a good thing?'

It's an interesting idea. The West Indies are separate nations that play together under one banner, due to common ancestral ground and not being up to Test level individually. A united Celtic Nations' team would be at least good enough to take on Bangladesh and give Zimbabwe a run for their money, and from there it could grow. Getting the Welsh on board would be the hard bit, but with the England and Wales Cricket Board trading out of the website 'ECB.com' it's pretty clear how the establishment view the Welsh role in their affairs.

'How many caps might Tony Lewis have had as captain of the Celts? Or Matthew Maynard?'

'Well none Dave, Maynard's English.'

'He'd have qualified by residency; after all those years living there he deserved a reward.'

Dave's idea has Scotland and Ireland uniting now at one day level and bolstering the team with a smattering from the Southern Hemisphere. This would produce a team of World Cup contenders serious enough to persuade the Welsh to throw their hand in on the side of the shorter inhabitants of the British Isles, and then united they apply for Test status. Given the composition of their current side, England would hardly be in a position to complain.

I like the idea, but I've been an England fan for thirty-seven years and lived in England for nigh on twenty, I would have to support both teams. It's part of who I am. When I cheer England's opponents in the football and am accused by English friends of small-minded, churlish racism, I can look my accuser in the eye and say how can that be true? I support England at cricket. I don't dislike the English, just the 15 lads on a stag-do they call a rugby team.

'Oh sure Stuart, even if the Celts unite, I'll always want England to beat Pakistan. Well, unless David Gower is made captain again.'

'Is that likely?'

'We must never forget the dark years.'

'Reckon he's still got it?'

'Now the West Indies have blown themselves out, he could probably scratch a few.'

We continue to dissect the concept of nationhood and what are in many cases just lines on a map, lines drawn by long-dead civil servants or kings with little regard for the people on the ground.

Just ask the inhabitants of Berwick-Upon-Tweed which country their town lies in, and you'll get views as divided as those in Kosovo. Are there characteristics and qualities you can claim are shared by a land or all that land's inhabitants? Hampshire Conservatives undeniably sit more comfortably beside Aberdonian Tories than they do with Sheffield socialists. Don't the landowners of Dumfries have more in common with their counterparts just over the border than the denizens of Glasgow? We conclude that these generalisations are a pointless exercise, a complete waste of everyone's time, and resolve to debate the matter more fully at a later date. How we're not Members of Parliament is an eternal mystery.

With identity issues on ice, we begin picking our eleven for the World Cup. This is more like it, a pub, a beer, some laughs and old-fashioned head-scratching of who should bat at three. And then I have the epiphany, I realise why I supported England, what it was that had led me down the English Country Garden path: discussions about the team. Even with all the modern coverage of world cricket on satellite TV, the English domestic game is the only one I know, so English selections are the only ones I have an informed opinion on. I support the team I can pretend to manage. And sometimes that's all it takes to feel a sense of attachment to a land: an appreciation of the local conditions, an understanding of the soil you plant your seeds in, what will grow, what fail, when the wind will blow and when the rains will come.

'Particularly the latter in the case of cricket, Stuart.'

'Indeed.'

'So what we're left with after all that, is bundle of memories, some scribbled match reports, a fleeting impression of Australia, an horrific overdraft and a faded carry-on bag of old prejudice.'

'And interviews, and photographs, and some great stories! And the envy of all our friends, Dave.'

'I don't have any friends. All I've got is handful of Australian coins and bad hair.'

'And you've still got your tan.'

'There is that.'

'Do you want this phone by the way?'

'What's wrong with it?'

'Nothing. Except it only works in Australia.'

'That's handy. Why don't you get it unlocked?'

'The guy in the shop laughed at me. He took one look and said it'd cost more to unlock than to buy a new one.'

'Bummer.'

'There you go, keep it; it's a souvenir of the trip.'

'I reckon we should burn it, put its remains in an urn and every two years—'

'Now you're talking.'

SCORECARDS

The Ashes 2010/11 – 1st Test
Toss won by England, who chose to bat

Played at the Gabba, Brisbane
Match drawn

England 1st innings		R	M	B	4s	6s	SR
AJ Strauss*	c Hussey b Hilfenhaus	0	2	3	0	0	0.00
AN Cook	c Watson b Siddle	67	283	168	6	0	39.88
IJL Trott	b Watson	29	62	53	5	0	54.71
KP Pietersen	c Ponting b Siddle	43	95	70	6	0	61.42
PD Collingwood	c North b Siddle	4	9	8	1	0	50.00
IR Bell	c Watson b Doherty	76	183	131	8	0	58.01
MJ Prior†	b Siddle	0	1	1	0	0	0.00
SCJ Broad	lbw b Siddle	0	1	1	0	0	0.00
GP Swann	lbw b Siddle	10	21	9	1	0	111.11
JM Anderson	b Doherty	11	38	22	2	0	50.00
ST Finn	not out	0	1	0	0	0	-
Extras	(lb 8, w 7, nb 5)	20					
Total	**(all out)**	**260 (76.5 overs 360 mins 3.38 runs/ov)**					

Fall of wickets 1-0 (Strauss, 0.3 ov), 2-41 (Trott, 13.6 ov), 3-117 (Pietersen, 37.3 ov), 4-125 (Coll'gw'd, 39.5 ov), 5-197 (Cook, 65.3 ov), 6-197 (Prior, 65.4 ov), 7-197 (Broad, 65.5 ov), 8-228 (Swann, 69.2 ov), 9-254 (Bell, 76.1 ov), 10-260 (Anderson, 76.5 ov)

Bowling	O	M	R	W	Econ
BW Hilfenhaus	19	4	60	1	3.15 (2nb, 2w)
PM Siddle	16	3	54	6	3.37 (2nb, 2w)
MG Johnson	15	2	66	0	4.40
SR Watson	12	2	30	1	2.50 (1nb, 3w)
XJ Doherty	13.5	3	41	2	2.96
MJ North	1	0	1	0	1.00

Australia 1st innings		R	M	B	4s	6s	SR
SR Watson	c Strauss b Anderson	36	113	76	6	0	47.36
SM Katich	c & b Finn	50	159	106	5	0	47.16
RT Ponting*	c †Prior b Anderson	10	34	26	1	0	38.46
MJ Clarke	c †Prior b Finn	9	76	50	0	0	18.00
MEK Hussey	c Cook b Finn	195	462	330	26	1	59.09
MJ North	c Collingwood b Swann	1	6	8	0	0	12.50
BJ Haddin†	c Collingwood b Swann	136	374	287	16	1	47.38
MG Johnson	b Finn	0	32	19	0	0	0.00
XJ Doherty	c Cook b Finn	16	43	30	2	0	53.33
PM Siddle	c Swann b Finn	6	7	11	1	0	54.54
BW Hilfenhaus	not out	1	16	10	0	0	10.00
Extras	(b 4, lb 12, w 4, nb 1)	21					
Total	**(all out)**	**481 (158.4 overs 662 mins 3.03 runs/ov)**					

Fall of wickets 1-78 (Watson, 25.2ov), 2-96 (Ponting, 33.2ov), 3-100 (Katich, 36.1ov), 4-140 (Clarke, 51.2ov), 5-143 (North, 52.5ov), 6-450 (Haddin, 145.3ov), 7-458 (Hussey, 148.6ov), 8-462 (Johnson, 152.3ov), 9-472 (Siddle, 154.4ov), 10-481 (Doherty, 158.4ov)

Bowling	O	M	R	W	Econ				
JM Anderson	37	13	99	2	2.67 (1w)				
SCJ Broad	33	7	72	0	2.18 (1nb, 1w)				
GP Swann	43	5	128	2	2.97				
ST Finn	33.4	1	125	6	3.71				
PD Collingwood	12	1	41	0	3.41 (2w)				

England 2nd innings		R	M	B	4s	6s	SR
AJ Strauss*	st †Haddin b North	110	267	224	15	0	49.10
AN Cook	not out	235	625	428	26	0	54.90
IJL Trott	not out	135	362	266	19	0	50.75
Extras	(b 17, lb 4, w 10, nb 6)	37					
Total	**(1 wicket declared)**	**517**	**(152 overs 630 mins 3.40 runs/ov.)**				

Fall of wickets 1-188 (Strauss, 66.2 ov)

Bowling	O	M	R	W	Econ
BW Hilfenhaus	32	8	82	0	2.56 (3nb, 1w)
PM Siddle	24	4	90	0	3.75 (3nb, 2w)
MJ North	19	3	47	1	2.47
MG Johnson	27	5	104	0	3.85 (1w)
XJ Doherty	35	5	107	0	3.05
SR Watson	15	2	66	0	4.40 (2w)

Australia 2nd innings		R	M	B	4s	6s	SR
SR Watson	not out	41	119	97	4	0	42.26
SM Katich	c Strauss b Broad	4	22	16	0	0	25.00
RT Ponting*	not out	51	96	43	4	1	118.60
Extras	(b 4, lb 1, w 1, pen 5)	11					
Total	**(1 wicket)**	**107**	**(26 overs 119 mins 4.11 runs p/ov)**				

Fall of wickets 1-5 (Katich, 5.2 ov)

Bowling	O	M	R	W	Econ
JM Anderson	5	2	15	0	3.00
SCJ Broad	7	1	18	1	2.57 (1w)
GP Swann	8	0	33	0	4.12
ST Finn	4	0	25	0	6.25
KP Pietersen	2	0	6	0	3.00

Close of play

25 Nov. Day 1 - Australia 1st innings 25/0	(SR Watson 9*, SM Katich 15*, 7 ov)
26 Nov. Day 2 - Australia 1st innings 220/5	(MKHussey 81*, BJ Haddin 22*, 80 ov)
27 Nov. Day 3 - England 2nd innings 19/0	(AJ Strauss 11*, AN Cook 6*, 15 ov)
28 Nov. Day 4 - England 2nd innings 309/1	(AN Cook 132*, IJL Trott 54*, 101 ov)
29 Nov. Day 5 - Australia 2nd innings 107/1	(26 ov) - end of match

The Ashes 2010/11 – 2nd Test
Toss won by Australia, who chose to bat

Played at the Adelaide Oval
England won by an innings and 71 runs

Australia 1st innings		R	M	B	4s	6s	SR
SR Watson	c Pietersen b Anderson	51	127	94	7	1	54.25
SM Katich	run out (Trott)	0	2	0	0	0	-
RT Ponting*	c Swann b Anderson	0	2	1	0	0	0.00
MJ Clarke	c Swann b Anderson	2	7	6	0	0	33.33
MEK Hussey	c Collingwood b Swann	93	299	183	8	0	50.81
MJ North	c †Prior b Finn	26	100	93	4	0	27.95
BJ Haddin†	c Finn b Broad	56	148	95	3	1	58.94
RJ Harris	lbw b Swann	0	4	1	0	0	0.00
XJ Doherty	run out (Str's/Cook/†Prior)	6	25	19	1	0	31.57
PM Siddle	c Cook b Anderson	3	24	21	0	0	14.28
DE Bollinger	not out	0	7	3	0	0	0.00
Extras	(lb 6, w 1, nb 1)	8					
Total	(all out)	245 (85.5 overs 377 mins 2.85 runs p/ov)					

Fall of wickets 1-0 (Katich, 0.4 ov), 2-0 (Ponting, 0.5 ov), 3-2 (Clarke, 2.1 ov), 4-96 (Watson, 28.3 ov), 5-156 (North, 54.4 ov), 6-207 (Hussey, 73.3 ov), 7-207 (Harris, 73.4 ov), 8-226 (Doherty, 79.3 ov), 9-243 (Siddle, 84.3 ov), 10-245 (Haddin, 85.5 ov)

Bowling	O	M	R	W	Econ
JM Anderson	19	4	51	4	2.68
SCJ Broad	18.5	6	39	1	2.07
ST Finn	16	1	71	1	4.43 (1nb, 1w)
GP Swann	29	2	70	2	2.41
PD Collingwood	3	0	8	0	2.66

England 1st innings		R	M	B	4s	6s	SR
AJ Strauss*	b Bollinger	1	4	3	0	0	33.33
AN Cook	c †Haddin b Harris	148	428	269	18	0	55.01
IJL Trott	c Clarke b Harris	78	213	144	11	0	54.16
KP Pietersen	c Katich b Doherty	227	428	308	33	1	73.70
PD Collingwood	lbw b Watson	42	92	70	5	0	60.00
IR Bell	not out	68	151	97	8	1	70.10
MJ Prior†	not out	27	25	21	2	0	128.57
Extras	(b 8, lb 13, w 8)	29					
Total	(5 wickets declared)	620 (152 overs 673 mins 4.07 runs p/ov)					

Did not bat SCJ Broad, GP Swann, JM Anderson, ST Finn

Fall of wickets 1-3 (Strauss, 1.3 ov), 2-176 (Trott, 48.3 ov), 3-351 (Cook, 96.4 ov), 4-452 (Collingwood, 117.4 ov), 5-568 (Pietersen, 146.2 ov)

Bowling	O	M	R	W	Econ
RJ Harris	29	5	84	2	2.89 (1w)
DE Bollinger	29	1	130	1	4.48 (2w)
PM Siddle	30	3	121	0	4.03 (1w)
SR Watson	19	7	44	1	2.31
XJ Doherty	27	3	158	1	5.85
MJ North	18	0	62	0	3.44

Australia 2nd innings		R	M	B	4s	6s	SR
SR Watson	c Strauss b Finn	57	174	141	10	0	40.42
SM Katich	c †Prior b Swann	43	108	85	6	0	50.58
RT Ponting*	c Collingwood b Swann	9	21	19	2	0	47.36
MJ Clarke	c Cook b Pietersen	80	170	139	11	0	57.55
MEK Hussey	c Anderson b Finn	52	154	107	5	1	48.59
MJ North	lbw b Swann	22	56	35	3	0	62.85
BJ Haddin†	c †Prior b Anderson	12	24	21	2	0	57.14
RJ Harris	lbw b Anderson	0	1	1	0	0	0.00
XJ Doherty	b Swann	5	17	9	1	0	55.55
PM Siddle	b Swann	6	28	22	1	0	27.27
DE Bollinger	not out	7	14	16	1	0	43.75
Extras	(b 5, lb 1, w 5)	11					
Total	**(all out)**	**304**	**(99.1 overs 392 mins 3.06 runs p/ov)**				

Fall of wickets   1-84 (Katich, 29.2ov), 2-98 (Ponting, 35.2ov), 3-134 (Watson, 46.2ov), 4-238 (Clarke, 79.2ov), 5-261 (Hussey, 85.2ov), 6-286 (Haddin, 90.5ov), 7-286 (Harris, 90.6ov), 8-286 (North, 91.2ov), 9-295 (Doherty, 95.1ov), 10-304 (Siddle, 99.1ov)

Bowling	O	M	R	W	Econ
JM Anderson	22	4	92	2	4.18
SCJ Broad	11	3	32	0	2.90
GP Swann	41.1	12	91	5	2.21
ST Finn	18	2	60	2	3.33 (1w)
PD Collingwood	4	0	13	0	3.25
KP Pietersen	3	0	10	1	3.33

Close of play

3 Dec. Day 1 - England 1st innings	1/0	(AJ Strauss 0*, AN Cook 0*, 1 ov)
4 Dec. Day 2 - England 1st innings	317/2	(A Cook 136*, K Pietersen 85*, 89 ov)
5 Dec. Day 3 - England 1st innings	551/4	(K Pietersen 213*, IR Bell 41*, 143 ov)
6 Dec. Day 4 - Australia 2nd innings	238/4	(MEK Hussey 44*, 79.2 ov)
7 Dec. Day 5 - Australia 2nd innings	304	(99.1 ov) - end of match

The Ashes 2010/11 – 3rd Test
Toss won by England, who chose to field

Played at the WACA, Perth
Australia won by 267 runs

Australia 1st innings		R	M	B	4s	6s	SR
SR Watson	lbw b Finn	13	72	40	1	0	32.50
PJ Hughes	b Tremlett	2	10	6	0	0	33.33
RT Ponting*	c Collingw'd b Anderson	12	11	10	3	0	120.00
MJ Clarke	c †Prior b Tremlett	4	13	10	1	0	40.00
MEK Hussey	c †Prior b Swann	61	139	104	9	1	58.65
SPD Smith	c Strauss b Tremlett	7	46	37	0	0	18.91
BJ Haddin†	c Swann b Anderson	53	119	80	6	1	66.25
MG Johnson	c Anderson b Finn	62	117	93	8	1	66.66
RJ Harris	b Anderson	3	8	5	0	0	60.00
PM Siddle	not out	35	69	59	3	0	59.32
BW Hilfenhaus	c Cook b Swann	13	25	12	3	0	108.33
Extras	(lb 3)	3					
Total	**(all out)**	**268**	**(76 overs 322 mins 3.52 runs p/ov)**				

Fall of wickets   1-2 (Hughes, 1.6 ov), 2-17 (Ponting, 4.5 ov), 3-28 (Clarke, 7.6 ov), 4-36 (Watson, 16.1 ov), 5-69 (Smith, 27.3 ov), 6-137 (Hussey, 40.4 ov), 7-189 (Haddin, 57.3 ov), 8-201 (Harris, 59.5 ov), 9-233 (Johnson, 70.3 ov), 10-268 (Hilfenhaus, 75.6 ov)

Bowling	O	M	R	W	Econ
JM Anderson	20	3	61	3	3.05
CT Tremlett	23	3	63	3	2.73
ST Finn	15	1	86	2	5.73
PD Collingwood	2	0	3	0	1.50
GP Swann	16	0	52	2	3.25

England 1st innings		R	M	B	4s	6s	SR
AJ Strauss*	c †Haddin b Harris	52	125	102	8	0	50.98
AN Cook	c Hussey b Johnson	32	91	63	3	1	50.79
IJL Trott	lbw b Johnson	4	7	8	1	0	50.00
KP Pietersen	lbw b Johnson	0	2	3	0	0	0.00
PD Collingwood	lbw b Johnson	5	25	17	0	0	29.41
IR Bell	c Ponting b Harris	53	133	90	6	0	58.88
MJ Prior†	b Siddle	12	62	42	1	0	28.57
GP Swann	c †Haddin b Harris	11	45	31	1	0	35.48
CT Tremlett	b Johnson	2	21	14	0	0	14.28
JM Anderson	c Watson b Johnson	0	7	6	0	0	0.00
ST Finn	not out	1	2	1	0	0	100.00
Extras	(b 8, lb 4, w 1, nb 2)	15					
Total	**(all out)**	**187**	**(62.3 overs 267 mins 2.99 runs p/ov)**				

Fall of wickets   1-78 (Cook, 24.1ov), 2-82 (Trott, 26.3ov), 3-82 (Pietersen, 26.6ov), 4-94 (Strauss, 31.3 ov), 5-98 (Colling'd, 32.3 ov), 6-145 (Prior, 46.4 ov), 7-181 (Swann, 57.1 ov), 8-186 (Bell, 61.1 ov), 9-186 (Tremlett, 62.1 ov), 10-187 (And'son, 62.3 ov)

Bowling	O	M	R	W	Econ
BW Hilfenhaus	21	6	53	0	2.52 (1nb)
RJ Harris	15	4	59	3	3.93 (1w)
PM Siddle	9	2	25	1	2.77 (1nb)
MG Johnson	17.3	5	38	6	2.17

Australia 2nd innings		R	M	B	4s	6s	SR
SR Watson	lbw b Tremlett	95	221	174	11	0	54.59
PJ Hughes	c Collingwood b Finn	12	51	31	1	0	38.70
RT Ponting*	c †Prior b Finn	1	17	9	0	0	11.11
MJ Clarke	b Tremlett	20	21	18	4	0	111.11
MEK Hussey	c Swann b Tremlett	116	296	172	15	0	67.44
SPD Smith	c †Prior b Tremlett	36	83	62	2	0	58.06
BJ Haddin†	b Tremlett	7	17	10	0	1	70.00
MG Johnson	c Bell b Collingwood	1	5	4	0	0	25.00
RJ Harris	c Bell b Finn	1	14	7	0	0	14.28
PM Siddle	c Collingwood b Anderson	8	33	26	1	0	30.76
BW Hilfenhaus	not out	0	8	5	0	0	0.00
Extras	(lb 6, w 4, nb 2)	12					
Total	(all out)	309	(86 overs; 390 mins 3.59 runs p/ov)				

Fall of wickets   1-31 (Hughes, 12.2 ov), 2-34 (Ponting, 16.1 ov), 3-64 (Clarke, 20.4ov), 4-177 (Watson, 50.2 ov), 5-252 (Smith, 68.4 ov), 6-271 (Haddin, 72.3 ov), 7-276 (Johnson, 73.3 ov), 8-284 (Harris, 76.2 ov), 9-308 (Siddle, 84.1 ov), 10-309 (Hussey, 85.6 ov)

Bowling	O	M	R	W	Econ
JM Anderson	26	7	65	1	2.50 (1w)
CT Tremlett	24	4	87	5	3.62 (1nb, 2w)
ST Finn	21	4	97	3	4.61 (1nb)
GP Swann	9	0	51	0	5.66
PD Collingwood	6	3	3	1	0.50 (1w)

England 2nd innings	(target: 391 runs)	R	M	B	4s	6s	SR
AJ Strauss*	c Ponting b Johnson	15	39	35	3	0	42.85
AN Cook	lbw b Harris	13	24	16	1	0	81.25
IJL Trott	c †Haddin b Johnson	31	85	61	3	0	50.81
KP Pietersen	c Watson b Hilfenhaus	3	36	23	0	0	13.04
PD Collingwood	c Smith b Harris	11	38	27	1	0	40.74
JM Anderson	b Harris	3	22	14	0	0	21.42
IR Bell	lbw b Harris	16	32	23	3	0	69.56
MJ Prior†	c Hussey b Harris	10	19	9	0	1	111.11
GP Swann	b Johnson	9	8	5	1	0	180.00
CT Tremlett	not out	1	12	3	0	0	33.33
ST Finn	c Smith b Harris	2	6	7	0	0	28.57
Extras	(lb 8, nb 1)	9					
Total	(all out)	123	(37 overs 167 mins 3.32 runs p/ov)				

Fall of wickets 1-23 (Cook, 6.1 ov), 2-37 (Strauss, 9.5 ov), 3-55 (Pietersen, 18.1 ov), 4-81 (Trott, 25.5 ov), 5-81 (Collingwood, 26.6 ov), 6-94 (Anderson, 30.5 ov), 7-111 (Bell, 34.1 ov), 8-114 (Prior, 34.4 ov), 9-120 (Swann, 35.4 ov), 10-123 (Finn, 36.6 ov)

Bowling	O	M	R	W	Econ
BW Hilfenhaus	10	4	16	1	1.60
RJ Harris	11	1	47	6	4.27
MG Johnson	12	3	44	3	3.66
PM Siddle	4	1	8	0	2.00 (1nb)

Close of play
16 Dec. Day 1 - England 1st innings   29/0   (AJ Strauss 12*, AN Cook 17*, 12 ov)
17 Dec. Day 2 - Australia 2nd innings   119/3   (SR Watson 61*, MKHussey 24*, 33ov)
18 Dec. Day 3 - England 2nd innings   81/5   (JM Anderson 0*, 27 ov)
19 Dec. Day 4 - England 2nd innings   123   (37 ov) - end of match

The Ashes 2010/11 – 4th Test
Toss won by England, who chose to field

Played at the Melbourne Cricket Ground
England won by an innings and 157 runs

Australia 1st innings		R	M	B	4s	6s	SR
SR Watson	c Pietersen b Tremlett	5	14	12	0	0	41.66
PJ Hughes	c Pietersen b Bresnan	16	59	32	2	0	50.00
RT Ponting*	c Swann b Tremlett	10	52	38	2	0	26.31
MJ Clarke	c †Prior b Anderson	20	89	54	2	0	37.03
MEK Hussey	c †Prior b Anderson	8	44	41	1	0	19.51
SPD Smith	c †Prior b Anderson	6	18	15	0	0	40.00
BJ Haddin†	c Strauss b Bresnan	5	23	16	1	0	31.25
MG Johnson	c †Prior b Anderson	0	8	4	0	0	0.00
RJ Harris	not out	10	39	23	2	0	43.47
PM Siddle	c †Prior b Tremlett	11	25	15	1	0	73.33
BW Hilfenhaus	c †Prior b Tremlett	0	10	8	0	0	0.00
Extras	(lb 2, nb 5)	7					
Total	**(all out)**	**98**	**(42.5 overs 195 mins 2.28 runs p/ov)**				

Fall of wickets 1-15 (Watson, 3.2 ov), 2-37 (Hughes, 13.1 ov), 3-37 (Ponting, 14.2 ov), 4-58 (Hussey, 25.2 ov), 5-66 (Smith, 29.3 ov), 6-77 (Clarke, 33.4 ov), 7-77 (Haddin, 34.5 ov), 8-77 (Johnson, 35.2 ov), 9-92 (Siddle, 40.3 ov), 10-98 (Hilfenhaus, 42.5 ov)

Bowling	O	M	R	W	Econ
JM Anderson	16	4	44	4	2.75
CT Tremlett	11.5	5	26	4	2.19 (1nb)
TT Bresnan	13	6	25	2	1.92
GP Swann	2	1	1	0	0.50

England 1st innings		R	M	B	4s	6s	SR
AJ Strauss*	c Hussey b Siddle	69	232	167	5	0	41.31
AN Cook	c Watson b Siddle	82	212	152	11	0	53.94
IJL Trott	not out	168	486	345	13	0	48.69
KP Pietersen	lbw b Siddle	51	127	89	7	0	57.30
PD Collingwood	c Siddle b Johnson	8	27	15	1	0	53.33
IR Bell	c Siddle b Johnson	1	19	13	0	0	7.69
MJ Prior†	c Ponting b Siddle	85	201	119	11	0	71.42
TT Bresnan	c †Haddin b Siddle	4	22	17	0	0	23.52
GP Swann	c †Haddin b Hilfenhaus	22	51	28	3	0	78.57
CT Tremlett	b Hilfenhaus	4	8	7	0	0	57.14
JM Anderson	b Siddle	1	5	6	0	0	16.66
Extras	(b 10, lb 2, w 3, nb 3)	18					
Total	**(all out)**	**513**	**(159.1 overs 700 mins 3.22 runs p/ov)**				

Fall of wickets 1-159 (Cook, 51.1 ov), 2-170 (Strauss, 55.3 ov), 3-262 (Pietersen, 86.3 ov), 4-281 (Collingwood, 91.3 ov), 5-286 (Bell, 95.3 ov), 6-459 (Prior, 141.1 ov), 7-465 (Bresnan, 145.4 ov), 8-508 (Swann, 156.3 ov), 9-512 (Tremlett, 158.1 ov), 10-513 (Anderson, 159.1 ov)

Bowling	O	M	R	W	Econ
BW Hilfenhaus	37	13	83	2	2.24 (1w)
RJ Harris	28.4	9	91	0	3.17
MG Johnson	29	2	134	2	4.62 (2nb, 2w)
PM Siddle	33.1	10	75	6	2.26 (1nb)
SR Watson	10	1	34	0	3.40
SPD Smith	18	3	71	0	3.94
MJ Clarke	3.2	0	13	0	3.90

Australia 2nd innings		R	M	B	4s	6s	SR
SR Watson	lbw b Bresnan	54	136	102	6	0	52.94
PJ Hughes	run out (Trott/†Prior)	23	49	30	2	0	76.66
RT Ponting*	b Bresnan	20	101	73	2	0	27.39
MJ Clarke	c Strauss b Swann	13	81	66	0	0	19.69
MEK Hussey	c Bell b Bresnan	0	9	7	0	0	0.00
SPD Smith	b Anderson	38	91	67	6	0	56.71
BJ Haddin†	not out	55	135	93	4	1	59.13
MG Johnson	b Tremlett	6	23	22	0	0	27.27
PM Siddle	c Pietersen b Swann	40	70	50	4	1	80.00
BW Hilfenhaus	c †Prior b Bresnan	0	5	4	0	0	0.00
RJ Harris	absent hurt	-					
Extras	(b 1, lb 6, w 2)	9					
Total	(all out)	258 (85.4 overs 354 mins 3.01 runs p/ov)					

Fall of wickets 1-53 (Hughes, 11.3 ov), 2-99 (Watson, 31.6 ov), 3-102 (Ponting, 35.4 ov), 4-104 (Hussey, 37.5 ov), 5-134 (Clarke, 52.5 ov), 6-158 (Smith, 61.5 ov), 7-172 (Johnson, 67.5 ov), 8-258 (Siddle, 84.2 ov), 9-258 (Hilfenhaus, 85.4 ov)

Bowling	O	M	R	W	Econ
JM Anderson	20	1	71	1	3.55 (1w)
CT Tremlett	17	3	71	1	4.17
GP Swann	27	11	59	2	2.18
TT Bresnan	21.4	8	50	4	2.30 (1w)

Close of play
26 Dec. Day 1 - England 1st innings	157/0	(AJ Strauss 64*, AN Cook 80*, 47 ov)
27 Dec. Day 2 - England 1st innings	444/5	(IJL Trott 141*, MJ Prior 75*, 136 ov)
28 Dec. Day 3 - Australia 2nd innings	169/6	(BJ Haddin 11*, MG Johnson 6*, 66ov)
29 Dec. Day 4 - Australia 2nd innings	258	(85.4 ov) - end of match

The Ashes 2010/11 – 5th Test
Toss won by Australia, who chose to bat

Played at the Sydney Cricket Ground
England won by an innings and 83 runs

Australia 1st innings		R	M	B	4s	6s	SR
SR Watson	c Strauss b Bresnan	45	182	127	5	0	35.43
PJ Hughes	cCollingwood b Tremlett	31	121	93	5	0	33.33
UT Khawaja	c Trott b Swann	37	120	95	5	0	38.94
MJ Clarke*	c Anderson b Bresnan	4	25	21	0	0	19.04
MEK Hussey	b Collingwood	33	113	92	2	0	35.86
BJ Haddin†	c †Prior b Anderson	6	15	13	0	0	46.15
SPD Smith	c Collingwood b Anderson	18	85	53	1	0	33.96
MG Johnson	b Bresnan	53	89	66	5	1	80.30
PM Siddle	c Strauss b Anderson	2	2	4	0	0	50.00
BW Hilfenhaus	c †Prior b Anderson	34	88	58	3	1	58.62
MA Beer	not out	2	23	17	0	0	11.76
Extras	(b 5, lb 7, w 1, nb 2)	15					
Total	**(all out)**	**280**		(106.1 overs 436 mins 2.63 runs/ov)			

Fall of wickets 1-55 (Hughes, 29.3 ov), 2-105 (Watson, 44.3 ov), 3-113 (Clarke, 50.6 ov), 4-134 (Khawaja, 58.6 ov), 5-143 (Haddin, 62.4 ov), 6-171 (Hussey, 79.6 ov), 7-187 (Smith, 84.2 ov), 8-189 (Siddle, 84.6 ov), 9-265 (Johnson, 99.5 ov), 10-280 (Hilfenhaus, 106.1 ov)

Bowling	O	M	R	W	Econ
JM Anderson	30.1	7	66	4	2.18
CT Tremlett	26	9	71	1	2.73 (2nb)
TT Bresnan	30	5	89	3	2.96 (1w)
GP Swann	16	4	37	1	2.31
PD Collingwood	4	2	5	1	1.25

England 1st innings		R	M	B	4s	6s	SR
AJ Strauss*	b Hilfenhaus	60	92	58	8	1	103.44
AN Cook	c Hussey b Watson	189	488	342	16	0	55.26
IJL Trott	b Johnson	0	6	6	0	0	0.00
KP Pietersen	c Beer b Johnson	36	87	70	4	0	51.42
JM Anderson	b Siddle	7	41	35	1	0	20.00
PD Collingwood	c Hilfenhaus b Beer	13	68	41	0	0	31.70
IR Bell	c Clarke b Johnson	115	296	232	13	0	49.56
MJ Prior†	c †Haddin b Hilfenhaus	118	237	130	11	1	90.76
TT Bresnan	c Clarke b Johnson	35	116	103	5	0	33.98
GP Swann	not out	36	47	6	3	1	138.46
CT Tremlett	c †Haddin b Hilfenhaus	12	31	28	1	0	42.85
Extras	(b 3, lb 11, w 5, nb 4)	23					
Total	**(all out)**	**644**		(177.5 overs 748 mins 3.62 runs p/ov)			

Fall of wickets 1-98 (Strauss, 22.2 ov), 2-99 (Trott, 23.3 ov), 3-165 (Pietersen, 43.2 ov), 4-181 (Anderson, 53.3 ov), 5-226 (Collingwood, 68.3 ov), 6-380 (Cook, 115.3 ov), 7-487 (Bell, 139.4 ov), 8-589 (Bresnan, 167.6 ov), 9-609 (Prior, 170.6 ov), 10-644 (Tremlett, 177.5 ov)

Bowling	O	M	R	W	Econ
BW Hilfenhaus	38.5	7	121	3	3.11 (1w)
MG Johnson	36	5	168	4	4.66 (2w)
PM Siddle	31	5	111	1	3.58 (1nb, 1w)
SR Watson	20	7	49	1	2.45 (2nb, 1w)
MA Beer	38	3	112	1	2.94 (1nb)
SPD Smith	13	0	67	0	5.15
MEK Hussey	1	0	2	0	2.00

Australia 2nd innings		R	M	B	4s	6s	SR
SR Watson	run out (†Prior/Pietersen)	38	51	40	7	0	95.00
PJ Hughes	c †Prior b Bresnan	13	74	58	1	0	22.41
UT Khawaja	c †Prior b Anderson	21	89	73	2	0	28.76
MJ Clarke*	c †Prior b Anderson	41	96	73	6	0	56.16
MEK Hussey	c Pietersen b Bresnan	12	66	49	1	0	24.48
BJ Haddin†	c †Prior b Tremlett	30	51	41	3	0	73.17
SPD Smith	not out	54	132	90	6	0	60.00
MG Johnson	b Tremlett	0	1	1	0	0	0.00
PM Siddle	c Anderson b Swann	43	85	65	4	0	66.15
BW Hilfenhaus	c †Prior b Anderson	7	14	11	1	0	63.63
MA Beer	b Tremlett	2	9	9	0	0	22.22
Extras	(b 11, lb 4, w 3, nb 2)	20					
Total	(all out)	281 (84.4 overs 343 mins 3.31 runs/ov)					

Fall of wickets 1-46 (Watson, 12.4 ov), 2-52 (Hughes, 19.2 ov), 3-117 (Khawaja, 37.3 ov), 4-124 (Clarke, 43.4 ov), 5-161 (Hussey, 53.6 ov), 6-171 (Haddin, 56.3 ov), 7-171 (Johnson, 56.4 ov), 8-257 (Siddle, 78.3 ov), 9-267 (Hilfenhaus, 81.3 ov), 10-281 (Beer, 84.4 ov)

Bowling	O	M	R	W	Econ
JM Anderson	18	5	61	3	3.38 (1w)
CT Tremlett	20.4	4	79	3	3.82 (2nb)
GP Swann	28	8	75	1	2.67
TT Bresnan	18	6	51	2	2.83 (2w)

Close of play

3 Jan. Day 1 - Australia 1st innings	134/4	(MEK Hussey 12*, 59 ov)
4 Jan. Day 2 - England 1st innings	167/3	(AN Cook 61*, JM Anderson 1*, 48 ov)
5 Jan. Day 3 - England 1st innings	488/7	(MJ Prior 54*, TT Bresnan 0*, 141 ov)
6 Jan. Day 4 - Australia 2nd innings	213/7	(SPD Smith 24*, PM Siddle 17*, 67 ov)
7 Jan. Day 5 - Australia 2nd innings	281	(84.4 ov) - end of match

About the authors

Stuart Croll is a sports journalist and writer who has worked for a host of newspapers, radio stations and websites, including BBC London, ESPN Cricinfo, and the Professional Darts Corporation. He has also written comedy for TV, radio and the Edinburgh Fringe Festival. Born and raised in Arbroath, he now lives in London.

David Alexander's life is a tragic secret, and he's keeping it that way until someone commissions the book on 'his 'tragic secret'. He has worked, occasionally, now and then, when anyone would let him, and mostly under cover of darkness or someone else's name. His interests include everything.